D0083665

The Cambridge Companion to Literature and Religion invites readers to consider how acts of reading that take both literature and religion seriously may illuminate our encounter with texts, authors, other readers, and the world itself. Drawing on both the dharmic and Abrahamic traditions, it offers close readings of exemplary texts, and, in a return to earlier uses of the word "religion," focuses on practices, rituals, sensibilities, liturgies, affects, and other rich, embodied aspects of various religious traditions. Written for those with interests in literature or religion, this Companion is an ideal resource for undergraduate and graduate students, as well as academic specialists.

Susan M. Felch is Director of the Calvin Center for Christian Scholarship and Professor of English at Calvin College. Her publications include *The Collected Works of Anne Vaughan Lock* (1999), *Bakhtin and Religion: A Feeling for Faith* (2001, coedited with Paul Contino), *The Emmaus Readers* (2008–2009, coedited with Gary Schmidt), *Elizabeth Tyrwhit's Morning and Evening Prayers* (2008), for which she won the Josephine A. Roberts Scholarly Edition Award, and *Selected Readings of Bible Stories* /圣经故事选读 (2011, co-authored with Xing Ling). Her *Elizabeth I and Her Age* (2009, coedited with Donald Stump) won the Teaching Edition Award from the Society for the Study of Early Modern Women. *Teaching and Christian Imagination* (written with David I. Smith) was published in 2016.

A complete list of books in the series is at the back of this book

CAMBRIDGE
COMPANIONS TO
LITERATURE

THE CAMBRIDGE
COMPANION TO

LITERATURE AND RELIGION

SUSAN M. FELCH
Calvin College, Grand Rapids, Michigan

CAMBRIDGE
UNIVERSITY PRESS

CAMBRIDGE
UNIVERSITY PRESS

One Liberty Plaza, New York, NY 10006, USA

Cambridge University Press is part of the University of Cambridge.

It furthers the University's mission by disseminating knowledge in the pursuit of
education, learning, and research at the highest international levels of excellence.

www.cambridge.org
Information on this title: www.cambridge.org/9781107483910

© Cambridge University Press 2016

This publication is in copyright. Subject to statutory exception and
to the provisions of relevant collective licensing agreements,
no reproduction of any part may take place without
the written permission of Cambridge University Press.

First published 2016

Printed in the United States of America by Sheridan Books, Inc.

A catalog record for this publication is available from the British Library.

Library of Congress Cataloging in Publication Data
Names: Felch, Susan M., 1951- editor.
Title: The Cambridge companion to literature and religion / edited by Susan Felch.
Description: New York : Cambridge University Press, 2016. | Series: Cambridge companions
to literature | Includes bibliographical references and index.
Identifiers: LCCN 2015045378| ISBN 9781107097841 (Hardback) |
ISBN 9781107483910 (Paperback)
Subjects: LCSH: Religion and literature. | Religion in literature. | Books and reading. |
Literature, Modern–History and criticism. | Religions. | BISAC: RELIGION / General.
Classification: LCC PN49 .C3557 2016 | DDC 809/.93382–dc23 LC record
available at http://lccn.loc.gov/2015045378

ISBN 978-1-107-09784-1 Hardback
ISBN 978-1-107-48391-0 Paperback

Cambridge University Press has no responsibility for the persistence or accuracy
of URLs for external or third-party Internet Web sites referred to in this publication
and does not guarantee that any content on such Web sites is, or will remain,
accurate or appropriate.

Revelation characterizes the world
just as much as natural laws do.

(M.M. Bakhtin)

CONTENTS

LORI BRANCH is Associate Professor of English at the University of Iowa, Iowa City. She is the author of *Rituals of Spontaneity: Sentiment and Secularism from Free Prayer to Wordsworth* (2007).

PAUL J. CONTINO is the Blanche E. Seaver Professor of Humanities at Pepperdine University, Malibu, California, and former editor of the journal *Christianity and Literature*. He is the editor, with Susan M. Felch, of *Bakhtin and Religion: A Feeling for Faith* (2001) and has published in journals and book collections.

SUSAN M. FELCH is Professor of English at Calvin College, Grand Rapids, Michigan, and director of the Calvin Center for Christian Scholarship. Among her books are *Elizabeth Tyrwhit's Morning and Evening Prayers* (2008), *Selected Readings of Bible Stories / 圣经故事选读*, with Xing Ling (2011), and *Teaching and Christian Imagination*, with David I. Smith (2016).

SUSAN HANDELMAN is Professor of English at Bar-Ilan University, Ramat Gan, Israel. She is the author of *The Slayers of Moses: The Emergence of Rabbinic Interpretation in Modern Literary Theory* (1982), *Fragments of Redemption: Jewish Thought and Literary Theory in Benjamin, Scholem, and Levinas* (2005), and *"Make Yourself a Teacher": Rabbinic Tales of Mentors and Disciples* (2012).

WILLIE JAMES JENNINGS is Associate Professor of Systematic Theology and Africana Studies at Yale Divinity School, New Haven, Connecticut. He is the author of *The Christian Imagination: Theology and the Origins of Race* (2011).

CLEO KEARNS teaches at New York University, New York. She is the author of *T. S. Eliot and Indic Traditions: A Study in Poetry and Belief* (1987) and *The Virgin Mary, Monotheism and Sacrifice* (2008).

JULIA REINHARD LUPTON is Professor of English at the University of California, Irvine. Among her books are *Citizen-Saints: Shakespeare and Political Theology* (2005), *Design Your Life: The Pleasures and Perils of Everyday Things* (2009), and *Thinking with Shakespeare: Essays on Politics and Life* (2011).

MICHON M. MATTHIESEN is Associate Professor of Theology at the University of Mary, Bismarck, North Dakota. She is the author of *Sacrifice as Gift: Eucharist, Grace, and Contemplative Prayer in Maurice de la Taille* (2013).

MUSTANSIR MIR is University Professor of Islamic Studies at Youngstown State University, Youngstown, Ohio, and coeditor of the journal *Studies in Contemporary Islam*. His recent books include *Iqbal* (2006) and *Understanding the Islamic Scripture: A Study of Selected Passages from the Qur'an* (2008).

SUSANNAH BRIETZ MONTA is the John Cardinal O'Hara, C.S.C., and Glynn Family Honors Associate Professor of English at the University of Notre Dame, Notre Dame, Indiana. She is the editor of the journal *Religion and Literature* and the author of *Martyrdom and Literature in Early Modern England* (2005).

ZHANGE NI is Assistant Professor in the Department of Religion and Culture at Virginia Tech, Blacksburg, Virginia. She has published in the *Journal of Religion* and the *Harvard Divinity Bulletin*.

IOANA PATULEANU is an independent scholar and has published in book collections and journals.

RICHARD K. PAYNE is Dean of the Institute of Buddhist Studies, Berkeley, California, and the Yehan Numata Professor of Japanese Buddhist Studies. He is the author of essays in edited collections and journals as well as the editor-in-chief of the Buddhism section of Oxford Bibliographies.

MATTHEW POTTS is Assistant Professor of Ministry Studies at Harvard Divinity School, Cambridge, Massachusetts. He is the author of *Cormac McCarthy and the Signs of Sacrament: Literature, Theology, and the Moral of Stories* (2015).

SUSAN VANZANTEN is Professor of English at Seattle Pacific University, Seattle, Washington. Among her books are *Postcolonial Literature and the Biblical Call to Justice* (1994), *Truth and Reconciliation: The Confessional Mode in South African Literature* (2002), and *Mending a Tattered Faith: Devotions with Dickinson* (2010).

ROWAN WILLIAMS is the Master of Magdalene College, Cambridge, and was the 104th Archbishop of Canterbury. Among his books are *Christian Imagination in Poetry and Polity* (2004), *Dostoevsky: Language, Faith and Fiction* (2009), *Faith in the Public Square* (2012), and *Meeting God in Mark* (2014).

JAMES MATTHEW WILSON is Associate Professor of Religion and Literature at Villanova University, Villanova, Pennsylvania. His recent books are *The Violent and the Fallen* (2013) and *Some Permanent Things* (2014).

CHRONOLOGY OF RELIGIOUS FOUNDERS AND TEXTS

B.C.E.

ca. 1500–700	Vedas composed
ca. 800–600	Brahmanas composed
ca. 800–150	Hebrew sacred writings composed
ca. 600–400	Early Upanishads composed
ca. 500–150 C.E.	Sutras composed
566	Birth of the Buddha (long chronology)
448	Birth of the Buddha (short chronology)
ca. 400–100	Later Upanishads composed
ca. 300–300 C. E.	Mahabharata composed
ca. 280–130	Hebrew writings translated into Greek (the Septuagint)
ca. 200–200 C. E.	Ramayana composed
ca. 150–68	Creation of the Dead Sea Scrolls

C.E.

4	Birth of Jesus of Nazareth
ca. 50–125	New Testament writings composed
ca. 100	Bhagavad Gita composed
ca. 200	The Mishnah composed
ca. 350–1350	Puranas composed
ca. 400	Bible translated into Latin by Jerome (the Vulgate)
ca. 500	The Gemara composed
ca. 500–700	Tevaram collection compiled
ca. 500–900	Early Tantras composed
ca. 570	Birth of Muhammad
610–632	Revelations of the Qur'an
983	First printing of Chinese Buddhist canon
1054	Great Schism marks permanent split between Church of Rome and Church of Constantinople
1517	Luther posts the 95 theses; beginning of the Protestant Reformation

SUSAN M. FELCH

Introduction

In the first half of the twentieth century, French philosopher Simone Weil wrote: "Workers need poetry more than bread. They need that their life should be a poem. They need some light from eternity. Religion alone is able to be the source of such poetry."[1]

Weil was not naïve, and she penned these words with open eyes. She had seen poverty, injustice, and impending war. She was not given to conventional religious or aesthetic sentiments. Yet against her own inclinations, she had found herself drawn to God and to spiritual practices – indeed to a reorientation of her life – although she never formally became a member of a religious community. Her essays, notebooks, and letters remain a testament to her desire for light and her efforts to become attentive to God in the lives of other people, in liturgical and everyday rituals, and in the beauty of an often-marred world.

The Cambridge Companion to Literature and Religion begins by acknowledging, with Weil, that human beings need poetry and they need religion, and these two needs are intimately conjoined. It offers a *companion* for those who want to read literature and religion within the same intellectual and affective frame. It is not a handbook or guide or survey; it makes no pretense of offering a comprehensive map to either of those capacious fields "literature" and "religion," nor of delimiting their boundaries. Rather, as a companion, it invites us to consider how acts of reading that take both literature and religion seriously may illuminate our encounter with texts, authors, other readers, and the world itself.

The tasks assigned to the writers of each chapter were straightforward, although they were not easy: reflect on your assigned topic, treat with equal rigor literary and religious concerns, and explicate one or more literary works. In other words, each author was asked to undertake an act of reading that incorporated at least one literary text and one religious tradition, however broadly or narrowly "literary" and "religious" might be construed.

I.

The decision to offer a companion that illustrates some of the varied inter-relationships of literature and religion, rather than a volume that provides a comprehensive map of their terrain, was not mere modesty. It was realism. Individually considered, "literature" and "religion" are each enormous academic fields; together they constitute a vast landscape of inquiry, enlarged by the generative and problematic conjunction that links them.

In the past hundred years, "and" has proven an hospitable word, inviting scholars to consider every period of literary history, every genre, every national literature and subset thereof in relationship to a variety of religious traditions. It is not difficult to find conference papers, articles, and books on Shakespeare and religion, the influence of Buddhism on modernist texts, the turn to religion in contemporary fiction, postsecularity, Islam and emerging African writers, and the like. There appear to be few boundaries in the landscape inscribed by literature and religion; so long as a critic can demar-cate a text, an author, or a methodology as having literary and religious concerns or, converting absence into presence, as resisting literary and reli-gious interests, she is welcome to join the conversation.

Yet this generative, hospitable "and" also obscures the problematic genealogies of the terms that it links. The categories of "literature" and "religion," as we understand them today, have troubled histories, the former originating in the eighteenth century to become a field of study in the nineteenth-century research university, the latter emerging as part of the intellectual project to find a universal essence among various faith traditions. "Religion" is particularly worrisome because, as Wilfred Cantwell Smith noted in *The Meaning and End of Religion*,[2] it deformed the earlier sense of the word, which designated practices of piety and worship, into a label for abstract structures of beliefs. A universal essence called "religion" could now be studied via its instantiation in various "religions," each of which more or less conformed to the ideal. The *practice* of religion thus became the *study* of religion or religions, a homogenizing and universalizing move that was often resisted by practitioners of a particular faith tradition, "those who live their culture immediately," to borrow Slavoj Žižek's turn of phrase.[3]

Recent work by scholars of world religions has continued the critique. Talal Asad, for instance, astutely reads the genealogy of religion as a modern historical object that takes Christian conceptual frameworks as its norm and yet dismisses earlier instantiations (for instance, the values of physical pain and self-abasement) as archaic.[4] The universalizing of concepts formed by the values of liberal democracies, theological modernism, and a critical reason that casts religion as a private rather than public discourse perpetrates an intellectual imperialism that distorts not only non-Western religions but also many historical and contemporary Christian communities of faith. From a philosophical perspective, Paul Griffiths argues in *Religious Reading: The Place of Reading in the Practice of Religion*[5] that to be religious means to give a religious account of the world that is marked by three elements: it is comprehensive; it concerns issues of central importance for human thriving; and it is unsurpassable, by which he means that a practitioner holds a religious account as true in a deep and fundamental way not just for herself but for others as well. Although "account" might be read as abstract belief, Griffiths intends for it to be understood in more richly embodied ways. To offer a religious account, therefore, is not merely to articulate its contours but rather to engage its ritual practices, sensibilities, cultural mores, ethics, and forms of piety, as well as its beliefs.

Despite the difficulty of defining religion, the term can still serve as a useful placeholder to designate what social scientists call "communities of belief and practices oriented around claims about the ultimate grounds of existence."[6] Although this definition sounds austere, its acknowledgment that religion concerns real people, in social groups, who both believe and act in purposeful ways that engage matters of ultimate significance goes some way towards relieving the Western Academy's predilection for conceptual analysis, critical distance, and the privatization of religion.

In addition to problems of scope and genealogy, the "and" of literature and religion has also signaled an ambiguous and unstable hybrid. What precisely constitutes the relationship between the two terms? Should we talk, for instance, about religion and literature, about literature and religion, or about religion in literature, to name just three possibilities? Are we interested in a religious reading of a literary text? A theological reading? A literary reading of a sacred text? An exposition of the ways in which a religious culture has shaped a particular author or text? A theologically inflected literary theory or cultural criticism? All of these approaches and more have been embraced – and rigorously critiqued – under the generous rubric of "the study of literature and religion."

And yet despite these problems, the academic study of literature and religion continues to flourish. A brief survey of its institutional history in the Anglophone world may serve as illustration. In 1950, the Divinity School at the University of Chicago established a graduate program in Theology and Literature, followed in subsequent years by programs at Vanderbilt, the University of Virginia, and other schools in North America. In 1956, the Conference on Christianity and Literature was organized, and twenty years later its members, along with other interested faculty, proposed Religious Approaches to Literature (now the Forum on Religion and Literature) as a formal entity within the Modern Language Association. In 1977, *NDEJ: A Journal of Religion in Literature* (now *Religion and Literature*) began publication, and ten years later the British journal *Literature and Theology* published its first issue. Although some academic programs in literature and religion have closed their doors, others have opened in recent years, including the Literature and Religion Research Network in the Institute of Advanced Study at the University of Warwick, the Society for Religion and Literature at Durham, which morphed into the International Society for Religion, Literature and Culture in 2000, and the Centre for the Study of Literature, Theology and the Arts at the University of Glasgow. Seminaries, such as the Graduate Theological Union in California, offer advanced degrees in Art and Religion, and the American Academy of Religion hosts an Arts, Literature, and Religion section. Many universities and seminaries offer individual courses and encourage research in literature and religion, outside of formal degree programs. Washington University in St. Louis now lists Literature and Religion as one of its focal "interests and approaches," and as recently as May 2012 the University of California at Irvine held an inaugural conference for the study of literature and religion.

This brief institutional history is exemplary, not exhaustive, but it suggests both the capaciousness of the field "literature and religion" and its current vitality, despite the definitional difficulties. It also points to two default positions in the current configuration of the academic field of "religion and literature": a preponderance of Anglophone scholarship and a decided tilt toward texts and theories that are inflected by Western Christianity and its aftermaths, traditionally Protestantism but more recently Roman Catholicism as well.

2.

This *Companion* reflects, in the selection of texts and religious traditions considered in its chapters, the dominance of both American-British literature and Western Christianity in the contemporary Academy. At the same time, however, it is alert to the dangers of assuming that these default positions are either necessary or self-defining. Nearly every chapter wrestles with questions of definition and plots its own position with some care. Rather than considering "religion" as an abstract or universal entity, authors articulate and speak from within particular dharmic or Abrahamic traditions, which they seek to explain and illustrate. Selected literary texts are understood to be exemplary, not canonical. Even the notion of religion and literature as an academic "field," with its concomitant implications of tidy boundaries, tight furrows, and predictable harvests is questioned. Readers should not assume a uniform set of assumptions, terms, theories, or texts nor agreement among the authors. Readers can expect a stance that deeply engages both literary and religious concerns within the same frame of reference.

Because one of the crucial interstices within the discourse of literature and religion lies at the point of reading practices, Part I examines three perspectives on the act of reading: theological, confessional, and postsecular, asking what work each term can do to map the relationships among texts, authors, and readers. Part II takes up a set of topics that are particularly suggestive when appropriated by both literary and religious sensibilities: ethics, dwelling, imagination, sacrifice, and repetition. These chapters allow readers to eavesdrop as thoughtful critics engage texts within an intellectual and affective frame that embraces both religion and literature. Parts I and II are largely informed by the Abrahamic religions, particularly Christianity. Part III of the *Companion*, however, invites authors to reflect on particular practices, beliefs, and religious traditions within and beyond the Abrahamic religions and overtly to challenge the categories of "religion" and "literature." These chapters seek to counter the modernist paradigm of reducing religious particularity to instantiations of an abstracted religious essence and to offer fresh perspectives on the enterprise of religion and literature from inside various faith traditions.

3.

In "Theological Reading," the first chapter in Part I, Rowan Williams asks whether we might rehabilitate theological readings in the twenty-first century, not as statements of dogma but as harbingers of language that allow us to seek the face of God and the face of other human beings. He wonders why three British plays produced since 2006 – David Edgar's *Written on the Heart*, Mick Gordon and A.C. Grayling's *On Religion*, and Alexi Kaye Campbell's *The Faith Machine* – have so insistently conjoined the cultural memory of religion with anxieties about the inability of contemporary language to do justice to our full humanity. "What does a thoroughgoing secularity prohibit us from saying?" he asks, "and why is the resultant discourse not nearly enough?" Perhaps it is not nearly enough because the world we inhabit is "deeper and more troubling" than we have acknowledged it to be and, despite our manipulations, has proved to be replete with "obligations and relations we have not chosen." Theological reading, Williams suggests, may educate us to see in texts this deeper, more troubling, and richer world. A world that exceeds us, a world of gift, requires not merely technological but theological and imaginative language, which is most potent when it is most evocative.

James Matthew Wilson, on the other hand, proposes in his chapter on "Confessional Reading" a robust return to the transcendental triad – truth, beauty, and goodness – as the necessary guarantor of art. He argues through a reading of Oscar Wilde's *The Picture of Dorian Gray* and a reconsideration of the New Criticism that trying to protect aesthetics by excluding the seemingly extraneous categories of truth and goodness evacuates art of its substance, reducing it to mere subjective feelings. If we want to retain beauty, he concludes, we will need its companions truth and goodness. As Wilson demonstrates throughout the chapter, all readings, including the most avowedly secular, are confessional, in that they proceed necessarily on the basis of prior assumptions. What he argues is that the transcendental triad, which is congruent with although not necessarily predicated on religious belief, provides the basis for a more deeply aesthetic experience of the text, as well as one more attentive to the beauty of its surface. For Wilson, because faith does not stop short of the fact of God, it "jams open the gates," allowing human reason to plumb the depths of aesthetic, metaphysical, and theological forms "without confusing them or leaving any of them behind in the process, in a dynamic and fruitful communication."

Zhange Ni poises her consideration of "Postsecular Reading" between theological and confessional readings. As she notes, "Postsecular reading follows theological reading to challenge the hegemonic universalism of 'secular' reason and joins confessional reading to address the failures of the protectionist exclusionism of 'secular' aesthetics." Ni, like Williams and Wilson, is suspicious of the easy dichotomy between the "religious" and the "secular." But she challenges both traditional religions and canonical literature in her reading of the popular *Hunger Games* trilogy. Wilson's universal categories do not sit easily with the postsecular investment in fluidity, multiplicity, angular particularities, and non-Western habits of thought and life, as well as its critical focus on the intertwining of politics and religion. Through an examination of the two "secular sacreds" in the *Hunger Games* – the modern liberal state and the autonomous individual – and the failed bildungsroman of its heroine, Ni explores the possibility of alternative spiritualities that the novel trilogy never fully achieves.

4.

Part II holds up five resonant terms to religious and literary scrutiny: ethics, dwelling, imagination, sacrifice, and repetition. Though distinct in methodology and scope, the chapters together offer a tapestry of readings in which religious and literary concerns interweave, modify, and enrich one another.

Susan Felch triangulates among religion, literature, and ethics under the rubric of the human desire for purity. She reads Mary Gordon's novel *Pearl* and its predecessors, the medieval Pearl poem and Nathaniel Hawthorne's short story "The Birthmark," as quests for purity that are both deeply ingrained in the human soul and that can go horribly awry. Within the Christian tradition that marks these three works, ethics alone, whether understood as the fulfillment of obligation or the cultivation of virtuous habits, is insufficient for a good life. The desire for purity, an "extravagance that exceeds the economy of dutiful actions," reveals a desire to live well within a capacious divine-human relationship in response to God's call. It also reveals the desire for religion's excess, the "something more" that the merely secular, as Rowan Williams notes, cannot adequately say. Purity, Felch notes, "repositions ethical decision-making by changing the question from 'What should I do?' to 'What is asked of me?'" Spelling out what might be asked of me is the task undertaken by these writers, who deal in all the messy particulars of fictional lives that mirror lives in the world. Novels, short stories, and narrative poems, as Mary Gordon puts it, dwell amidst "the sheer difficulty of actual human deliberation."

It is these arts of dwelling that are explored by Julia Lupton in Chapter 5, as she juxtaposes Heidegger's essay "Building Dwelling Thinking," Shakespeare's late play *Pericles*, and the biblical book of Jonah to consider how human bonds are established "out of and around our requirements for shelter, sustenance, and succor." These bonds draw on lines of affiliation with the *mishkan* and temple of the Hebrew Bible, the *ecclesia* of the New Testament, and the intimate, indwelling exchanges of the Eucharist, but also act to "reclaim institutionalized sacred spaces and sacred times for common use." In particular, Lupton thinks through the contingency, sojourning, and estrangement that thread their way through the biblical stories, *Pericles*, and the openness to the divine created by Heidegger's "four-fold" schematic as pointing toward human dwellings that shelter and sustain but that also make room for political plurality, creativity, and openness. These are dwellings that "edify," that constitute "a form of daily theology," and we come to understand them as we allow the spheres of religion and literature to modify one another. To dwell well, Lupton concludes, "is to inhabit one's world with a sense of purpose, modesty, and gratitude; to live lightly in the structures that lend us a sense of duration; to use the opportunities for deliberation, exchange, and collective problem-solving that our architecture affords us; and to acknowledge and attempt to redress the forms of displacement that fund every act of place-making through works of justice and love."

Displacement, dwelling, justice, and love are certainly critical elements in Toni Morrison's novel *Beloved*, which Matthew Potts reads in Chapter 6.

But Potts focuses attention on our too easy commerce with the word "imagination." Useful as it has come to be in bridging literary and religious reflection, imagination – the making sense of received images and signs – especially in *Beloved* is fraught. The novel, Potts claims, is "about the task of imagining a liveable future while burdened by the weight of a dead past." But such a task is beyond the capacity of the protagonist Sethe, whose "devious brain" is locked into the memory of her young daughter's death. Although it is possible to read the interventions of other characters in the novel as attempts to release Sethe and allow her to move through imaginative recall to healing, truth, and a future, Potts wants us to reckon with "the costly and unavoidable consequences" of imagination. What, he asks, is to prevent an imagined truth from exacting a heavy toll on real bodies? This is the question that lingers at the end of *Beloved*: has a ghost been exorcised or has another young woman been sacrificed? Has imagination found a way to heal or only to repeat the trauma of the past? Is it possible, in fact, that the novel both serves as a warning against imagining into reality our own desires and leaves us to consider "the absolute intractability of sacrifice"?

The sacrifices that thrum though *Beloved*, those thrust upon the characters and those undertaken willingly, are troubling to contemporary readers. In Chapter 7, Michon Matthiesen acknowledges that sacrifice is often seen as "a symptom of the pathological suffering, violence, and abuse that either should be expunged from religion" or as reason enough to abandon religious traditions, especially Christianity with its theology of the cross. Through her reading of *A Prayer Journal* and "A Good Man Is Hard to Find," however, Matthiesen argues that Flannery O'Connor demonstrates "the productive and transformative potential" of redemptive suffering and sacrifice, even or rather especially in a Western therapeutic culture. O'Connor herself read the Spanish Carmelites, Teresa of Avila and John of the Cross, and Thomas Aquinas, and through their mediation learned to discipline her aesthetic and spiritual practices. Matthiesen demonstrates that the painful purification O'Connor sought as a means of coming closer to God was as productive for her art as for her spiritual life. Indeed, her artistic vocation was part, although not the whole, of her spiritual vocation, and her stories sought to depict the potential for healing – recognized or not – that may come through painful suffering, even death. As Matthiesen concludes, using O'Connor's own words, "If suffering is a 'healing' that leads the person to their highest good, earthly life takes on 'the character of a hospital; and death has something of the nature of a discharge from that hospital.'"

In the Christian tradition, prayer is sometimes called "the sacrifice of praise." Susannah Monta, in Chapter 8, examines the uses of repetition in prayer, liturgy, and poetry, seeing it as a point of convergence that allows both literature and religion to retain their own integrity while bringing them into close relationship "through traits, habits, practices, and qualities central to each." Repetition, she points out, "structures and motivates religious ritual," which recalls and reenacts significant moments in a religious tradition and also renews and sustains tradition by re-presenting practices or holy lives that are meant to be imitated. The repetition of sounds, stress, words, and lines, as well as the use of allusion and other less-exact forms of repetition, are integral to literary texts and work particularly to break patterns of linear time and to make readers aware of their "polytemporal commitments." Monta's reading of three devotional lyrics, the medieval "Suddenly Afraid," Robert Herrick's seventeenth-century "His Litany to the Holy Spirit," and Mary Sidney's translation of Psalm 150, show how "repetition may serve as a fine-grained, embodied, practice-based way to talk about tradition and traditioning, and about the interplay between the universal and the particular." Even in literature that is not overtly religious, she suggests, repetition may serve to "broach religious horizons, insofar as it raises questions about temporality and finitude, ritual performance, permanence and change, origins and originality, the givenness of language, and the nature and possibilities of meaning."

5.

At the conclusion of Part II, Susannah Monta warns against "the academic domestication of religious poetry as simply historical artifact," a warning heeded by the writers in Part III. Each chapter in this section explicates a particular dharmic or Abrahamic religious tradition – or rather one or more of its strands, since no faith tradition is homogenous – as it intersects with literary texts generated from within that tradition. Although the authors are careful to contextualize literary works within their religious and cultural milieus, they do not encapsulate these works in fossilized environments. Given the large archives of literary works inflected by various religious traditions, it behooves us to learn how better to read them; at the same time, however, local reading practices often generate productive encounters with other, more distant literatures as they challenge assumptions, raise new interpretive questions or reinvigorate old ones, and suggest alternative modes of intellectual inquiry.

In Chapter 9, Cleo Kerns interrogates both Western ways of reading Hindu texts and the word "Hinduism" itself. Counterintuitively, she argues that modern attempts to discard the term "Hinduism" as a Western fiction are themselves a form of Orientalism that position Indian religion as a polytheistic "other" against the West's unitary monotheism, a distortion of both religious traditions. Positively, she urges readings of Hindu texts, including the popular Bhagavad Gita, that recognize aesthetic experience as an invitation to immediate apprehension of the divine. As she notes, some forms of Hindu art "are regarded as sufficient and effective forms of spiritual practice in themselves," in contrast to much of Western art that finds itself – at least at times – in tension with the Abrahamic religions. In fact, to separate the "sacred" from the "secular" in Hindu literature is to miss the point that the interactions of religion and literature are often symbiotic as they engage the principle of *maya*, or illusion, the awakening from illusion, and the realization of the ontological identity of the deep self with the divine. Art itself can precipitate spiritual awareness, and Kearns shows how *kavya* a classical literary genre, and the traditional aesthetic theory of *rasa* provide the vocabulary and conceptual rigor for understanding the interplay of affective, intellectual, aesthetic, and spiritual experiences within and beyond Hindu literature.

Richard Payne's analysis of Buddhist literature in Chapter 10 similarly begins by noting that Buddhist texts "require readers to become familiar with cultural traditions and reading practices markedly divergent from their own," and he urges readers to resist the temptation to universalize religious themes. Because many of the often anthologized Buddhist texts have been chosen for their apparent congruence with core Western values and then misread through those same lenses, Payne offers a primer on reading/performing a lesser known genre: the tantras, which give a central place to prescriptive ritual practices and which eschew the large philosophic questions of Western religion and its dominant narrative of Edenic creation, fall into sin, and return to paradise. Rather than a moral narrative structure, Buddhist texts construct an epistemic narrative of ground (ignorance), path (training), and goal (the realization of impermanence). In the Vairocanābhi-sambodhi-tantra, ground and goal are seen as one, such that the path becomes not an awakening to the reality of impermanence but rather the making real to the practitioner that he or she has already been awakened. The appropriate reading practice for the tantra is, therefore, a ritual technology of gesture and speech, the latter understood not semantically as sounds that convey linguistic information but rather as a cosmogenic force. Such rituals, Payne concludes, enable "practitioners to realize their own body, speech, and mind as identical with the body, speech, and mind of a buddha," as they cultivate a religious reading sensibility suitable to the tantra and its cultural context.

Both Kearns and Payne point out that the sacred texts of the dharmic traditions have porous boundaries, unlike the bounded texts of the Hebrew scripture, the Christian Bible, or the Muslim Qur'an that distinguish sharply between revelation and commentary. Susan Handelman, however, in Chapter 11 pushes back against the very notion of "text." She tells of a rabbinical student who offered his teacher an "interpretation of the text," to which the rabbi responded, "It's not a 'text.' It's your mother!" A Jew, Handelman argues, always relates to sacred writings in the same "intimate, personal, reciprocal, and complex" ways as he would to his family. Handelman then reads midrashic accounts of two encounters between Moses and God in the Torah to illustrate the "urgent personal encounter, reciprocity, argument, questioning, and continuing search" that characterize Jewish reading practices, which return again and again to the primary narrative. These returns reveal, Handelman suggests, not just different glimpses of God, but glimpses of the different faces of God, "a God who is always larger than our grasp," to echo Rowan Williams' conclusion. Throughout the chapter, Handelman pays close attention to terminology – religion, text, literature, and interpretation – and to the vagaries of translation, both semantic and cultural. To read Hebrew is to decipher, sound out, and vocalize the three-letter roots that constitute its word-hoard. Reading, she reminds us, "is a form of calling out and being called, called to account and summoned to be transformed," which is why she prefers to call Jews "People of the Mouth," not "People of the Book." This restless, personal, oral way of reading need not be limited to midrash, for, as Handelman asks, "Can we ever really know without eros? Can we ever deeply understand a work of literature without somehow loving it?" – with a love that matures through questions, conflicts, and doubts.

In a complementary fashion, Lori Branch and Ioana Patuleanu in Chapter 12 argue that learning to read with an Eastern Orthodox sensibility allows readers to access love as a critical resource and "to speak about connections of literature to life that go beyond ideology replication and critical distance." A desire to do just this, they claim, is evident in the Academy today. Branch and Patuleanu structure their essay around explicating "the living literariness of Orthodox spirituality," in which believers, through liturgical song and prayer, and through ascetic practices and sacramental participation, move along a path of salvation that recognizes as its goal the return to paradise. Reading Chapter 12 in tandem with Chapters 9 and 10 on the dharmic traditions makes clear the distinction between an epistemic journey from ignorance to realization and the moral, salvific journey of the Abrahamic religions. Repentance, healing, freedom, and participation in the life of God form the rhythm of Orthodox spirituality, a rhythm that pulses through daily existence, in the twenty volumes of liturgical poetry and song that structure the year, and within the fiction that arises from this tradition. Orthodox liturgy is literary and Orthodox literature is liturgical, insofar as it works with other elements of temporal materiality to mediate "my ongoing conversation with my Creator." The model for such mediation is God becoming flesh in the man Christ Jesus; consequently, the work of such writers as novelist Alexandros Papadiamandis and memoirist Nicolae Steinhardt, which limn the everyday world of loss, betrayal, and disappointment as well as extraordinary sites of suffering and yet radiate an incandescent hope, can best be described, Branch and Patuleanu argue, as incarnational realism. These writers, and others, they suggest, follow the model of Christ in that they are "undeceived about human fallenness yet in love with the human ability, even amidst vicious weakness and suffering, to reorient one's heart and mind – to set out toward Paradise and to tarry with the transcendent divine, immanent in the created world."

Incarnational realism is also a term that Paul Contino, in Chapter 13, invokes to illuminate the charism, or particular gift, of Roman Catholic fiction and its near relatives. In a sweeping reading of Augustine, Dante, Dostoevsky, and contemporary novelists, Contino points to a number of themes – "the realistic acceptance of limits, the proper place of suffering, the fallen yet sacramental beauty of creation, the inspiration of the saints, and the gift of grace" – that are anchored in the enfleshing of God in Christ. "The concrete Catholic thing," as Pope Francis terms it, can be seen in the ascents to God that characterize Augustine's *Confessions* and Dante's *Commedia*, the upward journey rooted in divine grace and the assistance of fellow Christians who are themselves being conformed to the image of Christ. Contino's reading of Dostoevsky's "Cana of Galilee" chapter in *The Brothers Karamazov* demonstrates how fiction is particularly adept at disclosing "the wholeness of things," at inviting readers to participate in the earthly and the infinite, the human and divine, the suffering and joy, the solitary and communal experiences that constitute reality. His survey of contemporary Catholic and catholic fiction makes real that participation by showing "the variety of possible forms that 'the good life' of holiness can take, for in each work the path to sanctity is particular to that character" – and in that very particularity lies the heart of incarnational realism.

The heart of Islamic literature, as Mustansir Mir makes clear in Chapter 14, is its intricate relationship with the Qur'an, which stunned and impressed its original hearers with its literary beauty and linguistic dexterity. Islamic literature seeks both to emulate the Qur'an's verbal excellence and to respond to its spiritual and moral vision. Mir's reading of a medieval Arabic poem, *The Wine Ode* (*al-Khamriyya*) by the Egyptian Sufi 'Umar ibn 'Ali ibn al-Farid, and a modern Urdu poem, *Satan's Advisory Council* (*Iblis ki*

Majlis-i Shura) by the South Asian poet-thinker Muhammad Iqbal, shows their preoccupation with Islamic themes. *The Wine Ode* focuses on personal spiritual enlightenment, converting the Islamic prohibition against drinking alcohol into a metaphor for the "human-divine intimacy achieved through drinking the wine of divine love." *Satan's Advisory Council*, on the other hand, takes as its subject the creation of a body politic based on the Islamic principles of "an ethically fair and socially equitable system." Despite their differences in scope, tone, and topics, both *The Wine Ode* and *Satan's Advisory Council* draw on the Qur'an and on the sensory beauty and order of the created world, as a repository of signs that point to God, in order to promote a relationship of love between God and humans and a society that is just for all people.

Questions of justice are central for Willie Jennings, who takes a measured account of Protestantism in Chapter 15. He is appreciative of the word-based vernacular culture generated by the sixteenth-century reformation yet cognizant of its potential deformities, given the historical lineage of Western colonialism and slavery that maps onto the rise of Protestant Christianity. In his reading of Protestant culture, as illustrated by Isaac Watts' hymnic revision of Psalm 147, Jennings shows how "the legacy of the Protestant literary imagination is mixed. Translation, pedagogy, and nationalist visions can prove both liberating and, when infected with the racial semiotic, enslaving." He works out the complications of the Protestant literary enterprise under three headings: the choice presented to colonized peoples of either assimilation or cultural nationalism, the development of a "biblical-like devotion" to rising national literatures, and the production of a "relentless individualism." These three complications, Jennings argues, leave Protestantism with a "mangled literary space" replete with tragedy, possibilities, and the posing of this question: "Can a world formed by the word also be reformed through that word?"

Susan VanZanten answers with a nuanced "yes" in Chapter 16 as she considers two literary works from the Christian global South: Afua Kuma's Pentecostal Protestant oral poem, *Jesus of the Deep Forest*, and Chimamanda Ngozi Adichie's bildungsroman about a young African Roman Catholic woman, *Purple Hibiscus*. Working with the terms hybridity, proselytization, and conversion, VanZanten shows that the latter best describes the religious practices and literary production of World Christianity: "In postcolonial theory, hybridity begins with the imposition of a colonial identity (or literary form), but in World Christianity, the material, literary, and social practices of a local culture are pointed in a new direction as the old is transfigured into something new." European Christianity is not simply mimicked in a subversive fashion; Christianity itself finds a new form in the African context. For the convert, current beliefs and practices are redirected but not abandoned, as illustrated by Madam Kuma's choice of genre, the Akan *apae*, a sophisticated and highly esteemed form of Ghanian orature, and her ascription of African titles to honor Jesus. Similarly, Adichie's critique of a colonially imposed Roman Catholicism is balanced by her depiction and valorization of authentic African Catholic practices and devotion. Rather than a capitulation to European Christianity, the religious and literary forms of World Christianity, VanZanten suggests, reveal a rich and deep engagement with the embodied particulars of particular cultures.

6.

Despite the plurality of approaches, literary works, and theoretical positions offered in this *Companion*, three prominent threads can be discerned, woven throughout the chapters. First, every author is acutely aware that no literary or religious term is innocent. From Zhange Ni's rejection of the postsecular as "a descriptor for the reemergence of repressed religion after a secular age" to Susan Handelman's "it's not a text, its your mother," the writers remind us that the linguistic tools we use, the words we choose to frame a question, the discourse to which we resort will inevitably shape the way we read and the conclusions we reach. When we deal with a hybrid field, as in the literature and religion, it is a matter of integrity and justice to consider our language carefully, to respect terms preferred by practitioners, and to recognize that no one person can speak for an entire genre or an entire faith tradition. For this reason, the authors in the *Companion* are careful to define and locate the religious and literary theories and approaches that they use and to broach translations with great care. The Hebrew *y-sh-v*, Julia Lupton tells us, is usually translated "dwell" but also means "to sit" and roams semantically among acts of sojourning as well as permanent residence. *Dharma*, says Cleo Kearns, "is notoriously hard to translate; it has aspects of natural law or regulated natural occurrence, aspects of ethical normativity or the 'golden rule,' and aspects of the values of terms like *path, calling* or *duty*." Richard Payne's explication of *buddhavacana*, the speech of the Buddha, is linked to issues of authority and practice, not simply to verbal pronouncements. Susan Handelman shows that the Hebrew root *y-r-y* from which the word Torah is derived, can mean "to aim," "to proclaim," "to teach," and that another close root *h-r-y* means to conceive or generate. Her conclusion is that Torah "is not reducible to 'religion,' or 'literature,' or 'text,' or 'law.' It's generative learning and living in relation to God, the word, the world, and one other."

"Learning and living" is a rather good summary of the second thread woven throughout this *Companion*. In a return to earlier uses of the word "religion," the authors focus not so much on belief systems or theoretical abstractions as on practices, rituals, sensibilities, liturgies, affects, and other rich, embodied aspects of religious traditions. Without setting up an unsustainable dichotomy between body and mind, actions and intellect, they quietly insist that all vibrant religious traditions are multifaceted and that traditions themselves are internally heterogenous, particularly with respect to how practitioners live out their commitments. The various ways in which Christianity is read in this volume, for instance, range from James Matthew Wilson's reinscription of a Trinitarian aesthetics and Michon Matthieson's rehabilitation of redemptive suffering to claims from the rival traditions of Eastern Orthodoxy and Roman Catholicism to the same term "incarnational realism" to the distinct inflections of Protestantism as racially compromised in Willie Jenning's essay and as locally liberating in Susan VanZanten's. Andrew Walls has memorably suggested that if you visited in quick succession a series of mainstream Christian communities that have flourished over the past 2000 years, you would find variously a tight knit family offering animal sacrifices in the Jewish temple, individuals standing in ice-cold water up to their necks while they recited Hebrew psalms, and white-robed dancers healing the sick. None of these is an obscure sect, but rather each was an orthodox Christian community in first-century Palestine, seventh-century Ireland, and twentieth-century Nigeria.[7] Worship of Christ, recognition of the Bible as the primary religious text, sacramental practices, and a sense of covenant relationship with ancient Israel and other Christians knit these disparate communities into the genre of "Christian," but it was their local embeddedness that drew and maintained adherents.

In a similar way, literary works reveal, persuade, and draw readers into their orbit not through abstractions but in the concrete process of fashioning sounds, rhythm, words, characters, and storylines that cannot be resisted. It is literature, not history or philosophy, Philip Sidney famously claimed in his *Apology for Poetry*, that pulls children in from play and lures old people away from the comfort of the fire. Or as Julia Lupton suggests in this volume, to approach religion and literature bilaterally, as offering forms of wisdom, is perhaps to find in them "schemes for cohabitation in a world in which we dwell together, precariously."

Third, the particular conjunction of religion and literature seems to mitigate against drawing tight demarcations between texts and world. While it is true that Jonathan Culler, speaking for much of the twentieth century's high theory, warns against "the unseemly rush from word to world," religious-literary/literary-religious readings cannot resist pushing beyond textual boundaries into the world of real bodies, real action, real justice and injustice.[8] More than a rehabilitation of the trope of literature as a secondary world, this urgent march from word to world is couched as a necessary ethical response, motivated by aesthetic religious concerns. Early in the *Companion*, Zhange Ni presses the point that postsecular readings necessarily blur the "artificial boundaries between textual ideas and the conditions of social lives," making us both complicit in the brutality and domestication portrayed in the *Hunger Games* and uneasily attentive to the real hunger games played out in everyday life. Susan Handelman concludes in Chapter 11, "What and how can literature tell us about the great mysteries of life? How much can it know and reveal, and where are its limits? Do literature and criticism also have a mission in the world to redeem and save?" Lori Branch and Ioana Patuleanu suggest that literature itself may become "a place of revelation and repentance," and Mustansir Mir shows how the poetry of Muhammad Iqbal, beautiful on its own terms, is intended to foster social change.

Religion and literature are not identical spheres of human endeavor; they may not always be allies. But in this *Companion* they join hands to engage readers in encounters with that which can be said, but not plumbed or exhausted, and with that which lies beyond expression. Religion and literature, separately and together, look to both heaven and earth. "We have a heavenly country," Simone Weil said, "but in a sense it is too difficult to love, because we do not know it.... Let us love the country of here below. It is real; it offers resistance to love. It is this country that God has given us to love. He has willed that it should be difficult yet possible to love it."[9]

Notes

1 Simone Weil, *The Notebooks of Simone Weil*, trans. Arthur Wills (London: Routledge & Kegan Paul, 1956), 2:596.

2 Wilfred Cantwell Smith, *The Meaning and End of Religion* (San Francisco, CA: Harper San Francisco, 1978; 1962).

3 Slavoj Žižek, *The Puppet and the Dwarf: The Perverse Core of Christianity* (Cambridge, MA: MIT Press, 2003), 7.

4 Talal Asad, *Genealogies of Religion: Discipline and Reasons of Power in Christianity and Islam* (Baltimore, MD: Johns Hopkins University Press, 1993); *Formations of the Secular: Christianity, Islam, Modernity* (Stanford, CA: Stanford University Press, 2003).

5 Paul Griffiths, *Religious Reading: The Place of Reading in the Practice of Religion* (Oxford: Oxford University Press, 1999).

6 Daniel Philpott, "Has the Study of Global Politics Found Religion?" *Annual Review of Political Science* 12.1 (2009): 183–202.
7 Andrew F. Walls, "The Gospel as Prisoner and Liberator of Culture," in *The Missionary Movement in Christian History* (Maryknoll, NY: Orbis Books, 2009), 3–15.
8 Jonathan Culler, *Structuralist Poetics: Structuralism, Poetics, and the Study of Literature* (Ithaca, NY: Cornell University Press, 1976), 151.
9 Simone Weil, "Forms of the Implicit Love of God," in *Waiting for God*, trans. Emma Craufurd (New York: Harper and Row, 1973; 1951), 178.

PART I

Reading Practices

I

ROWAN WILLIAMS

Theological Reading

Discussion about the relation of theology to the creative imagination has blossomed in recent decades within English-speaking scholarship. Journals such as *Literature and Theology* in the United Kingdom and *Christianity and Literature*, the Notre Dame *Journal of Religion and Literature*, and *Image* (which includes the visual arts) in the United States have developed as platforms for serious and broadly ranging debate not only over religious themes in various kinds of imaginative work but also around the nature of the imaginative process itself. Research projects drawing together literary and intellectual history have welcomed the contribution of theologians and historians of theology; monographs on the religious hinterland of particular writers, monograph series on the interaction between the two realms, university departments, and chairs (from Chicago and Virginia and Baylor to Glasgow and London and Chester) concentrating on these frontiers all seem to be flourishing. Paradoxically, in a period when public religious affiliation is far from strong in Western Europe and not as strong as it used to be in North America, there is no shortage of interest in the ways in which religious categories appear as vehicles for serious imaginative exploration.

Apart from the high profile of religious – and specifically Christian – themes in the fiction of Marilynne Robinson or the poetry of Geoffrey Hill, several new plays produced in London since 2006 have very deliberately set out to reflect on religious faith and language. In what follows, I shall be looking at three examples. The first is David Edgar's *Written on the Heart*, a high-profile production in 2011 by the Royal Shakespeare Company that deals with the interactions of political power and spiritual integrity around the final revisions to the text of the Bible of 1611, contrasting the tormented conscience of the saintly but consumingly ambitious Lancelot Andrewes with the ghostly presence of William Tyndale, martyr and critic of the hierarchy. In 2006, Mick Gordon and A.C. Grayling collaborated on a play entitled simply *On Religion*, which looked at the tensions within a "secular" family set up by one character's conversion to Christianity, priestly vocation, and untimely death. And in 2011, Alexi Kaye Campbell's *The Faith Machine* presented, within a complex network of relationships, questions both about capitalism and personal ethics and about the tension within the Church between principle and pragmatism.

These dramas all suggest some of the areas in which religious believing and belonging continue to attract, repel, challenge, and baffle a secular culture. In what follows, I shall be using these three texts to tease out further what it is that still allows religious tradition and, in the British context, the somewhat fuzzy residual image of the life of the church as institution and cultural furniture, to work as a creative datum for imaginative life. Understanding how this works is, I shall argue, central in any adequate thinking about how theological reflection might find its way back into public discourse more generally; the risk is always of a theological rhetoric that has no serious way to engage with what puzzles or torments people wrestling with meaning, compromise, loss, and ultimate honesty.

I.

Written on the Heart begins from the problems confronted by the translators of the 1611 Bible in rendering words from Greek and Hebrew whose conventional translations had come to carry heavy theological freight. Faced with the choice between "church" and "congregation," for example, or "heal" and "save," or "withdraw" and "separate yourselves," there is no innocent or objective version available. To claim that a word means simply what it meant in the original context, and so to strip it of the associations of historical use, is an inflammatory and political decision. And to look for renderings that minimize offence or allow of ambiguity is equally a political strategy, a way of saying "thus far and no further" to reform of the Church of England. These are not academic issues: "If we render elders 'priests', in fifteen years we may consign the godly to the fire," says one Puritan-inclined scholar.[1] But this very specific and political dilemma is, in the play, opened out into a wider anxiety about the nature of language as mediation.

Tyndale in his prison cell awaiting execution refuses to amend his version, protesting: "I must break the glass wherein we see God's face?" (31). The original text is transparent to God. Yet believing this requires us also to think of the text as *already* "written on the heart," ready to be awakened by the written text – whose meaning is thus clear to the self-aware heart. And this leaves us with a potentially painful quandary. The text itself is swallowed up in the heart's self-recognition; *difficulty* is dissolved by our transparency to ourselves. As Tyndale's doubting young Catholic interlocutor (later to reappear as a Protestant archdeacon) puts it, it becomes possible for someone to look into the text and see only difficulty, and into the heart and find only emptiness, if there is no interpretative community to settle meanings. Tyndale brushes this objection aside, but the play returns to the question.

A scene in an Elizabethan parish dramatises this with a spirited quarrel about the breaking of painted windows: reformation means doing away with the faces that intrude between the heart and the face of God, so that instead of images decorating the parish church there will be *texts*. Such texts – as Tyndale insists in a scene where his ghost returns to confront Lancelot Andrewes, spokesman of conciliation and political balance – must not be muffled by "majesty" of diction and phrasing;[2] their force is in their intelligibility to all. But, although Andrewes is prompted to ask the anguished question of whether he is himself without a genuine spiritual witness in his heart, the play evokes poignantly the sense of danger that attends unmediated vision. Andrewes finally backs away from his aspiration to succeed the Archbishop of Canterbury because he does not want to spend his "remaining days at breaking bones" (97) – ironically echoing the words of the Puritan parish clerk whom he has visited in prison much earlier in the play, and who says that he does not want to spend his life "breaking windows" for the sake of the Reformation (56). "I will stay here," says Andrewes, "in this place, beneath these windows, with the beauty of these words, which John tells us were from the beginning. For I would see darkly" (97).

Wanting to "see darkly" means, for Andrewes, not wanting to see the future, the fate of the culture he cares about; but it also means that he fears to see God "face to face." The last exchange in the play brings back Tyndale, as Andrewes meditates on the translation of the creation narrative in Genesis. Tyndale prompts him to revisit Coverdale's phrasing: "'And darkness was upon the face of the deep, and the spirit of God moved,' again, 'upon the face of the waters'. [*Pause*] The sea a glass in which we see God's face." Tyndale ripostes, "God's face a glass in which man sees himself." The simple reader of Scripture reads and sees, knowing as he is known. Andrewes admits, "I would not so see him," but Tyndale replies enigmatically, in the play's closing words, with his hand on the folios of translation, "Yet – I am still here" (98). It is a tantalizing conclusion. At one level: Tyndale's dangerous insistence on the text's transparency and its efficacy in making us know ourselves still survives the attempt to soften the impact of scripture through the majesty and musicality that Andrewes longs to hear (and longs to hide in). At another level: the claim to see clearly (God or oneself) is, as Andrewes knows, the root of breaking bones as well as windows. The fragile work of language moulded so as to contain rather than intensify contradiction may be all we have between us and violence, as Andrewes has earlier warned the young William Laud, who is already thinking about what force beyond language may be needed to enforce conformity.[3]

David Edgar, in his own notes on the play, observes that language – unlike visual imagery – requires the hearer or reader to *work*, to join in what the words are doing. We have to collaborate in imagination, and it is just this active dimension to a culture of the word that helps to generate a modernity of questioning and intellectual expansion. Yet the play itself dramatizes some of the ways in which the very activism of linguistic performance and involvement can generate a distinctively modern kind of violence – the violence that comes from claims to unmediated knowledge of self or of the world. A text that is received as the unmediated word of God is both almost unimaginably liberating – because in it, as Tyndale says, we can at last see our own faces – and alarmingly volatile in its effects. And rather than offering a direct and unqualified apologia for a culture of the word, the play seems to probe more deeply. Tyndale is "still here" in the heavily mediated, politically and ecclesiastically nuanced solutions that Andrewes and others have crafted: there is within these words the unsettling possibility that perhaps we *can* be honest, perhaps we can see God face to face and ourselves likewise. But Andrewes' questions are weighty enough also to be "still here," questions about the dangers of imagining that there can be a language valid beyond the changes of a temporal existence, a "heavenly perfection here on Earth," a free and complete consensus of perception and understanding within a community that has passed beyond the possibility of conflict (96).

So this is a play that uses the very idea of a holy and transparent text to ask about language and mediation. The seriousness of Tyndale's presence and challenge in the play is to do with his passionate desire that everyone should have access to God – and so to themselves: hieratic speech, which accompanies hierarchical authority and distracting visual imagery, denies the powerless person that most basic of powers, the capacity to see and articulate who they are. The holy text is the unanswerable proclamation that all can have this power. The notion of an inspired book that awakens what is latent in all is a crucial moment – culturally as well as theologically speaking – in the evolution of the modern mind. In effect, it offers meaning independently of authority: the pivotal point of Enlightenment universalism. But that universalism is capable of becoming a new and even more troubling tyranny. It can create an absolutism of those who believe there is nothing to *learn* in the negotiations of actual history; the rejection of an authoritative past, a tradition, a process of distilling insight, leads to the claim here and now of unchallengeable rationality and the consequent exclusion from the human conversation of those who do not share the sense of a wholly transparent present knowledge or perception.

Edgar's drama takes the theological confrontation between tradition and reformation as a starting point for reflecting on the workings of "modern" language: when meaning is liberated from hierarchical control, what is the price paid in violence? The Bible of 1611, Edgar suggests, is a sort of icon of this unresolved and unresolvable dilemma, making its claim to be the transparent "glass" in which we see God and ourselves, yet hedging this round with the awareness of the risks that lie within any rejection of historical mediations of meaning. Edgar does not quote it, but Miles Smith's famous preface to the King James Bible, written on behalf of the translators, has some pertinent thoughts on why there can be no final translation of a text and how a good translation, alerting readers to the ambiguities of its own rendering, may prompt a further stage of hermeneutical development.[4] The sacred text both affirms that meaning is accessible to all and denies that it can be crystallized in one reading or one reader's reading. So long as language remains, the glass is in some degree darkened, and this may be a necessary defence against the violence of apocalyptic clarity.

2.

Apocalyptic clarity is certainly one of the themes of *The Faith Machine*. Sophie, the moral lodestone of the action, is the daughter of an Anglican bishop, Edward, who has resigned his office in protest at the homophobic attitudes and disciplines of his church. She separates acrimoniously from her partner, Tom, when he takes on an advertising contract with a pharmaceutical company that has been conducting lethally dangerous tests of their products in Africa. She becomes a journalist, making high-risk trips to war zones in Asia, where she is eventually killed. The opening scene, depicting the quarrel between Sophie and Tom and set (with a touch of symbolic overdetermination echoed elsewhere in the play) on September 11, 2001, makes it plain that her moral intensity is a channelling of her father's ethical passion. Later in the play (though this is set chronologically earlier), we see him defending his resignation from office to an African colleague: "the covert fascist in everyone appreciates clearly defined categories, not those murky shades in between," he says, excoriating the Church's obsession with fixing and morally assessing sexual identities and behaviours.[5] His Kenyan friend, bridling at the charge of fascism, turns the argument around, accusing Edward of imposing a new colonialism, whose main effect will be the destruction of the Church in the African context and of colluding with an uncritical culture of entitlement (45). It is Edward who is the one who cannot manage diversity and the actual – unsteady – pace of historical change. Apocalyptic clarity, it seems, is the enemy of the world as it is; but it is Tom's appeal to "the world as it is," in a later confrontation with Sophie, that alerts us to the corruption that may be hidden in any appeal to "natural" processes of compromise or delay. Tom accuses Sophie of "not having lived her life at all" because of her obsession with being and doing right: none of us has made the world the way it is, and we have to take the slender chances of happiness that we are offered through human love, accepting that the rest is "fucking atoms, fucking things, animals fucking animals in the fucking dark, eating each other, ... fucking appetite that's all, ruthless and indiscriminate" (95).

What is most interesting for our present concerns is that Sophie's renewed challenge to Tom – nine years after their earlier break-up – is prompted by a bit of literary criticism. She has reread the novel that Tom wrote years before and realized that, callow as it is, it was written for a reason, and realized also that whatever reason there once was has eroded. Tom's absorption into the world of advertising has "had something to do with words losing their definitions, their intrinsic meanings ... words like *success* and *happiness* and *aspiration, believe in better*, and that once the words went, then everything else did too and that things lost their shape and you weren't able to distinguish what was true from what wasn't and ... everything became not about what you were but about the way you were perceived, not about what connected you to others but about what *separated* you" (93–94). In this world, decisions are "weightless"; there is nothing to talk about, no word or act truly connects either with other speakers or with the world itself.

The moral crisis of rampant capitalism, as Sophie sees it, is a crisis of language. When everything is reduced to its exchange value, its price, words lose substance. The common world in which we share perception in language and *offer* perception for possible language we might share, the sense of a common agenda in a world we can understand only in relation and collaboration – all this is what is lost in Tom's "world the way it is," the world of animals eating each other. It's no use thinking of human love as the one worthwhile (nonexchangeable) thing in this dystopian environment, because that cannot of itself (as the play makes clear) survive without a soil to grow on in common perception, and that soil needs to be a language that struggles with a givenness quite unlike what Tom thinks are the "givens" of the world.

Sophie is not a person of religious faith, but in the last scene, after her death, someone recalls her saying that she is a "faith machine": whatever a Darwinian vision of nature red in tooth and claw might suggest, some people inherited in their machinery something that made them need to believe.

"Against all empirical evidence," some, like her, "continue to believe in the human being" (110). Earlier in the play, we have seen her friends sorting through her library, occasionally picking out quotations from books. At one point, the Ukrainian housekeeper reads from Tolstoy: "Become, at the fearful price of abnegation, what you could be," and asks, significantly, what "abnegation" means (104–105). A little later, Agatha (a young African student) picks up a King James Bible and quotes to Tom, "What good shall it profit a man shall he gain the whole world?" (112). Sophie's "abnegation" is difficult, almost incomprehensible to those around, but these words and phrases are presented as fragments shored against ruin, the remains of a culture in which it made sense to speak of sacrifice. At the very end, when Agatha asks Tom who he is, *He thinks long and hard* and eventually replies, "The missing man. Let's call me the missing man" (113). The loss of Sophie's language is the loss of a particular kind of human face, we could say; Tom can recognize that he is "missing" but has no obvious resource for recovering himself.

The theme of fractured language has already been flagged in the descent into dementia of Sophie's father. He proclaims "I AM LIFE," comes out with scattered biblical phrases, and tells Sophie and Tom that he is writing a book and leaving notes for it "Everywhere. Under the bed. In the hole" (82). But when Tom inadvertently comes across one such piece of paper, it is blank. The play's imagery pushes steadily towards the concluding picture of a last fragile residue of meaningful language, embodied in Sophie's story and legacy. The rather artificial scene where her friends go through her books is a way of indicating what has formed her own speech and sense. They will go to Agatha, it seems, who, formed in a Bible-reading family in Uganda, at least knows how to *read* – or perhaps we could say, knows how to *be read*. She has not yet lost the sense that there can be a text that shows you yourself, the kind of text that David Edgar's Tyndale wants to put into the hands of every ploughboy. But the culture inhabited by Tom, "the world as it is," is confronted only by fragments, blank paper or stray words from a demented man. As in Edgar's play, we are presented with a profoundly uncomfortable map of our language: the moral certainties of Edward and Sophie, their apocalyptic clarity, are unsettling and certainly not without shadow, yet the fracturing or dissolution of their world, their speech, leaves us with a "missing man." Sacred text, here understood less specifically than in Edgar's play, understood as the general moral and imaginative canon represented by Sophie's books (Tolstoy, Kierkegaard, Plato, Neruda, Forster, Shakespeare ...), is a glass in which we see if not God's face then at least a human face, a Blakean "Human Form Divine," a face that could be ours. Yet that clarity is not without cost: not simply the obvious cost of "abnegation" but some kind of cost in terms of a patience with the contingent and untidy. Sophie's self-description as a faith machine is telling: it is as though faith is indeed a genetic determination, setting some people apart from others, with mutual incomprehension as a result.

3.

On Religion is a drama about mutual incomprehension. Tom, a young lawyer, has converted to Christianity and is exploring a vocation to the priesthood, to the horror and dismay of his mother, Grace, a prominent scientist and antireligious polemicist. His Jewish father and agnostic girlfriend look on in some bemusement as the conflict becomes increasingly bitter – at least on Grace's side. Tom's death in a terrorist incident provokes the worst conflict of all, when Grace furiously resists the idea of a requiem mass for her son and alienates Ruth, Tom's partner. Ruth remembers her own atheist father's funeral where "we didn't say a word because it wasn't right. Because he would have hated it. So we said nothing. And it wasn't enough. It really wasn't. Not nearly."[6] She wants at least to have Philip Larkin's "Churchgoing" read; Grace refuses, and at the funeral Ruth reads instead "This be the verse" ("They fuck you up, your mum and dad . . ."). Much later, at Tom's grave, there is a kind of reconciliation, as Ruth presses Grace to speak honestly to her dead son. Grace finally pours out her confusion: she has sensed in Tom's birth the center of her being radically moved towards another and her own self-loathing healed, yet she has also deliberately withdrawn from him so that he will learn that "we're on our own," a message she says she was never taught. She – painfully – acknowledges the "splinter in the mind" which believes that Tom "got what you deserved. You got the poem you were looking for" (83). He has died because of violent and murderous religion, despite his passion to overcome bad religion with good; he has earned this horribly ironic fate. Grace's intense shame at this "splinter" is at the root of her rejection of pity or love from those around her. But it is also her own acknowledgement of the inadequacy of her "reasonable" vocabulary in the face of the nightmares of actual human experience.

Throughout the play, Tom's inarticulate but deeply felt and quirkily expressed commitment is verbally contrasted with Grace's carefully phrased and inexorable argumentation. Tom wants to be "an enlightenment person" and also religious, while Grace insists that this is a contradiction and a self-indulgent contradiction: *any* form of religious language "provides cover" for fanatics. Tom argues that "in the real world where religion is present everywhere," there is no chance of persuading people to abandon faith; it is as ubiquitous as sex and aggression. The best we can hope is to refuse the zero-sum game between "pure enlightenment thinking and bad religion" (49–53). And faith is still worth holding to because it, like human love, is more than "the list of things": as a commitment to another person is not just another conclusion from a bundle of evidence, so God is not a thing among other things (57–59, 75–76). For Tom, Christianity is the language he speaks: like any language it can say and show things that others can't. So it is possible to hold that this is the "best" language without refusing truth or validity to the others. "If you see them as languages, Christianity doesn't contradict Islam just as English doesn't contradict French" (68). The problem comes with a language that quantifies everything, that sees the "lists" as the essence of what is to be talked about; Grace is the true fundamentalist in such a framework (53).

The question posed by the debates in this play is to do with whether any attempt to formalize a language for what is not said at Ruth's father's funeral is incipiently or implicitly a "cover" for apocalyptic certainty. Something is missing, but supplying words for that something starts off the whole murderous business of dogmatism and rivalry. Like the other dramas we have examined, *On Religion* does not offer any resolution; the shocking (melodramatic?) death of Tom at the hands of religious fanatics may be too facile an irony, although it allows Grace a powerful monologue, as if it were acknowledging the excessiveness of that irony. She comes close to admitting her own apocalyptic clarity, while at the same time recognizing the excess at the center of her personal response both to gift (the birth of her son and its decentring effect on her) and to loss. There is very palpable strain in her attempt to speak to her dead son, but she becomes increasingly direct as she becomes increasingly agitated. Ruth asks her with affectionate mockery, "Who are you talking to you mad woman?" (83). It is as though madness is the only language possible for the excess of feeling Grace finally recognizes: addressing her absent son in the context of consecrated ground – "A serious place for serious people," as Grace says, in ironic homage to Larkin. The implication is perhaps that, if religious language is ever to find a place as something other than a potentially dangerous ideology, it must be in this register, the unreasonable and counterfactual address to what is absent rather than anything that has a descriptive claim. We are (very properly) left unclear as to whether this is the language for which Tom has been willing to sacrifice career and even family, whether (if it isn't) it amounts to the same as the language of the fundamentalists who kill him, and whether it can count as the sort of commitment that is briefly evoked again at the very end of the play, when Tom's father Tony gives Ruth the paper napkin on which Tom once wrote reasons for and against marrying Ruth – the process he had described to Ruth so as to show why "that list could never add up to what I was about to do." (58).

4.

At the surface level, all three dramas show a kind of secular nostalgia: religious language allows a dimension of human identity and, importantly, human accountability to be articulated, and its loss as a cultural presence is a loss of something real. None of the plays is written from the point of view of faith; none is simply hostile to it, although the nexus of religion and violence is consistently invoked. But what is intriguing is the way in which the cultural memory of religion – the immediate memory of a religious upbringing in *The Faith Machine* – functions as a vehicle for anxieties about how to do justice in human speech to certain elements in our humanity.

Very roughly, the plays prompt the question of whether there is a language which allows us a measure of self-transparency that will liberate us from the self-images that are variously imposed on us. If human speech cannot ever do this, are we left with "the world as it is," the "weightlessness" of Tom in *The Faith Machine*, or the ultimately oppressive (self-oppressive) rational individualism of Grace, conscientiously burying her intuition that in giving birth her ego has been recentered and deliberately inducting her child into a world where "we're on our own"? The secular nostalgia is for a world in which there is somewhere, somehow, a "text" which speaks truthfully about who we are and can be recognized by us as such, as "written on the heart." But these are also dramas that carefully warn about the risks of committing to any particular claimant to such a status: what is lost by commitment, it is implied, is some kind of appropriate irony, some sort of humility, even; a proper caution about final clarity, a valuing of space for irresolution or at least a resolution less than final.

Critical reception of all these dramas was uneven: a good deal of respect in some quarters for the substantiality of the questions raised, a good deal of exasperation in others at the excessive didacticism and (especially in *The Faith Machine*) what was seen as "priggishness" in some characters. The deaths of Sophie in *The Faith Machine* and Tom in *On Religion* are, as I have hinted, open to the accusation of melodrama, and the postmortem trawl through Sophie's books is an excuse for a sentimental review of one kind of ethical/literary canon, a Great Books summary for the wistful humanist. All three make high demands on the audience in their cross-cutting of time sequences, confusing and not obviously necessary to the advance of the action. But the more unsympathetic critics were overlooking some of the deeper consistencies in each play, and most particularly – so I have been suggesting – their concern with what speech itself can and cannot do in a secular environment. And it is this concern that is of most interest for anyone reflecting on the frontier between religious belief and the world of literary imagination.

Looking at this frontier is not a matter of seeking religious residues, coded reminiscences of faith, or theological patterning in ostensibly secular texts but attending to the issue so insistently pressed in these three plays: what does a thoroughgoing secularity prohibit us from saying? And why is the resultant discourse not nearly enough? The plays maintain a precarious balance, recognizing the fact of moral loss yet putting all the imaginative arguments against a certain sort of commitment. But this is itself already a commitment, and thus already a refusal.

The theologian looking at these plays might want to raise a variety of points about the characterization of religious language. Say, for example, that the hints at the end of *On Religion* could be systematized as follows: there is a role for religious speech as a simple performance of unmanageable emotion in language, but no role for a third-person discourse about realities that might "justify" the use of such a register. As soon as we attempt to justify, we are on the road to a covert or overt fascism – a claim that the world is thus and not otherwise which would in turn justify the exclusion or annihilation of those who do not accept that they inhabit the same world. But this leaves religious language with no real work to do as a shared reality, and if it does not operate at this level, how can it effectively work against "the world as it is"? It will relate only to what the *individual* senses cannot be spoken, and so it will be an expression of precisely the nostalgia that this kind of secularity invites: *if only* we could speak in relation to a frame of reference that is not "the world as it is," we could construct a world in the process of exploring speech together. But what would make such construction possible would be the acknowledgement that we are all dealing with a *common* moral challenge, a humanity that can be uncovered in any human being if there is some word that brings it alive.

But here is the crucial point at which the resources of traditional theological speech can be deployed to respond to the anxiety that keeps surfacing, the anxiety that reference to a shared world of more dimensions than "the world as it is" will push us towards violence. If there is a communication whose source is "outside" the world of determinate agencies and objects (granted the inadequacy of the spatial metaphor here), it is by definition beyond the ownership of any speaker or group of speakers; it will always, however authoritatively defined for the time being, invite further thought/speech. As we have seen Miles Smith arguing in his preface to the

King James Bible, it will always be capable of fresh *translation*. And while the history of revealed religion is full to overflowing of distortions of this in the name of whatever authority currently prevails, the fact is that just such a process of translation has characterized that history – though it has never simply led to an abandonment of the conviction that there has been provided a "glass" in which to see the human and the divine face. Andrewes' seeing darkly need not be an agnostic aestheticism turned in on itself, not a stark alternative to Tyndale's confident hope for a universally shared human self-understanding. What makes the difference is the continuing fact of corporate religious discernment and argument, as well as corporate worship (including corporate and personal silence) and the reflection that flows from it.

Between innocent speech, free from any risk of violent distortion, and nakedly ideological speech, defined by its claim to power, there is something else. These three plays reflect an uneasy, perhaps even half-conscious, suspicion that clarity about the human condition is as much of a problem as total confusion about it, so that a speech which claims to set out a coherent picture of human destiny or nature or vocation is always already so compromised, so ideological or violent or exclusive, that it cannot be accepted and committed to. But if that speech is also a way both of recalling speakers to an ultimate reticence or humility before what is spoken of and of finding access to a resource of grace and absolution in the wake of inevitable failure – if it is the speech that Eliot is feeling his way towards in the *Quartets*, for example – it cannot be written off in advance as irredeemably "violent." The transparency to self and God that is involved becomes not a triumphant comprehension, a successful map of the territory, but a series of keys to recognition. A text which speaks like this will be one that allows enough partial recognition at a time to enlarge the scope of self-awareness and self-questioning in a way that opens up new levels of recognition and new readiness to seek, patiently, what is recognizable in the speech of others.

The sense of *being engaged* by a reality that is not to be exhausted by this or that mapping of the world of things does at least two things. It keeps before us the conviction that there is something with which we all "have to do," a world whose contours are as resistant and difficult as the physical world we are more familiar with, and so it sustains the belief that human conversation is always overflowing the limits of the meanings that "the world as it is" imposes, the world of (geographically and culturally) local interest or of apparently value-free competition between lonely selves. Put in stronger terms, Geoffrey Hill writes of the "necessary formal alienation" belonging to serious poetry (578): the alienness of the poem leaves the reader feeling as though "brushed past, or aside, by an alien being" (566). In the poem, something has "come to itself" more fully than the reader has done, and so exerts an authority (resented, ignored, welcomed, fought ...) in putting the reader's world in question.

In examining the three plays we have been concentrating upon here, we have seen the unease that surrounds the "alien," that which is more realized in itself than we (the majority) are; religious language has this in common with poetry, that it is ultimately not about what an audience has requested but proposes, verbally embodies, a world of obligations and relations we have not chosen. What distinguishes religious speech even from most poetry, however, is the affirmation that this world of obligations and relations is also an effective source of absolution or healing once we have acknowledged the loss or damage we bring to it and inflict upon it. If there are general lessons to be learned here for the study of religion and literature overall, they have to do with how theology educates us as readers in the widest sense. We learn not to look for religious echoes, doctrinal subtexts, or symbolic residues but to ask about how a text proposes a world whose internal connections are deeper and more troubling than the world as it is, as it has been made; we bring to bear a certain familiarity with the kinds of connection that are perceptible in a world related radically to gift and absolution, a theologically informed world; we read the lives of poetic speakers, fictional figures, dramatic voices with this familiarity in mind, restlessly asking to what extent this is a glass in which we see ourselves more fully, how far it takes us forward in "coming to ourselves." Nostalgia for lost moral connections is not enough, but its forms and expressions are suggestive; after all, if there is a "missing man" in contemporary literature, we should bear in mind that "missing" things are things that *belong*. And it is not just a narrowly religious paradox that it seems to be the most "alien" speech that can restore to us something of that more durable belonging.

Notes

1 David Edgar, *Written on the Heart* (London: Nick Hern Books, 2011), 14. Subsequent page references are to this edition and are noted parenthetically.
2 I shall be returning at the end of this chapter to Geoffrey Hill's lectures on "Alienated Majesty" (*Collected Critical Writings*, ed. Kenneth Haynes [Oxford: Oxford University Press, 2008], 493–580), where the notion of "majesty" is recast in terms of an alienness of pitch and verbal density that refuses to be accommodated in the familiar world of the reader. References are to this edition.
3 Edgar, *Written on the Heart*, 93–94: note the use again of the glass/mirror analogy, as Andrewes first says that Laud is a "glass in which I see myself," and then that "Tomorrow is a glass in which no man can look with certainty," and Laud replies, "Except that he looks there to determine what to do today."

4 "The Preface to the Authorized (King James) Version, 1611," in *Documents of the English Reformation*, ed. Gerald Bray (Minneapolis, MN: Fortress Press, 1994), 413–436.
5 Alexi Kaye Campbell, *The Faith Machine* (London: Nick Hern Books, 2011), 42. Subsequent page references are to this edition and are noted parenthetically.
6 Mick Gordon and A.C. Grayling, *On Religion: A Theatre Essay* (London: Oberon Modern Plays, 2006), 64. Subsequent page references are to this edition and are noted parenthetically. The play was performed in New York in 2008 as *Grace* and is now sometimes referred to by that title.

JAMES MATTHEW WILSON

Confessional Reading

In his preface to *The Picture of Dorian Gray* (1891), Oscar Wilde offers the reader a manifesto for modern aestheticism, a philosophy of beauty that is essentially a concern for form – for beauty and the manifestations of beauty in themselves.[1] According to Wilde, the integrity of form and therefore the integrity of a work of art can be secured only by excluding the concerns of philosophy and ethics, of truth and goodness, which always threaten to harness what is beautiful for the service of something extrinsic and secondary to it. "Form is absolutely essential," we are later told (209), but as importantly: nothing else is. "Beautiful things mean only beauty," says Wilde, and therefore there "is no such thing as a moral or an immoral book. Books are well written, or badly written. That is all" (1). "All art is quite useless" precisely because aesthetic form, the dimensions of the beautiful thing, is the final and highest reality: there is nothing more ultimate than beauty and so nothing outside itself that it should serve, and this form resides in "surface and symbol" (2).

Wilde's manifesto for modern aestheticism is a confession, and in *The Picture of Dorian Gray* Wilde offers two confessional readings of the protagonist by Lord Henry Wotton and Basil Hallward that begin in the presumption that artistic form can be protected only by way of exclusion. In the novel, we witness two versions of aestheticism coordinated by beauty's respective conditions of surface and symbol and represented by the noble lord and the diligent painter, both of whom vie for the soul of that innocent, "unspotted" beauty, Dorian Gray. How they initially understand what it means to have a concern for form, and where Wilde has it lead them, provides a cautionary tale regarding the whole enterprise of literary study and indeed of any aesthetic activity defined by its concern for form and understood as a "secular," that is to say, as a separated and self-grounding mode of inquiry premised on an act of exclusion. Cautionary, I say, because such an enterprise will by its nature collapse on itself. Wilde's novel begins by establishing its concern for form, for beauty, to the exclusion of the whole of reality, above all the knowledge of truth and adherence to the morally good; when it finally ends, beauty has been excluded, too. It therefore provides us an occasion to offer an alternative aestheticism, and so an alternative account of literary study, that proposes specific principles of Christian faith accessible to human reason as a necessary guardian of art itself.

I.

At the start of Wilde's tale, we meet Lord Henry, a conscientious aesthete of surfaces. Early in the novel, he admonishes Dorian,

> People say sometimes that beauty is only superficial. That may be so, but at least it is not so superficial as thought is. To me, beauty is the wonder of wonders. It is only shallow people who do not judge by appearances. The true mystery of the world is the visible, not the invisible. (33)

Aesthetic form, the proportionality of a thing that manifests itself to the senses, is the cause of wonder and locus of mystery, for it gives itself to be sensed and known only as an integral whole irreducible to its parts.[2] An encounter with form is a cause of wonder, exciting us to attention, and in its integrity – its refusal to be known as a series of abstracted parts – it enchants, in the sense of holding us in contemplation over the impenetrable (because there would seem to be nothing to penetrate) mystery of its appearance.

In calling thought "superficial" here, Henry paradoxically dismisses a concern with truth, as known by reason, as inferior to one for beauty; to dwell in the mystery of visible form is superior to knowing merely the dull facts of truth. But if thought is more superficial than material surfaces, it must, finally, be more beautiful as well. This much Henry suggests in the succeeding pages, as he offers us something like a hierarchy of superficial beauties in a parody of that articulated by Plato in the *Symposium* and the neo-Platonist Plotinus in *Ennead* VI. For these ancient philosophers, the mind enters into the mystery of beauty by passing *through* sensible or material forms to those that the soul's vision alone can see: from moral beauty to the beauty of the soul, and on to a reality that Plato calls Beauty Itself, simple, eternal, and intelligible, and which Plotinus explicitly states is an intelligible light beyond all form.[3]

In Henry's reformulation of the hierarchy, we perceive beyond sensible beauty per se an immoral beauty: he praises sin as "the only real colour-element left in modern life" (43). And, beyond even this, a rapture of pure ideas, which he first hints at in declaring, "I can believe anything, provided that it is quite incredible" (9). The beauty of an idea is categorically distinct from its truth; indeed, its credibility would be like a smudge of ashes on its otherwise brilliant face. We witness this aesthetics of thought some chapters on, as Henry toys over dinner with the minds of his often moralizing, philanthropic, and utilitarian aristocratic companions – all of whom, in their concern for goodness, are less human than the true aesthete. After reporting several of Henry's paradoxes, Wilde enters into a typically purple rhapsody to convey the full sensation and effect of Henry's wit:

> He played with the idea and grew wilful; tossed it into the air and transformed it; let it escape and recaptured it; made it iridescent with fancy and winged it with paradox. The praise of folly, as he went on, soared into philosophy, and philosophy herself became young, and catching the mad music of pleasure, wearing, one might fancy, her wine-stained robe and wreath of ivy, danced like a Bacchante over the hills of life, and mocked the slow Silenus for being sober. Facts fled before her like frightened forest things. (61–62)

Immorality is paradoxically elevated to the visible – color – and philosophy, in shedding its cloven-footed dependence on facts, becomes a pure music of thought. Paradoxes are supposed to reveal a truth behind apparent contradiction, but for Henry it is clear that the appearance of contradiction causes the irreducible surface of ideas to become iridescent, vital, and intoxicating like a dancer. The mystery of the visible draws what is properly understood as spiritual and beyond the senses back into itself until sin and thought themselves become brilliant surfaces. Henry would seem to be concerned with aesthetic form as surface and to the exclusion of all else, in awe before it, and reverently refusing to go beyond it.

Wilde contrasts this contemplative dwelling on surfaces with Basil's ostensibly more "Platonic" concern with form as symbol. Basil's love of Dorian's beauty is tied specifically to its manifestation of the *eidos*, the simple and eternal idea of Beauty Itself. We are referred repeatedly to the "merely visible presence" of Dorian as a revelation of the ideal (21, 24). Henry reflects on Basil's words at the same dinner where he introduces us to his philosophy of paradox, marveling that "the mere shapes and patterns of things" were "refined" so that they gained "a kind of symbolical value, as though they were themselves patterns of some other and more perfect form whose shadow they made real" (55). It was Plato, he recalls, who first proposed that sensible things were but imperfect participants in the eternal ideas that are alone fully real. Basil insists on a "harmony of soul and body" (16), and yet it becomes clear that he can understand Dorian's beauty only as the expression of the insensible *eidos*, that is to say, of an absolute and intellectual form. Dorian's beauty is exclusively symbolic, and Basil fears that were

Dorian to lose his innocence, he would cease to be "the visible incarnation of that unseen ideal" (166–167). Basil's aestheticism is fundamentally a concern for ideal form.

2.

Wilde does not long leave us in suspense regarding the fragility of both these modes of aestheticism. Dorian has, of course, been given eternal youth through some chemical or spiritual mystery, so that the ravages of age and ruination of his soul deform the portrait of him Basil has painted rather than his actual body. But Basil soon senses a disconnection between the ideal of which Dorian's appearance was a symbol and the pristine appearance itself. He cannot explain it to himself, and it disturbs him. Long before he confronts Dorian in one last hope of seeing his soul and reassuring himself that aesthetic form really is nothing other than a subordinate expression of moral and intellectual beauty (222), Basil feels he has lost Dorian and so accepts that this symbolic theory must be incorrect. He confesses to Dorian, with evident sorrow, "Form and colour tell us of form and colour – that is all" (168). Aesthetic form has grown mute and inert, collapsing until it no longer signals those higher, genuinely real forms that are ideas. It has lost all mystery and has ceased to be what Basil once understood as beauty.

Henry's aestheticism, of which Dorian is soon made a disciple, seems to prove more enduring, but in fact its own fragility has been intimated from the beginning. Henry enjoins Dorian to be "always searching for new sensations" and proclaims his aesthetic philosophy a "new Hedonism" (34). He iterates, "One could never pay too high a price for any sensation" (85), and Dorian echoes, "I am always ready for a new emotion" (117), vowing not to "sacrifice any mode of passionate experience" (192). Taken together, such passages indicate that Henry and Dorian's concern for form is not genuinely in respect to the thing itself but only in respect to form as received into subjective experience. As with any hedonism, the sensation comes to outweigh categorically the form that stimulates it. Form withers into feeling, a series of ever-changing sensations that is a kind of oblivion.

Dorian's life comes to appear like the leaky jug Plato describes in his *Gorgias* – incessantly in need of the new and different because it cannot attain a stable plentitude (494a). He will murder Basil, killing decisively any connection between the visible and ideal, between the experience of surfaces and the stability of the soul. But, more decisive for his fate than this actual murder, he will also and finally kill the connection between aesthetic form and sensation:

> Ugliness that had once been hateful to him because it made things real, became dear to him now for that very reason. Ugliness was the one reality. The coarse brawl, the loathsome den, the crude violence of disordered life, the very vileness of thief and outcast, were more vivid, in their intense actuality of impression, than all the gracious shapes of art, the dream shadows of song. (273–274)

Henry's aestheticism fails to be sufficiently superficial because surface itself, aesthetic form, ceases to matter in itself. Form collapses and outworn beauty gives way to striking ugliness, leaving the "new Hedonism" with only the principles of change and sensation. Such a concern for the beautiful is at last revealed as exclusively a desire for stimulation.

Theodor W. Adorno remarked long ago that the aestheticism of Wilde's age always drew the work of art back into the pose and personality of the artist.[4] It never concerns itself with form as such. I propose that *Dorian Gray* offers us more than just such a historical lesson; it expresses an epistemic and ontological problem that confronts every serious effort to encounter and understand a work of art or to read a work of literature. Both Basil and Henry's modes of aestheticism are initiated by an act of exclusion. Symbol is separated from surface, and surface from symbol, yes, but also the form as such, the being of beauty, is cloistered from reality as a whole. If aesthetic form were also taken as an instance of truth or goodness, such a theory proposes, its integrity as art, where the form itself manifests beauty, would be compromised. This leads us to presume that aesthetics is essentially "secular," that is to say, that it is an autonomous field of knowledge that collapses either as soon as anything else is allowed to impose itself from the outside or, more importantly, as soon as it is acknowledged that form is by its own nature not simply an appearance of beauty, but also an instance of truth and goodness as well. A secular aesthetics therefore excludes concerns of truth and goodness because it holds that any acknowledgment of these things would distract us from the beautiful and finally deform or conceal it from us.[5]

3.

The problems of an exclusionary or autonomous modern aestheticism are replicated in the history of modern philosophy. Wilde attempts to conceive of aesthetics as a realm of beauty apart from the whole of being, concerned with form but independent of everything else. As Etienne Gilson argued many years ago, modern philosophers have repeatedly tried to establish philosophy as separate and self-grounding, and in each instance they have failed. Despite their different methods, their common error was to exclude philosophy's fundamentally metaphysical dimension;[6] philosophy is not so much a method as it is a recognition of being. In the wake of these failures, philosophy took several paths that might be understood as separate but ungrounded, as if it could get at reality more adequately without addressing the question of what it means for something *to be* real in the first place: first pragmatism, and then, in recent decades, the competing linguistic turns of analytic and continental poststructural philosophy. Wilde's aesthetes detach aesthetic form from the rest of being; modern philosophy attempts to detach truth from being. In recent continental philosophy, we see that this project has "collapsed" into an effort to do philosophy without truth; it takes pleasure in the play with ideas much as Lord Henry does in the novel.

Literary criticism with its supposed concern for form has followed these trends in philosophy closely, if with some delay. Although I cannot explore the scope of this history in much detail, I would like to sketch its arc and suggest ways in which it shows how prescient is the cautionary tale offered in Wilde's novel.

In the first half of the last century, John Crowe Ransom, the southern poet, "agrarian," cultural critic, and professor of literature, emerged as a promising figure in the effort to establish literary criticism as a genuinely aesthetic enterprise. Having studied in England after the First World War, he discovered both German Idealism and the Romantic "minority tradition" in English theology and literary criticism that runs from Wordsworth and Coleridge through John Henry Newman and on to Matthew Arnold and C.S. Lewis.[7] This tradition encouraged Ransom to think of communal and religious life as an essentially poetic reality, where myth is the irreducible expression of a people's self-understanding and understanding of spiritual realities. Poetry itself was thus in a sense the archetype and highest expression of communal religious life. Ransom would create a Christian fundamentalist and agrarian adaptation of this vision in *God Without Thunder* (1931), where he argues that "Myth resorts to the super-natural in order to represent the fullness of the natural."[8] Although the tradition in which he wrote had many weaknesses, one senses that Ransom envisioned aesthetic form as having an irreducible beauty, but also saw it as having depths and splendor that revealed its participation in truth (myth) and goodness (community and politics). If reality was poetic, then truth, goodness, and beauty must somehow converge in what we might call the great poem of the whole as it finds expression in concrete, historical being. Ransom wished to defend culture as this complete poem and saw modern developments such as industrial capitalism or "scientific naturalism" as harmful acts of exclusion. Modern persons concern themselves only with material reality as the domain of truth or only with economic productivity as the measure of goodness; they overlook the peculiar and particular forms that constitute a culture and that finally must be understood in terms of beauty.

In his most influential book, *The New Criticism* (1941), Ransom attempted to refine emergent literary theory so that it was genuinely open to the whole of form.[9] He called for an "ontological critic" who could recognize without reducing the distinctive being of literature. In the process, Ransom introduced an untenable dualistic theory of form that divided a poem between "logical structure" and "irrelevant ... texture" (220), but the intention behind this crude distinction between prose or scientific content and formal or poetic surface was nevertheless to preserve the whole of the poem in all its "local particularity" (221). The New Criticism, as Ransom first practiced it, promised an aesthetic theory that gave attention to the form of the figure but maintained a genuine openness to its broader significance. The more he probed the distinction between structure and texture, however, the more radically did aesthetic form come to reside in "texture" alone, whose particularity could be maintained only to the extent that it could not be universalized, that is, to the extent it was rendered irrelevant to the work as a whole and so refused to become comprehensible to the naturally universalizing human intellect of the reader.

This was perhaps an inevitable conclusion given Ransom's beginnings in a Kantian philosophy that presumed all aesthetic terms were properly subjective and therefore already alien impositions on the particularity of the work of art itself.[10] Having begun in openness to the form, the New Criticism reached the height of its influence as an aesthetics of exclusion.[11] Though Ransom began his career with a concern for form as something that speaks to the whole of reality and so is by nature open to it, he attempted to understand this concern in dualistic terms, and dualisms by their nature proceed by way of exclusion: in his case, some parts of a work of literature were properly aesthetic, the rest was not. The domain of aesthetic form shrank in his hands until it was too minute to seem of much importance. The New Criticism came to appear as an overly refined intellectual exercise, aesthetic form an unimportant object suitable only to the classroom, and literature a department of inquiry isolated from the rest of human life. The concern for form that begins in an act of exclusion ends in the collapse – the loss of significance – of form itself.

Since the decline of the New Criticism in the second half of the twentieth century, there has been a proliferation of literary theory, various in detail, but finally resolving into two lasting trends.[12] At the end of the twentieth century, literary theory came to be identified with "Theory," that is to say, with literary criticism that derived from the philosophies of language of continental poststructuralism. The integrity of aesthetic form was denied: words were nothing but "floating signifiers" fraught with indeterminacy. One sees in its attraction a variation on the late aestheticism of Dorian, wherein artistic form becomes a mere occasion for subjective sensation, an experience of thrill that finally owes nothing but its occasion to its object.

"Theory" retreated somewhat at the turn of this century, only to be partly absorbed, partly displaced by what might generally be deemed a radically historicist positivism. Beginning with Stephen Greenblatt's new historicism and Jonathan Dollimore's cultural materialism, literary form was denied any intrinsic significance. As happens to Basil after his partial disillusionment with Dorian, literary form becomes mute in itself but could be made to speak as an expression of the ideology of its cultural moment. For Basil, art comes to mean nothing but itself; for this trend in literary criticism, literature becomes just one more historical fact expressing its own age. Most contemporary literary scholarship denies literature its status as an aesthetic object, as something for whose form we should be especially concerned, and treats it rather as one more tile to be interpreted within the inert mosaic of the history of "ideology."

What might be deduced from this short history is that a concern for aesthetic form that begins with an act of protective exclusion, whether of surface from symbol or of form from the whole of reality, will consistently lead to the collapse of form. The critic Denis Donaghue once noted how strange it was that form is rarely considered in contemporary aesthetic discourse: "strange, because form is the distinguishing characteristic of art."[13] But perhaps it would be truer to say that, from Wilde onward, we have not had any aesthetic discourse at all, because none of it has exhibited the one trait that would seem essential to the aesthete: the concern for form. This becomes clear if we consider that, while aestheticism may be modern, a concern for the aesthetic is ancient.

4.

As Rémi Brague has argued, Western civilization's characteristic embrace of the aesthetic has always entailed an openness to the whole.[14] It does not merely "digest" works, taking what it finds valuable in them within the horizon of its expectations and discarding the rest, but rather seeks to include within itself the whole of works that were originally foreign (107–108). Its "aesthetic attitude" refuses all "separation of form and content" so that "content quite obviously permits the protection of the form" (103). A classic work of literature, he tells us, is thus understood to be "inexhaustible," by which we mean one "from which one can always extract new ideas." Classics "will always have something to teach us" and so "must be preserved in all their literalness" (103–104). Brague's thesis is that this inclusiveness and refusal to reduce or collapse what is judged beautiful is not only the trademark of the West as "Roman" in the historical sense, but also as Roman in the Catholic Christian sense. Catholic faith, he suggests, is a source and guardian of the aesthetic.

To why this should be we now turn in order to sketch out a confessional reading of a different sort, one that continues the Christian-Platonist or *philosophia perennis* tradition in which, as Basil's aesthetics imperfectly suggests, form is the principle of intelligibility of all being; form causes a thing to be *what* it is and so to be knowable as such.[15] This tradition offers a paradox perhaps not dreamed of in Henry's philosophy, but one which I invite the reader to entertain: form, the specifying principle of a being, is also the cause of its truth, goodness, and beauty. Although truth, goodness, and beauty are rationally distinct (they can be understood separately), they are one in the form and in being.[16] The effort to hold form apart as aesthetic, far from proving a genuine concern for form, will always cause it to be understood as something other than and less than itself: at first an iridescent surface or an invisible ideal, but then, a muted symbol, an objective surface absorbed by the appetites of mere subjectivity. When we begin by dividing beauty from truth or goodness we conclude by cutting it off from being as well: beauty loses its reality, and aesthetics has no longer a form proper to its care.[17]

The account of form, being, and reason I offer here is in one sense specifically confessional; I will make explicit the way in which its major claims do not derive from but are deepened by a Catholic understanding of the Holy Trinity (God as Father, Son, and Holy Spirit) as not only a creedal claim about the nature of the divine, but also as a paradigm of the structure of creation. But my account is not something only a Catholic could accept. I believe that it in fact explains why the aesthetic, the concern for form, should have a claim on us in the first place and that it also can explain why supposedly "secular" accounts of the aesthetic have consistently failed, because they conclude by "collapsing" the concern for form. In brief, it can make sense of Wilde's aestheticism as well as its failure, and can do so in such a way that vindicates the historical experience of form and beauty as valuable dimensions of reality.

5.

Let me begin by offering a summary of my position, before unfolding it in more detail. Catholic faith guards form and beauty not by an act of exclusion; rather, because it recognizes both the "ceaselessly self-transcendent orientation" of reason to what lies beyond itself[18] as well as the self-giving intelligibility of being,[19] this faith jams open the gates, as it were, ensuring that reason will not wither into a false modesty or self-contempt and that the mystery of being will not be flattened until its form appears irrelevant to reason in its particularity and no longer bears meaningful depths within. An aesthetics opened by faith will therefore become capable of exploring the depths of aesthetic form, in whose recesses will be found the object of metaphysics, being in its fullness, and will even be able to press on further into its own interior, where it may discover and contemplate the formal object of faith, the revelation of God. This, it should be stressed, is not to argue that being and revelation are circumscribed by and reducible to the form of works of art but, rather, that because being is essentially analogous, human reason may proceed from aesthetic to metaphysical and on to theological forms and see them, without confusing them or leaving any of them behind in the process, in a dynamic and fruitful communication.[20] Faith does not merely supplement the concern of reason for aesthetic form; it guarantees to reason that aesthetic form is a true beginning for reason[21] and, further, urges it on to its proper exercise and full latitude.[22] In brief, what Catholic faith discloses gives to the human mind a reason for recognizing and contemplating aesthetic form in a way that it could undertake – indeed, has undertaken – on its own, but on which course it has often made false turns (as in the cases of Basil and Henry, of Ransom and poststructural theory) and, in consequence, despaired.

If one cannot preserve the integrity of the subject of aesthetic reading by an act of "secular" exclusion, then how *can* one preserve the integrity of the concern for form that is aesthetics and so also allow the form of works of art to reveal themselves as having an integrity of their own? The only way to preserve the wholeness of any field of knowledge is not by way of a hygienic act of exclusion but by a rigorous openness to the whole of which every such field is ultimately a part.[23] A genuine concern for form would have to be one that embraces the whole, which means a concern for its being (integrity), its appearance (beauty), its purpose (goodness), and its meaning (truth). Moreover, it would have to remain open to the whole in its concrete particularity as well as in its invisible depths, as is often expressed by the German term *Gestalt*.[24]

In sum, a genuine aesthetics cares for the form as bearing an irreducible polarity within the integrity of the *Gestalt*, the form, so that it never ceases to be itself but is at the same time always epiphanic, revelatory of infinitely more than itself.[25] The form itself is a whole and is one that is always already transcending itself and standing in relation to other wholes and the whole of reality as such. Everywhere there is form there is being, everywhere there is being is reality – and nothing is real except being.

6.

If aesthetics is an explicit thematic concern for form as the beauty of being, what must be in place for it to maintain this openness to the whole of reality and to avoid collapsing in on itself? There are three conditions. First, we need an anthropology adequate to protect the full scope of human reason, which is the whole of reality (all being); otherwise, we will be tempted to presume a priori that human knowledge may attain certain aspects of reality but never the whole. To apply the reason in the concern-for-form of aesthetics would then seem either outside its powers (beauty as beyond reason) or beneath its powers (as is the case when, for instance, we think of reason as a fine calculating machine for quantities but incapable of exploring the highest realities). John Paul II argued in his encyclical *Fides et Ratio* (1998) that all human beings by nature ask questions about the fundamental nature and purpose of their lives (§1). They are in this sense philosophers, and philosophical reasoning is the chief resource by means of which they set about that inquiry (§3). Thus, for philosophy to *be* itself, it must have above all a *sapiential dimension*, that is, an orientation to "search for the ultimate and overarching meaning of life" (§81). For this, we need reason, but when reason will accept into itself only those principles that it can demonstrate and denies the possibility of "always go[ing] beyond what it has already achieved" (§42), when, that is, it attempts to be self-grounding and absolutely separate and closed to what is beyond itself (§46), it falls into rationalism. Rationalism is not, therefore, a theory that says reason can know reality, but, to the contrary, it says that it can achieve only certain limited tasks. When reason rests content with modest tasks and ceases to address itself to the whole of reality – especially the highest realities – then difficult matters such as the nature of beauty tend to fall into contempt or despair.

To meet this first condition, human reason must be understood as having three essential aspects. First, far from being self-grounding, our knowledge of the indemonstrable first principles that we need for the act of reasoning is but one testimony that reason is in fact ground*less* precisely because, at its base, we find not bedrock but light. Reason is a faculty that comes into being only because it has first been illuminated. Beneath and within the *ratio* of discursive reasoning lies the light of *intellectus*, the immediate principles that orient and make possible that reason's often halting journey toward truth.[26]

Second, reason moves toward Being, toward the whole of reality. But the whole of reality is not just the total assemblage of beings (universal being) but also their principle and cause, Being Itself. And so reason must have still a third aspect; its inquiry is by nature "always open – at least implicitly – to the supernatural";[27] in touching being it is already in contact with God as absolute being. Plato explored this orientation of reason to the absolute in the *Republic*, but, in the confessional reading that I am advocating, faith in God the Father and Creator of all things not only reveals to us that the source of the light of reason is the imprinting in our nature of the light of the divine mind, but also leads us to the highest principles of being – and on to Being Itself who is God. "It is faith," writes John Paul, which "stirs reason to move beyond all isolation and willingly to run risks so that it may attain whatever is beautiful, good and true. Faith thus becomes the convinced and convincing advocate of reason" (§56).[28] Human reason is illuminated and self-transcending because its nature is a divine gift and its true object is the inexhaustible depths of Being.

If the first condition for maintaining an openness to the whole of reality is a proper anthropology, then a proper understanding of being is our second condition. Modern philosophy tends either to deny its natural metaphysical dimension or to critique it along with human reason in order to reveal both as abyssal: we propose truth as the object of reason, but never reach it; we propose being as what is real but find it slips out of reason as soon as we try to grasp it. We need not only an anthropology that says the rational animal is oriented to being, but also a metaphysics that can account for why created being has been given existence, and in turn gives itself to be known. Reason may go in search of being, but it does not acquire it as a possession so much as receive it as a gift. If we refuse to recognize what is as created gift and a gift that can be understood, reality will come to appear as flat and passive *quanta* offering nothing to be known and therefore ready to be possessed, reduced to sensation, and dominated by our will. Art itself will become mute.

Only a conception of being as love, as given and self-giving, which a confessional faith recognizes as finding its archetype in the dynamic vision of the Holy Spirit as the procession of the love between Father and Son in the Trinity, realizes the full meaning of being as the very term of the real. And only if being and reality are one can it be the case that beauty as a property of being becomes worthy of our concern. In it appears the mystery of love – a mystery we do not solve by reducing it to a finite thing comprehended or devoured as an object of our appetite, but which we contemplate as a reality that gives itself to be beheld.

We have indicated, however, that more than just a proper anthropology and a metaphysics of being as gift is required for an aesthetics open to the whole. A third condition presents itself: the understanding of form as constitutive of beings, and of form as the *Gestalt*, as a unity-in-difference of the concrete individual thing and the universal idea to which it gives expression. A being is beautiful because of its unrepeatable particularities, but those particularities are themselves expressive of what is eternal and absolute. The Christian-Platonist tradition speaks of beauty as form and splendor: the figure and all the figure reveals. Neither can be excluded. Otherwise, after the fashion of Basil, we will be tempted to pass beyond form in concrete being to the abstract idea beyond it, or after the fashion of Henry, we will presume that beauty is superficial and has no depths to reveal. Human reason can recognize this for itself, because of course it experiences the beauty of being as a matter of routine[29] and remains unsatisfied with efforts to explain that beauty merely in terms of concrete particularity or universal types.[30]

This understanding of *Gestalt* is something human beings have frequently grasped on their own. We often talk of the highest, most abstract ideas as beautiful and delight in thinking of them as if they were a precious jewel held before our gaze. Conversely, when we encounter the beauty of a good story, we routinely presume that its very specificity, its capacity to represent the most minute and individual details somehow helps it to convey something more than those particular details. But faith bears upon reason to show us how central the irreducible unity of the universal and particular, the concrete and the absolute, really is. For Christ, the son of God, both fully man and fully divine, two irreducible natures in one person, is the archetype of all form: "a true form placed before the sight of man."[31] Faith in the mystery of the incarnation, in the Eucharist, and in the resurrection of the flesh, reveals that, as Balthasar puts it, "the poets" were right, "content and form are inseparable," and we may "possess the infinite within the finitude of form."[32] Just as the incarnation is a mystery enfolded within the mystery of the Trinity, so is the polarity of form, its universality and particularity, a mystery at the heart of being.

7.

The doctrine of the Trinity, received in faith, therefore reveals to us the full scope of reason, the gift of being as reality, and the difference-in-unity of form, though reason was already open to, without being capable of realizing, all three of these conditions on its own. Faith also guards these truths on their behalf. An emblem of this paradox, as others have observed, appears in the First Vatican Council's dogmatic constitution, *Dei Filius*.[33] There, we read that "Holy Mother Church holds and teaches that God, the beginning and end of all things, can be known with certitude by the natural light of human reason from created things."[34] As the document indicates, this is a dogmatic assertion. It is a proposition of faith that reason should have so great a power and scope that it can know God as the creator and purpose of human beings and of reality as such. Faith demands of reason that reason fulfill itself – and does so at just that moment (1870), when modern rationalism was markedly confident of its power to master and dominate the world even as it had come to doubt its capacities for the sapiential and metaphysical tasks that had formerly been understood as its vocation and glory. It may be then that, as a matter of history if not in principle, only faith, as a challenge thrown down by God, can guard reason and being – and along with them, the object of aesthetics, form – preserving them from collapsing upon themselves and falling into contempt. For this reason, I have described faith as a guardian who jams open the gates of reason and guides us on the proper path to a true aesthetics, an aesthetics that concerns itself with not this or that aspect of form but with form as a whole and, finally, with the whole of reality, created and uncreated.

Notes

1 Oscar Wilde, *The Picture of Dorian Gray* (Milwaukee, WI: Wiseblood Books, 2014). Subsequent page references are to this edition.
2 For a consideration of the distinction between sensible aesthetic beauty and intelligible beauty, see Jacques Maritain, *Art and Scholasticism and the Frontiers of Poetry*, trans. Joseph W. Evans (Notre Dame, IN: University of Notre Dame Press, 1974), 24–25, and *Creative Intuition in Art and Poetry* (New York: Meridian Books, 1957), 163–164. On the conditions of beauty, including integrity and proportion, see James Matthew Wilson, "John Paul II's *Letter to Artists* and the Force of Beauty," *Logos: A Journal of Catholic Thought and Culture* 18.1 (2015): 46–70.
3 Plato, *Complete Works*, ed. John M. Cooper (Indianapolis, IN: Hackett Publishing, 1997), *Symposium* 211e–212a; Plotinus, *The Enneads*, trans. Stephen MacKenna (London: Penguin Books, 1991), 54. One might be surprised to hear of the soul or the mind as having "vision," but of course, beyond our faculty of imagination, we are all accustomed to saying to someone who has obscurely stated something, "I don't follow your words, but I *see* what you mean."
4 Theodor W. Adorno, *Aesthetic Theory*, trans. Robert Hullot-Kentor (Minneapolis, MN: University of Minnesota Press, 1997), 239.
5 On this idea of the secular, see Bruno Latour, *We Have Never Been Modern*, trans. Catherine Porter (Cambridge, MA: Harvard University Press, 1993).

6 Etienne Gilson, *The Unity of Philosophical Experience* (San Francisco, CA: Ignatius, 1937), 241–257.

7 Stephen Prickett, *Romanticism and Religion* (Cambridge: Cambridge University Press, 1976), 8.

8 John Crowe Ransom, *God Without Thunder* (London: Gerald Howe, 1931), 67.

9 John Crowe Ransom, *The New Criticism* (New York: New Directions, 1941), x–xi. Subsequent page references are to this edition.

10 John Crowe Ransom, *The World's Body* (Baton Rouge: Louisiana State University Press, 1968), 343.

11 For an account of Ransom's critical withering from a somewhat different perspective, see James Matthew Wilson, "The Fugitive and the Exile: Theodor W. Adorno, John Crowe Ransom, and the Kenyon Review," in *Rereading the New Criticism*, ed. Miranda B. Hickman and John D. McIntyre (Columbus: Ohio State University Press, 2012), 83–101.

12 For an account of the most interesting proliferation in the wake of the New Criticism, see Frank Lentricchia, *After the New Criticism* (Chicago, IL: University of Chicago Press, 1981).

13 Denis Donoghue, *Speaking of Beauty* (New Haven, CT: Yale University Press, 2003), 121.

14 Rémi Brague, *Eccentric Culture: A Theory of Western Civilization*, trans. Samuel Lester (South Bend, IN: St. Augustine Press, 2009), 93. Subsequent page references are to this edition.

15 Louis Dupré describes this classical principle as follows: "If there is one belief the Greek thinkers shared, it must be the conviction that both the essence of the real and our knowledge of it consists ultimately of *form*. Basically this means that it belongs to the essence of the real to *appear*, rather than to hide, and to appear in an orderly way. By envisioning the real as such as harmonious appearance, the Greek view displays a uniquely aesthetic quality, expressed as much in architecture and sculpture as in philosophy" (Louis Dupré, *Passage to Modernity: An Essay in the Hermeneutics of Nature and Culture* [New Haven, CT: Yale University Press, 1993], 18). To be "formless" in this sense means neither to exist nor to be knowable.

16 Thomas Aquinas, *Summa Theologica*, vol. 1. Trans. Fathers of the English Dominican Province (New York: Benzinger Brothers, 1948), I.5.4.

17 Hans Urs von Balthasar, *The Glory of the Lord*, 7 vols. (San Francisco, CA: Ignatius, 1983–1990), 1.30.

18 John Paul II, *Fides et Ratio* (Boston: Pauline Books and Media, 1998), §23.

19 D.C. Schindler, *The Catholicity of Reason* (Grand Rapids, MI: Eerdmans, 2013), 105.

20 To make aesthetic form the criterion of metaphysical and theological form would be to enslave the latter to material conceptions of beauty rather than allowing them to unfold according to their own proper form and order. This practice has been justly decried as a mere "aesthetic theology" (Balthasar, *The Glory of the Lord*, 1.79). We shall see later that Wilde's Lord Henry gives us an aesthetic philosophy that fails to be either a genuine aesthetics or a genuine philosophy.

21 Plato, *Phaedrus*, 249d, 250d.

22 Ibid., 246c.

23 A field of knowledge is itself a whole with its own proper autonomy (John Paul, *Fides et Ratio*, §45), but as such it is a whole ordered to a larger whole, just as every human being is a whole unto itself but also as ordered to the whole of society (see Jacques Maritain, *The Person and the Common Good*, trans. John J. Fitzgerald [Notre Dame, IN: University of Notre Dame Press, 1966], 56).

24 The Swiss theologian Hans Urs von Balthasar argued for an adaptation of the idea of *Gestalt*, as first described in German idealist philosophy, as essential to any philosophy's understanding of form. The *Gestalt* is "the figure and that which shines forth from the figure" (Balthasar, *The Glory of the Lord*, 1.20). As such, we never leave the concrete form behind in order to be transported to the depths (1.118). "The form as it appears to us is beautiful," he writes, "only because the delight that it arouses in us is founded on the fact that, in it, the truth and goodness of the depths of reality itself are manifested and bestowed" (1.118).

25 See Schindler, *The Catholicity of Reason*, 71, 73, 105.

26 Aquinas, *Summa Theologica*, I.79.10; cf. Balthasar, *The Glory of the Lord*, 1.139.

27 John Paul, *Fides et Ratio*, §75.

28 On faith as the orienting principle of reason, see E.F. Schumacher, *A Guide for the Perplexed* (New York: Harper Perennial, 1977), 39–49.

29 See Wilson, "John Paul II's *Letter to Artists*."

30 See W.K. Wimsatt, "The Concrete Universal," in *The Verbal Icon* (New York: Noonday Press, 1954), 69–83.

31 Balthasar, *The Glory of the Lord*, 1.153.

32 Ibid., 1.154; 155.

33 Schindler, *The Catholicity of Reason*, 262.

34 Interdisciplinary Encyclopedia of Religion and Science, "Dogmatic Constitution 'Dei Filius,'" chapter 2. Available at http://inters.org/Vatican-Council-I-Dei-Filius.

3

ZHANGE NI

Postsecular Reading

In the undergraduate religious studies courses that I teach, I often ask students why they show up, if not just for the sake of required credits. The answer is always, "I want to understand what's going on in the news." And religion is certainly in the news. The public visibility and awareness of religion in current global affairs compels us to engage the "postsecular" question, although we may or may not be entering a postsecular age if that term is a descriptor for the reemergence of repressed religion after a secular age. This designation implies that religion and the secular can be conceptualized as neatly bounded and easily separable entities, or even consecutive stages on an evolutionary ladder, a questionable assumption.[1]

A better way to define the postsecular is to see that religion and the secular are not polar opposites but have always been interdependent since their coemergence in the modern West. Although defined as apolitical, interior piety by the normative claims of secularism, religion has never been completely contained inside this model. Claiming the separation of church and state or state neutrality toward different religious traditions, secularism itself has proved to be a problem space that is already implicated in religious questions.[2] The postsecular, therefore, is not merely disenchantment with secularism, but rather an effort to reconsider and reconfigure symbolic assumptions, cultivated sensibilities, and power relations associated with religion and to question the secular's claim to epistemic, affective, and moral-political supremacy. The postsecular is particularly attentive to the fluidity of religion as a constructed category, to the varieties of nonmodern, non-Western religious traditions, and to the flourishing of new types of "spiritual" (although almost invariably embodied) practices.

Postsecular reading follows theological reading to challenge the hegemonic universalism of "secular" reason and joins confessional reading to address the failures of the protectionist exclusionism of "secular" aesthetics. But rather than working within the comfort zone of one literature and one religion, postsecular reading ventures outside those boundaries to question the formation of the sacred or sacralization in a whole range of interlinked "secular" spheres. Postsecular reading asks the reader to encounter the world and human lives as radically more than what secular modernity has made them – even more than what a text, given its inevitable limits and situatedness, may possibly imagine – and to embrace a rigorous openness to the wholeness of reality, including the multiplicity of faith commitments, the alterity of religious traditions beyond the model of confessional communities, and the intertwined power relations of religion and politics.

In the first decade of twenty-first century, scholars such as John McClure and Amy Hungerford began to read contemporary American literature as a terrain for tentative, open-ended "partial faith" or "belief in belief" rather than in God.[3] In the second decade, a new wave of scholarship further broadened the scope to read world literature, postcolonial literature, popular literature, and various non-Western national literatures in relation to diverse projects of religion-making and secularism.[4] For instance, Talal Asad and Saba Mahmood studied Muslim protests in the *Satanic Verses* affair and the Danish cartoon controversy, urging us to pay attention to the multiplicity of reading/writing practices.[5] Tracing new contours and constellations of religion and the secular by traversing high art and mass entertainment, Gauri Viswanathan proposed that we study popular culture to quest for what has been rejected by *both* orthodox religion *and* normative secularism.[6] In this regard, fascination with popular movies, TV shows, and comic books may very well capture the spiritual expressions, embodied practices, and political imaginations of our contemporary world.[7]

It is the turn both to the postsecular and to popular culture that I wish to examine in this chapter by analyzing the popular franchise *The Hunger Games (HG).*[*] *The Hunger Games* trilogy by Suzanne Collins – *The Hunger Games* (2008), *Catching Fire* (2009), and *Mockingjay* (2010) – and their movie adaptations (2012–2015) are caught between upholding and problematizing secular assumptions regarding our collective and individual lives. Tracy Fessenden has appropriately warned against turning literature into a "secular" site for "sacred" authority and reinscribing old categories and their delineations.[8] The *HG* trilogy, however, helps us to question traditional definitions of both sacred and secular as well as the sacralization of the secular in the modern world. It enacts two types of sacralization – the sacredness of the modern state and the sacredness of the modern individual – that are simultaneously put into conflict with each other

---

[*] The reader should be aware that "spoilers," i.e., important plot points, are revealed in this chapter.

and sutured together by the cult of romantic love. A postsecular reading of the trilogy exposes the unsteady polarization and interdependence of the two secular sacreds within the novels, but also undermines the division between textual ideas and actual social lives to gesture toward the potential limned in the trilogy for a new humanity beyond traditional religious or secular categories.

I.

The *HG* trilogy is at once a dystopian narrative and a bildungsroman. It tells the growing-up story of a girl named Katniss Everdeen, who lives in future America and is caught up in a killing game staged by the totalitarian state Panem. The three novels gradually unfold the drama in which this girl eventually brings down that regime, pitting the sacredness of the modern individual against the sacralization of the modern state. The *HG* trilogy seems to be a "secular" text, if the word "secular" refers to what remains after the subtraction of religion. The *HG* trilogy is not the *Harry Potter* series and does not bother to invent a magical or supernatural realm. However, the *HG* trilogy is actually postsecular because it sheds light on the mutual penetration of the sacred and secular orders by depicting *both* a God-like secular state *and* the inviolable sacredness of the person in secular humanism. It also presents romantic love as a new form of spirituality shared by the audience of the hunger games inside the story and readers/viewers of the text. The *HG* trilogy is not fully postsecular, however, because it does not challenge some secular understandings of state politics and personal sensibilities, especially in pre-senting the downfall of the evil Panem and the maturation of heroic Katniss as two sides of the same coin. That is to say, it remains "secular," if we take secularism to be a set of normative claims about progress and the valuation of individual consciousness that shape, if not dictate, our lives.

The commercial success of the *HG* trilogy is phenomenal. What are we fascinated with? The gory brutality of the hunger games or Katniss' selfless devotion to her loved ones? Why do we have to choose? The mixture of a sadistic pleasure in horror and violence and a much more "proper" yearning for compassion and benevolence corresponds to the subterra-neous intertwining of the sacralization of politics and the sacredness of the individual despite their deadly (although facile) conflict. What we see in Panem, the fictional totalitarian state in future America, is the sacralization of the modern nation-state where capital has taken the form of an all-encompassing spectacle. This spectacle is the annual hunger game. Panem of the hunger games is a dystopian imaginary that stands in stark contrast to various modern theories of the state, which present it as the necessary political mechanism to control "religious" violence and the indispensible basis of modern civilization founded on capitalism. The very persistence of dystopian imagination, not to mention the popularity of apocalyptic themes in contemporary literature, undermines the progressive view that the modern world has witnessed a commitment to reason, the refinement of feelings, and the decline of violence and suffering.[9] The dystopian Panem exaggerates the worst possibilities of the modern state and crushes what has been promised since the Enlightenment: individual autonomy, moral progress, and human flourishing. As many readers of the trilogy have noticed, Panem is not just an authoritarian or totalitarian state. Panem, controlled by the Capitol (the capital), ruled by a President, and consisting of thirteen Districts that correspond to thirteen industries, is a demonic doppelgänger of the democratic state, capitalist economy, and the Weberian industrial society.[10]

Panem is not just a social-political institution, that is, the state of the capital, but also the abstract totality of the Capitol and the thirteen Districts, in other words, a national identity. This state not only creates its nation but also exercises a wild sovereignty that sacralizes itself. There is no divine existence or supernatural power in Panem, but Panem itself is God. There is no belief in Panem, considering the Capitol's addiction to consumerism, the Districts' struggle for survival, and Katniss' experience of doubt and disillusionment, although love seems to be a new faith, the complexity of which will be explored later. The godless, faithless Panem is the omnipotent, omnipresent, and omniscient God that demands sacrifice. The annual hunger game is the state ritual, the ritual sacrifice, of Panem. The sacralization of the state is complete.

This game is Panem's commemoration of its triumph in a civil war when the Districts rebelled against the Capitol in vain. Two tributes, one boy and one girl between the ages of twelve and eighteen, from each of the twelve Districts, with the exception of the controlling Capitol and District 13, which has gone underground, are selected in a lottery-like reaping process. These young tributes arrive in the Capitol, receive one week's training to become gladiators, and are sent into a camera-saturated arena to fight each other until one last survivor walks away. Their battle is broadcast live. The entire nation is compelled to watch. The victor/survivor is worshiped as a pop culture idol and made to tour the country to keep up the flames of excitement. For citizens of the Capitol, the annual hunger game is *the* show that combines sports, fashion, gambling, tourism, and reality television. These games perpetuate the spectacle they live in and would die for. However, real children die in the same games. The mere entertainment for the Capitol is simultaneously the fear and trembling of the District people, who are always at the mercy of Panem the God.

That Panem is, or at least aspires to be, the omnipotent, omnipresent, and omniscient God can be seen by looking carefully at the arena. Panem builds the arena to exercise its omnipotent power over life and death. Preparations for and the aftermath of the game help to build the omnipresent national body of Panem. Techno-scientific media linking the arena and the entire country throughout the game season render Panem omniscient; it is a society of surveillance and of spectacle.

First, Panem has the sovereign power to stage the hunger games. It builds the arena, a self-enclosed mini-world, and forces the young tributes to fight the Hobbesian "total war" inside. The arena makes possible Panem's omnipotent power, which is the right to demand sacrifice and go beyond the political and natural law. The political law allows an exemption that is not universal and is therefore not valid. The ruling class located in the Capitol is exempted from the game, which draws only from the Districts. Citizens of the Capitol enter the arena only after the game, as tourists. And although there is no magic or any supernatural power in the trilogy, Panem transcends the natural law inside the arena, which is full of deadly "special effects." Gamemakers in the control room create inclement weather and monster-mutations to make the tributes' fight more difficult and exciting to the audience. When gamemakers play with computer simulation and genetic engineering, Panem plays God.

The artificially constructed and remotely controlled arena replicates what Hobbes meant by the "natural condition of man." The fight inside the arena is clearly his "total war" of everyone against everyone else. However, in the trilogy, the "natural" condition is not just a human construct but rather a state project. Panem reverses the conceptualization of Leviathan. According to Hobbes, it is the commonwealth, or the more well-known Leviathan, that comes into being as a result of social contract and that steps in to end the natural condition or the total war by appropriating and monopolizing violence. To the contrary, Panem acknowledges its origin in a civil war and perpetuates its foundational violence by manufacturing the natural condition and staging the total war inside the arena. The arena is the norm of Panem's political configuration. The fight to death inside the arena, the hand-to-mouth labor of the Districts, and the endless consumption of the Capitol all have the human body as their source and target. Panem exercises its sovereign power over the bare life of its people. Since Giorgio Agamben argues that the concentration camp is the hidden matrix rather than the exemption of modern bio-politics,[11] we cannot help raising this question: is the arena another hidden matrix for our, not just Panem's, politics?

Second, Panem controls not only its people but also geography and historiography. It claims to be omnipresent, that is, a cosmic presence.

Readers of the trilogy have noticed that the fictional universe of the text is absent of any country other than Panem and void of any prehistory before the Dark Days of the first civil war. The bio-spatial-temporal totality of Panem is produced by a whole series of pre- and postarena events, beginning with the national reaping and culminating in the national victory tour. The hunger game is first and foremost an annual ritual. The calendar year of Panem is divided into the game season and the waiting period. The cyclical game is a regeneration ritual that ensures the "eternal return" of Panem, to borrow the term from Mircea Eliade.

Reaping marks the beginning of the game season and constitutes Panem's population census. Everyone must attend the ceremony in a public square, with children between twelve and eighteen forming several rows, their name cards placed inside two glass balls (for the two genders). The state power of Panem reaches every individual in the Districts, marks them by age, and picks the tributes in the name of fate. However, fate is actually the sovereign power of Panem that pretends to be the whimsical will of the cosmos. While fate picks the tributes, the entire population is reaped into Panem.

The reaping process continues when tributes take the bullet train to the Capitol and then, wearing glamorous makeup and outfits, ride chariots into the training center. This parade of the tributes/chariots, resembling the parade of the nations in the opening ceremony of the modern Olympic games, is meant to display the identity of each District (or, industries) and the unification of all these Districts and the Capitol into Panem. This parade is also a demonic parody of the Senate, because the Districts, which the tributes represent, are united into Panem, like the United States of America.[12]

The United Districts of Panem emerge from the fight in the arena. The only survivor becomes the ultimate representative of the twenty-four tributes representing the twelve Districts. He or she represents the unified identity of Panem. The reversal of the prearena train ride and chariot parade is the postarena victory tour. The ultimate representative travels from the Capitol, all the way through the twelve Districts, back to his or her crowning ceremony in the Capitol. Although Panem has an air force, tributes always take the train. The railway system is the blood vein of Panem's national/geographical body. The railway takes tributes and goods from the twelve Districts to the Captiol, and victors and soldiers (ironically called Peacekeepers) from the Capitol to the Districts. During the final tour, the victor/survivor has to chant this slogan wherever he or she visits: "Panem today. Panem tomorrow. Panem forever." Not only the entire population and landscape but also time is reaped into the omnipresent Panem.

Third, Panem is panentheistic, meaning that God penetrates the world but transcends it as well. Panem reaps and stays beyond its people, land, and history. To maintain absolute control, it has to see all from above. The sovereign structuring principle of the theologico-political requires a site of perfect vision; political/theological sovereignty requires omniscience.[13] The arena where Panem exercises its omnipotence must be camera-saturated. It must become a panopticon. Covered by cameras for surveillance and entertainment, the Eye of Panem never blinks in or outside the arena. What connects the arena and the entire territory of Panem is not just the train ride back and forth but also, in an even more effective way, the television, an omniscient network of camera eyes and TV screens. Like participation in the national reaping, watching the hunger games on television is compulsory. Everyone sees through the Eye of Panem, which sees everyone seeing. The essence of television is that the eye of the camera and the eyes of the spectator are two and that the viewers see something from a point of view other than their own.[14] There is thus a radical asymmetry between viewers and the camera. The eyes of the viewers are not allowed to look back at the Eye of Panem, although they must always look through that Eye.

However, Panem's accomplishment of omnipotence, omnipresence, and omniscience also initiates the reverse process of disintegration. The abstract totality of Panem cracks from within. The divide between the Capitol and Districts is incorrigible. Guy Bebord is right in pointing out that we remain separated in the very act of being united into spectacle.[15] While citizens of the Capitol relish the schadenfreude of viewing brutal killings, District kids like Katniss have no taste for the Capitol-style extravagance and sentimentality. The war is not so much between Panem and District 13 as between the sacralization of the modern state and the sacredness of the modern individual. It is worth noticing that among the rebels against Panem there are stylists, camera crews, and even gamemakers. They have violated the asymmetry of the Eye and looked back at Panem precisely because they helped to create it, and they cannot bear what they see. They work for District 13 instead and fight spectacle with spectacle. One case in point is the moment when Katniss appears on television after having survived the seventy-fourth hunger game. Before being forced to fight again, her snow-white wedding dress morphs into a burning black mockingjay costume right in front of the audience of Panem. Her stylist, Cinna, who secretly works for the rebels, designed the spectacular dress to declare war.

2.

The girl on fire becomes an emblem of the sacred modern individual. The trilogy itself leans toward a secular reading that identifies with the autonomous and authentic self while condemning totalitarianism, thus choosing one secular sacred over the other. A postsecular reading, however, probes for the complexity and ambiguity inherent in the text and in the everyday lives of humans outside the text. Katniss is a symbol of rebellion against the dystopian Panem, but this paradigmatic modern – and secular – individual is also implicated in the modern state that manipulates intimate relations and shapes individual lives. Her story is a contemporary bildungsroman that undergirds – and, rather unwittingly, undermines – the sacredness of the modern individual.

In his study of the modern European bildungsroman, Franco Moretti demonstrates that these texts have given rise to a modern self marked by social mobility and psychological interiority.[16] Following his lead, Jed Esty argues that the unbridled dynamism of capitalist modernity as crystallized in the figure of the restless youth was tentatively folded into the formation of the nation that coincided with the golden era of classical bildungsroman; however, this momentary equilibrium collapsed when European nation-states developed into colonial empires. Anti-bildungsromans in which prot-agonists (women, the disenfranchised in Europe, and the non-Western other) suffer stagnation rather than develop into their mature selves mushroomed in modernist literature and non-Western literatures in the twentieth century.[17]

Seen in this context, the *HG* trilogy continues the bildungsroman tradition because Katniss is portrayed as a girl of inner authenticity and outer mobility (or, transgression). But it is also an anti-bildungsroman because it twists the utopian promises of the state and capital into the dystopian Panem that does not allow the proper development of its people, let alone human flourishing. Given her young age, female gender, dubious ethnicity (in the original novels), and working-class background, Katniss is the other in multiple senses, that is, the multiple others who live beyond the limited utopia of Enlightenment humanism. However, reading Katniss simply as the Other may shift our attention away from the ways in which she is presented and received as a paradigmatic modern individual, and as a result precludes the possibility of wrestling radical otherness from the thickness of her story. This radical otherness would read the *Hunger Games* as a post-bildungsroman in which the values of psychological interiority and autonomous individuality are recognized as historical, Westernized constructs. Saba Mahmood's *Politics of Piety*, Lila Abu-Lughod's *Do Muslim Women Need Saving?*, and Nirmala S. Salgado's *Buddhist Nuns and Gendered Practice*, among other texts, have pointed out the secular limits of global feminism and of the discourse of liberal humanism behind it.[18] They question the validity and viability of assumptions such as autonomy, empowerment, and sympathetic identification and endeavor to do justice to women's lived experiences in nonsecular symbolic universes evolving around Muslim submission or Buddhist nonself. Such a postsecular alternative is not developed in the *Hunger Games*, as we shall see later, but it is at least suggested. The titular subject of the novels, the hunger games, constitute a collective ritual, an ongoing narrative, and bodily disciplines that, although enacted negatively, shape what Asad calls a "discursive/material tradition."[19] These games, in other words, are presented only in relation to the dystopian political regime of Panem. Moreover, they are disrupted not simply by an autonomous heroine, but rather by a heroine who herself symbolizes the sacred individual. As a result, alternative sources and routes of resistance are only dimly evoked in the novels, lost in the glory of the girl on fire.

In the trilogy, the adorable girl Katniss is true to herself, committed to loved ones, and dauntless under the pressure of state violence. She preserves her inner authenticity against the encroachment of heteronomous impositions. Out of a truly compassionate, humanitarian spirit, she volunteers to fight the hunger game in place of Prim, her younger sister, who is reaped as a tribute. At the very outset of the text, her volunteering challenges the logic of Panem's reaping. She breaks rules and rejects scripts. Even before volunteering at the reaping, she dares to hunt in forbidden areas. Inside the arena, she collaborates with Peeta, a fellow tribute from District 12, to the point of committing a double suicide to protest against the game. During the victory tour afterward, she makes defiant gestures, triggering riots across Panem that later escalate into the second civil war. She stands against the omnipotent, omnipresent, and omniscient Panem and even maintains her sanity against revolutionary fury, for there is an uncanny affinity between the popular sovereignty of revolution and the wild sovereignty of Panem. The collective will of revolution may very well replicate what it overthrows. To destroy Panem and its possible revolutionary revival, Katniss dares to go insane by shooting President Coin, leader of District 13, although her initial task is to assassinate Panem's President Snow.

Among scholars who read the *HG* trilogy, Anna Mae Duane is one of the few who is not sympathetic toward the portrayal of Katniss. She sees in Katniss' volunteering as tribute a conflation of "a nineteenth-century model of sympathetic giving ... and a modern neoliberal story of plucky individuals who can win the competition for resources and applause." Hence she is deeply worried that "[e]namored by a story in which individual initiative and gambled bodies can win an escape from suffering, even the best-intentioned human rights activists can seek to celebrate the agency of individual players at the expense of ignoring the systemic power of what we could well call the global hunger games."[20] Duane's critique points to an important postsecular move – the blurring of artificial boundaries between textual ideas and the conditions of social lives, the quest for what has not been imagined and the question of why it is not imaginable. How different are we the readers/viewers, who take delight in the brutality of the games or the selfless devotion of Katniss to protect the weak against power, or both, from the complicit audience in the Capitol? How do we account for the commercial success of the franchise, which readers and viewers have fueled, recognizing that the cultivation of sensibility is politically, ethically, and not simply aesthetically motivated?

Duane's concern that celebration of the individual may obfuscate our sensitivity toward systemic power is worth highlighting. Moreover, since the sacredness of the modern individual and that of the modern state are mutually dependent, celebration of the individual works to conceal that link so that the global hunger games outside the text go on not just despite but precisely owing to the collapse of Panem inside the text. The story of Katniss and her victory over Panem becomes a security vault that contains the disturbing fact that Panem and its hunger games are close to, rather than opposite from, our everyday living, in which horror adds spice to aesthetics and entertainment, while violence is not without certain valence. In short, the *HG* franchise has become popular because it presents the world as it ought to be according to secular humanism and liberal politics, leaving out what does not fit. Traces of the repressed, however, are discernible.

3.

Within the text, the disturbing dystopian imagination of Panem and its hunger games makes the story of Katniss unstable from the bottom up. The trilogy has to enact a romantic love triangle to restore a certain sense of balance. Love seems to be a new spirituality that is genuine and universal, traversing the divide between the Capitol and Districts and bringing together the fictional and real worlds.

In contemporary Young Adult literature, the *HG* trilogy is often compared with the *Twilight* series that immediately preceded it. They share a romantic triangle between one girl and two boys. For many readers, the main plot of the *HG* trilogy is *not only* the conflict between Katniss and Panem *but also* her choice between Peeta and Gale. Treating conflict and war in the political realm as the indispensible larger context for a girl's self-formation achieved through selecting her Mr. Right is by no means merely sentimental, because it helps to illuminate the interdependence of the two sacreds and destabilize the affirmation of one over the other. Two candidates compete for Katniss' love: Peeta the bread boy and Gale the rebel boy.

Katniss eventually marries Peeta and has two children with him, choosing love and family instead of rage and revolution. Gale leaves, because the military attack he orchestrates to defeat the state apparatus of Panem is responsible for the death of Prim, Katniss' younger sister. Katniss' separation from Gale and union with Peeta, a movement away from violence and toward benevolence, is the much-desired trajectory of the paradigmatic modern individual that secular humanism celebrates and that, in turn, helps to stabilize the modern nation-state.

However, in a postsecular reading there is always more. The romantic relationship between Peeta and Katniss originates in an intentional misinterpretation and is manipulated by the state of Panem. The separation of Gale and Katniss is also a textual sacrifice that safeguards the "legitimate" characterization of the girl. Gale's exile stands for what must be left out to keep Katniss within the model of psychological interiority, transgressive mobility, and moral progress toward more civility and less suffering that is paradigmatic of the modern individual. Stories of romantic love, a cult claiming passionate devotees, function to truncate the inexhaustible complexities of our lived reality and fit a simplified representation into the limits of secular humanism, which has taken on an unquestioned sacredness.

The story of Peeta and Katniss demands critical attention first. Katniss and Peeta are children of the hunger game. They hardly speak to each other before fighting in the arena, although it is revealed later that Peeta has always been secretly in love with Katniss. Katniss is prepared for the brutal game, because as a fatherless girl responsible for the livelihood of her sick mother and younger sister, she has to hunt and has become a seasoned archer. Peeta the gentle boy survives as well, because he knows how to disguise himself and disappear right in front of his enemies. Katniss and Peeta are also smart enough to team up against other tributes. They are never short of unexpected tactics. Their last resort is especially impressive. They will not allow a single ultimate representative of Panem to emerge and decide to commit double suicide. They are not in love but in solidarity, determined to deprive the game of its victor/survivor.

Indeed, the romantic love between Katniss and Peeta is a misinterpretation that the melodrama-hungry audience in the Capitol (and readers/viewers of the trilogy) savors. President Snow, head of Panem, endorses this misinterpretation and forces the boy and the girl into a fake affair, because romantic love is the best smokescreen to make invisible other types of human connectivity, such as the bond of District people against the Capitol. Surprisingly, what Panem is least afraid of is the seemingly most powerful romantic love. It even uses love and other intimate relations to control the tributes. During the seventy-fifth hunger game, gamemakers release jabberjays (mutant birds that imitate human voices) to distract tributes with (simulated) tortured screams of their loved ones. In the third and final book, when the rebels rescue Peeta from his imprisonment in the Capitol and bring him back to Katniss, he tries to throttle her because he has been "brainwashed." Apparently this episode aims to show how sacrilegious Panem is, by violating the sanctity of inner emotions. However, the text neither gives specifics about how Panem does brainwashing nor explains how Peeta recovers from it. It is simply given that state power is able to penetrate into the most intimate recesses, that psychological interiority has always been shaped by social, cultural, and political conditions that are external to it. The text touches upon the constructedness of psychological interiority and suggests the mutual dependence of the modern state and the modern individual, but it then steers away by letting the mysterious "natural" course take over. Peeta just "naturally" recovers from the intervention of the state to become Katniss' family guy again, the role ironically dictated by the state in the first place.

President Snow does not want to see Gale and Katniss together and forces Katniss to pair with Peeta, threatening her with the life of Gale. Later, it is the text that does not want them together, either. Katniss and Gale have been close since childhood, having lost their fathers in the same mining accident. They are hunting partners before the hunger games and fight side by side in the civil war. They can be read as one person, with Gale embodying the violence that founds and sustains Katniss' humanist integrity and humanitarian project. Katniss must leave Gale because she must deny the rage and hatred she shares with him. Their shared experience simply contradicts the civilizing agenda to reduce violence and eliminate suffering. After the first civil war, District 13 manages to stay underground because its nuclear power is able to checkmate the Capitol. Then the rebels win the second civil war because they play Panem's game better than Panem does. Consumed by hatred, Gale, among many others, of course, does not refrain from arranging "uncivilized" attacks on civilians and framing Panem for what the rebels do. The rebels even consider continuing the hunger games but reaping only from the Capitol. Katniss is among those who vote for this "inhuman" proposal. Both Katniss and Gale kill, but Gale goes beyond the limits (murdering Prim and other innocent civilians) to make his own exile necessary, Katniss' integrity possible, and humanist principles legitimate. The text sacrifices Gale, mirroring Katniss' assassination of President Coin. Coin's death and Gale's exile are intended to terminate Panem for good, at least in Katniss' life. Both are acts of sacrifice demanded by the sacredness of the modern individual, who would never stage a hunger game but paradoxically has emerged from it.

Both stories, Katniss and Gale and Katniss and Peeta, however, point beyond themselves toward another Katniss, an unknown girl struggling with paradoxes (the intertwining of suffering and entertainment, violence and benevolence, and collective power and individual strength) and striving for alternatives. This unknown Katniss is perhaps the true child of the hunger games. Two very practical questions might help us to invoke the other side of this potential, postsecular self that is not contained by the sacred state, the sacred individual, or the sacred cult of romantic love: What helps Katniss stay alive against all odds? What defeats Panem in spite of its overwhelming power? The answer is not Katniss' relationship with Peeta, reduced to a simple romantic love affair. Instead, bodily discipline, everyday tactics, and human solidarity – collective rituals that both sustain and destroy life – enable her to survive the hunger games and the civil war. Similarly, it is not a conventionally transgressive individual who overthrows Panem. Instead, the powerful Panem falls to rage, scheming, and violence – collective rituals that maintain and undermine political regimes – the symbol of which is Gale, who must be exiled. To read Katniss' story as a postsecular post-bildungsroman, rather than as a conventional romance, is to fold back into her character the resources of everyday life that Peeta (not Mr. Right) stands for and the moral complexity that warriors like Gale (not Mr. Exile) have to confront. In this regard, the title of the trilogy is more revealing than the popular readings it has invited. The trilogy is not entitled *Katniss' Adventures in Panem*, but *The Hunger Games*.

In the trilogy itself, the two story lines of romantic love not only push Katniss from revolutionary rage to domestic order but also eclipse Katniss' relation to Prim and Rue, two other girls. Although some readers may hail Katniss' choice of the apparently feminine Peeta over the traditional type of masculine hero Gale as a feminist gesture, it is to be stressed that behind the two boys there are two dead girls. Katniss is a strong woman character, but she is first and foremost a modern individual defined by romantic love, heterosexual family, state power, and the global neo-liberal order. The two other girls, Prim, in whose place Katniss volunteers to fight the hunger game, and Rue, a tribute from District 11, with whom Katniss fights side by side, both die young. Rue is killed in the game; her solidarity with Katniss ignites in the latter the sparkle of revolution. However, the same solidarity between Katniss and Peeta is distorted into romantic love. This amounts to a second killing of Rue, who is not allowed to grow up into maturity, not to mention pointing toward an alternative future for Katniss. Likewise, corresponding to Katniss, an embodiment of nineteenth-century sympathy, her younger sister Prim is clearly a Victorian angel in the house, especially since she grows in the second and third novels into a caring nurse. However, toward the end of the story, Prim is killed by the bomb Gale has designed. Her death determines the separation of Katniss and Gale. What has to be sacrificed is not only Gale but also Prim, so that Katniss may be relieved of moral ambiguity, at least to an extent, and enter the heterosexual domestic realm rather than embracing female homosociality.

Both Rue and Prim are textual devices that decide a particular unfolding of the plot in one and not another direction, rather than fully developed characters. They must die because the trilogy is Katniss' bildungsroman, that is, the bildungsroman of the sacred individual who is presented as an individual available for romantic love. Although Katniss is celebrated as the adolescent, female, not necessarily white, and working-class other, no alternative alliance is visible along the lines of gender, race, or class, considering the immature death of other girls who are weak and meek in the first place. On a more fundamental level, collective lives and embodied practices are not allowed to grow beyond the confines of a brutal killing game. The state of Panem inside the text and the world outside both revere the inviolable individual and foster the cult of romantic love to co-opt the multiple others and preclude radical otherness from being articulated.

4.

The *HG* trilogy is not fully postsecular because although it sheds light on the blurred boundaries of secular and sacred and the rise of new spiritualities, it leaves unchallenged the discourse of secular humanism that sustains the power of the state through upholding autonomous individuals caught up in romantic relations as the only foundational form of human connectivity. Panem, the fictional falling of which ensures its longevity in the world outside the text, is least afraid of the purportedly most powerful romantic love. And Katniss' story has yet to be transformed into a post-bildungsroman.

A post-bildungsroman does not simply pit the autonomous individual against the social-political-economic powers that demand it into being and annul its development at the same time. The post-bildungsroman is not simply a story of personal development or arrested development, but rather explores the growth of the person beyond the limits of secular humanism or beyond the sacredness of the secular self to which the *HG* trilogy subscribes. The trilogy could have presented the marginalized female homosociality or the solidarity of other human collectivities as an alternative spirituality that complements, if not challenges, the cult of romantic love. These alternative spiritualities (although "spirituality" may not be an appropriate word) are what Mahmood, Abu-Lughod, Salgado, and others have explored in their accounts of the real stories of Muslim and Buddhist women in the Middle East and Southeast Asia. These women, drawing on everyday practices and tactics, build up various types of social relations that challenge the constrictive narrative of the sacred state, the sacred individual, and sacred romantic love. Other challenges to the Western secular sacreds have come from scholars who note the imaginative intertwining of revolution and romantic love and the formation of the crowd instead of the individual in modern Chinese literature and visual arts.[21] What a popular text in contemporary America is incapable of envisioning may be seen more clearly in literatures conditioned by other religious and political contexts.

A postsecular reading of the *Hunger Games* pushes us to study the porous divides, shifting contours, and fluid configurations in the trilogy, but it also pushes us into comparative readings that pluralize religion and literature, resist reductive truth claims, and press outward into a widening circle that begins, rather than ends, here and now. A postsecular reading challenges us to take up the ethical and political burden of looking beyond this textual world to a diversity of ontological realities and to the real social conditions that enable real persons to live well in the real world.

Notes

1 Regarding the "postsecular" in relation to religion and the secular at both theoretical and empirical levels, see Gregor McLennan, "The Postsecular Turn," *Theory, Culture & Society* 27.4 (2010): 3–20; Philip Gorski, et al., eds., *The Post-Secular in Question: Religion in Contemporary Society* (New York: New York University Press, 2012); and Craig Calhoun, Eduardo Mendieta, and Jonathan VanAntwerpen, eds., *Habermas and Religion* (Cambridge, UK, and Malden, MA: Polity Press, 2013).

2 For relevant scholarship, see Talal Asad, *Genealogies of Religion: Discipline and Reasons of Power in Christianity and Islam* (Baltimore, MD: Johns Hopkins University Press, 1993); *Formations of the Secular: Christianity, Islam, Modernity* (Stanford, CA: Stanford University Press, 2003); Tomoko Masuzawa, *The Invention of World Religions, or, How European Universalism Was Preserved in the Language of Pluralism* (Chicago, IL: University of Chicago Press, 2005); Markus Dressler and Arvind-Pal S. Mandair, eds., *Secularism and Religion-Making* (Oxford and New York: Oxford University Press, 2011); Hussein Ali Agrama, *Questioning Secularism: Islam, Sovereignty, and the Rule of Law in Modern Egypt* (Chicago; London: University of Chicago Press, 2012); and Matthew Scherer, *Beyond Church and State: Democracy, Secularism, and Conversion* (New York: Cambridge University Press, 2013).

3 John McClure, *Partial Faiths: Postsecular Fiction in the Age of Pynchon and Morrison* (Athens: University of Georgia Press, 2007); Tracy Fessenden, *Culture and Redemption: Religion, the Secular, and American Literature* (Princeton, NJ: Princeton University Press, 2007); and Amy Hungerford, *Postmodern Belief: American Literature and Religion since 1960* (Princeton, NJ: Princeton University Press, 2010).

4 See Zhange Ni, *The Pagan Writes Back: When World Religion Meets World Literature* (Charlottesville and London: University of Virginia Press, 2015); Justin Neuman, *Fiction Beyond Secularism* (Evanston, IL: Northwestern University Press, 2014); Manav Ratti, *The Postsecular Imagination: Postcolonialism, Religion, and Literature* (London and New York: Routledge, 2013); and Erdağ Göknar, *Orhan Pamuk, Secularism and Blasphemy: The Politics of the Turkish Novel* (London and New York: Routledge, 2013). The journal *Comparative Literature* ran a special issue, "Reading Secularism," in 2013 (65:3).

5 Saba Mahmood, "Religious Reason and Secular Affect: An Incommensurable Divide?," in *Is Critique Secular?: Blasphemy, Injury, and Free Speech*, ed. Talal Asad et al. (Berkeley: University of California, 2009), 64–100.

6 Gauri Viswanathan, "Secularism in the Framework of Heterodoxy," *PMLA* 123.2 (2008): 466–476.

7 B.J. Oropeza, ed., *The Gospel According to Superheroes: Religion and Pop Culture* (New York: Peter Lang, 2005); Jeffrey J. Kripal, *Mutants and Mystics: Science Fiction, Superhero Comics, and the Paranormal* (Chicago, IL: University of Chicago Press, 2011); and Victoria Nelson, *Gothicka: Vampire Heroes, Human Gods, and the New Supernatural* (Cambridge, MA: Harvard University Press, 2012).

8 Tracy Fessenden, "The Problem of the Postsecular," *American Literary History* 26.1 (2014): 154–167.

9 Talal Asad also questions this view in his article "Reflections on Violence, Law, and Humanitarianism," *Critical Inquiry* 41.2 (2015): 390–427.

10 For existing literature on the *HG* trilogy, see Balaka Basu, Katherine R. Broad, and Carrie Hintz, eds., *Contemporary Dystopian Fiction for Young Adults: Brave New Teenagers* (New York: Routledge, 2013); Sean Conners, ed., *The Politics of Panem: Challenging Genres* (Rotterdam: Sense Publishers, 2014); and Deidre Anne Evans Garriott, Whitney Elaine Jones, and Julie Elizabeth Tyler, eds., *Space and Place in the Hunger Games: New Readings of the Novels* (Jefferson, NC: McFarland, 2014).

11 Giorgio Agamben, *Homo Sacer: Sovereign Power and Bare Life*, trans. Daniel Heller-Roazen (Stanford, CA: Stanford University Press, 1998).

12 The *HG* trilogy is often compared with the Japanese movie *Battle Royale* (2000), in which the government of a dystopian Japan selects a class of high school students to fight their "hunger game." The discipline power of school education, which is also a form of state apparatus as studied by Louis Althusser and Michel Foucault, is featured in the Japanese "hunger game."

13 Stefanos Geroulanos, "Transparency, Omnipotence, and Modernity," in *Political Theologies: Public Religions in a Post-secular World*, ed. Hent de Vries and Lawrence E. Sullivan (New York: Fordham University Press, 2006).

14 Jenny Slatman, "Tele-vision: Between Blind Trust and Perceptual Truth," in *Religion and Media*, ed. Hent de Vries and Samuel Weber (Stanford, CA: Stanford University Press, 2006): 216–226.

15 Guy Debord, *The Society of the Spectacle*, trans. Donald Nicholson-Smith (New York: Zone Books; Cambridge: Distributed by MIT Press, 1994).

16 Franco Moretti, *The Way of the World: The Bildungsroman in European Culture*, trans. Albert Sbragia (London and New York: Verso, 2000).

17 Jed Esty, *Unseasonable Youth: Modernism, Colonialism, and the Fiction of Development* (New York: Oxford University Press, 2012).

18 Saba Mahmood, *Politics of Piety: The Islamic Revival and the Feminist Subject* (Princeton, NJ: Princeton University Press, 2005); Lila Abu-Lughod, *Do Muslim Women Need Saving?* (Cambridge, MA: Harvard University Press, 2013); and Nirmala S. Salgado, *Buddhist Nuns and Gendered Practice: In Search of the Female Renunciant* (New York: Oxford University Press, 2013).

19 See Talal Asad, "Thinking about Tradition, Religion, and Politics in Egypt Today." Available at http://criticalinquiry.uchicago.edu/thinking_about_tradition_religion_and_politics_in_egypt_today/.

20 Anna Mae Duane, "Volunteering as Tribute: Disability, Globalization and *The Hunger Games*," in *Disability, Human Rights and the Limits of Humanitarianism*, ed. Cathy J Schlund-Vials and Michael Gill (Burlington, VT: Ashgate, 2014), 63–82, 65.

21 Tie Xiao, "In the Name of the Masses: Conceptualizations and Representations of the Crowd in Early Twentieth-Century China," dissertation, University of Chicago, 2011; Andy Rodekohr, "Conjuring the Masses: The Figure of the Crowd in Modern Chinese Literature and Visual Culture," dissertation, Harvard University, 2012; and Liu Jianmei, *Revolution Plus Love: Literary History, Women's Bodies, and Thematic Repetition in Twentieth-Century Chinese Fiction* (Honolulu: University of Hawai'i Press, 2003).

PART II

Intersections

4

SUSAN M. FELCH

Ethics

In the Western cultural imagination, ethics, religion, and literature exist at an uneasy crossroads, a crossroads often marked by mutual suspicion.

Ethics is suspicious of literature for a variety of reasons, although two such reasons surface with some regularity. First, say ethicists, literature is fictive and therefore must be, at some level, fraudulent. Second, literature stirs the emotions and so can incite and prolong unregulated and disordered desire. Plato's view of literature is more nuanced than his censorship of poets might suggest, but their ban is real nevertheless. And it is not as though these ethical worries have no basis in fact. Every genocide begins with a good story – a compelling narrative about the inhumanity of its victims that incites neighbor to kill neighbor. Literature professors love to talk about the deeper truths revealed by stories, but stories can also propagate – and prop up – horrendous lies. Stories are not necessarily true, but they are powerful, as Plato well understood.

On the other hand, literature, particularly contemporary literature, is often suspicious of ethics. Few epithets are as demeaning to an author as "pedantic," a term critics find useful when they sniff out moral agendas in a poem or novel. Many twenty-first century readers agree, perhaps unthinkingly, with Archibald MacLeish: "A poem should not mean / But be," itself a baldly didactic claim.[1]

Sometimes these ethical worries about literature and literary worries about ethics are elided with religious concerns. Among the poets Plato bans from the Republic are those who tell false stories about immoral, duplicitous, and violent gods.[2] When Augustine, in the *Confessions*, berates himself for crying over Dido, he worries that his empathy for a fictional tragedy will displace sorrow over his own distance from God.[3] English translations of the Bible from the fourteenth century onward inveigh against the "vain imaginations" of human thought that may substitute fantasies for true words about God and the world. And yet narratives and lyrics, stories and poems, are integral to religious accounts, as the chapters in Part III of this volume demonstrate. Most, if not all, religious traditions understand themselves through one or more overarching narratives. There is a story or stories to be told of how a community practices its faith. At the same time, literature neither exhausts nor is coextensive with religion. Laws, physical rituals, and social practices are also endemic to religious traditions; a faith tradition always exceeds its narratives and lyrics, even as it is bound to and expressed by them.

But modern ethics is itself often suspicious of such robust faith traditions, particularly when these traditions claim a transcendent basis for ethical norms and behaviors. When Matthew Arnold argued in the nineteenth century that "most of what now passes with us for religion and philosophy will be replaced by poetry," he was motivated in part by the disjunction he saw between the organized religion of his day and its ethical failures.[4] In the triad ethics/religion/literature, the second term could, he thought, be easily, and without consequence, abandoned. One hundred fifty years later, it is the philosophers rather than the poets who exclude religion from ethics, arguing for biological and psychological altruism and other virtues based solely on immanent evolutionary processes.[5] Secularization theorists, from Durkheim onward, perhaps unwittingly enact Nietzsche's dictum that "Those who have abandoned God cling that much more firmly to the faith in morality."[6]

I.

And yet as the grand narrative of secularization has come increasingly under attack from proponents of postsecularity in the West and from thinkers outside the Anglo-American-Western European axis who contest its universalizing claims, there is a growing global sense that Western, modern explanations of life are somehow "not enough."[7] To use Charles Taylor's terms, even those who search for "fullness" (a sense of significance, value, and meaning in life) entirely within the "immanent frame" (a "natural" order that can be understood on its own terms, apart from the transcendent) find themselves "cross-pressured" (caught between the haunting echo of transcendence and the necessity of constructing meaning amidst a plethora of options).[8] It may not be easy to imagine transcendence in the twenty-first century, but it is equally difficult to erase its trace.

It is not just twenty-first century humans, however, who find themselves at the uneasy crossroads of literature, religion, and ethics. In the Christian tradition, the Gospel of John tells this story of conflict: Jesus comes to eat at the home of his friends in Bethany – Mary, Martha, and Lazarus.[9] When Mary takes a small jar of expensive perfume, pours it over Jesus' feet, and wipes his feet with her hair, the dinner party is incensed. The extravagant gesture seems not merely wanton but unethical. "Why wasn't this perfume sold and the money given to the poor?" one of the disciples remonstrates. Yet it is precisely the extravagance, the gesture that points to a fullness beyond an immanent ethics, that Jesus commends. It is telling that the narrative in John says that the fragrance of the perfume, evanescent but inescapable, filled the whole house. Such extravagance exceeds the economy of dutiful actions; it is the uncontainable residue of devotion, an intense fragrance that will not be denied. It is, in defiance of cultural sexual norms, an act of purity, an embodiment of Kierkegaard's dictum: "Purity of heart is to will one thing."[10]

Purity as remainder and supplement becomes then a way to pry into the affiliation of religion and ethics, not least because the notion of purity, like Mary's jar of perfume, has fallen into disrepute. Consider, for instance, Salman Rushdie's description of Los Angeles in *Shalimar the Clown*:

> The daughter of the murdered man was a woman who hated good weather, but most of the year the city offered little else. Accordingly, she had to put up with long monotonous months of shadowless sunshine and dry, skin-cracking heat. On those rare mornings when she awoke to cloud cover and a hint of moisture in the air she stretched sleepily in bed, arching her back, and was briefly, even hopefully, glad; but the clouds invariably burned off by noon and then there it was again, the dishonest nursery blue of the sky that made the world look childlike and pure, the loud impolite orb blaring at her like a man laughing too loudly in a restaurant.[11]

Rushdie is here not primarily concerned with the weather. Instead, he is worried that purity, rather than being a pathway to God, is a mirage, a harmful illusion, "the dishonest nursery blue of the sky that makes the world *look* childlike and pure" while the sardonic sun mocks our innocence (emphasis added). "'Purity' is a slogan that leads to segregations and explosions." Rushdie has said. "Let us have no more of it. A little more impurity, please; a little less cleanliness; a little more dirt. We'll all sleep easier in our beds."[12]

"Purity" can be a code word for exclusion, self-righteousness, and terror. But a desire for purity and cleansing is linked ineluctably to many, if not most, religious traditions, although we must be careful not to elide distinct faith traditions or to confuse translation of the term "purity" for identical concepts or practices. Purity may signal a turning away from things of this world, a willing alignment of one's will with that of God's, ritual practices, or attention to the consequences of one's actions and thoughts. It may take an individual or a more social bent. Nevertheless, a desire for some form of purity appears in many religions. As understood in the Shinto tradition, for instance, the attainment of *makoto no kokoro*, a sincere heart, or *sei-mei-shin*, the pure heart, is most to be desired.[13] In this context, sincerity of heart means to abandon one's own willfulness in order to be in harmony with the social whole. *The Laws of Manu*, a Hindu text, summarizes the chapter on purification rituals thus: "The limbs are cleaned by water, and the mind is cleaned by truth; the soul of a living being is cleaned by learning and inner heat, and the intellect by knowledge."[14] "Those who have attained the Guru's wisdom / Are pure in heart and speech," says a Sikh text.[15] The Qur'an states that "God loves those that purify themselves."[16] The *Dhammapada*, from the Buddhist *Khuddaka Nikaya*, says that "Doing no evil, / Engaging in what's skillful, / And purifying one's mind: / This is the teaching of the buddhas."[17] The Hebrew Psalmist asks, "Who shall ascend the hill of the LORD? And who shall stand in his holy place?" To which the reply is made, "The one who has clean hands and a pure heart; who does not lift up his soul to what is false, and does not swear deceitfully."[18] In the Christian gospel accounts Jesus says, "Blessed are the pure in heart, for they shall see God."[19]

And herein lies the dilemma of purity: for this fragrance of religious devotion may also seem to constitute, if not a vice, at least a temptation to act wickedly in a complex, pluralistic world.

2.

Mary Gordon's novel *Pearl* takes up this difficult relationship of purity and plurality as it is worked out in the lives of a mother, a daughter, and a substitute father.[20] Maria Meyers, a fifty-year-old mother, lapsed Catholic, and intrepid worker for social justice, lives on the edge of Harlem. She has built an impeccably ethical life: she supervises daycare facilities for the children of low-income, working parents, sends her daughter to a mediocre local public school, supports Democratic politicians, rejects her father (a conservative Catholic businessman who made a modest fortune selling religious kitsch), and participates in free but not overly promiscuous sex and drugs. She has sacrificed family relationships and an upscale professional career for the sake of her ethical commitments. Pearl, Maria's twenty-year-old daughter, is a college student, born of her mother's four-week liaison with a Cambodian civil rights activist who presumably was martyred when he returned to his home country in the 1970s. Joseph Kasperman, a widower and Maria's oldest friend, is the son of her father's housekeeper. It is Joseph, not Maria, who has carried on the family business, providing the additional income that allows Maria and Pearl to live comfortably in New York City.

The action of the novel begins on the evening of Christmas day, 1998, when Maria receives a phone call from the American embassy in Dublin. A woman's voice tells her that Pearl, who is in Ireland for her junior year abroad, has chained herself to the flagpole at the embassy and appears to be in the late stages of starvation. Pearl ferociously fights off attempts to help her. She pulls out her feeding tubes and suffers the indignities of having her hands tied to the hospital bed and the tubes physically sewn onto her nostrils. When Maria and Joseph rush to her bedside, she refuses to see them. The novel then traces the intricate patterns of cause and effect, guilt and responsibility, memory and action that have reunited this ersatz holy family around a hospital bed.

We are drawn almost immediately to Pearl, whose name simultaneously invokes the biblical story of the pearl of great price, for which a man joyfully sacrificed all that he had;[21] the small daughter of Hester Prynne and Arthur Dimmesdale in Nathaniel Hawthorne's *The Scarlet Letter*; and the eponymous heroine of the medieval poem *Pearl*. As readers, we quickly learn that Gordon's Pearl is on a quest for purity beyond the ethical dimensions of her mother's life, for we, unlike Maria and Joseph, are privy to Pearl's own actions, decisions, and thoughts. Although – or perhaps because – Pearl has been raised as a quintessentially globalized, secular child, she experiences the need to be pure as more compelling than the need for food or water. As the author herself has noted, the self-starvation of anorexic and bulimic girls – and by extension Pearl's refusal of food and drink – may perhaps better be understood as a desire for purity than merely as a strategy for control.[22] And Pearl, the narrator tells us, feels a great sense of purpose and joy as she stops eating, "the joy of pure statement, pure act" (19).

Pearl interprets her mother's ethical agenda as a rapacious pluralism, a greedy desire to consume the entire world by bossing it about. In contrast, Pearl longs simply to make one small wrong right by sacrificing herself. She conspicuously uncouples her fast from the ethical directives of the Irish political prisoners, although she imitates their method. For Pearl, purity enables her to say "no" – to herself and her family, to the temptation to excuse her own harsh words to Stevie Donegan, a mentally challenged boy who adores her, and ultimately to life itself. But purity also enables her to say "yes" to sacrifice undertaken willingly, even eagerly, on behalf of Stevie. Both the "no" and the "yes" go beyond ethical duty to answer what Pearl only dimly realizes to be a religious quest, a quest for fullness. Pearl intends her sacrifice to bear witness against the violence of insult, to mark "the human will to harm" (16), to speak by her death for one person, who would otherwise remain mute and ignored. It is this single act of devotion, Pearl reasons, that will make her life count:

> Her death was the vessel of her hope. She could use her death as she could not use her life. Her death would be legible, audible. Her life, she believed, was dim and barely visible; her words feeble whispers, scratches at the door.
>
> As she gave up eating, this sense of purpose, the joy of pure statement, pure act, took her over. She felt at rest. In emptying herself, she was turning from body to idea, the idea that a chosen death could serve as a marker for a wrongful death. (19)

If we feel a certain icy isolation at the heart of Pearl's desire for purity – a weariness with the multiple demands and clawing possessiveness of relationships and therefore an isolation that strikes us as somewhat immature and selfish – Gordon does not allow us easily to dismiss Pearl's vision of her own quest. As a result, much as Hawthorne's Pearl is able to crack open the self-serving assumptions and secrets of the adults around her, so too the fragrance of Gordon's Pearl illuminates Maria and Joseph's motivations.

For Pearl is not the only one who longs for purity. Maria's greedy capaciousness seems to Joseph to mark more a love of excess than a thoughtful pluralist ethics. In a memorably visceral scene, he sits across from Maria at a restaurant as she eats a rare steak, plunging each piece into a pyramid of salt before chewing it with gusto. Watching her, he becomes too ill to eat his own chaste, unbuttered roll (255–259). But Pearl understands that her mother does not so much love excess as that she loves excessively, and thus often foolishly. Maria's grand schemes to right the world's wrongs, her decisive actions, her confidence that she knows the precise needs of every person is a form of perverted purity, an obsessive desire to channel the fecundity of the world into a single and proper direction. Maria is, the narrator tells us, "a woman in love with movement" (57). And although Pearl must protect herself from such consuming mother-love, she also understands that it is *love*, and so learns to trim Maria's excess without thwarting it.

Joseph, too, longs for purity but his is neither the single-minded religious purity desired by Pearl nor the omnivorous activist purity of Maria but rather a purity that is quiet and beautiful and still, like the white marble statues he adores. Joseph equates purity with clarity – the clarity of his dead first wife's beautiful singing voice, the clarity of Pearl's vision. And Joseph, like Pearl, is willing to sacrifice. He gave up his own vocational ambitions to promote his first wife's singing career; he is willing now to devote himself to Pearl as a celibate husband. To maintain the purity of another's great vocation, whether it be music or moral insight, he is willing to become the guardian of that treasure – to give up all he has to cherish the pearl of great price. But the problem is that as soon as he grasps the treasure of purity, it vanishes. His first wife, Devorah, gives up her concert career for the mundane pleasures of house and garden, and Pearl recoils from his offer of marriage, seeing the cloister he offers as the prison it will become.

The desire for purity and the impossibility of attaining it are inextricably twined together in this novel, as are the demands of ethics and religious devotion. In the Christian tradition, from within which Gordon writes, ethics are not autonomous; an ethical life does not consist of checking off a list of duties or even finding the balance between two extremes. Instead, an ethical life is formed in response to God's call. A Christian seeks to align her life with God's call to love him with all her being and to love her neighbor as herself. Both the desire to love God and neighbor and the failure to do so are bound together, which is why rituals of humility, repentance, cleansing, and reception of grace are central to the practice of Christianity. Insofar as purity becomes a merely ethical rather than a religious quest, it is quickly perverted into violence and terror. But purity as religious devotion repositions ethical decision-making by changing the question from "What should I do?" to "What is asked of me?" Agency is subtly shifted, from the self as autonomous actor to the self as graced respondent: I feel the weight of both imperatives – to desire purity and to acknowledge my inability to achieve it.

The novel *Pearl* presses upon us the claim that even in a consciously secularized world the longing for purity is deep-seated and cannot be eradicated from the human soul. It will out, if only in the desire for pure spring water, chemical-free organic foods, extreme sports, or a vegan diet. Ya-Katey, Pearl's father, says to Maria, "I fear purity. . . . If we should have a child it would be very very impure: Jewish, Russian, Cambodian, Catholic, and Buddhist. A real mess. I am in love with the idea of mess. The mess is our only hope against the tyranny of the pure" (95). And Ya-Katey has every right to fear the tyranny of the pure, the murderous purification rites of Pol Pot and the Khmer Rouge. Yet it is Ya-Katey's "very very impure" daughter Pearl who, in turn, desires purity more than her own life. Joseph, her substitute father, understands that she is on a religious quest. He reflects that Pearl "would not have the word *atonement* in her vocabulary. But why, he wonders, would anyone have imagined that an impulse so deep, so ancient, would evaporate because it had not been nourished by the proper word?" (104).

When Joseph recognizes the need for a religious word – atonement, to-be-made-one-with – he recognizes that understanding purity merely as a way to control our chaotic environment by imposing rules of inclusion and exclusion is an insufficient explanation of its cultural pervasiveness.[23] While the desire for order may invade the desire for purity, the novel nudges us to consider that order and control may not lie at its heart. Perhaps an obsessive need to control the world is a perversion of purity, an invasive species as threatening to the moral environment as kudzu or purple loose-strife to a natural ecosystem. Rather than order and control, perhaps whole-heartedness and integrity are the proper synonyms for, or definitions of, purity. Certainly what Pearl is searching for is a sense of completeness, rightness, at-oneness, purpose for a life that seems thin, fractured, and shadowy – so permissive, free, and plural that it has no substance. Indeed, although Maria does not recognize this similarity, her daughter resembles no one quite so much as the virgin martyrs her mother abandoned along with her Catholic school uniform. Yet virginity, as Kathleen Norris notes, has at its core not sexual inexperience, but rather wholeheartedness. It is not passivity, much less a rejection of the world, but rather a state of being "that returns to God in wholeness. This wholeness is not that of having experi-enced all experiences, but of something reserved, preserved, or reclaimed for what it was made for. Virginity is the ability to stay centered, with oneness of purpose. . . . [virginity] could be named 'singleness of heart.'"[24]

3.

I see this desire for purity, for wholeheartedness, for integrity in my students. It is this longing that fosters unhappiness with the incommensurate distance between dream and reality – whether that be in the stories they imagine but cannot quite write or the relationships that promise more than they can ever deliver. But it is also this longing that fuels their imagination and their loves, that motivates them to sacrifice well-paying jobs for volunteer service, to think nothing of spending all night talking to a needy friend, or to buy their clothes at Goodwill rather than the Gap.

Because although purity may be defined as whole*heart*edness, it is inevit-ably incarnated in real bodies. Ethics may be considered abstractly; purity requires attention to actual, physical bodies. Pearl's desire to bear witness, to leave a mark on the world leads through the orifices of her own body. The Hebrew Levitical code prescribes elaborate rituals for washing bodies. The Qur'an allows sand to substitute for water to ensure that rites of purification are not neglected. In the *Kojiki*, an early Shinto text, the deity Izanagi performs a meticulous ritual cleansing that concludes with his wash-ing first his left eye, then his right eye, and finally his nose.[25] It would be wrong simply to dismiss such attention to physical pollution as a deep-seated Gnosticism that despises the body; instead, the body is cleansed so that it may participate fully in religious devotion.

Nor is the body lost when religious texts move the locus of purity from the outward to the inward self. It is true that the Hebrew Psalmist tells us that

God has "no delight in sacrifice; were I to give a burnt offering, you would not be pleased. The sacrifice acceptable to God is a broken spirit; a broken and contrite heart, O God, you will not despise," and the Torah commands the Israelites to "Circumcise, then, the foreskin of your heart, and do not be stubborn any longer."[26] The *Dhammapada* reminds Buddhists that "Not by matted hair, not by clan, / Not by birth does one become a brahmin. / The one in whom there is truth and Dharma / Is the one who is pure, is a Brahmin."[27] A Sikh psalm similarly reads, "Pilgrimage and penance and free-will giving / Gain for one no single grain of merit, / Unless one harken and his heart be loving, / Cleansed within by a meditative bath."[28] Jesus, like the prophets before him, repels external gestures that fail to touch an inner reality: "Do you not see that whatever goes into the mouth enters the stomach, and goes out into the sewer? But what comes out of the mouth proceeds from the heart, and this is what defiles. For out of the heart come evil intentions, murder, adultery, fornication, theft, false witness, slander. These are what defile a person, but to eat with unwashed hands does not defile."[29] And the apostle Paul makes it clear that regulations such as "Do not handle, Do not taste, Do not touch" have only "an appearance of wisdom in promoting self-imposed piety, humility, and severe treatment of the body, but they are of no value in checking self-indulgence."[30]

Yet purity and purification rituals remain firmly attached to bodies, to the congruence between spiritual alignment with God and concrete, public actions. Hypocrisy – the bane of true believers, the delight of religious naysayers, and the stuff of many a novel – is, quite simply, this lack of congruence between inner and outer lives. Religion is meant to foster moral living, even while it is not reducible to ethics. In a Christian text that draws together devotion and ethics, the apostle James says, "Religion that is pure and undefiled before God, the Father, is this: to care for orphans and widows in their distress, and to keep oneself unstained by the world."[31] Purity of heart can be expressed only through actions that demand bodily response.

But this very embodiment of purity also witnesses to its instability. Bodies that are washed become dirty again; widows and orphans do not disappear once they have been fed. The quest for purity is always a *quest*; the very nature of our decaying bodies means that we cannot achieve purity in the here and now. Surely that is the stark point of Father Zossima's stinking corpse in *The Brothers Karamazov*.[32] While his followers expect the pure, sweet scent of a saint to waft up from his dead body, what they smell is the stench of mortality. Purity is not a thing, an entity that can be attained or sustained in this world, and this is perhaps its greatest mystery: although we long for purity, we cannot have it this side of the grave. The quest for purity both draws our hearts to act rightly and chastens our confidence that we can ever fully act in ethically pure ways.

4.

Perhaps nowhere is this paradox more poignantly explored than in Nathaniel Hawthorne's "The Birth-Mark." In this story, Aylmer, who believes that he deeply loves his beautiful wife Georgiana, nevertheless longs to eradicate the birthmark that mars her almost-flawless cheek. "[Y]ou came so nearly perfect from the hand of Nature, that this slightest possible defect – which we hesitate whether to term a defect or a beauty – shocks me, as being the visible mark of earthly imperfection," he tells her. To which she quite wisely replies, "Shocks you, my husband! . . . You cannot love what shocks you!"[33]

Undeterred by her warning and consumed by his quest for purity, however, Aylmer persuades Georgiana to withdraw from the world into the cocoon of his laboratory. After a series of "mortifying failures" (772), he concocts an antidote that his wife willingly drinks; but as the birthmark slowly fades, so, too, does her life. Hawthorne notes, "As the last crimson tint of the birthmark – that sole token of human imperfection – faded from her cheek, the parting breath of the now perfect woman passed into the atmosphere, and her soul, lingering a moment near her husband, took its heavenward flight," and then adds, "Thus ever does the gross Fatality of Earth exult in its invariable triumph over the immortal essence, which, in this dim sphere of half-development, demands the completeness of a higher state" (780).

This longing for a purity that we cannot have, indeed, as Hawthorne would have it, this *demand* for purity that necessarily escapes us, witnesses that this world, with its ethical demands, is only a proximate good. Because purity cannot be fully possessed now, our longing for it makes us homesick. "I am not at home in this world, which I believe to be a place of harm," Pearl writes to her mother (17). The desire for purity gently loosens our tight grip on ourselves, our ambitions, our possessions, our relationships, our ethical systems. It gives us a glimpse into wholeheartedness, where clean hands accompany a pure heart. It helps us see the fullness beyond the finest ethical system, the most dutiful and upright person.

Because purity cannot be attained, it cannot be hardened into an end, a *telos*. Purity is iconic; it is a way of seeing through to God. It is not purity of heart that is the ultimate goal of Christian faith, but rather the sight of God that purity of heart enables. The evanescent fragrance of Mary's perfume fills the house, but it illuminates the figure of Christ. When purity is no longer a desire but a possession, it becomes pathology or perversion. Purity attests to both the necessity and the impurity of our moral efforts, and thus the need for humility, repentance, forgiveness, and grace. Purity linked to mercy opens onto vistas of plenty and joy.

5.

In the medieval poem *Pearl*, the dead heroine, who is now the very embodiment of purity in her heavenly existence, comforts her grieving father not with talk of narrow corridors or disciplined devotion but by conjuring images of plenitude and diversity. She tells him that in heaven the many-membered body of Christ refracts the light of divine life, and Jesus' parable of the workers in the vineyard is fulfilled.[34] Although some have served God for many years on earth while others came late to spiritual awakening, all are crowned in heaven with a purity that is at once simple and whole without being uniform or the same. "The court of the kingdom of God alive," Pearl continues,

> Has a virtue self-distinguishing:
> For every one of all who arrive
> Of the whole realm is queen or king;
> And yet no other shall he deprive,
> But rejoice in others' inheriting.[35]

Heavenly purity thus reflects the classic Christian doctrine of the simplicity of God, an attribute of plenitude in which all good is united in the divine person.[36] As Anselm of Canterbury noted, "You are life and light and wisdom and blessedness and eternity and many suchlike good things; and yet You are nothing save the one and the supreme good."[37] Purity reflects the wholeness and integrity of God and comes as a divine call to an integrated, loving ethical life. But such wholeness cannot be achieved in the here and now; it can only be sought.

The great sin of the narrator in the medieval poem, as for Joseph in Mary Gordon's *Pearl* and Aylmer in Hawthorne's story, is to grasp and hoard the treasure that belongs only to God, namely, a person made in God's image, to pervert an ethical love of neighbor into possession of neighbor. The medieval narrator wishes to repossess his Pearl, to pull her back from the plenitude of heaven and thus to reduce her purity to a commodity. Joseph wishes to enclose his Pearl in a union that will violate not only her full personhood but also the proper intimacy of marriage. Aylmer wishes not so much to perfect his wife as to possess her perfection. In contrast, the great virtue of Gordon's Pearl is that, like Mary of Bethany, she is willing to splurge, to open her hand, to empty her jar of perfume, to expend her life for a single person, Stevie Donagan.

It is always a temptation to confuse the virtues with virtuosity, to imagine that we can by dint of hard work and concentration perform virtuous deeds splendidly if not quite perfectly. Purity by its very nature, with its gestures toward wholeheartedness and single-mindedness, tempts us more than most to the hubris of virtuosity. At this point Simone Weil's distinction between *will*, the gritted-teeth determination to get things right, and *attention*, the active but quiet expectation that God will get things right, may be helpful.[38] Will, for Weil, is an act of pride; attention is a gift of the spirit. Yet attentiveness – the soul's preparation for attention – can be cultivated by story, by fiction, and by literature.

6.

Why turn to literature when we want or need to think about ethical questions? Martha Nussbaum argues that when we consider ethical values and behavior, we need to feel our way through literary texts alongside any rational arguments. Literature, she says, traces "the history of a complex pattern of deliberation, showing its roots in a way of life and looking forward to its consequences in that life. As it does all of this, it lays open to view the complexity, the indeterminacy, the sheer difficulty of actual human deliberation."[39] And it is this deliberate inquiry – which embraces mind, body, emotions, feelings, and all the messy difficulties of the real world – that best illuminates the way we ought to live. Similarly, Mary Gordon argues that "the moral good of fiction stems mainly from a habit of mind it inculcates in the reader," for fiction is "uniquely qualified to combat the sound bite. It says to us that the truth of human beings is often more complicated than we think. What we might like to call the truth is often made up of several truths, including the first thing we thought, its opposite, and something in between. Some things cannot be known without careful pondering; horror can sometimes be averted only if we take our time to look and think and look and think and look and think again."[40] It is not that writers of fictions are by definition always serious ethical thinkers or that readers of fiction, prose or poetry, thereby become better, more moral persons. Gordon herself has said the "notion of an unencumbered, devoted, directed singular life has always been very much in my imagination, although I don't live that way. I can't."[41] But literature does train us in the habits of attentiveness and allows us to wander in secondary worlds where wise and unwise choices, moral and immoral actions, brave and cowardly decisions, evocative and bland language unspool around us. It invites us to exercise our moral and spiritual muscles and to attend to characters who do the same.

And so to return to our story: almost unnoticed in the flurry of the narrative, but not in the structure of the novel, is Pearl's absent father, Ya-Katey. A doctor, an intellectual, a man in love – he knows that to return to Cambodia means certain death and probable degradation and torture. But return he does. When Maria asks him, "Must you go back?" he replies, "Yes, I can't be safe here in this dream while my people are living a nightmare" (97). It is her father's body that we see most clearly in Pearl's slim frame and dark eyes, but it is also his heart we hear in her commitment to bear witness even to death.

At the end of the novel, Pearl, too, determines to travel, her purity leavened with love, for having relinquished her quest for pure statement, pure act, she must now learn not how to die, but how to live. "I've had a lot of ideas," she confides to Joseph, "things I'd like to do before I go back to school. After I go to Cambodia, maybe I'll travel around Asia. And then I think I'd like to work on a farm. I'd like to learn about animals. Maybe I'll come back here, I have a friend whose family has a farm" (352). And so she chatters her way back into the muddy messiness of the world.

Literature, too, dwells in this muddy messiness. In the twenty-first century, a world of sophisticated, accessible communication and weapon technology, the longing for purity may too easily be perverted into the desire to control and manipulate through genocide and terror. But the longing itself cannot, and should not, be suppressed. Mary Gordon's novel suggests that we have abiding human concerns with right relationships, ethical actions, purity, sacrifice, and transcendence, although the context for these concerns – and therefore the shape that they take – may alter dramatically As we learn to glimpse purity rather than grasp it, she suggests, we may also learn to discipline our desire with obligation and sacrifice. It will necessarily be a pilgrimage.

"We will leave Joseph walking down the corridor," says the narrator, "And we will leave Pearl and Maria to themselves. We will hope for the best" (354).

Notes

1 Archibald MacLeish, "Ars Poetica," in *Collected Poems 1917–1982* (New York: Mariner, 1985), 107. But see Lawrence Buell's introduction to the special issue of *PMLA* devoted to Ethics and Literary Study for a survey of the renewed interest in ethical approaches to literature, shaped by traditional moral thematics, contemporary philosophers' turn to literary texts, concerns for ethical forms of life raised by Jacques Derrida and Emmanuel Levinas, Michel Foucault's late work on subjectness and agency, critiques of skepticism, and heighted awareness of professional ethics ("Introduction: In Pursuit of Ethics," *PMLA* 114 [1999]: 7–19).

2 Plato, *Complete Works*, ed. John M. Cooper (Indianapolis, IN: Hackett Publishing, 1997), *Republic* 2.3.

3 Saint Augustine, *Confessions*, trans. Henry Chadwick (New York: Oxford University Press, 1991), 1.13.21.

4 Matthew Arnold, "The Study of Poetry," in *English Literature and Irish Politics*, ed. R. H. Super, *The Complete Prose Works of Matthew Arnold*, vol. 9 (Ann Arbor: University of Michigan Press, 1973), 161–162.

5 See, for instance, the Jean Nicod lectures by Kim Sterelny, published as *The Evolved Apprentice: How Evolution Made Humans Unique* (Cambridge: MIT Press, 2012).

6 Friedrich Nietzsche, *The Will to Power*, trans. Walter Kaufmann and R. J. Hollingdale (New York: Random House, 1967), Aphorism 18, p. 16.

7 For a survey of postsecular thought, see Chapter 3.

8 Charles Taylor, *A Secular Age* (Cambridge, MA: Belknap Press, 2007); see, esp., chapter 16.

9 John 12:1–8.

10 Søren Kierkegaard, *Purity of Heart Is to Will One Thing: Spiritual Preparation for the Office of Confession*, trans. Douglas V. Steere (New York: Harpers, 1948).

11 Salman Rushdie, *Shalimar the Clown* (New York: Random House, 2005), 4–5.

12 Salman Rushdie, "What This Cultural Debate Needs Is More Dirt, Less Pure Stupidity," *The Times* (December 10, 2005). Available at www.timesonline.co.uk/article/o,,1072=1918306,00.html.

13 Stuart D.B. Picken, *Historical Dictionary of Shinto* (Lanham, MD: Scarecrow Press, 2002), 58.

14 *The Laws of Manu*, trans. Wendy Doniger with Brian K. Smith (New York: Penguin, 1991), 5.109, p. 111.

15 From the *Sri Rag* in *Selections from the Sacred Writings of the Sikhs*, trans. Trilochan Singh, et al. (London: Goerge Allen & Unwin, 1960), 70.

16 *The Koran*, translated with notes by N. J. Dawood. Revised 5th ed. (London: Penguin, 1990), 9:108, p. 144.

17 *The Dhammapada*, trans. Gil Fronsdal (Boston and London: Shambhala, 2005), verse 183, p. 49.

18 Psalm 24:3–4, Revised Standard Version; subsequent citations are taken in modified form from this version.

19 Matthew 5:8.

20 Mary Gordon, *Pearl* (New York: Pantheon Books, 2005). All references are to this edition.

21 Matthew 13:45–46.

22 Mary Gordon, "'Pearl': A Tale of Motherhood and Martyrdom," interview by Terry Gross, *Fresh Air*, NPR, January 31, 2005.

23 See, for instance, Mary Douglas, *Purity and Danger: An Analysis of Concepts of Pollution and Taboo* (New York: Praeger, 1966). Douglas argues that "ideas about separating, purifying, demarcating, and punishing transgressions have as their main function to impose system on an inherently untidy experience" (4).

24 Kathleen Norris, *The Cloister Walk* (New York: Riverhead Books, 1996), 201, 200. The quotations are from a Benedictine sister.

25 *Kojiki* 1:11, from *Kojiki*, trans. Donald L. Philippi (Princeton, NJ: Princeton University Press, 1969), 68–70.

26 Psalm 51:16–17; Deuteronomy 10:16.

27 *The Dhammapada*, verse 393, p. 101.

28 From the *Japji* of Guru Nanak Nirankari, a Sikh sage, in John Clark Archer, *The Sikhs in Relation to Hindus, Moslems, Christians, and Ahmadiyyas: A Study in Comparative Religion* (Princeton, NJ: Princeton University Press, 1946), Psalm 21, p. 126.

29 Matthew 15:17–20.

30 Colossians 20–23.

31 James 1:27.

32 Fyodor Dostoevsky, *The Brothers Karamazov*, trans. Richard Pevear and Larissa Volokhonsky (New York: Farrar, Straus and Giroux, 1990), 3.7.1, pp. 327–337.

33 Nathaniel Hawthorne, *Tales and Sketches* (New York: The Library of America, 1982), 765; references are to this edition. For a reading of this story within the rubric of beauty, see Denis Donoghue, *Speaking of Beauty* (New Haven, CT: Yale University Press, 2003), 13–17.

34 Matthew 20:1–16.

35 *Pearl* in *Medieval English Verse*, trans. Brian Stone (Baltimore, MD: Penguin Books, 1964), 154.

36 Much of contemporary philosophical theology misunderstands the simplicity of God as an abstract singularity that denies divine distinctions, reduces God to a property, and denies his personhood. In contrast, the traditional understanding of God's attributes sees them as a way of expressing the full, illimitable life of the personal God; God does not *possess* attributes but *is* his attributes, such that if any were removed, he would cease to be God; cf. Anselm of Canterbury, "On the Procession of the Holy Spirit," in *Anselm of Canterbury: The Major Works*, ed. Brian Davies and G.R. Evans [Oxford: Oxford University Press, 1998], 393).

37 Ibid., 100.

38 Simone Weil, "Attention and Will," in *Gravity and Grace*, trans. Emma Craufurd (London: Routledge and Kegan Paul, 1952), 105–111. See also "Reflections on the Right Use of School Studies with a View to the Love of God," in *Waiting for God*, trans. Emma Craufurd (New York: Harper & Row, 1973), esp. p. 111.

39 Martha Nussbaum, *The Fragility of Goodness: Luck and Ethics in Greek Tragedy and Philosophy*, rev. ed. (Cambridge: Cambridge University Press, 2001), 14.

40 Mary Gordon, "Moral Fiction," *The Atlantic Monthly* (Fiction Issue 2005): 93–96; quotes from p. 96.

41 *Conversations with Mary Gordon*, ed. Alma Bennett (Jackson: University Press of Mississippi, 2002), 23.

5

JULIA REINHARD LUPTON

Dwelling

In earlier eras, "dwell" and "dwelling" were not especially literary words. Variations occur more than eighty times in the plays of Shakespeare, and his clown Audrey in *As You Like It* would not have called it "poetical": "I do not know what 'poetical' is. Is it honest in deed and word? Is it a true thing?" (III.iii.14–15).[1] Today, "dwell" and "dwelling" have indeed become "poetical," thanks to their frequent appearance in the King James Bible and the impact of Martin Heidegger's 1951 essay "Building Dwelling Thinking." A Google search of "dwelling" yields a mix of etymological and semantic, architectural and legal, and religious and charitable hits, often around housing and hospice, disclosing a zone shaped by literary diction, design discourse, and congregational projects aimed at living (and dying) well. In this chapter, I follow the migrations of dwelling in religion, philosophy, and architecture. I then turn to dwelling in the Book of Jonah and Shakespeare's rewriting of Jonah in his late play *Pericles*.[*] The arts of dwelling establish human bonds out of and around our requirements for shelter, sustenance, and succor. Acts of dwelling focus on members of the household but extend – or pointedly refuse to extend – to neighbors and strangers. Dwelling cultivates a sense of place while incorporating an awareness of transit into the practices of home-making through stories of arrival and departure, images of plenty and dearth, and scripts of valediction and benediction. In exploring dwelling's work with and on its own limits, I demonstrate a bilateral approach to religion and literature in which each sphere modifies the other in a manner that invites artistic experiment, imaginative recreation, and communal reconstitution. To read religion with and as literature is to approach Scriptural texts in a nonsectarian and postsecular mode; to read

---

* My thoughts on Jonah and *Pericles* owe much to Elizabeth Allen and the participants of the graduate seminar we taught together in fall 2014 at the University of California, Irvine, on *Pericles* and Jonah. I develop my reading of *Pericles* and dwelling in my book manuscript, "Shakespeare Dwelling: Habitation, Hospitality, Design."

literature with and as religion is to access poetic texts not primarily historically or formally, but as offering schemes for cohabitation in a world in which
we dwell together, precariously.

I.

In English Old Testaments, the word "dwell" most frequently translates the
Hebrew root *y-sh-v*, which also means "to sit."[2] *Yoshev* is attached to acts
of sojourning as well as permanent residence; in Genesis 4:20, Yaval is "the
father of such as dwell in tents, and of such as have cattle." In Leviticus, the
Israelites are told that the Sabbath must be observed "in all your dwellings,"[3] playing on the resonance between *Shabbat* and *yoshev* as forms of
active restfulness that must be extended to strangers, servants, and cattle.[4]
Although dwelling is often coupled with the desire for security (the Lord
"delivered you out of the hand of your enemies on every side, and ye dwelled
safe"),[5] dwelling is always tinged by itineracy, exposure, and estrangement.
The holiday of Sukkot, in which Jews recreate the Exodus from Egypt by
camping out in temporary huts for a week, stitches the memory of
wandering in the desert into the security of stable settlement: "Ye shall dwell
in booths seven days; all that are Israelites born shall dwell in booths."[6]

"Dwell" also translates *shoken*, originally linked to temporary sojourning
but increasingly transferred to God's modes of indwelling.[7] In Exodus, God
tells Moses, "And let them make me a sanctuary [*mishkan*] that I may dwell
[*v'shakanti*] among them."[8] The *mishkan* or traveling ark of the covenant,
built according to the exacting standards spelled out in Exodus 25–27,
focalizes human attentiveness and communal gathering as building materials
that make God's presence immanent. *Shoken* is the root of *shekinah*, literally
"the Dwelling," which names God's hovering presence above the wandering
Israelites in Exodus and became a key idea in Jewish mysticism, whose
techniques of prayer, song, and ritual observance aim to make God's presence tangible.[9]

If the primary senses of dwelling evoke cohabitation and copresence,
dwelling in the Hebrew Bible always folds distance, wandering, and
estrangement into the promise of proximity. Job finds himself derided by
those who used "to dwell [*lishkon*] in the cliffs of the valleys, in caves of the
earth, and in the rocks,"[10] their lowly habitations offering up metaphors of
his own extreme condition. In another passage, Job complains, "They that
dwell [*garē*] in mine house, and my maids, count me for a stranger: I am an
alien in their sight."[11] Here the word translated as "dwell" is derived from
the Hebrew word for stranger, *ger*.[12] Leviticus 19:34 institutes the rule of
neighbor-love in a related play on estrangement and dwelling: "The stranger

[*ha-ger*] that dwelleth [*haggar*] with you shall be unto you as one born among you, and thou shalt love him as thyself; for ye were strangers [*gerim*] in the land of Egypt." From the earthbound, alienated *guwr* to the house-holding *yoshev* to the heavenly *shochen*, dwelling institutes provisional forms of permanence around the memory and prospect of itinerancy.[13]

In the New Testament, God and man come to dwell in each other through the intimate exchanges of the Eucharist: "He that eateth my flesh, and drinketh my blood, dwelleth in me, and I in him."[14] Here, "dwelleth" translates the Greek *menei*, from *menó*, to stay, abide, dwell; to sojourn, tarry (as a guest); to lodge.[15] In communion, ingestion makes a double sojourn and undergoes a mutual metabolism. When the communicant eats and drinks God, he dwells in her for a short time, but since the eaten is greater than the eater, her digestive-symbolic action incorporates her into the body of the church that Christ heads. She hosts the Host in order that the Host host her.

In an explicitly architectural metaphor, St. Paul tells the Corinthians, "Ye are the temple [*naos*] of the living God: as God hath said, I will dwell in them, and walk in them: and I will be their God, and they shall be my people."[16] Here "dwell" translates *enoikēsō*, with its root in *oikos*, or household, while *naos* (temple, sanctuary) comes from *naiō*, to dwell.[17] Paul identifies the church with the congregation of the faithful rather than with a particular building. Although he may be challenging the authority of the Temple and the Jewish Christians in Jerusalem, he also reasserts his own Jewishness by restating the Israelite idea that God will "dwell among them" through the forms of copresence cultivated around the desert-built *mishkan* in Exodus 25:8.

2.

Heidegger's essay "Building Dwelling Thinking" was initially addressed to a gathering of architects, engineers, and philosophers who had assembled in Darmstadt in 1951 to consider the task of rebuilding bombed cities and accommodating refugees from the East after World War II.[18] Heidegger begins by declaring that he will not attempt to give "rules for building," the main line of architectural theory that stretches from Vitruvius' *De Architectura* (first century BCE) to Le Corbusier's *The Radiant City* (1935). Instead, Heidegger subordinates *building*, which concerns engineering, to *dwelling*, the ensemble of routines of living through which human beings meet and exceed the needs of life. Dwelling collects those phenomena that knit human activity and enskillment to the spaces in which people live, labor and rest.

In one of the more mystical passages of his essay, Heidegger associates dwelling with the erection of the "fourfold" (*das Geviert*) formed by earth, sky, mortals, and the divinities. The fourfold sketches the rudimentary form of a dwelling, with its floor, roof, walls, and enclosed interior, dimensions that orient its inhabitants in relation to the constraints and resources of their physical situation. "Earth" and "sky" encompass the environmental features of land and climate as well as floor and ceiling; "mortals" concerns humans as those who inhabit the sheltered middle; and "divinities" gestures toward those forms of alterity, creativity, and expectation not fully accommodated by either the natural world or human sociability, yet implied by the stresses and benefits of their interaction. The divinities take shape in the abyss of our interdependence on each other and the natural world for our survival and flourishing. The meaningful gathering of mortals within a space of neediness, exposure, and necessity helps cultivate human openness to the divine as one means of encountering and acknowledging our own finitude. Heidegger refers not to humans but to mortals, a concept the ancient Greeks used to distinguish humans from immortals. A similar recognition of human limits in relation to the divine is captured in the Judeo-Christian tradition by the word "creature," that tremulous being that owes the fact and shape of its existence to forces other than itself.[19] In Heidegger's scheme, poetry measures the space between earth and sky as the dimension both proper to and other than human existence: dwelling poetically entails acknowledging "the way in which the god who remains unknown, is revealed as such by the sky."[20] In this account, poetry practices a kind of immanent negative theology that manifests divinity in its hidden or self-concealing state, recalling the hovering, tent-like, and ambient forms of divine indwelling courted by the *Shekinah* in the Jewish tradition.

In *The Concept of Dwelling* (1985), architect and theorist Christian Norberg-Schulz developed the architectural implications of Heidegger's essay. For Norberg-Schulz, "dwelling consists in orientation and identification": *orientation* is directional and deictic, a question of pointing and wayfinding, while *identification* is metaphoric and imagistic, concerned with meaning and value. He proposes a "figurative architecture" that would "satisfy the need for dwelling, in the existential sense of the word" by rendering more tangible and visible the syntax (orientation) and semantics (identification) of the places in which people live.[21] He reads Heidegger's fourfold in terms of the several dimensions of architecture, with earth designating the ground on which buildings are erected; sky indicating the upward movement of construction; mortals naming human-scaled routines and activities; and divinity suggesting the more-than-human frame of architectural aspiration. Architecture for Norberg-Schulz is a form of poetry that helps man dwell by gathering together disparate meanings and action-possibilities into a coherent world.[22] Whereas architecture carefully conceived and sited (an English cottage, a Pueblo cave dwelling, an Amsterdam canal house) supports and solicits thoughtful habitation, dwelling (cooking, eating, sleeping, working, greeting, sharing), conducted with a sense of receptivity to the qualities of place, the mortality of creatures, and the relative duration of things, in turn shapes the shelters that humans erect.

Although dwelling primarily evokes domestic architecture, Heidegger's fourfold also implies ecclesiastical spaces that solicit and support the moods appropriate to worship. Whether the aim is high church awe or low church fellowship, buildings designed for religious congregation are "edifying" in the Pauline sense drawn out by philosopher of architecture Karsten Harries: originally meaning simply "to build or construct," "edify" in the New Testament translates *oikodomeo* (from *oikos*, household, and *domeo*, to build). "Edification," Harries writes, "came to mean to build up the church or soul, to provide something like spiritual shelter."[23] Homes, too, are "edifying" when they incorporate contemplative spaces, meaningful décor, portals to sky and earth, or furnishings dedicated to hospitality into their floor plans and traffic patterns. Jewish, Christian, and Muslim prayer regimens include blessings before and after meals, petitions and thanksgivings upon rising and going to bed, the benediction of children and dependents, and formulas of greeting and leave-taking (*shalom, ma-ʿas-sa-laa-mah,* farewell, adieu, goodbye). Designed to exercise care, acknowledge others, express gratitude, build trust, and recognize as well as manage risk, these domestic prayers mark the creaturely, communal, and temporal thresholds that constitute dwelling as a form of daily theology.

In its construction and maintenance of scenes of belonging, the discourse of dwelling that issues from ancient Scripture, vernacular building forms, and postmodern architecture shares motifs and impulses with pastoral and georgic genres and the romanticisms of place and presence to which they are prey. Yet by also incorporating technicity, mortality, sojourn, and resettlement into settings riven by economic and ecological dependency, dwelling also gives space to the alienation from self, others, and God expressed by Job and bequeathed to modernity as the discordant attunement to both existential and historic estrangements. Architectural movements such as brutalism visualize the drift within dwelling in a manner at odds with Norberg-Schulz's more lyric sensibility, yet are nonetheless concerned with expressing the meaning of materials and the quality of human flow. The architecture of transience tracked by Charlie Hailey in *Camps: A Guide to 21st Century Space* documents a range of responses to disaster and displacement, from Katrina to Guantánamo, that probe dwelling in its most precarious forms.[24]

Whether exercised according to centuries-old building traditions or thrown up in the face of flood, famine, war, or economic injustice, dwelling concerns the human dimensions of architecture and the environmental conditions of human sociability and aggression. Dwelling harbors the range of means – spatial and linguistic, culinary and sumptuary – by which persons and communities strive to make their incompleteness bearable and sharable, sometimes by acknowledging and more often by disavowing the forms of displacement through which dwelling erects its temporary structures. In the pages that follow, I look at the dynamics of dwelling in the Book of Jonah and Shakespeare's *Pericles* and then conclude by considering dwelling in and as the collective art of theater.

3.

The Book of Jonah is not on the face of it much concerned with dwelling: the word does not appear in its few pages, and the reluctant prophet who gives the book its name spends most of the story very far away from home. Yet the text is organized around a series of linked locations – ship's hold, whale's belly, and booth or leafy shelter – that call upon the range of issues touched upon in my theo-architectural gloss of dwelling, including the risks of sojourning, the discovery of spaces for worship, and the plenitude and precarity of creaturely existence. The Book of Jonah is an animating source for Shakespeare's *Pericles*, and its affinity with drama makes it an interesting test case for considering theater as an instrument for collective exploration and creative edification (*oikodomeo*) around issues of housing, healing, immigration, and sanctuary.

Robert Alter describes the Book of Jonah as a "Late Biblical" work, composed sometime between the fifth and the second centuries BCE and characterized by its doxological and stylistic divergences from biblical texts of the First Commonwealth (1004–586 BCE).[25] Notable is the Book of Jonah's universalism: the prophet, accustomed to preaching at home, is called by God to chastise the Ninevans, historic enemies of Israel. Formally the Book of Jonah is distinguished from earlier biblical texts by its employment of fantastic and folkloric elements that draw the text closer to Job, Ruth, and Esther than to the Prophets.[26] We will later see Shakespeare drawing upon these romance qualities in *Pericles*, another "late work" that travels long distances and tests verisimilitude in staging living parables of dwelling in the teeming world of creation.

Although other Biblical prophets resist their vocation, only Jonah "actually tries to flee to the other end of the known world."[27] The book opens with God's call to Jonah: "Arise, go to Nineveh, that great city, and cry against it;

for their wickedness is come up before me" (1:2). Jonah responds by fleeing westward to Tarshish, identified with various cities in Asia Minor, including Paul's native town of Tarsus, as well as locales as far away as Carthage, Sardinia, and Spain. The ship that takes Jonah on his way presents the first built space of the book, a kind of floating tent that at once enables and visualizes Jonah's state of radical transit. When a storm threatens the ship and sends its gentile crew into a panic, Jonah himself "was gone down into the sides of the ship; and he lay, and was fast asleep" (1:5). Jonah's deep and sequestered slumber amid the turbulence manifests the depressive disconnection, what John Calvin calls his "stupor almost brutal," brought about by his flight from vocation.[28] When the sailors cast lots to determine the cause of the danger, the results point to Jonah as the problem, and he volunteers to be cast into the roiling waters; already *at sea* in his own life's journey, he is willing to drown in order to save the sailors from destruction.

His death is prevented, however: the Lord "prepared a great fish to swallow up Jonah" (1:17) and its innards constitute the second temporary dwelling place taken up by Jonah in the tale. In the belly of the beast he sings a psalm of thanksgiving (likely added by a later editor), in which he contrasts the temple mount in Jerusalem as the proper site of God's dwelling ("I am cast out of thy sight; yet I will look again toward thy holy temple") with the depths in which he now finds himself: "The waters compassed me about, even to the soul: the depth closed me round about, the weeds were wrapped about my head. I went down to the bottoms of the mountains; the earth with her bars was about me forever: yet hast thou brought up my life from corruption, O LORD my God" (2:4–6). The poem mixes terror with wonder: Jewish mystics believed that a "Tzohar-like pearl" was suspended in the belly of the whale, illuminating the underwater world for Jonah to see and admire.[29] The whale's cavernous interior is both an anticipation of hell and a sacred space prepared by God for the salvation and edification of his prophet. As Elizabeth Allen has pointed out, the medieval rendering of the Book of Jonah in the poem "Patience," ascribed to the so-called Pearl Poet, depicts the whale's jaw as a "munster dor" [cathedral door] and his belly as a "bour" [bower], blueprints that overlay Jonah's intestine environs with ecclesiastical and pastoral building forms.[30]

When Jonah ends his prayer, "the Lord spake unto the fish, and it vomited out Jonah upon the dry land" (2:10). The Lord once more enjoins Jonah to go to Ninevah, and he now obeys, preaching for three days as he walks from one end of the vast city to the other. The people respond by dressing themselves and their animals in sackcloth. Jonah is angry at God, either because he has spared gentiles rather than Israelites or because his mercy has rendered Jonah's prophesies into untruths. In a funk, Jonah leaves the city and builds the third dwelling place of the narrative: a booth (*sukkah*) where he sits (*yesheb*, linked to *yeshab*, dwell) waiting to see what will transpire in the city. (Compare Job, who also sits on his dunghill in an act of ritual *shiva* or sitting-in-mourning.) God now sends a vine that weaves a green canopy over Jonah's head, the man-made shelter and the God- and nature-built shade joining together in a single edifice. At dawn, God sends a worm to destroy the vine, and Jonah, exposed to sun and wind, complains, again Job-like, "Better my death than my life." God explains his action: "'Thou hast had pity on the gourd, for the which thou hast not laboured, neither madest it grow; which came up in a night, and perished in a night: And should not I spare Ninevah, that great city, wherein there are more than sixscore thousand persons that cannot discern between their right hand and their left hand, and also much cattle?" (4:10–11). The book ends on this question, leaving us to ponder just how Jonah might go about answering it with his actions.

God has created a living allegory in space and time, a parable about creaturely life that engages the growth patterns, climate spikes, and agents of creaturely life in an act of divine poiesis. The universalism of the Book of Jonah extends not only to the God-fearing gentile sailors and the God-trusting Ninevans, but also to plants, worms, beasts, and the environmental conditions in which they flourish and fade. Each of its three scenes of precarious dwelling is characterized by mobility (ship and whale), creatureliness (the belly of the fish, the shade of the plant), exposure to the elements (stormy waters and desert winds), and intense affective washes (depression, gratitude, anger, despair) that respond to the symphony of weather orchestrated by God.

The Book of Jonah's inclusive scenography made it ripe for messianic dreaming within Judaism, which imagined the end of days as a universal banquet held beneath a sukkah built from the skin of the leviathan, a scene that borrows both the whale and the booth from Jonah's repertory of temporary housing forms.[31] The Book of Jonah provides the *haftarah*, or prophetic reading on Yom Kippur, the Jewish Day of Atonement, thanks to its themes of transgression and return as well as its universal reach.[32] Ecumenical theologian Rosemary Reuther notes that the Book of Jonah was written after the return of Jewish leaders from the Babylonian exile and "was meant to promote tolerance and coexistence of Jews with other communities within the Persian empire."[33] Reuther's own commentary is posed in the context of the Israeli-Palestinian conflict; her aim is to hold Israel accountable to its own universalist aspirations. In the Christian tradition, the Book of Jonah's scenes of gentile righteousness have been used to support typological and even anti-Jewish appropriations of the story by promoting a universalism that is more coercive than consensual. Thus the

Ordinary Gloss, a widely used medieval biblical commentary, attributes Jonah's flight to his bitter knowledge that "whenever the Gentiles believed, Judea would be blinded."[34] Calvin is more careful, noting the special place of Israel in the history of salvation: "it remained ever true, that God had not done to other nations as he had to the Jews, for he had revealed to them his judgments (Psalm 157:20)."[35] Here, Calvin echoes Paul's reassurance to the Jewish Christians in Romans that Israel – and Israel's literature – enjoys a special place in providential history (Rom. 1:16). Jonah's ecumenical capacities are more fully realized in Jean Bodin's 1588 dialogue, *Colloquium of the Secrets of the Sublime*, which includes the tale of "a most hazardous sea voyage" in which each passenger on the tempest-tossed ship prays in his own language to the same God.[36]

The resources of the Book of Jonah for ecumenical, nonsectarian, and postsecular reflection concern not only the text's address to Jews and gentiles, but also its disclosure of scenes of vulnerability and drift that bear more existentially on humanity's creaturely condition. To dwell well is to inhabit one's world with a sense of purpose, modesty, and gratitude; to live lightly in the structures that lend us a sense of duration; to use the opportunities for deliberation, exchange, and collective problem-solving that our architecture affords us; and to acknowledge and attempt to redress the forms of displacement that fund every act of place-making through works of justice and love. The literature of dwelling is dedicated to these themes in order to build the forms of respect, attention, and care that flow from them. The Book of Jonah's strangely vibrant landscape tells the story of a prophet who has little to prophesy; Jonah's story instead is one of exposure to the elements, wandering in the streets, and retreat into temporary lodgings of the most transient and porous kind. (Recall that Heidegger's essay on dwelling was composed in response to the housing crisis brought about by the influx of postwar refugees.) It is easy to imagine that Jonah asleep in the ship's hold is a migrant stealing passage to a new life, that his tossing overboard is the work of human smugglers, that his sojourn in the whale's belly is a form of incarceration, or that his booth outside Nineveh is a skid-row shack assembled from cardboard boxes and a shopping cart. Such predicaments are taken up in modern homeless shelters and charitable organizations that identify their care for the stranger with Jonah's plight,[37] and they also count among the resonances tapped by Shakespeare in *Pericles*.

4.

Pericles is the first of Shakespeare's late romances. The play was most likely coauthored with George Wilkens, a tavern-owner and minor playwright who also published a novelized form of the drama in 1608. Based on the story of Apollonius of Tyre narrated in Gower's *Confessio Amantis* (c. 1386) and chorally framed by the character of Gower himself, *Pericles* is a self-consciously archaizing play that draws on saints' lives and miracle plays along with Greek romance. *Pericles* was likely performed in a recusant (nonconforming Catholic) household in Yorkshire in 1610, along with a "seditious interlude," a play about Saint Christopher, and *King Lear*, implying the play's appeal to Catholic readers.[38] In Thomas Betteridge's formulation, the play yearns for "a pre-confessional world in which liturgical words, the language of faith, united rather than divided Christians."[39] *Pericles* can be read as mapping Jonah's concern with the relationship between Jews and gentiles onto the division between Catholics and Protestants in a period of religious terrorism and state surveillance. Read more broadly, the father's catatonia, like Lear's heath rants or Job's dunghill decrepitude, invites us to consider the perils of aging, disease, and mental illness, while the daughter's sale into sex trafficking evokes the plight of adolescents exposed to exploitation and neglect.

The first half of the drama tracks the wanderings of young Pericles, prince of Tyre, whose initial solving of a riddle concerning father-daughter incest leads him into a precipitous flight from persecution, self-knowledge, and sovereign rule. After surviving a shipwreck, he marries a princess named Thaisa, who gives birth to their daughter Marina during a second storm on their way back to Tyre. When Thaisa appears to die in childbirth, the sailors insist that her body be thrown overboard. Pericles leaves his daughter in Tarsus to be raised by the rulers there and returns alone to Tyre. The second half of the play focuses on the travails of Marina. Her beauty and artistic gifts inspire jealousy in her stepmother, who orders her murder on the shore. One act of violence is averted by another: pirates kidnap Marina and sell her into sex slavery in Mytilene. In the brothel she not only talks her way out of defloration, but also secures enough money to start a school for girls in a "leafy shelter" at the island's edge (21.40).[40] Pericles arrives on a ship, sunk into a deep depression by the news of Marina's demise. After she draws him out of his stupor, they travel to Ephesus, where Thaisa has preserved herself as a priestess in the Temple of Diana.

Pericles has long been associated with the Book of Jonah.[41] Jonah's flight from his calling to preach to the Ninevans colors the fugitive character of Pericles' behavior in the first half of the play. The tossing of Thaisa's body overboard echoes the dumping of Jonah into the sea, while Pericles' elegy marking his wife's watery interment near "the belching whale" (11.61) recalls Jonah's psalm of thanksgiving. Jonah's Tarshish is associated with the Tyre and Tarsus of *Pericles*, and Jonah's depressive retreat into the bottom of the ship resembles Pericles' shipbound catatonia.[42] What has not been noted in comparisons of Jonah and Pericles, however, is the extent to which Marina's "leafy shelter" might recall Jonah's booth. Lysimachus, the governor of Mytilene who will marry Marina at the end of the play, describes her situation to his visitors from Tyre as he boards their ship in the harbor of Mytilene:

> She in all happy,
> As the fairest of all, among her fellow maids
> Dwells now i'th'leafy shelter that abuts
> Against the island's side. (21.38–41)

"Leafy shelter" suggests a form of minimal architecture, like Viola's willow cabin, Lear's hovel, or Jonah's sukkah. True to her name, Marina has chosen to build her academy (from *akedēmia*, the grove outside Athens where Plato taught) as close to the shore as possible. It is, literally, a "halfway house," open to the elements, perched between sea and city, and functioning as a sanctuary. Mytilene harbors a history of female educators: the city is on the island of Lesbos, where Sappho ran her school for women. Randall Martin associates Marina's school with the house-churches of Priscilla and Aquila at Ephesus and Corinth.[43] Marina's decision to dwell and teach outside the city also picks up on Jonah's soft architecture, while her capture by pirates, her exposure to urban danger, and her suburban building project suggest the housing crises suffered by Jonah. If Pericles activates Jonah's flight from knowledge and acknowledgment, Marina discovers within Jonah's story the chance for personal and social healing through the arts of edification, in the double sense of building and teaching.

Earlier in the play, her shipwrecked father had courted her royal mother by bringing a single "withered branch that's only green at the top," labelled with the motto *"In hac spe vivo*. 'In that hope I live'" (6.46–8). Messianic Marina has taken her father's solitary bough and multiplied it into a leafy house of hope, crafting the conditions for her own survival but also for the edification and succor of others. A new Jonah as well as a new Sappho, Marina's *hortus inconclusus* dramatizes her cosmopolitan origins, her sense of environmental connectedness, and her prophetic interest in ministering to the social body.

Both Mytilene and Ninevah are cities of sinners who are nonetheless capable and worthy of conversion, and in both texts, these opportunities for redemption are conceived in environmental as well as human terms. The last words of the Book of Jonah are *behamah rabah*, "much cattle," words that appear as the end of a question, the syntax of hope. Shakespeare and Wilkens turn to the Book of Jonah in order to explore the floating worlds and salty vernaculars of sailors and fishermen, discovering in their demanding taskscapes distinctive ways of life, allegories of existential exposure, and patterns of social exploitation, the latter captured in the fishermen's "pretty moral" of big fish eating little fish in the predatory ecology of early capital (5.76). In both texts, the stories of prophets and princes shelter other fates of vagabondage and human trafficking, homelessness and shanty towns, refugeeism and sanctuary. In both texts, the sukkah's loose structure shelters a range of affects (fear, hope, anger, dismay, regret) and possible comportments (patience, resilience, hospitality, care) that continue to proffer blueprints for ways of dwelling in the world. And both works are concerned with performance as a simultaneously interpersonal and architectural art. God educates Jonah by building a festival folly whose baseless fabric constitutes its meaning, while *Pericles* identifies its leaky, leafy sites of transit (ship, shore, brothel, shelter) with the open building forms of the theater. By freely mixing Jewish and Pauline motifs in a fluid Hellenistic geography, *Pericles* accesses Jonah's uneasy universalism in a world on its way to Christianity but not Christian yet, in order to imagine another world beyond the schisms of contemporary Christendom. *Pericles* draws on Jonah's Yom Kippur themes of transgression, atonement, and forgiveness in an allusive terrain built up from the deposits left by multiple religious traditions. In *Pericles*, Shakespeare reads the Book of Jonah in order to practice an abounding secularism, a humanism that draws on religion's brooding depths and dwelling's symbiotic rhythms in order to support the effort of recognizing one another in a shared world that requires our care.

5.

The Book of Jonah has often been called "dramatic," thanks to its three-part structure and its reliance on dialogue. Jonah sometimes appeared in medieval Corpus Christi plays and other civic-ecclesiastical performances; in Shakespeare's time, Jonah also showed up in vernacular ballads, wall paintings, and at least one play.[44] In more recent decades, many dramas and musicals have been based on the Book of Jonah; although most are for children and many address particular faith groups, several attempt, like *Pericles*, to integrate a range of materials and performance styles for mixed audiences. In December 2014, the Guthrie Playhouse in Minneapolis, next to the Mississippi River, wanted to stage a December show that would be open to religious interpretation, not belong to a particular denomination, and "use either the building or the landscape in the project."[45] The result was a site-specific play that incorporated local musical groups, the river environs, and ancient and modern as well as religious and secular motifs in a comprehensive reimagining of Jonah's journey. In another ambitious citywide project conducted in the same year, LA Opera commissioned a new work based on the Book of Jonah and performed by more than fifteen professional and amateur musical groups at the Cathedral of Our Lady of the Angels.[46] A rather different cycle of efforts appears in the 2015 volume *Resettlement: Drama, Refugees and Resilience*, which documents a series of applied theater interventions for families displaced by war and poverty from Burundi and Ethiopia to Logan, Australia. Although unrelated to either Jonah or Pericles, these actions used "tall tales and legends" to process trauma, build resilience, and attempt the work of resettlement by asking all of its cocreators to exercise the theatrical virtues of attention, courage, empathy, imagination, and acknowledgment.[47]

Are not Jonah and *Pericles* also a species of refugee theater, insofar as they use folklore and fairy tale in tandem with liturgy and drama to probe the resources for dwelling at the limits of human place-making? The character of Gower opens *Pericles* with what might be read as a manifesto for such community experiments:

> To sing a song that old was sung
> From ashes ancient Gower is come,
> Assuming man's infirmities
> To glad your ear and please your eyes.
> It hath been sung at festivals,
> On ember-eves and holy-ales,
> And lords and ladies in their lives
> Have read it for restoratives.   (1.1–8)

Shakespeare's Gower links the Hellenistic story of Apollonius of Tyre (renamed Pericles in Shakespeare and Wilkens' version) with the stories shared through collective song and holiday at "festivals" such as "ember-eves" (the night before a religious fast), and "holy-ales" (church picnics and fundraisers), celebrations under attack by Puritans for their pagan elements and general rowdiness. Gower's sounding of these vernacular performance traditions supports the "postconfessional" project of Shakespeare's late plays, which recreate the aesthetic, emotional, and communal plurality of medieval literary and liturgical forms in response to the schisms of confessional Christianity.[48] Betteridge characterizes Shakespeare's late plays as "Catholic plays, not Protestant or Roman Catholic."[49] I would prefer an even broader word, such as "messianic" or "Abrahamic," to describe the inclusive, pluralizing, creaturely, and historically layered landscapes of these testamental works. Shakespeare's recourse to prophetic writings such as the Book of Jonah and wisdom literature such as the Book of Job as well as his ongoing engagement with the story of Abraham and Isaac reveal his receptivity to the Hebrew Bible in a mode that is not simply typological.[50]

Both the Book of Jonah and *Pericles* dramatize dwelling as the assemblage of architectural and ecological features brought together by the lived routines and symbolic investments of human habitation in its sojourning character and edifying import. Both texts draw on multiple faith traditions and thematize religious pluralism in order to craft ecumenical spaces for intersubjective acknowledgment and worldly attunement. Gower's invocation of festival forms at the opening of *Pericles* and the Book of Jonah's rich history in liturgy and community theater from late antiquity and the Middle Ages to the present indicate the way in which works of literature can be used to explore the challenges to dwelling faced by particular social groups and to experience our unevenly shared immersion as human beings in creaturely existence. When I study *Pericles* with groups of older adults, we work together to enact and expand the play's themes of aging, mental illness, and public health, and we practice declamation, interpretation, and discussion as keys to mental agility and spiritual refreshment as well as community formation.[51] This work connects us in an odd way to that Catholic household in Yorkshire that hosted the play in 1610 as part of its own arts of dwelling. In both cases, acts of theater pursued in not-quite-public settings address with an unusual directness the identities, expectations, and experiences of those gathered in its intimate circle of disclosure. In a different way from formal theater, applied theater is an exercise in trust.

When approached collectively, whether in classrooms, basements, libraries, theaters, or halfway houses, literature aims to become what Shakespeare's Gower calls a "restorative." A restorative is a drug or medicine that enhances health, mood, or memory. Poetry is such a restorative, Shakespeare's Gower claims, especially when digested in community. Both the Book of Jonah and *Pericles* practice the work of dwelling as the slow and painful process of affirming human relationships within a renewed alertness to place. Both texts invite their readers to understand trees as buildings and buildings as trees: as structures that take root and offer shelter, that establish locales and visualize connections, for a time. Both texts, the one through liturgy and the other through theater, solicit embodied acts of listening that build comportments of trust, attention, and care. Art on its own can neither restore the capacities eroded by age and infirmity nor redress the injuries wrought by social injustice. The very imperfection of poetic repair, however, a theme in both works, can itself become the occasion to affirm our mutual beholdenness within environments that are neither impervious to concern nor resistant to action. "*In hac spe vivo.* 'In that hope I live'": the motto hanging from the shipwrecked prince's withered branch names the messianic margin shared by the Book of Jonah and *Pericles*, and cultivated by the art of dwelling poetically.

Notes

1 *As You Like It*, ed. Alan Brissenden (Oxford: Oxford University Press, 1993).
2 See *yashab*, Strong's Concordance 3427. There are 1082 occurrences in the Hebrew Bible. Unless otherwise noted, English translations of the Bible are from the King James Version at Bible Gateway (www.biblegateway.com); Hebrew text and commentary is from the *Jewish Publication Society Torah Commentary* (hereafter JPS Commentary), in several volumes, supplemented by the Interlinear Bible and Strong's Concordance available at Bible Hub (http://biblehub.com).
3 Leviticus 23:3.
4 Exodus 20:10.
5 1 Samuel 12:11.
6 Leviticus 23:42.
7 Strong's Concordance 7931, "*shakan* or *shaken*: to settle down, abide, dwell." See JPS Commentary to Exodus 25:8, which notes the link between *mishkan* (sanctuary), *sh-k-n* (dwell in tents), and *shekinah* (divine presence).
8 Exodus 25:8.
9 Max Kadushin, *The Rabbinic Mind* (Binghamton, NY: Binghamton University Press, 2001; 1952), 233–235.
10 Job 30:6.
11 Job 19:15.
12 Strong's Concordance 1481: *guwr*, "to sojourn … to dwell as a newcomer." Strong's 1616: *ger*, sojourner, alien, temporary dweller.
13 My thanks to Chava Lion for advice on Hebrew words for dwelling.
14 John 6:56.
15 Strong's Concordance 3306.
16 2 Corinthians 6:16.
17 Strong's Concordance 1774: *enoikeó*: to dwell in. Strong's Concordance 3485: *naos*, a temple.
18 Adam Scharr, *Heidegger for Architects* (New York: Routledge, 2007).
19 On creatureliness, see Eric Santner, *On Creaturely Life* (Chicago, IL: University of Chicago, 2006), and Julia Lupton, "Creature Caliban," *Shakespeare Quarterly* 51.1 (Spring 2000): 1–23.
20 Heidegger, "Poetically Man Dwells," in *Poetry, Language, Thought* (New York: Harper, 2001), 220.
21 Christian Norberg-Schulz, *The Concept of Dwelling: On the Way to Figurative Architecture* (New York: Rizzoli, 1985), 7.
22 Ibid., 17.
23 Karsten Harries, *The Ethical Function of Architecture* (Cambridge: MIT Press, 1997), 11.
24 Charlie Hailey, *Camps: A Guide to 21st Century Space* (Cambridge: MIT Press, 2009).
25 Robert Alter, *Strong as Death Is Love: The Song of Songs, Ruth, Esther, Jonah, Daniel* (New York: Norton, 2015), Kindle e-book, location 43.
26 Ibid., location 72.
27 Ibid., location 2624.
28 Calvin, *Commentary on Jonah* (Amazon Digital Services, 2012), 1:5.

29 Howard Schwartz, *Tree of Souls: The Mythology of Judaism* (Oxford: Oxford University Press, 2004), 87.

30 "Patience," in *Complete Works of the Pearl Poet*, trans. and ed. Casey Finch (Berkeley: University of California Press, 1993), lines 268, 276, 437, glossed by Elizabeth Allen, professor of English, graduate seminar at UC Irvine, fall 2014.

31 On the role of the Leviathan in the messianic banquet, see Schwartz, *Tree of Souls*, 145–148. Schwartz notes that Jews eat fish on the Sabbath because "eating fish anticipates the feast of Leviathan." The origin of this messianic motif is Job 40:30 (41:6 in KJV), a line relevant to both Jonah and *Pericles*: "Will bands of fishermen make a banquet of him?"

32 Joseph Dov Soloveitchik, *Reflections of the Rav: Man of Faith in the Modern World*, ed. Abraham R. Besdin (New York: KTAV Publishing House, 1989), 141–145.

33 Rosemary Radford Reuther and Herman J. Reuther, *The Wrath of Jonah: The Crisis of Religious Nationalism in the Israeli-Palestinian Conflict*, 2nd ed. (Minneapolis, MN: Fortress Press, 2002), xx.

34 "The Ordinary Gloss on Jonah," trans. and ed. Ryan McDermott, *PMLA* 128.2 (2013): 428.

35 Calvin, *Commentary on Jonah*, notes to Jonah 1:1–2.

36 Jean Bodin, *Colloquium of the Seven about the Secrets of the Sublime*, 6–8. Cited in Sheiba Kian Kaufman, "Neither East nor West: Early Modern Mutualisms and the English Stage," dissertation prospectus, UC Irvine, 2013.

37 Examples include Jonah's House Food Pantry, Carlsbad, NM; Sign of Jonah Partnerships in Healing, Washington, DC; Jonah's Loving Heart Rescue, Beverly Hills, CA; Project Jonah, New Zealand; and Jonah's Place, Houston, TX. The Jonah House Community was founded by a group that included Philip Berrigan and Elizabeth McAlister on the principles of nonviolence, resistance, and community. See also *Children of Jonah: Personal Stories by Survivors of Suicide Attempts*, ed. James T. Clemons (Herndon, VA: Capital Books, 2001).

38 Richard Wilson, *Secret Shakespeare: Studies in Theatre, Religion and Resistance* (Manchester: Manchester University Press, 2004), 271–293; Suzanne Gossett, Introduction, *Arden 3 Pericles* (London: Thomson Learning, 2004), 87–90.

39 Betteridge, "Writing Faithfully in a Post-Confessional World," in *Late Shakespeare 1608–1613*, ed. Andrew J. Power and Rory Loughane (Cambridge: Cambridge University Press, 2013), 225. On *Pericles* and Catholic narrative and dramatic forms, see Peter Womack, "Shakespeare and the Sea of Stories," *Journal of Medieval and Early Modern Studies* 29.1 (Winter 1999): 169–187.

40 *Pericles*, ed. Roger Warren (Oxford: Oxford University Press, 2003).

41 Hannibal Hamlin, *The Bible in Shakespeare* (Oxford: Oxford University Press, 2013), 122.

42 The editor of the Soncino edition of *The Twelve Prophets*, ed. A. Cohen (London: Soncino Press, 1994), associates Tarshish with Tyre (138n). George Abbott identifies Tarshish with Tarsus, the birthplace of Paul. *An Exposition upon the Prophet Ionah* (London: Richard Field, 1600), 34.

43 Randall Martin, "Shakespearean Biography, Biblical Allusion and Early Modern Practices of Reading Scripture," *Shakespeare Survey* 63 (2011): 222–223.

44 Lynette R. Muir, *The Biblical Drama of Medieval Europe* (Cambridge: Cambridge University Press, 1995), 193, 217. On Jonah in ballads and wall paintings, see Tessa Watt, *Cheap Print and Popular Piety, 1550–1640* (Cambridge: Cambridge University Press, 1994), 116. Thomas Lodge and Robert Greene's Jonah play, *A Looking Glass of London* (London: Thomas Creede, 1594), includes an incest scenario whose royal transgressors are killed by thunderbolt, like the incestuous king of Antioch in *Pericles*. My thanks to Erin Kelly for alerting me to this play.

45 www.twincities.com/stage/ci_27118309/do-musical-jonah-and-whale-they-had-just. Other examples of modern Jonah plays designed for community engagement and performance include *Jonah and the Whale*, music by Dominick Argent, "A Dramatic Oratorio with libretto in English, adapted from anonymous medieval English, the Biblical Book of Jonah and Psalm CXXX, sea shanties, and work songs." Carl Gerbrandt, *Sacred Music Drama: The Producer's Guide* (AuthorHouse, 2010), 40–41.

46 Composer: Jack Perla; librettist: Velina Hasu Houston; conducted by James Conlon as part of LA Opera's Cathedral Project, 2013–2014. www.laopera.org/season/13=14Season-at-a-Glance/Jonah/.

47 Michael Balfour et al., *Resettlement: Drama, Refugees and Resilience* (London: Bloomsbury, 2015), 69, 70.

48 Betteridge, "Writing Faithfully," 226.

49 Ibid., 225.

50 Kenneth Jackson, *Shakespeare and Abraham* (South Bend, IN: Notre Dame Press, 2014).

51 My reading partners include Laguna Woods Shakespeare Society; Osher Institute for Lifelong Learning, Irvine chapter; and Laguna Beach Senior Center.

6

MATTHEW POTTS

Imagination

It is intuitive that literary fiction should depend upon imagination. Christian theology, on the other hand, has typically approached the imagination with somewhat more caution. This is perhaps because anxieties over the foundations of Christian truth claims have traditionally complicated theology's imaginative sense. Whereas truth might be understood by theology as either revealed by God or discovered through reason, Christians have rarely warmed to the notion of truth as conjured by human imagination. Whatever the role of the imagination in Christian theology – and who could deny such a role in the monumental work of figures like Augustine of Hippo or Julian of Norwich or Karl Barth – most Christians would resist referring to theological or scriptural writings as mere fictions or imaginations.

Conventional intuitions notwithstanding, in recent years the imagination has come usefully to bridge literary (especially fictional) writing with theological (sometimes scriptural) reflection in a manner that might prove illuminative for the study of religion and literature at large. As critical theory has progressively reconsidered the simple givenness of any proposed truth, theology has found its own anxieties less singular. Consider Toni Morrison's reflections here on the practice of literary writing in her essay, "The Site of Memory":

> On the basis of some information and a little bit of guesswork, you journey to a site to see what remains were left behind and to reconstruct the world that these remains imply. What makes it fiction is the nature of the imaginative act: my reliance on the image – on the remains – in addition to recollection, to yield up a kind of truth . . . Fiction, by definition, is distinct from fact. Presumably it's the product of imagination – invention – and it claims that freedom to dispense with "what really happened," or where it really happened, or when it really happened, and nothing in it needs to be publicly verifiable, although much of it can be verified . . . [But] the crucial distinction for me is not the difference between fact and fiction, but the distinction between fact and truth.

> Because facts can exist without human intelligence, but truth cannot . . . The
> approach that's most productive and most trustworthy for me is the recollec-
> tion that moves from the image to the text. Not from the text to the image.[1]

Toni Morrison's argument here – that verifiability is separable from truth,
that truth itself is complicit with human invention, that it arises in the
dialogic movement from image to text, from imagination to writing – is an
account that resounds throughout much contemporary thought and perhaps
especially in Christian theology.

Of course, recognition of the imagination's role in religious thought is not
an insight peculiar to our age. In fact, the "interpretation of religion as a
form of imagination is in fact nothing new at all."[2] Since the rise of modernity at least, imagination has served as a useful notion with which to delimit
religious thought, and this always in opposition to more scientific or secular
approaches to knowing. As Garrett Green argues, both "those critics who
have opposed religion as the great enemy of science and the apologists
who have tried to defend it against 'scientific' critique have shared an
underlying assumption that religion is a form of imagination."[3] In other
words, science and religion have often been recognized in modernity as
antagonists, and for good or ill, imagination is always on the side of the
angels.[4] But when philosophers of science such as Thomas Kuhn rehabilitated the scientific imagination against reductive forms of positivism in
the mid-twentieth century, "familiar dichotomies between what counts as
subjective and objective, theory and fact, interpretation and observation"
blurred and forced "a fundamental rethinking of the relationship between
science and religion."[5] As these lessons resonated beyond the philosophy of
science into several schools of inquiry, nearly all of them were incorporated
at one time or another into some forms of Christian theology.[6]

What late twentieth-century theory introduces then is not a rethinking of the
religious imagination but a rethinking of the imagination in general.
Postmodernity asserts that there is no view from nowhere, that each subjective
insight will be historically and socially situated, that there is no mode of
knowledge or thought left unfiltered by interpretation.[7] Imagination is therefore not some whimsical invention set aside from rigorous thought. Rather, it
inspires and conspires with thinking itself. Imagination in late modernity is
understood as foundational to "the production of meaning itself," rather than
"merely reproductive of some absent meaning."[8] The imagination makes,
rather than merely refigures, meaning. In postmodernity, human thought is
as much construction as perception; or, rather, perception itself is regarded as a
constructive engagement with the world.[9] And once imagination has been
recognized as instrumental to the production of all sorts of human knowing,
religious imagination can come in out of modernity's cold.

If it is correct that truth is discovered – in Morrison's words – in the movement from image to text, then the image that moves Christian theology "is, materially, the paradigmatic image of God embodied in Jesus Christ."[10] Christian theological reflection is a work of the human imagination: it is making sense of the world through a foundational image that is inherited and assumed. From given sign to constructed sense, from foundational image to human imagination, the movement of theology mimics the motions of all rational thought. For postmodern Christian theologians, theological reflection is, in Morrison's words, an imaginative reconstruction at the site of memory, a working from image to text. Green, for example, suggests that "the common but inadequate dichotomy of 'fact' and 'fiction' prevents a proper understanding of how fictional narratives" – including scriptural ones – "function as normative."[11] What is given to the theologian "is not a foundational experience, but a religious paradigm: a normative model of 'what the world is like,' embodied in a canon of scripture and expressed in the life of a religious community."[12] The story of Jesus, written and received, grounds the Christian imagination. Or in David Tracy's words, the Christian imagination is established upon "the encompassing . . . *event* of Jesus Christ as God's ownmost self-manifestation."[13] As Tracy elaborates, "Christianity does not live by an idea, a principle, an axiom, but by an event and a person – the event of Jesus Christ occurring now and grounded in none other than Jesus of Nazareth."[14] But insofar as this event and person grounds Christian thought and life, it does so through the workings of human memory and the imaginative constructions of human community. Theologians make sense of the world they encounter by imaginatively reconstructing the memory of Jesus, an image written, recalled, and received by the tradition they have assumed as an inheritance. Again, in an echo of Toni Morrison, these recollections may stir dangerous memories, but the work of Christian theology – like the work of any other imagination – occurs at the site of this memory, in search of an imagined truth.

I find these arguments from theology largely persuasive. If I take any issue with them, it is not directly in what they have claimed, but in what they have left unclaimed or failed to claim sufficiently. While I agree that reconsiderations of the role of imagination in the production of human knowledge are largely welcome ones, I believe these ideas have often been too warmly received by Christian theology. I don't worry that these postmodern notions are wrong; rather, I worry that theology sometimes regards itself as too easily rehabilitated by these ideas, that it has not fully reckoned with the costly and unavoidable consequences of its own imagination. I agree with Green, Tracy, and others that the memory, event, and image of Jesus can be understood to ground Christian truth claims. But I want also to ask at what cost these claims might come. Indeed, I believe that the memory, event, and image of Jesus in particular demand just such a question. And in order more fully to ask this question, we turn now to Toni Morrison's indispensible novel *Beloved*.

I.

It may be that there is no more important twentieth-century American novel than *Beloved*. But whatever else it is, *Beloved* is a book about memory, about how memories persist in the present and haunt the world of human knowing. It is also, perhaps, a book about the task of imagining a livable future while burdened by the weight of a dead past. What's so startling about *Beloved* is how literally that past lives in the novel, how robustly its memory is imagined. Briefly, *Beloved* is a ghost story. The protagonist of the story, a former slave named Sethe, is haunted by a child whose name the reader never learns. The ghost is called Beloved since this is the only word Sethe can afford to have carved on the toddler's headstone. Several years prior to the action of this novel, Sethe escaped slavery in Kentucky and came to a small community of African-Americans on the outskirts of Cincinnati, but when her slave-driver Schoolteacher arrived to abduct her, Sethe attempted to murder her own children to keep them from being returned to the plantation. She reached for her two-year-old daughter first and drew a handsaw across the child's throat before being halted by a neighbor, Stamp Paid. Schoolteacher, having witnessed the killing, abandoned Sethe as damaged goods. Following a short prison term, Sethe returned to the same community outside Cincinnati and settled there, her home haunted by the ghost of her child. The haunting has taken its toll: her mother-in-law Baby Suggs has died of grief and her surviving sons Howard and Bugler have run away. Only Sethe's youngest child, Denver, newly born at the time of the killing, remains with Sethe.

These events, however, are recollected, not told in the present tense; the action of the novel is set several years later, once Denver is almost fully grown and she and Sethe have become accustomed to their insular life at 124 Bluestone Road. In her daily life, Sethe struggles "to remember as close to nothing as [is] safe."[15] Unfortunately,

> [her] brain [is] devious. She might be hurrying across a field, running practically, to get to the pump quickly and rinse the chamomile sap from her legs. Nothing else would be in her mind . . . Just the breeze cooling her face as she rushed toward water . . . Then something . . . and suddenly there was Sweet Home rolling, rolling, rolling out before her eyes, and although there was not a

leaf on that farm that did not make her want to scream, it rolled itself out before her in shameless beauty . . . Boys hanging from the most beautiful sycamores in the world. It shamed her – remembering the wonderful soughing trees rather than the boys. Try as she might to make it otherwise, the sycamores beat out the children every time and she could not forgive her memory for that. (6–7)

The complications and persistence of memory for Sethe, its tendency to consume the present, is clear here. Even when set at her mindless daily tasks, Sethe's world can be transformed by memory into the Sweet Home plantation, and that transformation is not one over which she has any control. Even when she wants to recall Sweet Home's horror for the sake of the memory of those lynched boys, she sees only its lovely trees and its gently rolling hills. Tellingly, these imaginations are no less real for being imagined. As Sethe explains to Denver, "Some things go. Pass on. Some things just stay. I used to think it was my rememory . . . But it's not. Places, places are still there. If a house burns down, it's gone, but the place – the picture of it – stays, and not just in rememory, but out there, in the world" (43).

Morrison's own words echo here. An image exists at the site of memory, and the search for truth means visiting that site and interpreting that image. But this imaginative work is a relentless burden, one that mires Sethe in the past. Sethe's brain is "not interested in the future. Loaded with the past and hungry for more," it leaves "her no room to imagine, let alone plan, for the next day" (43). Sethe's present is her past, her imagination cannot extend into the future. To Sethe, "the future [is] a matter of keeping the past at bay. The 'better life' she believe[s] she and Denver [are] living [is] simply not that other one" (51). For Sethe, the primary task of each day is therefore just the "serious work of beating back the past" (86).

But all this changes, at least briefly, when a fellow Sweet Home ex-slave, Paul D, arrives at 124 Bluestone. Paul D stirs the memories Sethe daily works to beat back, and she tells him about her last days at Sweet Home, her rape and lashing and the stealing of her breastmilk. In response, Paul D trembles, kisses the scars on her back, holds her bare breasts in his hands, and allows her to rest just long enough to weep. Sethe reflects that perhaps "this one time she could stop dead still in the middle of cooking a meal . . . and feel the hurt her back ought to. Trust things and remember things because the last of the Sweet Home men was there to catch her if she sank" (21). The responsibility for her breasts, she wonders, is "at last . . . in somebody else's hands" (21). With Paul D's arrival, a future opens and Sethe can begin to imagine a next day. But as Paul D holds her, the house begins to pitch and a table rushes across the floor toward him. He takes it up by two legs and bashes it around the house shouting "Leave the place alone! Get the hell out! . . . She got enough without you!" (22). Paul D outlasts the ghost's tantrum until the house ceases its lurching. In the relative quiet that follows, "Sethe, Denver, and Paul D [breathe] to the same beat, like one tired person. Another breathing [is] just as tired" (22). And then, suddenly, that fourth and separate breath ceases. The past is beaten back; the ghost is gone.

Or so it seems. Denver, Paul D, and Sethe spend a short time together in relative peace, but upon returning together one day from a fair they see a woman sitting on a stump near 124 who calls herself Beloved. She takes up house with the small family and becomes desperate for Sethe's attention. Relaying memories to Beloved becomes for Sethe

> a way to feed her . . . Sethe learn[s] the profound satisfaction Beloved [gets] from storytelling. It amaze[s] Sethe (as much as it please[s] Beloved) because every mention of her past life hurt[s]. She and Baby Suggs had agreed without saying so that it was unspeakable . . . Even with Paul D, who had shared some of it and to whom she could talk with at least a measure of calm, the hurt [is] always there . . . But . . . she [finds] herself wanting to, liking it. Perhaps it [is] Beloved's distance from the events itself, or her thirst for hearing it – in any case it [is] an unexpected pleasure. (69)

We might consider this another liberation for Sethe. Memory is no longer unspeakable for Sethe; unexpectedly, it has become pleasurable instead of painful.

But these good feelings quickly fade and Beloved's desire for Sethe's memories begins to overtake the household. Denver immediately recognizes this woman as the fully grown ghost of her sister, now present in corporeal form. And Beloved desires Denver's memories too – at least insofar as they reconstruct Sethe's past. Denver speaks, Beloved listens, and the two do "the best they [can] to create what really happened, how it really was," something only Sethe really knows (92). There is a complicated and collective working of imagination upon memory here, one that the text describes as well as performs. Though neither actually holds Sethe's memory, Denver and Beloved together create Sethe's story, they imagine it into reality, so much so that the narrative of escape that the text itself offers as Sethe's own is the one shared here between Denver and Beloved. Once again, as Morrison has stated above, the truth in this case is the one invented in the movement from image to imagination, at the elusive site of memory.

Beloved haunts Paul D with the past, too. If Paul D represents the possibility of imagining a future, then Beloved frustrates his future in her desire for Sethe's past. As Beloved consumes Sethe's attention, Paul D steadily moves away from Sethe both emotionally and physically, until at last he takes to sleeping in a shed behind the house. Once he's relocated, Beloved comes to Paul D in the middle of the night asking him to touch her "on the inside part and call" her by her name (137). Unlike Denver, Paul D is never quite convinced of Beloved's ghostliness. When she comes to him, Paul D rejects and scolds her, but it's because he knows that if he feels the "need to see the nature of the sin behind him . . . he too [will] be lost" (137). Sexual temptation here is aligned with a temptation to look backward, to be lost in that backward glance. Despite Paul D's resolve to move forward, he does turn back toward Beloved, he does touch her inside part and call her by her name.

Interestingly, it does not occur to Sethe for some time that this strange woman might be her resurrected child. Once Paul D has left 124, however, Sethe overhears Beloved humming a tune she recognizes as her own, and the pieces in her brain suddenly settle "into places designed and made especially for them" (207). In an instant, Sethe recognizes Beloved as her daughter, and the fully present memory of that child begins entirely to overtake Sethe's world. As Sethe reflects,

> I don't have to remember nothing. I don't even have to explain. She under-
> stands it all . . . Dearly Beloved, which is what you are to me and I don't have to
> be sorry about getting only one word . . . I can forget it all now because as soon
> as I got the gravestone in place you made your presence known in the house
> and worried us all to distraction. I didn't understand it then. I thought you
> were mad with me. And now I know that if you was, you ain't now because
> you came back here to me and I was right all along. There is no world outside
> my door. I only need to know one thing. How bad is the scar?   (216–217)

Indeed, the past has returned so completely to Sethe she need neither recall it nor beat it back. It is a past so fully alive in her present that it literally consumes her. Once Sethe has "seen the scar . . . the little curved shadow of a smile in the kootchy-kootchy-coo place under her chin" – once she's touched it and stared at it, her only concern is to meet Beloved's insatiable desires for sweets and stories (281–282). Sethe grows dangerously thin while Beloved grows "bigger, plumper by the day" (281). Sethe pleads "for forgiveness, counting, listing again and again her reasons: that Beloved was more import-ant, meant more to her than her own life. That she would trade places any day. Give up her own life, every minute and hour of it, to take back just one of Beloved's tears" (284). But Beloved rejects these pleas, and while Sethe wastes away Beloved "[eats] up her life, [takes] it, [swells] up with it, [grows] taller on it" (295). There is no world outside 124 for Sethe anymore, no world beyond this mother's memory of a murder.

The propensity of memory to consume the present and overcome the future is clear. Pictures of the past stir Sethe's imagination, but these pictures colonize her entire world through the relentless workings of imagination, such that her whole existence is reduced to the sight of the scar on Beloved's throat. Sethe is trying "to make up for the handsaw" but there will "never be an end to that" (295). But if there is no end to it, how can one move forward from the sight of that scar into the future? How can imagination turn toward a new day?

For a short period, a new day does seem to dawn. Paul D's exorcism is prefaced by Sethe's poignant hope that someone might be able to catch her if she sinks into her memory, that the responsibility for her violated body might be held "in somebody else's hands" (21). And for a while, this works. The ghost departs and Sethe, Paul D, and Denver live briefly with some sense of an open future. But when a flesh-and-blood Beloved moves back to 124 Bluestone Road, the stakes are raised and so must the collective response and responsibility. Because what seems to rescue Sethe in the end is just an amplified version of Paul D's initial exorcism. Sethe will be bodily taken into the hands of others; she will become others' responsibility. Although the memory of this murder has always haunted Bluestone Road, when Beloved appears and threatens Sethe, the community takes collective responsibility and determines to rescue Sethe from the past. Denver recognizes her mother is dying and steps out of their insular world in search of help. The ghost of Baby Suggs calls to her from the dead to do so. Stamp Paid reaches out to Paul D and solicits aid from others as well, most notably from a woman named Ella. Like Denver, Ella immediately regards Beloved as the ghost of Sethe's dead child. "You know as well as I do," she tells Stamp Paid, "that people who die bad don't stay in the ground" (221). And Stamp Paid can't disagree; "Jesus Christ himself didn't" (221). It is Ella who convinces the women of the community that Sethe must be rescued, and Ella's reasons have less to do with any affection for Sethe or sanction of Sethe's past than with a resolve to restrain the movements of memory in the present. When Ella hears 124 is "occupied by something-or-other beating up on Sethe," it infuriates her (302). Whatever Sethe's past, Ella doesn't "like the idea of past errors taking possession of the present," the possibility "of sin moving in on the house, unleashed and sassy" (302). If the past doesn't "stay behind, well, you might have to stomp it out," and Ella determines that in this case the past demands some stomping (302).

As the women gather at 3 p.m. on a Friday to march on 124, they ask Ella, "Shall we pray?" "Uh huh," Ella responds. "Then we got to get down to business" (302). They come to 124 praying and singing and kneeling, building "voice upon voice . . . a wave of sound wide enough to sound deep water and knock the pods off chestnut trees. It [breaks] over Sethe and she tremble[s] like the baptized in its wash" (308). Coincidentally, as the women arrive Denver's new, white employer Mr. Bodwin is also coming down the road. Consumed by memory, staring blindly through a scar, Sethe mistakes Bodwin for Schoolteacher. Sethe rises in rage to murder him, but the women surround and embrace Sethe, responding to her past and taking responsibility for her present. The women of Bluestone literally bear Sethe bodily in their arms as Paul D had once done. And in this melee of song, prayer, and community, Beloved vanishes.

Beloved is a complex novel, and this gloss of its themes – and especially of its conclusion – leaves much unsaid. Indeed, Sethe's redemption should be counted ambiguous at best. Though Denver seems altogether rejuvenated after these events and even Paul D appears mostly recovered, in the aftermath of this baptism of song and bodies Sethe remains broken and unstable. The possibility of a future for Sethe is still in question. "Me and you, we got more yesterday than anybody," Paul D tells Sethe. "We need some kind of tomorrow" (322). But the very fact of that future's possibility defines its character as future: it remains open, indefinite, neither foreclosed by memory nor predetermined by the past. When we finish the novel, we do not know what will become of Sethe and Paul D, but their future at least is not foreclosed by memory. "By and by all trace is gone," we are told (324). The past has once again been beaten back, leaving room for an imagined future.

It's tempting to align this conclusion with the theological preface I offered earlier, especially given the baptismal imagery that accompanies Sethe's rescue, Stamp Paid's recollection of the resurrected Christ, and the telling timing of Ella's good Friday intervention. Isn't this exactly what Green, Tracy, and others have described as the primary project of the Christian religious imagination? It is the wrestling of a community with a dangerous memory. It is the collective, common struggle to move from the site of memory toward some truth, to move together from image to text, such that the remembrance of real trauma might become a means of engaging the present and imagining a future. I must confess that I want this to be *Beloved*'s final word on imagination. But I fear a deeper critique haunts this text.

2.

For much recent theory, sense is understood to be actively made of, not passively received from, the world; meaning is given in received images and signs. Indeed, this linguistic, imaginative aspect of human thought is precisely the theoretical attribute contemporary theology has looked to in order to theorize its foundations. But there is also a demanding critical edge to the late modern linguistic turn. As Jacques Lacan has noted, if "I identify myself in language," then it is "only by losing myself in it like an object."[16] Lacan is notoriously opaque; the theologian Louis-Marie Chauvet helpfully explains that for Lacan linguistic signs "play a double and para-doxical function: they constitute the . . . advent of the subject, to the extent that the subject is represented in them; but also, and simultaneously, they constitute the . . . *exclusion* of the subject, to the extent that the latter is *only* represented in them."[17] Signs do represent us, but they only *re*-present us. Or as Terry Eagleton poetically puts it, the self "can be detected only negatively, in the lack which stirs at the heart of lan-guage."[18] Fair enough, but for Lacanian psychoanalysis, this lack has a particular significance with respect to remembered trauma and its lived repetition. "What is realized in my history," Lacan asserts, "is not the past definite of what was, since it is no more, or even the present perfect of what has been in what I am, but the future anterior of what I shall have been for what I am in the process of becoming."[19] The site of one's memory is not what happened yesterday (past definite), since that no longer exists, nor even what has happened to lead up to today (present perfect), but what will have happened tomorrow to make sense of this day once it has passed (future anterior). The past is not a firm ground upon which our presents and futures are precariously scaffolded. The past is gone. It is the world actually in front of us that continually conspires with memory in our sense-making.

This is all rather too abstract; *Beloved*, I think, makes Lacan's concern devastatingly concrete. At the beginning of the novel, 124 is haunted by a poltergeist. When Paul D shouts down its memory, the house calms. But then a woman comes. She appears to be Sethe's resurrected daughter, a corporeal form of Sethe's tragic past. But there are subtle clues she may not be. Indeed, Sethe is one of the last characters convinced. Before the pieces fall into place for Sethe, she tells Denver she believes Beloved has been "locked up by some whiteman for his own purposes, never let out the door" (140). She recalls that "something like this happened to Ella except it was two men – a father and son – and Ella remembered every bit of it. For more than a year, they kept her locked in a room for themselves" (140). Sexual slavery is the only way Sethe can explain Beloved's broken speech, her profound need, her odd behavior. But when she hears Beloved's humming, Sethe's devious brain clicks. Later on, Stamp Paid asks Paul D who he thinks Beloved might be. "She reminds me of something," Paul D responds. "Something . . . I'm supposed to remember" (276). Beloved resembles a memory he thinks he's meant to have. But Stamp Paid speculates instead that there was "a girl locked up in the house with a whiteman over by Deer Creek. Found him dead last summer and the girl gone. Maybe that's her. Folks say he had her in there since she was a pup" (277). But Sethe's and Stamp Paid's initial intuitions die away as Beloved's specter rises.

What if these intuitions were correct? If Beloved is a girl, not a ghost, if she is a real child who has been sexually enslaved by a white man for years and has arrived at 124 seeking rescue, then we must arrive at some unsettling conclusions. The central horror of this book is that awful handsaw, Sethe's sacrifice of her child in order to spare her from slavery. But if Beloved is a girl, not a ghost, then the sacrifice has been repeated. Ella – herself a victim of a similar history – cannot rightly see this wounded child. Sethe – who suspects as much at first – cannot rightly see this child. Denver cannot see her, Paul D can't see her, Stamp Paid – even for all his initial suspicions – can't see her either. Like Sethe mistaking Bodkin for Schoolteacher, they stare blindly at Beloved through a scar. They cannot see, they can only imagine. As the women of Bluestone Road rise against Beloved, cursing her and calling her the devil, they are surprised "by their absence of fear when they [see] . . . her" (308). Because, despite their worst imaginings, she is beautiful. She has "taken the shape of a pregnant woman, naked and smiling in the heat of the afternoon sun. Thunderblack and glistening . . . her belly big and tight . . . Jesus. Her smile [is] dazzling" (308). And then Beloved – beautiful, Jesus, full of life with Paul D's child – disappears without a trace in that uprising. She has been imagined into nothingness. If Beloved is a girl rather than a ghost, then it is not, as Ella worries, that a real past has come forward to possess the present. It is rather, as Lacan warns, that a real present, one pregnant with possibility, has been sacrificed to the ghost of a dead past in order that it might be made into some sense, in order that a memory might be redeemed.

There are profound implications to this reading. I am an American, male reader and student of literature. I am not white, but none of my ancestors was an enslaved African. The first few times I read *Beloved* I interpreted Ella and the others to be redeeming an unspeakable violence by their religious resolve. Like many other literary critics, I saw in the novel a tentative way forward, a risky path into the future Paul D and Sethe so dearly need.[20] And wouldn't that be nice for a nonblack, male reader like myself? Wouldn't it be convenient for my criticism if racial and sexual violence were ghosts awaiting exorcism in song? But if Beloved is an ordinary body rather than a resurrected one, then the stakes are troublingly raised. If Beloved is real, then I must confess that there may be something insidiously (if unwittingly) blinkered in my male, un-African-American imagination, in the ease with which I have seen redemption at this novel's conclusion – especially when what the novel may in fact be proclaiming is not the possibility of redemption but the absolute intractability of sacrifice.

I am also a student of Christian theology, and Beloved's disappearance unsettles my theological imagination too. "Disremembered and unaccounted for" at novel's end, Beloved "cannot be lost because no one is looking for her" (323). Imagined into nothingness, Beloved no longer fits the meanings we desire. Readers and characters alike allow her to "pass on," they forget "her like a bad dream" (323).

At the end of the first written gospel, in its earliest version, Jesus disappears entirely from the text. There are no resurrection appearances, no words of comfort and mission, no paracletian promises of ghostly presence, only terror and an empty tomb. In that first telling of the Christian story, Jesus no longer fits the meanings of his disciples, past or present. All that remains in Jesus' place is an absence, an open tomb, and the desire to make sense at the site of his memory.[21] Christ vanishes abruptly from Christian scripture only to arise gloriously in Christian imagination. But in mimicking the disappearing movements of Jesus, Beloved forces theologians to ask at what cost resurrection comes. The Christian tradition has been only too willing throughout its long history to disappear all sorts of others for the sake of its vision of Christ. Like Ella, Stamp Paid, or Sethe, we have often been so desperate to see Jesus that we have looked past the real need standing naked and vulnerable and beautiful and pregnant with possibility before us. We have exorcised human persons in order to make our imagined memories more real. Garrett Green and David Tracy are surely correct: theology is a practice of the imagination, a visit to the site of memory. But as theologians return again and again to the empty tomb of Christian recollection, Beloved urges a demanding question: whom shall we sacrifice to our imaginations?

Notes

1 Toni Morrison, "The Site of Memory," in *Inventing the Truth* (New York: Houghton Mifflin, 1995), 83–102.
2 Garrett Green, *Imagining God: Theology and the Religious Imagination* (Grand Rapids, MI: Eerdmans, 1989), 9.
3 Ibid., 10.
4 For a detailed and compelling account of this development in modern thought, from Kant to Hegel, through Coleridge, to Feuerbach, Marx, and Durkheim, see ibid., 9–27.
5 Ibid., 45.
6 Among many others, some prominent examples stand out. In addition to Garrett Green's work, David Tracy's *The Analogical Imagination* (New York: Crossroad, 1982) makes a similar argument using the insights of the hermeneutic tradition, while Ronald Thiemann's *Revelation and Theology: The Gospel as Narrated Promise* (Eugene, OR: Wipf and Stock, 2005) pursues a nonfoundational theology through recourse to the analytic philosophical tradition.

7 These assertions are not unique to the late modern West, of course; other traditions and other ages have made similar claims. Postmodern thought is unique in this regard perhaps only by virtue of its emphasis upon such assertions.

8 Tracy, *Analogical Imagination*, 128.

9 Nietzsche articulates this in a way that profoundly inspires much postmodern thought. See "On Immaculate Perception," in *Thus Spake Zarathustra* (New York: Cambridge University Press, 2006), 95–97.

10 Tracy, *Analogical Imagination*, 104.

11 Ibid., 6.

12 Ibid., 133.

13 Ibid., 313.

14 Ibid., 427.

15 Toni Morrison, *Beloved* (New York: Vintage, 2004), 6. Subsequent page references are to this edition.

16 Jacques Lacan, *Écrits: A Selection* (New York: W.W. Norton, 1982), 86. I should also note that the imaginary is (not uncoincidentally) a crucial category for Lacan, one profoundly related to issues of subjectivity, language, and signs, and one too complex to survey in summary here. See ibid., 1–7, 30–113, and 146–178.

17 Louis-Marie Chauvet, *Symbol and Sacrament: A Sacramental Reinterpretation of Christian Existence* (Collegeville, MN: Liturgical Press, 1995), 96.

18 Terry Eagleton, *The Trouble with Strangers: A Study of Ethics* (Malden, MA: Wiley-Blackwell, 2009), 84.

19 Lacan, *Écrits*, 86.

20 There are other Lacanian readings of *Beloved*. See, among others, Sheldon George's "Approaching the Thing of Slavery," *African-American Review* 45.1–2 (Spring/Summer 2012): 115–130. There are theological readings of the novel, for example, L. Gregory Jones' *Embodying Forgiveness* (Grand Rapids, MI: Eerdmans, 1995), 279–302. And there are morally tragic readings of it; see Eddie Glaude's *In a Shade of Blue* (Chicago, IL: University of Chicago Press, 2008), 17–46. Indeed, few contemporary novels are as widely read as this one. But no readings I have yet encountered fully reckon with what I regard and have here proposed as the novel's sacrificial sense of memory and imagination.

21 For an extended consideration of the empty tomb as a site of memory, see Michel de Certeau's "The Weakness of Believing," in *The Certeau Reader* (Malden, MA: Blackwell, 2000), 214–243.

7

MICHON M. MATTHIESEN

Sacrifice

Sacrifice is a fraught category for many twenty-first-century readers, and any effort to promote or preserve it surely calls for careful negotiation. In its religious and liturgical expressions, sacrifice is marked out for critique as a symptom of the pathological suffering, violence, and abuse that should either be expunged from religion or be the sufficient reason for abandoning religion as an artifact of a benighted past. Christianity, in particular, with its central figure of a crucified Christ and with a central ritual identified by some denominations to be *sacrifice*, bears the brunt of such attacks.

Feminist critiques of Christian sacrifice are distinctively sharp, claiming that sacrifice and atonement theory together perpetuate patriarchy and are conducive to a dangerous construct of fear-respect-love that encourages abuse in families and societies.[1] Pamela Sue Anderson pointedly argues that the very notion of sacrificial suffering connotes a pernicious, "self-destructive love." In her view, women especially must shun the Marian model in which they, repressively socialized into a passive love of a male God, are encouraged to say, *"fiat mihi,"* "Let it be done to me." In place of a love that encourages sacrificial suffering, Anderson proffers a liberated, Enlightenment-rational proposition of autonomous, nonsacrificial love.[2] Put bluntly, a free, equal, and rational humanity has no need of sacrifice. At least in the court of the Western world, the jury has largely decided that religion is more enlightened and more compassionate without it. But is this the case? And what is lost to Christianity in particular if the attempt to excise sacrifice – with all its unsettling and negative polyphony – is indeed successful?

1.

For a clear riposte to such critiques of sacrifice, and for insight into the productive and transformative potential of sacrifice, we can turn to the vision and writing of Flannery O'Connor. O'Connor's recently published

A Prayer Journal (2013; hereafter abbreviated as *PJ*), in which she explores her vocation as a writer, provides a remarkable framework for revisiting Christian sacrifice. The journal is written between the years 1946 and 1947, when O'Connor is in her early twenties. She is living in Iowa City, participating in the Writer's Workshop, and waking up – almost wildly – to her vocation as God's writer. She desires both God and artistic success, but she connects these desires with the need for grace and the necessity of sacrifice, understood in terms of suffering and ascetical practices.

Her view of the necessity of suffering for the Christ-lover is interpreted profitably through the lens of two significant theological traditions: those of the Carmelites and Thomas Aquinas. The Spanish Carmelites, Teresa of Avila and John of the Cross, depict the ascent to union with God as one propelled by love's desire and fraught with suffering. The desire for union with the all-holy God and the course to that union is, necessarily, accompanied by the pain of purification. Eleonore Stump, in her monumental monograph on human suffering, *Wandering in Darkness*,[3] masterfully unfolds Thomas Aquinas' vision of human suffering and its relationship to human flourishing, a flourishing measured according to the highest Good: increasing closeness to God. Reading O'Connor without such theological contextualization results in serious misreadings of her often startling fiction. Other chapters in this volume, especially those in Part III, demonstrate this same imperative of carefully situating authors in their confessional homelands.

It goes without saying that, since the mid-1960s, critical thought on O'Connor's work has proceeded without caesura.[4] A recent critical trend deliberately veers away from reading O'Connor through any theological lens – an approach viewed as limiting and "obsequious."[5] I argue, however, that such an approach is misguided, and particularly when trying to interpret human suffering in O'Connor's work, a suffering set undeniably in a Christian context. To be sure, the violence of O'Connor's fiction continues to disturb both ordinary readers and literary critics. O'Connor's own mother famously wished that her daughter would write about "nice people" and frequently asked Flannery's friends and professional acquaintances to use their influence to this end.[6] As I have witnessed among my students encountering O'Connor's stories for the first time, one of two major responses predictably emerges: either a strong repulsion, which shrinks from the strangeness and violence of her writings, or a kind of stunned joy, as if stumbling upon something unexpected, rare, significant, but elusive.

O'Connor frequently found herself in a position of defending the violent and grotesque in her writing as necessary to her craft. Wishing to communicate her Christian vision to a largely "hostile" readership that sees the "distortions" of the modern world as *natural*, O'Connor insists upon "evermore violent means." She acknowledges her tactics of writing to shock and to unsettle the complacent and erroneous vision of her readers: "to the hard of hearing you shout, and for the almost blind you draw large and startling figures."[7] Perforce, such a purification of vision cannot be accomplished without "cost" – to both the artist and the reader. It is precisely here that O'Connor's early journal helps to sharpen our sense of the painful cleansing that her stories intend. One may judge the violence in her fiction to be *excessive* – even a torture of the reader[8] – but not before recognizing that the God O'Connor longs for is even more *excessive* in his desire for union with the creatures he made; this is a God who wishes to make mystics of all humans and through a process inherently painful to fallen humanity.

Two thematic threads, ultimately entwined, dominate the pages of this journal. The first, and the one most forcefully articulated, is the expression of her desire for God, a desire she ardently wishes to be both augmented and purified. O'Connor's words in these passages on desire sound remarkably like a knowing Carmelite vision of growth toward union with God, a movement that underscores the need for great self-understanding, asceticism, and sacrifice. The second thread reveals O'Connor's emerging confidence in her vocation as a writer, an artist who will write as God's servant. It is a confidence, however, not unchallenged by anxieties of a destiny that might spell only mediocrity. What ties together these two prevailing topics is O'Connor's repeated plea for grace – grace to work, to trust, to love, and, especially, grace to *suffer*.

At twenty-two, O'Connor writes perceptively about the suffering that necessarily attends the purification of desire. In the pages of this journal, she more than once confesses that she is too weak to pray for suffering. The following entry articulates well, and not without a bit of drollery, the dilemma she confronts: "I am afraid of pain and I suppose that this is what we have to have to get grace. Give me the courage to stand the pain to get grace, Oh Lord" (*PJ*, 13). Grace purifies, but not without leaving "blood" in its wake. When O'Connor prays that her desire be animated, she asks particularly that it be *alive* in a way that "it will probably have to live in suffering" (*PJ*, 36). A living love must surely be one of vulnerability, one tried in fire: this is her early wisdom. That spiritual desire requires sacrifice and a willing asceticism O'Connor is quick to admit. Fearing that she shall reach the age of seventy and be no nearer to God and her artistic goals, O'Connor calls for a "revolution" that would demand of her "a 20th cen. asceticism," adding humorously, "at least when I pass the grocery" (28). Her ambivalence toward the pain required for spiritual perfection is reaffirmed in a story told by O'Connor's acquaintance and biographer,

W.A. Sessions. Sessions recalls asking Flannery, "Have you ever thought about what it would mean to be a saint yourself?" "'Oh yes,' she laughed, 'and the price to pay.'"[9] Even many years after composing her prayer journal, after she has endured the shock and painful reality of her lupus disease, O'Connor is yet contemplating (and with a dread) the suffering that accompanies spiritual growth. My point is simply to underscore that the rather brutal self-assessment of her desire for God, seen alongside the aversion to painful purification, does not negate necessarily the sincerity of her desires, but rather acknowledges the "cost" of possessing them.

O'Connor's desire for God appears hardly separable from her longing to be a serious and accepted author. Both her desire for God and for authorial success coalesce in a cry for the grace to accept the suffering that her calling requires. We do well to remember that the vocational struggle O'Connor records in this journal comes unaided by a Vatican II articulation of the ecclesial vocation of the laity.[10] O'Connor had a fairly clear sense that she was not called to religious life (*PJ*, 6, 23). In the journal we witness her attempt to discover a path yet unmarked, a path yet to be officially recognized by the Church as a way of participating in the sacrifice of the Christ she loves.

With the bold proclamation that she is a writer – "I must write down that I am to be an artist" – O'Connor releases a plea that she indeed become one: "I have prayed to You about this with my mind and my nerves on it and strung my nerves into a tension over it and said, 'oh God please,' and 'I must,' and 'please, please'" (*PJ*, 29, 3). The impassioned requests for the development of her talents are directed not solely at public success; she angles distinctively at being God's servant and instrument, even as the typewriter is her instrument. She wants to write God's story, the one divinely provided to her, and asks for God's assistance to make it "sound" and not "cheap" (*PJ*, 11). How delighted she would be if Christian principles would "permeate" her writings, but, she implores, "let there be enough of my writings (published) for Christian principles to permeate" (*PJ*, 5). Christian and godly, yes, but in the public eye, she pleads. Prompted, it seems, by a recent reading of Bernanos, she declares firmly that God "must be in all" her writing (*PJ*, 21). She asks for help in loving and bearing with work, expressing a willingness to "sweat for it" in the service of God. In her labors for God, she prays that she might be "intelligently holy" (*PJ*, 18).

Doubt and anxiety, however, likewise surface in the words of her prayer journal. In the same way that she detects mediocrity in her spiritual life, aching suspicions of a lackluster artistic talent also emerge. She alternately vows to battle such mediocrity to the death and to surrender to it if it be her "scourge" (*PJ*, 22, 27). In moments of artistic discouragement, she wonders if a lack of gratitude for God's previous assistance has caused the current "dry" patch:

> If ever I get to be a fine writer, it will not be because I am a fine writer but because God has given me credit for a few things He kindly wrote for me. Right at present this does not seem to be His policy. I can't write a thing. ... Right now I wonder if God will ever do any more writing for me. ... Perhaps I have not been thankful enough for what has gone before. (*PJ*, 23)[11]

The overall impression of O'Connor's journal entries hardly suggests an acquiescence to the mediocrity of her gifts – how can they be so if they come from God? – yet she is frank in acknowledging that the way to greatness can be had only by grace. And it is precisely in this request for grace that she knows herself to be but half-hearted.

In a fairly uncanny way, the young O'Connor knows clearly the costly price of the grace that will allow her to write with success. On 25 January 1947, she journals that both her God-given intellectual and artistic gifts, as well as the "delights" accompanying them, are as "visions" for which one must pay. More, with frankness she asserts that the "thirst" for such visions rarely carries an equal thirst for "the attendant suffering." At this point, we poignantly hear O'Connor "looking back" and remarking that she has already suffered – "not my share, but enough to call it that." Still, she avers that a "terrific balance" remains and prays for the grace to endure the "due": "Dear God please send me your grace" (*PJ*, 28).

2.

Under a single petition for grace, O'Connor's ardent desire for union with God conjoins with her equally fervent desire to serve that God as a writer. She ultimately recognizes that both spiritual and artistic perfection will be achieved through a costly grace that brings suffering, even as that grace works "whatever it does" supernaturally. From whence derives O'Connor's concept of a necessary tendering of sacrificial suffering for realized desires and graces received? Is O'Connor's God, as feminist theologians might purport, a dominating male figure who repressively and with violence demands her submission of will and delights in her suffering? O'Connor's journal gives no credence to this suggestion. Quite the contrary, in fact.

The prayer journal iterates a process of spiritual maturation that accords well with Carmelite teaching; namely, that a movement toward union with God – into the interior castle of the soul or an ascent up Mount Carmel – is attended inevitably by a purifying suffering, *inevitably* because of the fallen human will and its attachment to things earthly (and the spiritual sins, such as pride). At the beginning of his *The Ascent of Mount Carmel*, John of the Cross describes two important features of the journey of every soul to perfect union with God. First, such a journey can be pursued and achieved only "through love," and second, the soul on its way to such a union will experience "numerous and profound" "darknesses and trials, spiritual and temporal" (*Ascent*, Prologue, 1). Later in the *Ascent*, John sums up progress on the road to union, elaborating the "one thing necessary": "true self denial, exterior and interior, through the surrender of the self both to suffering for Christ" and to absolute detachment from things. He does not hesitate to characterize these trials as cruciform – a "living, sensory and spiritual, exterior and interior death of the cross" (*Ascent*, II. 8, 11). But again, the courageous confrontation of such suffering occurs only because of, and only through, a heart *fired* with love of God.

Teresa of Avila is equally vivid in portraying purifying difficulties on the path to union with God. In her *Interior Castle*, for example, Teresa identifies the devil's violent efforts – "he will gather all hell together" – to keep the soul from moving closer to God. This is nothing short of a real battle, and Teresa writes that souls must be "manly."[12]

Can we assume that the well-read, young Catholic intellectual of twenty-two knew the Carmelite spiritual tradition? I would argue that she did. For one, her private library reveals a certain predilection for the Carmelite mystics, and her later letters make reference to John of the Cross.[13] At the very least, O'Connor's desire to give herself entirely to God, a desire she feels impeded by a fear of suffering, is a clear reflection of the Carmelite law of the spiritual life – and not, I would urge, a reflection of a masochistic God. The object of O'Connor's desire aligns neatly with the Carmelite God of Love who enflames the soul disposed to surrender to him and brings her along a path of purification.

3.

If the Carmelite tradition helps to situate O'Connor's desires, Thomas Aquinas' approach to the problem of human suffering takes us further into the mystery of grace and its costliness. Thomas' treatment of human suffering in the context of human *flourishing* sheds light not only on O'Connor's prayer journal, but also, more suggestively, on the violence and suffering in her fiction. Can we securely propose the young Flannery O'Connor was shaped by Thomas Aquinas' worldview? On page 26 of her prayer journal we have but a teasing hint that St. Thomas was on her mind: the words "St. Thomas" appear in her hand, but then the remainder of the page has been excised. Whatever she was invoking in regard to St. Thomas in 1947, we shall never know; but we can be certain that Thomas' thought was not new to O'Connor in her graduate work. One of her undergraduate professors at Georgia State College for Women, George Beiswanger, was impressed with Flannery O'Connor's intellect and asserted in particular that she "knew Aquinas in detail."[14]

Her collected letters also reveal more than a mere passing interest in St. Thomas' work. In a letter to "A" (9 August 1955), for instance, she mentions reading Thomas every night for twenty minutes before going to bed.[15] Theologian Frederick Bauerschmidt inclines toward reading these lines in O'Connor's letter as a mere "joke."[16] To be sure, O'Connor's wit is active in the letter: she reports giving a "scholastic" response to her mother who tells her to put the *Summa* down and turn off the light. Still, I see no reason not to take O'Connor at her word – that she indeed is a "student" of St. Thomas – even though she also speaks of learning Thomas by "osmosis" and of being a Thomist "three times removed."[17] Further epistolary evidence discloses how frequently Thomas is a kind of theological loadstone for O'Connor and that she was reading with great admiration the "vigorous" Etienne Gilson, a leading scholar of Thomas in the twentieth century.[18] Perhaps her comment about being thrice-removed refers to the fact that she relies on a sound distillation of Thomas' thought, perhaps by someone like the eminent Gilson, over and above the fact that she was not a reader of Latin. More, her words may simply indicate a humility, a sense of ineptitude before his voluminous writings and brilliance, a sentiment shared by many Thomas Aquinas "disciples." At any rate, both her reading of Thomas and her reliance on Gilson seem to qualify O'Connor as competent in Thomas' worldview and theological vision.[19]

Eleonore Stump's masterful work *Wandering in Darkness: Narrative and the Problem of Suffering* presents a nuanced Thomistic theodicy that takes seriously questions of human flourishing and the desires of the heart.[20] Thomas' worldview and treatment of human suffering provide a way to understand the evil humans experience while, at the same time, maintaining belief in an omniscient, omnipresent, and all-good God. Put differently, Stump's interpretation of Thomas seeks a *morally sufficient* reason for God to allow human suffering, parsing morally sufficient in the following terms: the suffering experienced by individuals may be morally sufficient if it contributes to their flourishing, shaping them to be who they ought to be or allowing them to attain their heart's desires (or both, as Stump would have it).

> On Aquinas's views, if a good God allows suffering, it has to be for the sake of a benefit that outweighs the suffering, and that benefit has to be one that, in the circumstances, cannot be gotten just as well without the suffering; the benefit has to *defeat* the suffering.[21]

Importantly, Stump underscores that the benefit that defeats the suffering need not be transparent either to the sufferer or to others.[22] The suffering, however, will be directly linked to the flourishing of the individual.

But what constitutes human flourishing in Thomas Aquinas' worldview, and how do the desires of the heart enter the experience of human suffering? Suffering is a matter of what one cares about (health, security, politics, justice), what one desires (literary success, academic achievement, meaningful relationships – human and divine), and what the heart loves (one's children, one's friends, God). In Thomas' view, human flourishing is measured on a scale of values, at the top of which – and source for other goods – is union with God, a union that will be shared ultimately with others. Such a union would mean becoming like to God (deification), a participation in his being, a sharing in his divine nature.[23] If this is so, closeness and union to God, one that is ultimately shared with others, is thus the "best thing" for the human being; while, on the other hand, the absence of such union is the deprivation of human flourishing. St. Thomas holds that human freedom must allow for the possibility of never willing love of God and other persons. And because human beings do not perish at death, then a human may everlastingly choose to be at an unbridgeable distance from God. Such would be the worst possible thing that could happen to an individual; it would be the final impossibility of flourishing for the human creature.[24] In Thomas' view, then, the flourishing of the human depends upon an ever-increasing closeness to God, the very desire that O'Connor often articulates in *A Prayer Journal*, that is, the very thing, along with her writing, that she cares about most deeply. In sum, then, the Thomistic defense of suffering says that suffering is redeemed if it contributes to an individual's good, either by "warding off the worst thing for that person or in providing the best thing for that person."[25]

For a more complete picture, however, we must nuance these ideas of human flourishing, the heart's desire, and redeemed suffering. Stump suggests that human beings can be *mistaken* in their assessment of all three of these; that is to say, there can be an opacity about what constitutes my flourishing, my desires of my heart, and my suffering. Stump introduces a significant distinction between objective and subjective flourishing. By objective flourishing, we might understand that which an individual "ought" to be, that is, what obtains when an individual is "the best she can be"; this objective flourishing may or may not be consonant with what one cares about most deeply.[26] The example that Stump provides is memorable. John Milton cared deeply about the Puritan Party in England and desired to be politically active in its government. He envisioned that he would flourish through his commitment to Puritan politics. In fact, this desire kept him away from his poetic vocation for several years. We can surmise that had Cromwell's political power held sway for decades, *Paradise Lost* may never have been written. In some way, then, what one cares about may not necessarily be "equivalent to what one ought to be." But we need as well to consider the *subjective* element of flourishing, which includes the heart's desire. When one is deprived of that desire, suffering ensues. With the failure of the Puritan revolution, Milton lost his wealth and his goods and was confronted with possible imprisonment and death. In terms of his heart's desire, he suffered a deep subjective disappointment.[27] Stump stipulates further that what one thinks is their heart's desire may not have much intrinsic value (e.g., to own a new Jaguar); nevertheless, as long as it is what an individual cares about deeply, it is the loss of that thing or things that constitutes the "subjective side" of suffering and impedes flourishing.[28]

Oddly, it is also the case that our experience of suffering is not always transparent. Can it be that we at times do not know that we are suffering? Stump demonstrates that this is so, reminding us that suffering and pain are not simply equivalent. On a basic level, a person may not know immediately that he or she is no longer flourishing physically. A disease such as cancer can grow in the body for some time without inhibiting one's sense of well-being. The body suffers, and yet we do not know it. More profoundly, one can be mistaken about their heart's desire, about *what* that desire is or whether or not it is in their possession. Such error can derive from a lack of introspection, from an effort to repress what one cares most about, or from a conscious or unconscious decision to deceive oneself about what matters most. In other words, it is possible to be suffering and therefore not flourishing without being fully conscious of this reality.[29] Though these qualifications may appear counterintuitive and baffling, they are particularly significant, and not least because we can see them operative in O'Connor's fiction – and often in spades.

Thomas Aquinas thinks that the Christian is committed to a "generalized" acceptance of, or assent to, the suffering that can bring one closer to the highest good, namely, greater nearness to God. Such an assent is "tacitly included in the volitional component of faith, and it is explicitly part of sanctification."[30] In other words, Christianity acknowledges that growth toward perfection or optimum flourishing involves adversity, involves a fight against the self and the dragon. In her later essays, O'Connor relished Cyril of Jerusalem's words to those in formation for baptism, warning about the dragon that sits by the road watching, waiting, and ready to attack and devour. The Christian journey "to the Father of souls" necessarily passes by the dragon. About this adversarial dragon, O'Connor writes: "No matter what form the dragon may take, it is of this mysterious passage past him, or into his jaws, that stories of any depth will always be concerned to tell, and this being the case, it requires considerable courage ... not to turn away from the storyteller."[31] I am suggesting that Thomas Aquinas' vision of human suffering and flourishing is one that O'Connor must have known, if only, as it were, through "osmosis." Her prayer journal leaves little doubt of this: she asked to receive the "visions" necessary to her writing of godly stories, and she desired an asceticism that would bring her nearer to God. The full integration of these things for which she cared deeply and which would lead to her flourishing would be "paid" for through suffering. Of this she seemed quite sure – intuitively and theologically.

4.

In January 1950, only a short two and a half years after the writing of her prayer journal, O'Connor was first struck down with the disease (lupus erythematosus) that would take her life fourteen years later, at the age of thirty-nine. The disease, painful and crippling at times, with treatments wreaking havoc on her energies and capacities, would indeed cause her much suffering and hardship. But by all accounts, and as much as one can objectively judge, that suffering was defeated: O'Connor did indeed become a published and accomplished writer,[32] her talents deepening and her visions scintillating ever more sharply in the years she wrote. In terms of her illness, O'Connor memorably writes in a letter that she found sickness before death to be a "one of God's mercies."[33] Up to the very last weeks of her life, O'Connor worked indefatigably finishing and editing stories ("Revelation," "Parker's Back," and "Judgment Day"[34]) for her final book; yet she seemed also to approach death with acceptance,[35] having achieved, in and through her suffering, the desires of her heart revealed in her early prayer journal: an ever closer union with God and success as an author.

One might protest, and rightly, that it is not possible to judge that through her suffering O'Connor's desire for a closer relationship and union with God was obtained. How can such a claim ultimately be verified? Eleonore Stump acknowledges that one of the weaknesses of the Thomistic defense is its *relational* aspect. That is to say, it is difficult "to see" the redeeming benefit of suffering that is said to bring one closer to the highest good of union with God: "it might not be evident to anyone lacking a God's-eye view of the whole life of the sufferer."[36] Certainly, suffering can lead also to the disintegration of personality, and the sufferer may well be turned away from flourishing and from God. The Thomistic defense, with its insistence on the human free will, does allow that a sufferer may refuse the offer of grace, the nearness of God, and the refolding or integration of the heart's desires into the deepest desire of the heart. In Flannery O'Connor's case, however, this does not seem to be what happened. The letters of her final year of life reflect neither bitterness nor a refusal of the God whom she serves. Rather, they seem to carry on in O'Connor's usual sharp and witty vein, but with increasing descriptions of weariness and a request for prayers.[37] Of her last months, Sally Fitzgerald writes that O'Connor was "not so much stoical as quite serene; she had attained her personal form."[38]

5.

If one hesitates to make a final judgment about the moral sufficiency of suffering in O'Connor's own life, we may nonetheless gain an new entrée into the world of her fictional narratives by examining them through the lens of this Thomistic concept of human suffering and flourishing, which seems to rescue her characters from the "worst thing" that can happen to the human being.

I have chosen "A Good Man Is Hard to Find," one of O'Connor's best-known stories, because it is among her more unyielding works in terms of delivering a clearly redemptive account of suffering. The memorable grandmother of this story, given no proper name and thus universalized, is killed at point blank by the Misfit, a man "aloose from the Federal Pen." Can one argue that her suffering and violent death is somehow redeeming? Do we have any insight from the story that points to a growth in nearness to God, any achievement of the desires of her heart that suggests flourishing? Indeed, the evidence is spare. In the opening two pages of the story, the narrator reveals that this grandmother, conniving, judgmental, wishing always to be in control, is a "know-it-all" who considers herself a lady, and a righteous one at that. She dresses for the road trip to Florida in such a way that, in case of an accident, "anyone seeing her dead would know she is lady" (CW, 138). This desire for proper social recognition seems to indicate the shallowness of the grandmother's deepest concerns, a suggestion reaffirmed when, upon recognizing the Misfit, the grandmother says, "I know you wouldn't shoot a lady would you?" (CW, 147). Mistakenly, she imagines that her highest good lies in being perceived as a lady with social standing and high moral rectitude; ironically, the narrator reveals that those closest to her – her son, his wife ("deaf" to the grandmother), and the rude, comic-book-reading grandchildren – grant her no such respect. At more than one point, we hear the grandmother pining nostalgically for another age in which people were "nice" and "did right" (CW, 141, 139). The grandmother seems to live for those fleeting moments in which she "flourishes" by manipulating events and pontificating with her moral wisdom.

At the end of the story, after her son – "her only son,"[39] her "Bailey boy" – and the rest of the family are killed, the distraught and crumbling grandmother confronts the truth about her feeble moral position and the errant desires of her heart. As her son and grandson are taken into the woods to be shot, Bailey turns around at the edge of the forest and poignantly yells, "I'll be back in a minute, Mamma, wait on me!," which are the first words of love (such as they are) coming from him in the story. The grandmother orders him to come back "this instant," but recognizing her utter lack of power, she cries out in a "tragic voice": "Bailey Boy!" (*CW*, 148). O'Connor vividly demonstrates the grandmother's pain as her spiritual trial unfolds. Looking down upon the Misfit, who is crouching on the ground in front of her, the grandmother asks him if he ever prays. Then, as she hears two pistol shots from the woods, she begins a kind of chant (to both herself and the Misfit) – "Pray, pray ... pray, pray" (*CW*, 149). When the rest of the family, including the infant that she has been coddling on her lap, is taken out to the woods, the grandmother has difficulty speaking at all: she can only say, "Jesus, Jesus," in a way that "almost sounded as if she might be cursing," the narrator adds. The Misfit seems to concur, "Yes'm ... Jesus thrown everything off balance" (*CW*, 151). Surprisingly, even at this point, the grandmother again turns her hope to social respectability and leverage: "I know you come from nice people .... Jesus, you ought not shoot a lady!" (*CW*, 152)

It is only after hearing the gunshots that kill the remaining family that the grandmother's heart ultimately cracks. Again she calls out, "Bailey Boy, Bailey Boy!" She begins to understand that she loves and desires something, someone, beyond and more than herself; she recognizes that she has lost what she really desired: the life and love of her son and his family. No longer able to stand, she sinks to the ground, her pride expired, and the suffering of her heart literally crushing her. Looking at the Misfit now on his own level, she watches him agonize over not knowing if Jesus really did raise the dead. His fist hitting the ground, his voice high, angry, and cracking, the Misfit cries out: "Listen lady ... if I had been there I would of known and I wouldn't be like I am now" (*CW*, 152). What happens next enigmatically signals the grandmother's transformation. Her head clears, and she sees close to her own face the Misfit's contorted visage on the brink of tears. She murmurs the only words of true charity that surface from her in the story: "Why you are one of my babies. You're one of my own children!" Accompanying these words of empathy is a gesture of communion, as the grandmother reaches out and touches the Misfit on the shoulder; he recoils from the touch, as if bitten by a snake, and shoots her three times in the chest. The grandmother has seen in the Misfit her own brokenness, and that of her son and his family; she has heard the echo of her own spiritual languishing. The Misfit's words have stirred the memory of her deepest desire: to be with the Jesus who forgives sins, raises the dead, and exalts the souls of believers. In other words, the Jesus who "did what He said." At the point of a gun, the Misfit can bring the grandmother, who has been lying to herself, to others, and even to the Misfit ("I know you are a good man!"), to the point of truth: there is only one who has authority over life and death and the world, only one who is truly righteous, and he lies far beyond her categories of "good" and "nice."

Was this momentary epiphany of what her heart most deeply loves and of what can bring authentic flourishing sufficient to redeem the horrors she experienced – the ruthless killing of her only son and family, and then the violence of her own death? O'Connor's description of the grandmother in death suggests that we can answer this question affirmatively. The grandmother lays with her legs "crossed under her like a child's and her face smiling up at the cloudless sky" (CW, 152). In death, she again becomes child-like before a God who can, in mercy, admit her into his kingdom. The smile surely tells of the unexpected discovery of an inner peace. She sees, in an eternal last moment, her heart's deepest desire for a loving union with God and others. She has, through this violence, achieved "the best thing" and has been spared the "worst."[40] When we consider the worldview and defense of redemptive suffering in Aquinas, our perspective on the tragedy of death is also transformed. If suffering is a "healing" that leads the person to their highest good, earthly life takes on "the character of a hospital; and death has something of the nature of a discharge from that hospital."[41] Death is the not the worst thing; eternal separation from the heart's true desire is. The grandmother has experienced something of a hospital emergency room immediately prior to her own discharge from this life.

6.

I have suggested in this chapter that O'Connor's prayer journal from 1946 to 1947 provides insight into the theological and spiritual mindset of the young Flannery, as well as granting a fresh standpoint from which to see the violence and suffering in her fiction. O'Connor does seem to disclose in her fiction that suffering is redeemed through the gaining of the heart's deepest desire – a shared love and union with God. If this is so, her fiction is Christian comedy of a most profound sort. Her central characters are spared the "worst thing," gaining instead highest happiness in and through their suffering.

Notes

1 For a careful analysis of a feminist perspective on sacrifice and atonement, see Darby Kathleen Ray, *Deceiving the Devil: Atonement, Abuse, and Ransom* (Cleveland, OH: Pilgrim Press, 1998), esp. 43 passim. See also Stephen Finlan, *Problems with Atonement: The Origins of, and Controversy about, the Atonement Doctrine* (Collegeville, MN: The Liturgical Press, 2005), for an acerbic argument against sacrifice and a Christian atonement theory.

2 See, for example, Pamela Sue Anderson, "Sacrifice as Self-Destructive 'Love,'" in *Sacrifice and Modern Thought*, ed. Julia Meszaros and Johannes Zachhuber (Oxford: Oxford University Press, 2013), 29–47 (esp. 41–46). In terms of ritual sacrifice, Nancy Jay has judged Catholic eucharistic sacrifice to be unredeemably patriarchal, a liturgy in which women should refuse to participate: *Throughout Your Generations Forever: Sacrifice, Religion and Paternity* (Chicago, IL: University of Chicago Press, 1992).

3 Eleonore Stump, *Wandering in Darkness: Narrative and the Problem of Suffering* (Oxford: Oxford University Press, 2010). Hereafter cited as *WD*.

4 For an excellent history of the thematic trends in this corpus of literature, see Sura Rath's "Introduction," in *Flannery O'Connor: New Perspectives,* ed. Sura P. Rath and Mary Neff Shaw (Athens: University of Georgia Press, 1996), 1–11.

5 See, for example, Patricia Yeager, "Flannery O'Connor and the Aesthetics of Torture," in *Flannery O'Connor: New Perspectives*, 183–206, esp. 191; and Michael Kreyling, ed., "Introduction," in *New Essays on Wise Blood* (Cambridge: Cambridge University Press, 1995), 1–24.

6 See, for example, Brian Gooch, *Flannery: A Life of Flannery O'Connor* (New York: Back Bay Books, 2009), 317.

7 Flannery O'Connor, "The Fiction Writer and His Country," in *The Collected Works* (New York: Library of America, 1988), 806. Hereafter cited as *CW*.

8 See Yeager, "Aesthetics," 191–206.

9 W.A. Sessions, "Real Presence," in *Inside the Church of Flannery O'Connor: Sacrament, Sacramental, and the Sacred in Her Fiction*, ed. Joanne Halleran McMullen and Jon Parrish Peede (Macon, GA: Mercer University Press, 2007), 39.

10 See nn. 30–38 in *The Dogmatic Constitution on the Church: Lumen Gentium* (Boston: Pauline Books and Media, 1965), 56–66. In the last year of her life, O'Connor writes the following in a letter to Janet McKane (also single) about being single in the Church: "I'm rather glad the single folks, the left-overs as you call us, haven't been discovered by the Church. Think of the awful oratory that would flow over us …" (*The Habit of Being: Letters of Flannery O'Connor*, ed. Sally Fitzgerald [New York: Farrar, Straus and Giroux, 1988], 564; hereafter cited as *HB*).

11 See also an earlier entry in which she is reflecting particularly on prayers of thanksgiving and wishing she prayed such prayers more purely, more in the "form of self-sacrifice" (*PJ*, 12).

12 Teresa of Avila, *The Interior Castle*, trans. Kieran Kavanaugh and Otilla Rodriguez (Mahwah, NJ: Paulist Press, 1979), 51.

13 In her private library, O'Connor had on her shelf three works by the Carmelite Bruno de Jesus-Marie: *Love and Violence, St. John of the Cross*, and *Three*

Mystics: El Greco, St. John of the Cross, and *St. Teresa of Avila.* See Lorine M. Getz, *Flannery O'Connor: Her Life, Library and Book Reviews* (New York: Edward Mellon Press, 1980), 89. For references to John of the Cross in her letters, see *HB,* esp. 97, 113, 241, 337.

14 Gooch, *Flannery,* 114.

15 *HB,* 93–94.

16 Frederick C. Bauerschmidt, "Shouting in the Land of the Hard of Hearing: On Being a Hillbilly Thomist," *Modern Theology* 20.1 (2004): 163–183.

17 *HB* (To John Hawkes, 20 April 61), 439. I am rather more inclined to read the phrases in this letter as O'Connor's self-deprecating humor.

18 *HB,* 107.

19 Indeed, there has been important critical work addressing the influence of Thomas Aquinas upon O'Connor's fiction. I point the reader to Bauerschmidt's essay, cited earlier, in which he attempts to measure the Thomist features of this "hillbilly Thomist" writer. Bauerschmidt contrasts St. Thomas' serene, gentle-manly, and dispassionate writing in the *Summa theologiae* with O'Connor's own "ungentlemanly," passionate, and shocking fiction. Another literary critic, Helen R. Andretta, has traced Thomas' influence in terms of O'Connor's use of the hylomorphism in her stories, and most especially in "Parker's Back," where O'Connor, as it were, takes a stand against gnosticism as a fundamental denial of the incarnation and of a sacramental worldview. See Andretta, "Parker's Back," in *Inside the Church of Flannery O'Connor: Sacrament, Sacramental, and the Sacred in Her Fiction,* ed. Joanne Halleran McMullen and Jon Parrish Peede (Macon, GA: Mercer University Press, 2007), 41–63, esp. 48.

20 To be most precise, what Stump aims to present is not a *theodicy,* but a *defense.* That is, her efforts attempt "to tell a story about a possible world that contains both God and human suffering and that this is enough like the actual world that, for all anyone knows, this story *could* be true." Only a theodicy claims that what is described in the defense is *true,* actually the case. Yet, as Stump points out, one may indeed accept the defense as a theodicy (*WD,* 19, 389). My recapitulation of Stump's intricate argument, which includes a rich exposition of the biblical narratives of Abraham, Job, Samson, and Mary of Bethany – a "panoply of human suffering" – will perforce be selective and brief. I can only hope that it will be provocative enough to whet appetites for the entire book.

21 *WD,* 378.

22 *WD,* 13 and 459. As I will indicate later, this ignorance of the benefit is consonant frequently with an opacity in regard to one's flourishing and the cares of the heart.

23 *WD,* 386–388.

24 Stump also insists that the soul that loves moves toward union with God (and others), whether or not the soul recognizes that the *end* of their love is union with God. Thomas intends, however, "that if real love has its way and is not somehow driven off course, it will eventuate in shared union with God" (*WD,* 91, 387)

25 *WD,* 466.

26 *WD,* 10.

27 *WD,* 10, 468–469.

28 The objective and subjective side of flourishing and suffering need not be at odds: "What is the greatest good for a person on the scale for objective value can

converge with what is the deepest heart's desire for a person on the scale for subjective value for her; and, when it does, all the things a person cares about can be interwoven into a unity with the deepest desire of her heart and with her care for her flourishing" (*WD*, 453). I want to suggest that such a unity obtained for Flannery O'Connor.

29 *WD*, 12–13.

30 *WD*, 383.

31 "The Fiction Writer and His Country," *CW*, 806.

32 One clear indication of her recognition as an eminent author came in 1972, when her *Collected Stories* won the National Book Award in Fiction. Even within her short life, she was able to see some of that literary success, as, for example, when she witnessed *Wise Blood* being translated into French and "Revelation" receiving the O. Henry prize for fiction in 1964.

33 To "A," 28 June 1956, *HB*, 163.

34 See Gooch, *Flannery*, 360–373.

35 I discern an attitude of acceptance in at least two of O'Connor's late letters, one to Jane McKane (15 May 1964) and other to Cecil Dawkins (24 June 1964). In thanking McKane for having a Mass said for her, O'Connor wryly pens: "I do appreciate the Mass that will be said for my intentions by the Paulist fathers. I don't know what my intentions are but I try to say that whatever suits the Lord suits me" (*HB*, 577). Less than six weeks before her death, O'Connor writes to Cecil Dawkins that the doctors "expect [her] to improve, or so they say." But O'Connor adds, "I expect anything that happens …" (*HB*, 587).

36 *WD*, 460. Stump provides medical and psychological cases that give evidence of just such a benefit, namely, the sufferer growing close to God (*WD*, 455–460).

37 See, for example, *HB*, 560, 581, 592.

38 *HB*, 560.

39 This phrase, which appears in the opening sentences of the story, seems intended to echo Genesis 22, that poignant scene in which Abraham leaves, with his "only son," the one he loved, for the place of sacrifice on Mt. Moriah.

40 Not all readers agree with my interpretation of the details at the end of this story. Joanne Halleran McMullen, for instance, in *Writing against God: Language as Message in the Literature of Flannery O'Connor* (Macon, GA: Mercer University Press. 1998) sees ambiguity throughout the final scene of "A Good Man Is Hard to Find," 34–37, 45–49. Additionally, I have not dealt with the Misfit himself. Has he also been redeemed? It is indeed likely that he has been touched by grace, as O'Connor herself suggests in a letter to John Hawkes (14 April 1960) (*HB*, 389). But my interest here is with the characters who have, in the course of the narrative itself, suffered the pain of losing that which was dear to them.

41 *WD*, 466.

8

SUSANNAH BRIETZ MONTA

Repetition

How might we bring together the study of religion and literature? How ought (or oughtn't) we to conjoin these ways of making, finding, and thinking about meaning? For some, the simple fact that religion and literature intertwine in particular historical periods and cultures demands that they be studied in connection with each other. For others, literature provides an occasion for speculative religious thought, whereby literary texts are used to think about religious questions. Conversely, religious texts may be read with attention to their literary forms. But we might also think about religion and literature through their many points of convergence, allowing each area its integrity while bringing religion and literature into relation through traits, habits, practices, and qualities central to each. In the ways Western religion and literature are configured, those points of convergence include canon, belief (or disbelief), form, genre, ritual, and ways of relating to tradition and to authority.

I.

Repetition is especially promising as a point of convergence. It is central to many areas of religious thought and practice. Repetitive prayer features in Western and non-Western religious practices, and repetition structures and motivates religious ritual. Ritual may both recall – by remembering an earlier event – and, in many traditions, reenact – by making earlier events present again to the community ritually performing them. Repetition is related to exemplarity, in that particular instances – of sanctity, of a holy life or practice – point toward a "corresponding universal principle."[1] Repetition plays a role in the persistence and development of religious traditions. Within Christianity, the religion most relevant to the poets discussed later, theology's work arguably proceeds through adaptive repetition. The Christian theologian's goal is not novelty or originality per se, but the interpretation of given revelation, teachings, texts, and practices with respect to the particularities of his or her culture and time.[2] This is not pure repetition, to be sure, but processes of reinterpreting and renewing given truths do engage with repetition obliquely insofar as earlier texts and practices continue to resonate in new contexts.

Repetition is also critically important not only for the content but also for the form of literary texts. It thus has the capacity to open up large religious questions without blurring or evading literary texture. Repetition of stress, rhyme, syllables, tones, sounds, or syllable count structures traditional poetry in many languages.[3] Much contemporary English poetry, free from traditional rhyme and meter, nevertheless uses repetition to center and/or create boundaries for poems, as in the enduringly popular litany poem, structured by periodic returns to repeated words or phrases.[4] Pattern and variation, expectation and satisfaction: these remain integral parts of literary pleasure.[5] As in religion, so in literary history: repetition can connect new literary work to tradition, and exemplarity is of course a literary concern as well. With respect to both religion and literature, repetition may serve as a fine-grained, embodied, practice-based way to talk about tradition and traditioning, and about the interplay between the universal and the particular.

Repetition thus has the potential to ground the relations between religion and literature in phenomena integral to each. Of course, areas of overlap are not points of exact similitude: literary repetition need not have religious import. But it may broach religious horizons, insofar as it raises questions about temporality and finitude, ritual performance, permanence and change, origins and originality, the givenness of language, and the nature and possibilities of meaning. For instance, repeated words – as in the poetic refrains discussed later – are not easily interpreted as the self-expressive utterances of a fictional or dramatic poetic speaker.[6] Repetition may thus function as a guard against the imperial self. It reminds us that words come to us bearing poetic and linguistic histories; they are not purely ours to use as we wish. Or, in Mutlu Blasing's memorable formulation, poetry "remembers what the 'human' has forgotten: that he is not God."[7]

Repetition's polytemporal dimensions also have the capacity to move us beyond our selves, even as they engage us in our own time. For example, repeated refrains pace the unfolding of poems in time, and yet even as they mark linear time they also frustrate it: they bring the immediate past of reading (or hearing) into the present.[8] Similarly, repetition asks us to consider what words meant in the past, and what they mean *now*. Repeated words and forms (as in genres or rituals) lead us to expect what has not yet arrived and to measure what we hear, perform, or read alongside a past made present again. Patterns of literary imitation also raise questions of temporality, insofar as echoes of earlier works bring those works forward in time, into the reading and interpretation of other works. The extent to which temporal gaps are maintained or collapsed in that process may determine whether we perceive imitation as close to or distant from repetition. By its very nature, then, repetition engages time – past, present, and future – in ways that can be deadening or enlivening and in ways that move between fixity and flux. Always it asks us to think both in and beyond our own time.

Thinking about religion and literature together through practices of repetition thus requires that the reader be aware of her polytemporal commitments. We must be sensitive to the past, to history, for literary and religious repetition accrues significance in context. For two of the poems discussed later, for example, late medieval and Reformation-era debates about repetitive forms of prayer, liturgy, and devotion prove important. Careful literary-historical study has an ethical charge: we ought to strive to understand the past insofar as we are able. This is, fundamentally, the labor of respect. But repetition's capacity for polytemporality simultaneously highlights the past and reaches into the present. What Catherine Pickstock has called the "liturgical now" has its literary dimension, too.[9] We read poetry, and we practice ritual, in the present, as the poems discussed later recognize. We are not sealed off from what we read; it aspires to repeat itself through us, reaching toward our time.

In what follows, I give three lyric poems the time – or times – they seem to request. Dated from the late fifteenth to the mid-seventeenth centuries, these poems engage various dimensions of repetition: its relationships to time, exemplarity, and the givenness of language. They make overt use of repetition through thematic emphases, rhetorical figures, and refrains. They reflect upon the religious and theological dimensions of repetition as they do so (I use "theological," as all three address Christianity specifically). Repetition crafts a relation between religion and literature within the poems and between the poems' past and present readers. It is through this most literary feature that the poems do their religious thinking, and ask us to do ours.

2.

In the early Reformation, many reformers criticized devotional practices that asked devotees to count a certain number of repeated prayers. Such practices were often derided as deadening, mindless, and unstimulating either to thought or to devotional feeling. But in the late middle ages, repetitive prayer and passionate affective piety were not necessarily seen as inimical to each other. Counted repetitions were combined powerfully with affective meditation in popular devotional practices such as rosary prayer.[10] In fifteenth-century literary culture, imitation of prior models was a high literary value, and in devotional practice, imitation of exemplary figures, especially Christ and Mary, was critically important. The poem "Sodenly afraide" comes from this period of heightened concern with devotional emotion and repetition, imitation and exemplarity. Its anonymous author presents readers with a tableau: in a state halfway between waking and sleeping, a hard-hearted person encounters a weeping woman, who is soon revealed to be the Virgin Mary. The hard-hearted person's emotional transformation is rendered in the poem's sophisticated use of refrain. Because the poem is fairly short, I cite it in full;[11] a modernized text is included in Section 6.

> Sodenly afraide, half wakyng, half slepyng,
> And gretly dismayde – a wooman sate weepyng.

With favoure in hir face ferr passyng my reason,
And of hir sore weepyng this was the enchesone:
Hir soon in hir lap lay, she seid, slayne by treason.
Yif wepyng myght ripe bee, it seemyd than in season.
> 'Jesu!' so she sobbid –
> So hir soon was bobbid,
> And of his lif robbid –
Saying thies wordes, as I say thee:
'Who cannot wepe, come lerne at me.'

I said I cowd not wepe, I was so harde hartid.
Shee answerd me shortly with wordys that smarted:
'Lo, nature shall move the; thou must be converted;
Thyne owne Fader this nyght is deed' – lo, thus she thwarted –
> 'So my soon is bobbid,
> And of his lif robbid.'
> Forsooth than I sobbid.
Veryfyng the wordes she seid to me:
'Who cannot wepe may lern at me.'

'Now breke, hert, I the pray! this cors lith so rulye,
So betyn, so wowndid, entreted so Jewlye.[12]
What wight may me behold and wepe nat? Noon truly,
To see my deed dere soon lygh bleedyng, lo, this newlye.'
> Ever stil she sobbid –
> So hir soon was bobbid,
> And of his lif robbid –
Newyng the wordes, as I say thee:
'Who cannot wepe, com lern at me.'

On me she caste hir ey, said, 'See, man, thy brothir!'
She kissid hym and said, 'Swete, am I not thy modir?'
In sownyng she fill there – it wolde be noon othir;
I not which more deedly, the toon or the tothir.
      Yit she revived and sobbid,
      So hir soon was bobbid,
      And of his lif robbid –
'Who cannot wepe,' this was the laye,
And with that word she vanysht away.

The poem's first two lines describe fear but without invoking an agent who experiences either fear or the liminal state of consciousness, "half wakyng, half slepyng," to which the lines refer. This lack of an agent indicates that what follows will not be merely a first-person perspective on strange events. The movement beyond personal perspective grounds the poem's later use of refrain, for refrains are difficult to account for if we understand poetry primarily as the dramatic utterance of a real or imagined speaker (under what conversational circumstances might one repeat a refrain, without being considered mad, overly dramatic, or intoxicated?). The poem's formal, thematic, and devotional exploration of repetition is condensed in complex refrains found in the second half of its stanzas, in lines shaped by careful repetition and variation. Such repetition does not belong to what earlier critics might have called the poem's "speaker" – either to his or her agency or his or her time. Instead, highly ordered repetition is used to characterize disruptive experience, precisely because repetition exceeds linear time and overgoes the expression of any single persona.

That the refrain offers us repetition with variation is perhaps not a surprise: in preindustrial, premechanized cultures, there were no exact copies. Yet the poem uses careful variation to perform the replication of devotional emotion and, by the end, to invite its replication in us. The second stanza clarifies this replication as the poem's focus. The poem will not concern faith's propositional content, what is accessible to reason. Indeed, the poet carefully tells us that the "favor" or beauty of the woman's face is "ferr passyng my reason," the first apperance of the /I/ in the poem. True, the "enchesone," or cause, of the woman's weeping is perfectly logical: her son has been murdered and betrayed, "slayne by treason," enough to make anyone shed tears. But reason or logic alone is neither the poem's concern nor its method. The poem aims instead to rouse devotional passions, in the present time of its /I/ as well as the present of its readers, through the use of repetition.

The poem thus insistently interweaves emotion with repetition. The woman's son is first named in an emotive outburst – "'Jesu!' so she sobbid."

This emotional utterance begins the poem's complex refrain. The weeping woman is of course Mary. And she offers herself as an exemplar, inviting imitation: "Who cannot wepe, come lerne at me." "At" carries the sense of "from" and also suggests Mary as a site of exemplarity. The next appearance of the /I/ is coldly blunt: "I said I could not wepe, I was so harde hartid." Mary's sharp retort establishes kinship between the /I/ who speaks and the battered body in her lap, identifying the dead Jesus as "Thyne owne Fader." She then personalizes a repeated line: "So *my* son is bobbid" (emphasis added). These statements of relation bring the /I/ out of a focus on the self; the /I/ no longer expresses hard-heartedness but instead joins in the refrain's pattern: "Forsooth than I sobbid." The /I/, not Mary, sobs in this instantiation of the refrain; Mary, not /I/, describes the fate of Mary's son. The /I/ speaks language originating outside the self, taken from Mary; the /I/ enters that language, forming the self according to what is given, rather than simply using language for self-expression. The third stanza's refrain also varies the order of its three short lines. Elsewhere, the rhyme words are "sobbid," "bobbid," and "robbid," in that order. Here "sobbid" appears last, used to represent the speaker's imitation of Mary. The variation encodes response; it performs the claim to devotional affective imitation in each stanza's closing line. The poem subtly asks us to think about the literary response it seems to hope for, one characterized not by distanced, sterile evaluation – from a position above the text, so to speak – but by a performance of poetic repetitions. And these literary repetitions, in turn, engender devotion, a performance within the reader's present experience.

The fourth stanza highlights the breaking of time and space that Christiania Whitehead attributes to late medieval affective meditational practices, ruptures characteristic also of refrain itself.[13] After a lament (lashed with a bitter anti-Semitism that another surviving copy of the poem lacks), Mary insists on the immediacy of Jesus' death; he still lies bleeding "newlye" – recently, anew, now. Mary's immediate, present grief brings back the refrain: "Ever stil she sobbid." The line's complex temporality suggests both historical locatedness – in the past tense of "sobbid" – and timeless continuity – "Ever stil." This challenge to linear time is underscored in the stanza's penultimate line: "Newying the wordes, as I say thee: / Who cannot wepe, com lern at me." "Newying" may simply mean repeating, but it carries also the connotation of renewal and echoes the poem's making-present of Christ's "newlye" suffering body. The poem's reader is invoked, for the second time: the poem turns outward, inhabiting the present of its reader's repetition (or "newyng") of its words. Repetition in this poem seems designed to move the reader, to join past and present in a way that invites participation in devotional grief.

That participation is encouraged directly in the poem's penultimate line, which readers are asked to complete (we are surely able to do so, for repetition stimulates the memory). That line names the refrain as a "laye," a song. John Hollander notes that in much medieval song, the refrain was the part in which all were invited to join.[14] The poem thus enacts verbally what it desires to bring about in its readers: a devotional imitation of intense emotion, reaching from Mary to /I/ to "thee," the reader, an imitation that joins the past event of Christ's death to the reader's present meditation. The poem's emotional power and breaking of temporal boundaries are performed through repetition.

3.

Many of refrain's characteristics – its ability to mark and evade linear time; its resistance to models of poetry as self-expression, of either a historical or a fictional self – persist into later, Reformation-era work. During the Reformation, some hotter reformers condemned nearly all set liturgical prayer as mere "lip labor," inimical to the heartfelt expression that should characterize true prayer. The seventeenth-century poet and Anglican cleric Robert Herrick (1591–1674) would seem to have disagreed. The title of Herrick's "His Litany to the Holy Spirit" signals the poem's relationship to litanies, a form of repetitive prayer that persisted, through several reforms, in the Church of England's liturgy. The Roman Catholic "Litany of the Saints" invoked the intercession of saints through repeated formulae; given its support for the cult of the saints, it was controversial early in the Reformation. It was one of the first elements of the traditional Sarum Primer to be altered or dropped in reformed prayer books for the English market.[15] A revised litany, which drew upon Luther's litany of 1529, was published in 1544; it was the first English-language liturgy. That litany was further revised for inclusion in the Edwardian *Books of Common Prayer* (*BCP*) of 1549 and 1552, and again for the Elizabethan *Book of Common Prayer* of 1559. The *BCP* litany invoked only members of the Trinity and combined petitions to reduce the number of repeated responses. Even so it remained controversial; by the mid-seventeenth century some complained that it was an instance of deadening, papistically repetitive prayer.[16] During the seventeenth century the word "litany" acquired pejorative connotations; in addition to a liturgical form of prayer, it could signify a seemingly interminable list or lengthy, meaningless complaint.

As a Church of England clergyman with traditional religious sensibilities, one who mourned the dismantling of the Church of England in the 1640s,

Herrick found value in set liturgical prayer. His poem is not, of course, a liturgical litany but it draws on litanies' set, repeated responses. It signals its relation to litanies through extravagant use of repetition. Repetition appears in its refrain, in its sounds (hard "d" and "c" sounds recur), and in its meter (the stanzas never depart from an insistent trochaic tetrameter). The poem also uses anaphora extensively (the figure begins successive phrases, clauses, or lines with the same word). "When" initiates ten lines in this short lyric, signaling its concern with the time of death, the movement from time to timelessness. Another nine lines begin with "And," prompting the poem's accumulation of vivid deathbed details. Here is Herrick's "His Litany to the Holy Spirit":[17]

In the hour of my distress,
When temptations me oppress,
And when I my sins confess,
        Sweet Spirit, comfort me!

When I lie within my bed,
Sick in heart and sick in head,
And with doubts discomforted,
        Sweet Spirit, comfort me!

When the house doth sigh and weep,
And the world is drown'd in sleep,
Yet mine eyes the watch do keep,
        Sweet Spirit, comfort me!

When the artless doctor sees
No one hope but of his fees,
And his skill runs on the lees,
        Sweet Spirit, comfort me!

When his potion and his pill
Has or none or little skill,
Meet for nothing but to kill,
        Sweet Spirit, comfort me!

When the passing-bell doth toll,
And the Furies in a shoal
Come to fright a parting soul,
        Sweet Spirit, comfort me!

When the tapers now burn blue,
And the comforters are few,
And that number more than true,
        Sweet Spirit, comfort me!

When the priest his last hath prayed,
And I nod to what is said,
'Cause my speech is now decayed,
    Sweet Spirit, comfort me!

When, God knows, I'm toss'd about,
Either with despair or doubt,
Yet before the glass be out,
    Sweet Spirit, comfort me!

When the tempter me pursu'th
With the sins of all my youth,
And half damns me with untruth,
    Sweet Spirit, comfort me!

When the flames and hellish cries
Fright mine ears, and fright mine eyes,
And all terrors me surprise,
    Sweet Spirit, comfort me!

When the judgment is reveal'd,
And that open'd which was sealed,
When to thee I have appealed,
    Sweet Spirit, comfort me!

The poem offers a tight, even relentless treatment of a deathbed scene, much like those viscerally imagined in Reformation literatures on "good" deaths, or deaths offering evidence about the dying person's eternal fate (hopefully a heavenly one) and testifying to the reality of an afterlife. The poem takes its time establishing the spatial location of its /I/; we do not hear of a "bed" until the fifth line. What is clear from the beginning is a complex sense of time. In the first stanza, "When" and "In the hour" suggest futurity, but no "will" or "shall" modifies the stanza's verbs. Is the stanza about the future or the present? Does the speaker imagine or experience his death? This slightly dislocated sense of time persists. In the eighth stanza, for instance, present and future are blurred: the speaker imagines a "When" after an attending priest has prayed – plausibly, if not necessarily, in the future. But the stanza then insists on inhabiting the present: "'Cause my speech is now decay'd." Distress is intensified in the next stanza: "When, God knows, I'm toss'd about / Either with despair or doubt." The distinction between despair and doubt in Reformation theology was usually temporal, not qualitative: doubt becomes despair when doubt persists.[18] The ordering of the words may suggest a glimmer of hope – "doubt" would contain and restrict "Despair" – though it is only a glimmer. "Either . . . or" does not permit us to choose.

Refrains time and pace poems, marking their unfurling in the performative utterance of their reading (whether silently or aloud). Herrick's poem invests some relief for its grim imaginings of Furies, flames, and hellish ones in its refrain. The insistent linearity of "When" (not "if") and the steady accretion of deathbed agonies marked by "And" are juxtaposed with a simple, recurring petition: "Sweet Spirit, comfort me!" The plea's repetition, as in the litanies invoked by Herrick's title, is not mindless, as some seventeenth-century critics opined. It rather responds to the relentless march of time, the collapse of futurity and present into the certainty of death, through an ongoing renewal of prayer. This is evident in its form as well as its content: the refrain's trimeter shortens the stanza's tetrameter, pushing against accumulation, and its iambs are softer, less percussive, than the stanzas' trochees. The refrain remembers a single, unchanging response to the poem's frights, to its running out of time.

The final stanza brings together the "When" of linearity and the polychronicity of refrain. "When to thee I have appealed" suggests both the futurity of the appeal, in an imagined "When," and its certainty, for the line imagines a completed action. In the poem's final line, its narrative of inevitable death rests in its nonlinear refrain, in the poem's recurring plea for comfort. Refrain in this poem, as in so many, is an intensification of language's memory. Refrains remember themselves, their prior lives, their genealogies (including, in this instance, the genealogy of litany prayer itself). In Herrick's poem, as in "Sodenly afraide," refrain counts on the fact that language is not simply expressive of the self. In a poem in which the self steadily disintegrates as death encroaches, in which the self gradually comes to stand alone before an imagined judgment, refrain's exceeding of self-expression may offer a space of stability or stillness, beyond the frights to which the dying self is (or will be) subject. The refrain performs a careful balance between an urgent plea – its emotion is not dampened by its reiterations – and a renewal of the only hope for comfort, in the present and in the future, which the poem offers us.

4.

In the two poems discussed earlier, repetition pushes against linear time to foster affective commitment, religious imitation, devotional renewal, and, arguably, liturgically structured comfort. Religious ritual is not simply about comfort, of course; it is not therapeutic. The work of liturgy is the sanctification of time and space. Ritual enacts and shapes community; it can make, not just reflect, meaning; it remembers and renews. Certainly in the Christian tradition, ritual also enjoins praise. Repetition is central to praise; as Regina Schwartz argues with respect to Milton's *Paradise Lost*, "to praise the creation is ritually to reenact it."[19] Such reenactment also raises theological questions made especially pressing by the reformers' teachings: how may a sinful creature praise her creator; how may she give words that are always already given; how may her art fashion praise without succumbing to idolatry? For the poet Mary Sidney, repetition helps her offer praise through language that both depends upon divine donation and is unapologetically artful.

The Reformation period's rhetorical poetics used figures of repetition heavily. Such figures are prominent in Mary Sidney's translation of Psalm 150, the culmination of the psalter in a hymn of praise. Sidney's figures negotiate the simultaneously theological and poetic problem of human linguistic agency, a problem embedded in the imperative to praise. Germaine Warkentin has noted that the period's educational emphasis on rhetorical composition led writers to "accept that repetition, pairing, and deliberate inversion of poetic elements may advance the reading of a work as effectively as pure narrative."[20] Rhetorical figures, it seems, were not simply decorative; they were also prompts for cognitive exercise.[21] In other words, and given the focus of Sidney's poem, figures of repetition *do* theological work; they do not merely reflect theology.

Sidney's investment in rhetorical figures both draws upon and overgoes the many sources she consulted. One of the most widely known of those sources was the Geneva translation of the Bible, the most popular English translation of the later sixteenth and early seventeenth centuries. The Geneva translation of Psalm 150 uses anaphora heavily. "Praise ye the Lord" is its closing line, and variants of this imperative statement begin every verse: "Praise ye God," "praise ye him," and so on. The emphasis is firmly on command, the "exhortation to praise the Lord without cease," as the Geneva headnote to Psalm 150 specifies. Mary Sidney chooses an elaborate sonnet form for her translation, one that artfully performs the act repeatedly commanded in the Geneva text:[22]

> Oh, laud the Lord, the God of hosts commend,
> Exalt his pow'r, advance his holiness:
> With all your might lift his almightiness;
> Your greatest praise upon his greatness spend.
>
> Make trumpet's noise in shrillest notes ascend:
> Make lute and lyre his lovèd fame express:
> Him let the pipe, him let the tabret bless,
> Him organs' breath, that winds or waters lend.

Let ringing timbrels so his honour sound,
  Let sounding cymbals so his glory ring,
That in their tunes such melody be found,
  As fits the pomp of most triumphant king.

  Conclude: by all that air or life enfold,
Let high Jehovah highly be extolled.[23]

Sidney's first line surrounds "God" with imperatives of praise; the verbs
"laud" and "commend" frame the deity. The task of praise, then, is clear.
Yet the first stanza's careful repetitions are not simple imperatives, as in the
Geneva text. Instead, they respond to a critical theological question: whence
the language, whence the grace, to praise? For example, the exhortation that
humans employ "All your might" is related to, even prompts (within the
poetic line), God's "almightiness." But the verbal echo between "All your
might" and "almightiness" suggests that poetic effort is being encompassed
by, or folded into, God's power, much as the phrase "all your might"
becomes divine "almightiness" by dropping the (human) possessive
("your"). The following line works similarly. Human effort – "Your greatest
praise" – should be spent on, but is not equal to, his "greatness." "Great"
first appears in a comparative, "greatest": God demands the best of human
effort. The second occurrence of "great" is within the substantive "greatness," an ontological statement about the deity. The repetition suggests
circular movement: we give our greatest praise to Him, whose greatness
prompts that praise. Human efforts to praise and the absolute "great"
quality of the deity are linked through repetition, but without any suggestion
that the latter depends on the former.

 In the second stanza, Sidney considers human efforts at praise through
music. Humans act on and through musical instruments: we make trumpet
notes ascend shrilly or play lute and lyre to express fame (one traditional
function of lyric, of course). The Geneva Bible has "viol" and "harp" in
the passage corresponding to this stanza. Taking cues from early Calvin-
ists' hesitation about musical instruments in worship, the Geneva
translation's side notes stress that while instruments were used under the
old law, they are now banned in Christ's church. Rather than "viol" or
"harp," Sidney includes a contemporary instrument (the lute) and an
instrument associated with poetry from the classical period (the lyre,
Apollo's medium). The distance between old and new dispensations is
neatly closed in her poem, and, simultaneously, room is opened for lyric
praise. Yet her syntax and repetitions keep lyric carefully bound to the
divine. The stanza's last two lines use the figure anaphora. Both begin with

God – "Him." Repetitions of "let" in line 7 govern lines 7 and 8, and the verb shapes an ambiguous petition. On the one hand, Sidney's petition reads thus: "let the pipe and tabret bless Him." But the syntax ("Him let") is just ambiguous enough to suggest a secondary meaning: let Him bless the pipe, the tabret; let Him bless the organs' breath. "Let" also asks permission for praise. Does praise originate with us, or with God? Are we creative agents, or are we like passive instruments, inert without another's breath or motion? Do we speak, or do we echo? Repetition – and the ambiguities of "let" and of poetic syntax – allow Sidney to answer: yes.

The third stanza enfolds in its first two lines two figures of repetition: epanalepsis (the repetition of a word or words at the beginning and end of a line, phrase, clause, or sentence) and anadiplosis (repetition of the last word of a line, phrase, clause, or sentence at the beginning of the next one). Lines 9 and 10 of Sidney's poem offer an epanalepsis: they are framed by forms of "ring." Initially characterizing an action already under way, where "ringing" is almost an attribute of "timbrels," in line 10 "ring" comes close to signifying "echo" or "resound." In the corresponding passage, the Geneva Bible simply repeats "sounding cymbals" and "high sounding cymbals." With intricate rhetorical artifice, Sidney chooses instead to tuck anadiplosis within epanalepsis. She links the figures by varying the verb forms on which they're built in an exchange of sounds (first "ringing" followed by "ring," and in the interior of the lines we have the inverse: "sound" is followed by "sounding"). In Sidney's poem "sound" means both an action – the sounding forth of God's honor – and, in its repetition, a resounding. In the tunes of timbrels and cymbals a melody fit for the divine King will be "found." The formulation balances activity (finding) and passivity (what will be found). The sounding and resounding that the lines command, request, and (through repetition) perform will permit the voicing and the finding of appropriate praise.

The final line enacts another echo, as "high" Jehovah is to be "highly" extolled. "Let" is again ambiguous: the verb is poised between human and divine imperative, between a request that humans act and a petition offered obliquely to God. The substantive assertion of God's nature – "high Jehovah" – prompts praise even as its echo produces the adverb ("highly") modifying praise's character. The poem affirms the value of art: it insists on instruments and on intricate poetic lines. It also blurs distinctions concerning the origins of praise. Repetition's simultaneous ability to signify unoriginality and rhetorical artfulness allows Sidney to walk a delicate theological and poetic line. Unwilling to abase either her God or her art, Sidney praises through repetition's virtues.

5.

In each of these poems, repetition is a way to bring together, to think using the resources of, literature and religion. They were written in specific moments and for cultures concerned with affective meditation, devotional imitation, the value of set prayer, the cognitive work demanded by rhetorical figures, and the human capacity (or incapacity) to offer praise. Yet insofar as repetition presses against linear time, and implicitly against the academic domestication of religious poetry as simply historical artifact, these poems also aspire to speak in reading's "now" (even when that speaking may be disturbing, as with the anti-Semitism in one copy of "Sodenly afraide"). Perhaps another dimension of their "now" has to do with the contemporary methodological reflections they may provoke. When we give these poems time to unfold the complex interplay between religious and literary uses of repetition, they caution us against relating religion and literature in ways that rely nearly exclusively on historical contextualization or on poetry's summarizable content. If we are to bring religion and literature into authentic, deep relation, we might do so by carefully grounding the many broad links between literary and religious habits of thought, practice, and interpretation in the granular formal and linguistic particularities of a single utterance.

6.

"Suddenly Afraid"[24]

> Suddenly afraid, half waking, half sleeping,
> And greatly dismayed – a woman sat weeping,

With favor in her face far passing my reason,
And of her sore weeping this was the enchesone: [cause]
Her son in her lap lay, she said, slain by treason.
If weeping might ripe be, it seemed then in season.
     'Jesu!' so she sobbed —
     So her son was bobbed,   [beaten, insulted]
     And of his life robbed —
Saying these words, as I say thee:
'Who cannot weep, come learn at me.'

I said I could not weep, I was so hard hearted.
She answered me shortly with words that smarted:
'Lo, nature shall move thee; thou must be converted;
Thine own Father this night is dead' — lo, thus she thwarted — [retorted]

'So my son is bobbed,
And of his life robbed.'
Forsooth then I sobbed,
Verifying the words she said to me:
'Who cannot weep may learn at me.'

'Now break, heart, I thee pray! this corse lies so rulye,   [body; pitifully]
So beaten, so wounded, entreated so Jewly.²⁵
What wight may me behold and weep not? None truly,   [creature]
To see my dead dear son lie bleeding, lo, this newly.'
    Ever still she sobbed –
    So her son was bobbed,
    And of his life robbed –
Newing the words, as I say thee:
'Who cannot weep, come learn at me.'

On me she cast her eye, said, 'See, man, thy brother!'
She kissed him and said, 'Sweet, am I not thy mother?'
In swooning she fell there – it would be none other;
I not which more deadly, the one or the other.   [(know) not]
    Yet she revived and sobbed,
    So her son was bobbed,
    And of his life robbed –
'Who cannot weep,' this was the lay,
And with that word she vanished away.²⁶

Notes

1 Lorna Clymer, "Introduction," in *Ritual, Routine, and Regime: Repetition in Early Modern British and European Cultures*, ed. Lorna Clymer (Toronto: University of Toronto Press, 2006), 4.

2 In *Poetry and Apocalypse: Theological Disclosures of Poetic Language* (Stanford, CA: Stanford University Press, 2008), William Franke writes that "The re-situating of theological revelation in the existence and consciousness of an individual numbers among its consequences the shattering of revelation into an open set of reenactments or repetitions. The time and place of disclosure of truth depend on the particular protagonist immersed in the contingencies of a singular existence.... Revelation and repetition become mutually dependent moments: only in being repeated can revelation be realized and validated" (100).

3 Cecile Chu-chin Sun, *The Poetics of Repetition in English and Chinese Lyric Poetry* (Chicago, IL: University of Chicago Press, 2011), compares English and Chinese traditions to argue that repetition is fundamental to lyric.

4 Michael Dumanis, "An Aesthetics of Accumulation: On the Contemporary Litany," in *The Monkey and the Wrench: Essays into Contemporary Poetics*, ed. Mary Biddinger and John Gallaher (Akron, OH: University Press Publications,

2011), notes that repetition in a litany poem allows it to "keep perpetuating its motion endlessly" but also bounds the poem, in that it "can never fly all that far from its trigger" (45).

5 Mary Oliver, *A Poetry Handbook* (New York: Harcourt, 1994), notes that variation is perceivable only against pattern; J. Paul Hunter argues for repetition and variation as essential to literary pleasure ("Seven Reasons for Rhyme," in Clymer, *Ritual, Routine, and Regime,* 172–198).

6 Jonathan Culler pushes against situational dramatic readings of lyric ("Why Lyric?," *PMLA* 123:1 [2008]: 201–206) which attempt to assimilate lyric to the verisimilitude of actual speech in particular circumstances.

7 Mutlu Konuk Blasing, *Lyric Poetry: The Pain and the Pleasure of Words* (Princeton, NJ: Princeton University Press, 2007), 9.

8 John Hollander, "Breaking into Song: Some Notes on Refrain," in *Lyric Poetry: Beyond New Criticism* (Ithaca, NY: Cornell University Press, 1985), 73–89.

9 Catherine Pickstock, *After Writing: On the Liturgical Consummation of Philosophy* (Oxford: Blackwell, 1998).

10 Anne Winston-Allen, *Stories of the Rose: The Making of the Rosary in the Middle Ages,* 2nd ed. (University Park: Pennsylvania State University Press, 2005).

11 Manchester, John Rylands Library 18932 (Latin 395), fol. 120a–b, as reproduced in *English Medieval Religious Lyrics,* ed. Douglas Gray (Exeter: University of Exeter Press, 1992, 21–22); the poem is also found in Trinity College Cambridge 1450 (O.9.38), fols. 63b–64a.

12 In this context, the anti-Semitic use of "Jewlye" is to indicate cruel treatment; the Trinity manuscript has "fuly" ("foully") here.

13 Christiania Whitehead notes that the tradition of affective meditation is the key devotional context underlying the content and expression of many medieval religious lyrics and that affective meditation (and, I would add, lyric itself) tends to diminish "spatio-temporal difference" ("Middle English Religious Lyrics," in *A Companion to the Middle English Lyric,* ed. Thomas G. Duncan [Rochester, NY: D.S. Brewer, 2005], 101).

14 Hollander, "Breaking into Song."

15 Helen C. White, *The Tudor Books of Private Devotion* (Madison: University of Wisconsin Press, 1951), has helpful overviews of these early primers.

16 As one writer complained, the litany is simply "vain repetition . . . not a *stump or a limb of Dagon,* but the head of the *Masse-book*" (*The Anatomy of the Common-Prayer* [London, 1661, 25–26, printed with *A Short View of the Prelatical Church of England,* 2nd ed., first published 1641 as *The anatomie of the service book*]).

17 As reprinted from *His Noble Numbers* (1647) in *Ben Jonson and the Cavalier Poets,* ed. Hugh MacLean (New York: W. W. Norton, 1974).

18 Lisi Oliver and Susannah Brietz Monta, "Spenser, Wolfram, and the Reformation of Despair," *Journal of Literary Onomastics* 1 (new series, 2011): 9–30.

19 Regina M. Schwartz, *Remembering and Repeating: Biblical Creation in Paradise Lost* (Cambridge: Cambridge University Press, 1988), 91.

20 "Amoretti," in *The Spenser Encyclopedia,* ed. Donald Cheney et al. (Toronto: University of Toronto Press, 1992), 33.

21 This is one of the claims advanced by Sylvia Adamson in "Synonymia: or, In Other Words," in *Renaissance Figures of Speech,* ed. S. Adamson, G. Alexander, and K. Ettenhuber (Cambridge: Cambridge University Press, 2007), 17–35.

22 Sidney's octave is in two quatrains rhymed after the Italian fashion – ABBA ABBA – and the sestet is in the English form – CDCD EE.

23 Cited from *The Sidney Psalter: The Psalms of Sir Philip and Mary Sidney*, ed. Hannibal Hamlin, Michael G. Brennan, Margaret P. Hannay, and Noel J. Kinnamon (Oxford: Oxford University Press, 2009).

24 Manchester Rylands Library 18932 (Latin 395), fol. 120a–b; also found in Trinity College Cambridge 1450 (O.9.38), fols. 63b–64a.

25 In this context, "cruelly"; the Trinity manuscript lacks the anti-Semitism, using "fuly" ("foully") instead.

26 I have modernized the poem's spelling wherever it was possible to do so while still preserving its form. I have not modernized its vocabulary but have included brief glosses where a modern reader might need assistance. I am indebted to Katherine Zieman and Karen Saupe for their suggestions; any remaining errors are mine.

PART III

Traditions

9

CLEO KEARNS

Hinduism

The Western reader who sits down to read the literary works most Hindus would identify as classics is often in for a surprise, especially about the way in which religious and theological discourse cohabits with aesthetic expression and popular piety in these texts.[1] In the Hindu context the interaction between religion and literature is usually assumed to be benign and often symbiotic: literary expression reflects religious texts and values and religious specialists welcome the support of literary expression. In the Judeo-Christian world, by contrast, there is an inherent tension between religion – or more precisely revelation – and poetics: theologians and clergymen have often cast a nervous eye on the arts, and artists and writers find they must defy the clerics and their orthodoxies to express themselves fully. Blasphemy – or at least transgression – acts as a kind of strange attractor for Western artists, and it is often a major source of the energy that drives their choices of form, genre, and trope. It is not so in the canonical works of Hinduism: the Mahabharata (and its embedded lyrical drama, the Bhagavad Gita), the Ramayana, and the play *Shakuntala* to name only the most revered.[2]

1.

Before attempting to sketch the aesthetic and theological issues at stake in this difference, it is probably wise to canvas briefly the vexed question of the definition of Hinduism and its relationship to Sanskrit, the language in which these classics were originally written and performed. In the first place, religious studies specialists today generally like to repeat what has become a truism: that Hinduism is a relatively late and artificial portmanteau term whose frequent use is a colonial artifact under which are grouped a vast array of diverse religious views and practices. As such – or so the argument goes – Hinduism is no more than a convenient term imposed from without on phenomena that are otherwise quite disparate and cannot be addressed except on a case-by-case basis.[3]

It is arguably the case, however, that the term "Hinduism" is nevertheless indispensable, both as a gateway to understanding and as pointing to a conceptual unity and existential stance toward life among these practices and viewpoints that most Hindus themselves assume to underlie their religious traditions. Some such designation, in any case, seems to be necessary, if nothing else to represent the compelling religious vision of India in a form that can be grasped by those new to it, and many Hindus are quite content to be so described, provided this term is understood to refer to a *family* of spiritual perspectives and disciplines and not a fixed or reified category. It is a family indeed remarkable – until recently – for its pluralism, tolerance, and diversity of stances toward the divine, but at least one major scholar of Hinduism, Andrew Nicholson, has shown that the concept of a coherent worldview underlying its many manifestations not only may be discerned in but is also indigenous to the tradition, which is not the random congeries of incompatibles it might seem to Western eyes.[4]

From this point of view, the resistance to the word "Hinduism" itself smacks a little of Orientalism, of the Western projections according to which India and the East are seen as the home of a wild "polytheism" involving the worship of strange gods, often in aesthetically grotesque forms. The implicit contrast here is between this "polytheism" and a supposed "monotheism," cast as the happy home of defined if thorny belief in a single, indeed a quite singular God. This God may or may not exist, but he forms a useful point of reference and measuring stick, negative or positive, for art and for life as well. This binary opposition is misleading on many counts. On the one hand, it erases a profound monotheistic tendency in Hinduism, and on the other it implies that the Western traditions are far more monolithic than they really are.

It may be better then to think of Hinduism not as a forced and artificial colonialist term, but as a perfectly useful rubric and to see the religion to which it points not as a hodgepodge of competing cult and deities but as a relatively coherent phenomenon, characterized by an identifiable family of beliefs, values, and practice. By many if not most lights, these would include (1) reverence, to varying degrees, for the Sanskrit scriptures, the Vedas and Upanishads, for the language in which they are expressed, and for *sanskriti,* the culture and civilization built on that language; (2) acceptance of the principle of union with one divine essence, brahman, as the ultimate goal of religious practice; (3) high tolerance for differing forms of religious observance and understanding and for many forms of divine manifestation; and (4) emphasis on orthopraxis, ritual purity, and contemplation, rather than on orthodoxy, righteousness, and right teaching in the pursuit of this goal.

The Hindu reverence for Sanskrit is based on the way in which the nature of that language is understood. Many Sanskrit words and phrases are traditionally said to evoke and vibrate in tune with the nature of the qualities they name; indeed, an entire theory of the use of these words and phrases, called "mantras" for their special properties, has evolved in their wake. In this regard, the language itself is a special vehicle of meaning, and its intonation is a path to oneness with the divine. The arts which draw on Sanskrit and Sanskrit precedents, even in the vernacular, participate in this sacred dimension of the language and its culture.

The term *sanskriti* refers to the widespread, historically documented civilizational complex that spread from small kingdom to small kingdom throughout the subcontinent and into Asia many centuries ago and that endured for over two thousand years. It was characterized by a common set of cultural coordinates including reverence for the Vedas and Upanishads and for the body of lyric, drama, and epic that emerged in their orbit. These aesthetic expressions of dharma were often sponsored by kings and priests, but they had a strong popular appeal as well, one that carried over into vernacular texts and performances across wide and diverse regions and locales. Even though vernacular expression became vital and vibrant at many points in this construct, Sanskrit was essential both to spiritual practice and to literary production at almost all times, constituting a kind of gold standard of precision and evocative power.[5]

Here Westerners may be baffled or miss important points, for Abrahamic traditions do not often generate forms of art that are regarded as sufficient and effective forms of spiritual practice in themselves. The closest analogue here might be "icon-writing," as the sacred painting of saints as a focal point for worship is called in the Orthodox tradition, or perhaps Gregorian chant, although the latter is not construed theologically as a way of evoking divine presence in quite the same way that sacred chant (*kirtan*) is in the dharmic traditions.[6] Because of these and other differences, the classic literature of Hinduism can sometimes seem unduly pious and/or unduly didactic to Western eyes. The great epics, the drama, and even much lyric expression is permeated not with the principles and exhortations of the Vedas and Upanishads but with invitations to direct experience of divine truth, though not always in obvious or apparent ways.

The great literature in Sanskrit that forms the historical substrate of literary work in Hinduism, however, is not just a collocation of disguised sermons or morality tales. True spiritual awareness of the kind the dharma requires involves many things, including – as we shall see – the sensual perception of natural beauty, even in what appear to be deviations from the straight and narrow path. This perception can be cultivated; the sacred arts of music, dance, and literature exist to do just that. Indeed, these genres support and enhance one another. Stories are danced; dancing is music and chant; and poetry often entails all three.

Nor are irony and a sense of the mystery of human life and of the inexplicable persistence of human suffering far from the horizon of this literature. As the poet T.S. Eliot says, himself a student of the Sanskrit language and an extensive and close reader of its classic texts:

> Think
> Neither fear nor courage saves us. Unnatural vices
> Are fathered by our heroism. Virtues
> Are forced upon us by our impudent crimes.
> These tears are shaken from the wrath-bearing tree.[7]

These lines would make a very telling and appropriate epitaph to the Mahabharata, the great epic of India, where the best intentions falter into violence and chaos and the worst contribute to a profound and cosmic rebalancing of which we in the present time are both the inheritors and the victims.

Hindus today would often likely point further to an underlying consistent architecture for Hinduism, an architecture rooted in the concept of *sanatana dharma*, sometimes translated as "cosmic order" or "eternal way of being" and best expressed in *sanskriti*, the culture to which it gave rise. The word *dharma* is notoriously hard to translate; it has aspects of natural law or regulated natural occurrence, aspects of ethical normativity or the "golden rule," and aspects of the values of terms like *path*, *calling*, or *duty*. Though dharma is inherent in the cosmos and not revealed from above as in the Abrahamic traditions, the concept is parallel in many ways with that of Torah or even the "way of truth" spoken of by Jesus in the gospels, except that the latter are regarded as exclusive transmissions, at least initially. *Sanatana* dharma is dharma for everyone; civilization and culture are built on it, and so are individual destinies, wherever they are to be found, east or west, north or south.

2.

T.S. Eliot was only one of a number of Western poets who were deeply struck by the depth and power of literature in Sanskrit: the list extends from Goethe, who drew upon the classic drama *Shakuntala* for the framing of Faust and learned a trick or two in the process, to Emerson, Thoreau, and Whitman, who were even able to find inspiration in the rather arcane laws of Manu, which have defeated many a Western reader, and to the poets of the postmodern American oriental renaissance, Alan Ginsberg, Gary Snyder, Nathaniel Tarn, and Jane Hirshfield among them.

These examples, however, are not the whole or even the typical story of the reception of Eastern classics in the West. For many, these classics are extremely hard to respond to and to place. A number of differences in underlying principle and mode of operation between what are roughly called the Abrahamic and the dharmic religions underlie this difficulty. In terms of textuality, for instance, the sacred scriptures of the Abrahamic traditions – the Torah, the Bible, and the Qur'an – constitute what are known as bounded texts or closed canons; their boundaries are strictly drawn and their priority over all other forms of writing is jealously guarded and maintained. In what are by contrast called the dharmic traditions (primarily Hinduism, Buddhism, and Taoism), the scriptures are less reified, and the boundary between revelation and commentary or literary supplementation is more porous.

The Vedas, for instance, the ancient body of literature embodying spiritual truths shown to the rishis of old, are distinguished in theory from the later commentaries such as the Upanishads, the Brahamans, and the Puranas, but both are absorbed and cited in practice in ways that are much on a par. Furthermore, since revelation arises directly from within the human soul and not from history, prophesy, or the written word, many later commentaries may be read, accepted, and honored as having spiritual authority. To put this another way, in Hinduism *sruti*, the body of divine revelations, is indeed distinct from *smriti* or commentary, but they are not in competition, and neither is regarded as the direct expression of a divinity that "owns" and countersigns them, so to speak, as God "owns" or countersigns the discourse of the Bible or the Qur'an.[8]

The dharmic traditions are also on the whole famously less dogmatic than the Abrahamic ones. Because they are less dependent on written revelation, literary expression in their orbit does not carry the same potential for transgression as does writing in the shadow of the Bible or the Qur'an. The down side of this difference for Hindu tradition is that its relatively unconflicted orientation to the body of sacred writings from which it emerges can make it seem, from a Western point of view, unduly codified and subservient to the archaic elements in that corpus, frozen in time, so to speak, lacking in both innovation and the capacity to provide critique and renewal. "Where," Westerners seem constantly if tacitly to be asking themselves, "is the cutting edge of these monumental and no doubt admirable works?" Where are the concerns with challenges to authority, social injustice, and conventional morality, the breaking of received ideas and forms, and the continuous innovations Westerners have come to associate with high art and indeed with cultural production at all levels?

These questions famously – and often legitimately – haunt the work of the major contemporary Sanskritist, Sheldon Pollock, who, while deeply invested in the study of Sanskrit language and of sanskriti, seeks to challenge both the tradition itself and the uncritical piety through which it is often approached. Pollock holds that literary expression in Sanskrit, while fascinating, sophisticated, and often aesthetically pleasing, has often functioned as a vehicle of received wisdom and ideological support for kings and brahminical elites and that for reasons partly political and partly due to its internal way of working it has frequently stifled both dissent and innovation. For instance, Pollock's reading of what has become a major cultural artifact of Hinduism, the epic poem called the Ramayana, draws sharp attention to its role in supporting a view of kingship that was based in part on the "othering" of Muslims and the suppression of women and that now undergirds communalist and nationalist movements in India, some of them violent indeed.[9]

3.

Pace Pollock, whose project is in many ways admirable, though perhaps unduly driven by political correctness, and whose scholarly credentials are in no doubt, this approach to literary expression and religion in Hinduism is bound in many respects to miss the point. For the social values of Sanskrit literature arise not just from political mystification, of which there is a certain dimension in all great monuments of culture, but from assumptions about spirituality, textuality, and the functions of sacred and secular order quite different from those found in Judaism, Christianity, and Islam. The major metaphysical and theological principles that underlie this difference on the Sanskrit side are three: (1) the principle of *maya*, or illusion, and of the "forgetting" or ignorance of our true nature, which entraps us in its web; (2) the importance of the witness state and of the experience of the inner self (*atman*) as observer and knower that allows for waking up from that illusion; and (3) the ontological identity of the *atman*, with brahman, the divine. This last is indicated by the famous affirmation *tat tvam asi*, "that are thou," which Hinduism takes from the Vedas.

The first of these principles gives most high art in ancient sanskriti culture its central problematic: to trace and display how and why we fall asleep to reality in such a way that the sense of divine identity is lost and bewilderment and suffering ensue. The nature of this process is particularly clear when it occurs in terms of aesthetic experience as conceived in this tradition. The second principle, the importance of the witness state, indicates the essential move or step in awakening: the gaining of distance on the illusion even while we operate within it. The third principle indicates the firm assertion that is uncovered in this process: the complete identity of the inner self with the divine, both (and indeed the entire cosmos that manifests them) being fully immanent and fully transcendent to one another. Of course, for the Abrahamic reader, such an assertion produces its own frisson, for mystics and heretics have throughout many centuries been marginalized and worse for asserting this inner identity of human and divine, or at least with doing so without qualification.

But how do these axioms of maya, witness, and divine identity relate to classic traditional literature in Sanskrit? There are two places to look for answers to this question: the ancient classical literary genre known as *kavya* and the traditional aesthetic theory indicated by the technical and philosophical term *rasa*. *Kavya* is a major genre of literary expression in Sanskrit and indicates the expression of eternal truths in elaborate poetic language and highly codified, not to say baroque, meters and styles. Rasa is a term both for the aesthetic effort of a work of art and for the theory that guides and shapes it.

The purpose of *kavya* the ancients taught, is to show the workings of the four *purusharthas*, or goals of earthly life, according to the dharmic understanding of human nature. These are the pursuit of righteousness (*dharma*), material wealth (*artha*), pleasure (*kama*), and liberation (*moksha*). This list places mundane goals in sequence with, rather than in opposition to, the otherworldly or spirituals goals in a way Westerners sometimes find confusing. In a sense, this sequence is the outgrowth of the particular equanimity of Hinduism vis-à-vis dualistic moralistic concerns, an equanimity that arises from seeing all things as to one degree or another a manifestation of the divine (which is not at all the same thing as having "no morals," as is sometimes felt or assumed). This kind of sequencing enables works written in the *kavya* genre to deal with a full range of human and natural experiences and perceptions without undue angst or without the need constantly to assume or exacerbate the tensions between and among them. As Daniel Ingalls, a prominent Sanskrit scholar of several generations ago notes, *kavya* can take its subject matter from many sources, for instance, the epics (Ramayana or Mahabharata) or from history, but in doing so it must offer descriptions of the full range of phenomena of ordinary perception, including visions of "cities, seas, mountains, moonrise, and sunrise."[10] *Kavya* must charm the reader or viewer on all sides, and a note of the highlights of human life is always made. An exemplary list is offered. It must include "accounts of merry-making in gardens, of bathing parties, drinking bouts, and love-making. It should tell of the sorrow of separated lovers and should describe a wedding and the birth of a son.... It should describe a king's council, an embassy, the marching forth of an army, a battle, and the victory of a hero."[11]

Furthermore, *kavya* must make its point in an interactive way. Explanations, in the form of questions and answers between the narrator and the listener, are expected to be integrated into the performance to show how the fructification of the four purusharthas is exemplified in a given narrative segment. It is this kind of codification and unambiguous support both for the beauty of life and for its ultimate aim and meaning that generates an obstacle to the Western reader (or at least to the modern Western reader), who is in general skeptical of these values, distrustful of sententious exemplarity, and alert for a rejection of precedent and presentation of "original" expression.

A deeper exploration of the aesthetics of *kavya* is badly needed in the study of Sanskrit, one freer of the largely modernist assumptions that may not be tuned even to the full range of aesthetic expression in the Western tradition. The same might be said of the second way of approaching Sanskrit literature, the concept and expression called *rasa*, the crown jewel of Hindu aesthetics and philosophical reflection on the nature of art. This term is often said to be untranslatable, though I suspect this insistence has more to do with its association with classical Indian music, which has long been very difficult for Western ears to hear, rather than with anything hugely arcane about the theory itself. At its simplest, rasa is just a term for pure aesthetic experience, experience to be found in many forms but that is always in some ways sui generis. More expansively put, rasa is the theory and practice of the evocation of states of attention particular and proper to art, though having profound religious and theological aspects and implications as well.

To demystify this term a bit, rasa theory is or can be a useful way of speaking about an experience quite common in many cultures, even Western ones. Think of a film or a piece of music about a character experiencing erotic love that moved you deeply. You began to participate in the feeling being evoked, maybe even to the point of tears. You forgot, for a moment, your separate self and became one with the represented and representative experience of another. What is going on here? It can't be that you are experiencing what the actor or singer is experiencing, because you don't know what that is. In fact, their experience is most likely some version of "dear God, let me not muff that line or miss that note" rather than the emotion of love per se.

Nor can your experience really be love for the character portrayed, because you well know that such a character is an artificial construct and that if you were engaging with a real person, there would most likely be something else going on, something perhaps not quite so sublime; indeed, it is the safety of this knowledge that you are entering a fiction that allows you to relax into the experience. Nor is it just that you are reminded of a love affair of your own, for when this experience is at its height you have probably forgotten about yourself and what seem to be for the moment the rather mundane and tedious details of your own real love life. Furthermore, and fundamentally odd, is that while you are experiencing this emotion, even if it involves tears, you are actually experiencing pleasure and sometimes even what the European critic Roland Barthes called *jouissance*, or bliss. That bliss is rasa.

Several qualities of this experience have been noted, observed, and studied by Sanskrit critical theorists in a highly evolved discourse elaborated over many centuries. Among other things, the state of emotion you feel arises in part from within you. Though a number of objective factors do matter – the quality of the performance and your own comfort while watching among it – your response is not simply and unilaterally generated by some mechanical external process. In the case of the film that moved you, for instance, not everyone around you feels this poignant feeling, nor will even you reliably feel it every time you see that movie again. It is a weirdly contingent and personal state, a state that happens *between* you and the performance or screening and that is dependent to a great extent on your quality of attention and openness, on your willingness, as Samuel Coleridge said, to undergo a "willing suspension of disbelief." Of course, it is up to the artist to evoke this open and attentive state with the maximum skill, but even then it can be elevated or destroyed by your receptivity and even by some very random contingencies such as your physical comfort or the condition of your digestion.

This openness is conditioned by many subjective factors particular to you, as you have been shaped by your own culture, experience, and personal development. These include what I can only call – however unfashionably – your refinement of sensibility, your emotional maturity, and even to some extent – with a wince at the cliché – the depth level of your spiritual life. In any case, this is a very strange state indeed, this emotion that has neither an existing object nor an existing source, which is neither real nor not-real, that resembles or is related to what you might feel in actuality but that does not operate in quite the same way. It is this state that is called rasa. As Somadeva Vasudeva notes in his discussion of this term, a Sanskrit critical theorist would probably go on to note that what you are really doing while you are having this experience is *relishing* one of your own fundamental and natural states or *passions*. It is, however, a passion that has been *decontextualized* by its invocation on a stage or in performance and *transformed* into an aesthetic sentiment.

Rasa theory thus need not be an entirely remote way of framing the experience of art, even though Westerners don't often categorize or enumerate aesthetic experience in quite this way. You can probably think of at least one film you have seen that strongly evoked and worked with some particular passion: erotic love, perhaps, or wonder, fear, anger, or grief. As discussions of rasa in the Hindu tradition go on to note, you may have recognized that the feeling is strengthened by being relatively restricted to that one note or at least returning to it again and again. And you have probably sometimes even gone so far as to become conscious of the strange effect of aesthetic relish, decontextualization, and transformation with respect to that fundamental passion. For instance, when you leave the theater after a very bleak but brilliantly realized film noir, you are often not at all cast down; rather, you are oddly elated and for a moment even in some way liberated. When this happens, you are experiencing the effect of rasa and the phenomenon to which rasa theory points.

There are many modes of rasa, and what we might call the "rasa of *noir*" is only one of them. In the work of the great eleventh-century philosopher, sage, and aesthetician Abhinanvagupta, a number of them have been determined and enumerated. They are *passion, energy, revulsion, anger, playfulness, wonder, fear, grief,* and *world-weariness.* Again, there are many points of reference in Western art and aesthetics, though they are differently cast, and the application of the terminology of rasa here can be helpful. Aristotle's understanding of tragedy, for instance, can be seen as involving the decontextualization and transformation of the rasas of fear and grief; he called this experience purgation or catharsis.[12] As for actual productions, Shakespeare exploited the decontextualization provided by the theater to its maximum with respect to almost every one of the rasas, including to an unusual degree playfulness and world-weariness. (Think of the drooping form of Portia at the opening of *The Merchant of Venice.*) The formal recognition of these modes and their psychology and way of working might indeed inform and expand our appreciation of Shakespeare's art.

The concept and practice of rasa proper, however, unlike Western parallels, is explicitly animated by the theology and metaphysics of Vedic traditions. The ground of the work of rasa is provided by the three principles noted earlier: the principle of maya, or illusion, the witnessing principle, and the principle of identity between the deep self and divine. These are the pillars that enable the realization of essential and natural unity between atman and brahman, and rasa takes its effect from the way in which it evokes, prepares for, and sometimes precipitates the realization of this unity.

4.

In the context of the dharmic religions, aesthetic appreciation and spiritual practice are both ways of attaining this realization. Spiritual practice is no doubt the high road, but aesthetic appreciation is the skillful means, to borrow a Buddhist term, and art is in some ways the natural expression of that practice. It is skillful and natural because it deploys a temporary, small, and contrived illusion to bring about an awareness of a great and naturally occurring one: the cosmic illusion of any separation at all between brahman, the world, and ourselves. We sense, watching our film for instance, that we are all in union with the author and performers, and all cocreators of the experience depicted. Remarkably, this experience is somehow defanged of its power to bind and hurt in the process. Our passion here is transmuted in such a way that it cannot fundamentally harm or disturb us, threaten our freedom, or tie us back onto the wheel of repetition and despair, as so often seems to be the case with direct experience in the world. If we are lucky, gifted, or graced, we can then transfer this minor and contrived experience of release and nonseparation in the "little" theater or screen to what is no more than the "big" theater or screen of the world outside. The fruit of this transference is equilibrium. We see our experience, inside the theater and then outside, as an emanation of our own being and deep nature, to be enjoyed and savored at will, even in its multiple ironies and illusory detours from the right order of things, an order that is unchanging and will always reassert itself in time.

In the Abrahamic context, by contrast, things are not quite so straightforward. In the first place, the basic theological stances here are not witnessing and union, but submission and subordination, and the central problem is not ignorance or deviation from the nature and right order of things but the full scale breaking of that frame by sin. The work is not simply to clear the obstacles so that a primal unity can be sensed, but rather to provoke a recognition of the need for drastic repentance, reorientation, and change of direction. For in this orbit, the "fear of the Lord is the beginning of wisdom," as the Bible says.[13] One of the strongest prohibitions is the prohibition against fabricating objects and using them as a focus for contact with the divine. "Thou shalt not make unto thee any graven image," as another injunction from the Bible has it.[14] As a result, art – at least outside an authorized religious context – is often seen not as irenic but agonistic, and its hallmark is not equilibrium but the recognition of conflict. True, in the very greatest works, that conflict is often accepted and resolved, but not without some form of reversal and seldom without violence or at least without tears.

There is a further problem here. The making of art in the Abrahamic traditions can be seen not simply as a benign analogue to and participation in God's creation of worlds but as a challenge to his singularity and hegemony. God is here the model for creativity, just as brahman is in Hinduism, but the model requires complete originality, and complete originality is inherently challenging to God's divine sovereignty. To seek to mimic or – which God forbid – to replace his singularity with an original work of creativity is at least in potential a serious form of hubris or pride, and over it hovers a profound sense of wrongdoing and a certain fear of punishment. We have already noted this in terms of the special privileges given the Bible over other literary expressions of religion or spirituality, but it holds true as well of any form of "graven image" set up as numinous or compelling and not just ornamental, against which the Bible injunctions are, as has been said, extremely strong.

It is the tension between the human urge to original creation and the worship owed to God that led the great contemporary critic Harold Bloom to speak of what he called the "anxiety of influence" in Western art. This anxiety comes from seeing creativity as something that does not arise immanently from nature but comes from a place beyond it, a place of ultimate transcendent originality and primacy. Art is both about accessing this primal originality of expression and about the potential drastic consequences of claiming it for one's own. Even today, many major artists informed by Abrahamic perspectives, from gospel singers to opera stars, from novelists to painters and sculptors, experience a deep conflict between their religious understanding and the degree of sublimity and mastery they sometimes experience in their work. Michelangelo depicts himself as a sinner flayed in hell; Shakespeare's Prospero breaks his wand; Goethe's heroes come to understand that they have forfeited all claim to bliss through their lust for power.

Yet that experience of sublimity and mastery is inherent not only in the process of creating a work of art, but also in the process of appropriation or enjoyment by the listener, reader, or spectator, with his or her intense experience at once of passion and detachment. It is largely from defiance of this whole painful structure that the secular and "transgressive" arts of the contemporary period arise, and it is this deeply reactive and defensive motivation that makes their expression so often limited and – after an initial titillation – so empty of lasting interest. A certain danger thus hovers over the enjoyment of the arts in the West from which readers are not exempt.

The Western reader who turns to the literature of Hinduism, however, must lay aside a little of this expectation of angst and transgression and look for something else instead. Not that the literary expression of the dharmic religions is without either drama or tribulation; quite the contrary. But the effect of crises and trials it depicts, fiery though they may be, is less the evocation of Faustian defiance than the cultivation of what I have been calling equilibrium, or to use the Sanskrit term, *shantih*, a certain unembarrassed acceptance and even celebration of natural passion and the natural unfolding of life, an acknowledgment of the deep order beneath the way of the world, a sharp sense of the ironies with which such order is hidden and revealed, and satisfaction, if only provisional and temporary, of the desire for a divine and inspired detachment.

5.

So if we don't have angst and anxiety in dharmic literature – or not of the typical Western kind – what *do* we have? We have above all a very delicate interplay between stories and their narrators, scripts and their actors, which entices us to forget that these are representations and then reminds us, often with some delight, that they are merely highly effective manifestations of maya. In the Mahabharata, for instance, we are fully caught up into a world where battles abound, and we are tantalized again and again into taking sides and identifying with one or another party, only to find that in the next bit or in the framing story we are asked to loosen this identification and see the action from another perspective.

So often does this happen, with many stories within stories, that there is eventually a kind of weariness with the sheer oscillation, the sheer futility of trying to find a point of rest or harmony. There may be an underlying pattern here – the great Sanskritist Charles Malamoud thinks he has found one in the tragic demonstration of the necessity of sacrifice and revenge even while these generate an unending chain of suffering[15] – but if so, it is often lost in the swirl of gripping events and difficult situations which collapse and fold into one another. There is a deep relish of embedded stories and of multiple and multiply valid points of view. For if brahman is immanent, then nature is his body; and if every atman is brahman, then the divine unity can be reflected and refracted in as many ways as there are individual selves. The result is, in fact, given our openness and the storyteller's art, a profound recognition of the maya, or illusion, that underlies all conflict, whether within characters or between them, and a deep precipitation into the witness state. The Bhagavad Gita, or sacred song, a famous set piece that is at the heart of the epic, seeks both to catalyze and to give theological grounding to this recognition.

The Bhagavad Gita is one of the most read and frequently translated works of literature of the world, and features large in university curricula and in comparative studies in literature, religion, philosophy, and theology. A dramatic lyric embedded in the Mahabharata itself, whose conventional designation means "beloved song" or hymn, it consists of a dialogue between the warrior Arjuna and his teacher, charioteer, and guide Krishna. Krishna's teaching is a synthesis of many lines of thought extending from the Upanishads through the early Sankhya tradition to the yogic systems of meditation found also in Patanjali's yoga sutras. In presenting these converging perspectives, the poem moves back and forth from the practical to the visionary, from the intimacy of personal exchange to the grandeur of revelation, and from perennial wisdom to apocalyptic. The result is a classic of world literature, one central to a long line of poets and writers in the West from Emerson and Thoreau to Yeats and Eliot. In fact, Eliot referred to the Gita as the next greatest philosophical poem to the *Divine Comedy* and noted that the balance of mind Arjuna was able to attain in the midst of warfare was that of only a few "highly civilized" individuals in the world canon.[16]

Consisting as it does of only eighteen short chapters and having a definite formal and thematic unity, the Gita presents to the reader on the one hand the challenges of a deceptive simplicity, accessible to all, and on the other those of an extremely anomalous and apocalyptic vision, attainable only through profound changes in epistemology and perception. The poem begins with an immediate and recognizable existential problem: the necessity of joining battle that, however righteous, is being waged against one's own kin and in which they may lose their lives. When we meet him in this context, Arjuna is overlooking that battlefield, to which he is called by his destiny, but he has fallen into despair. Krishna must rouse him, persuade him that he is the servant of divine mandates that lie beyond the mundane realm, and convince him to join the fray. If he does so cleanly, without attachment, with equilibrium of mind and with true devotion, Krishna promises, no guilt will adhere to him and the outcome, beyond his control in any case, need not concern him.

The intersection of ethical, political, and transcendental obligations and motives, the agony of their contradictions, and the need to act nonetheless are universal and instantly recognizable problems. Aeneas faced them, Dante faced them, Hamlet faced them, and all found relief from paralysis, if not resolution, in acceptance of destiny: as the *Paradiso* has it, "in His will is our peace."[17] That peace emerges from recognizing that surrender and self-offering trump even the most bitter mandates of fate.

The Gita's next move, however, may be compared less to these literary Western analogues than to scriptural and revelational ones, to Job and/or to John of Patmos. These analogues come to mind – or come to mind once we recover our equilibrium – in reading the famous chapter 11 of the Gita, the apocalyptic chapter in which we see, with Arjuna, Krishna drop his avatar and reveal his own true nature. Arjuna, in response to an overwhelming question that exceeds the terms of any he has been asked before, asks to be given a glimpse of the "real nature" of the divinity to whom he is supposed to surrender all. Krishna then creates for him a special heightened consciousness that will allow him to see this reality. Having done so, Krishna unveils himself and speaks in his own voice as time itself, savage, destructive, and obliterating of lives, particularities, and identities in an annihilation beyond all conventional categories of thought. "Time and I, world destroying, grown mature, engaged her in subduing the world. Even without thee [thy action], all the warriors standing in the opposing armies shall cease to be" (11.32).

The effect on Arjuna here is neither equilibrium nor peace of mind but sheer terror, the terror that attends the sublime, the *mysterium tremendum* of both West and East. "When I see Thee touching the sky ... with the mouth open wide, ... my inmost soul trembles in fear and I find neither steadiness nor peace, O Vishnu!" (11:24–30). Here, as in the case of Job, there is no cognitive relief, no ethical resolution, no salve for the conscience or the heart. The task for the reader is to bring into the same frame of reference the exhortation to steadiness and devotion in the prior part of the poem and the extreme and destabilizing challenge to ordinary categories of thought and feeling at this point. That this frame-bending unity of vision can in fact be achieved has long been the testimony of spiritual seekers in both biblical and Vedic traditions, and in both cases that resolution happens only *hors-texte*; indeed, how could it be otherwise?

6.

For an equally complex, though again deceptively simple, worldview we may look to *Shakuntala*, the great drama attributed to Kalidasa and regarded as one of the treasures of Sanskrit literature. The play is perhaps a little neglected, at least in modern times, though still revered, as it always has been, in traditional quarters. (I suspect this slight neglect is, in part, due to its innocent and long-suffering heroine, whose appearance of feminine passivity and victimization, while deeply qualified in the author's vision, does not endear easily to current values and mores, at least on a surface reading.) Nonetheless, *Shakuntala* is a supreme achievement, heralded alike in the East and the West, and its author has been compared by serious critics to Virgil and to Sophocles, though he needs no Western validation. The American poet A.W. Ryder said it best: "We know that Kalidasa is a very great poet, because the world has not been able to let him alone."[18]

In *Shakuntala*, the dramatic form is used to evoke a state of witness to erotic passion, and its susceptibility to obscuration generates a deep sense of the role of sexual desire in the divine play of maya and awakening. The action is framed by a prologue in a way that is highly contemporary, in a series of conscious mediations reminiscent of Brechtian distancing, and it is followed by an unfolding drama that includes and often foregrounds a series of discrete lyric epiphanies. The ensuing plot entails the encounter of the young semi-nymph and spiritual being Shakuntala with a great king who is out hunting and has come upon her hermitage. There follows a delicious evocation of their courtship, his affirmation of her as his wife in a private pledge, her pregnancy, his disavowal of her, and their reconnection through the likeness of the son born of their union to his father.

Kalidasa is able to turn this plot into an occasion for a most poignant evocation of the enchanted quality of extreme eros, the ecstasy of its mutual consummation, and the pain of its frequent failure to be honored in the "real world." Eros in this instance is neither distrusted nor in essence oppositional to spiritual practice; it is rather somewhat orthogonal to religion, operating in a different sphere and along a different trajectory. Shakuntala, when she first feels the power of desire, says it seems a feeling out of place in a hermitage, but the king, also experiencing that power, takes pains before marrying her to be sure that she has not taken a formal vow of celibacy, and his later relationship to her Brahmin protector is one of courtesy and submission. Here are no star-crossed lovers, no heroes torn between love and duty, no heroines disgraced by sexual experience or its threat, only a young woman, secluded with and betrothed to a lover for whom she feels great passion, appearing to importune him when he returns to the public sphere and she seems to have no warrant for doing so. The king's rejection of her is based on a relapse into a kind of worldly oblivion, not on sin.

It is easy to think of Western analogues to this tale that operate in a very different way, analogues in which sexuality, spirituality, and worldly duty rend the characters apart both internally and in their relationship with each other, and in which outright sin, and not a kind of slumbering dullness of perception, break them apart. We need only think of Aeneas and Dido, of Dante and Beatrice, of Romeo and Juliet. Here in these Western tales of love, the resolution is a true agon involving huge destruction of human life and ultimately a surrender to the inscrutable ways of the divine. Nothing in the hero's world, human or natural, provides support for this trial by fire. In *Shakuntala* there is an ordeal indeed, an ordeal in which the poet focuses more vividly on the suffering of the heroine than the hero, but the resolution is an awakening and a recognition, not a searing conflict, and it is a resolution both the natural world and human nature conspire to forward.

7.

Let me conclude by acknowledging fully that there are, in the great artistic achievements of both East and West, exceptional places where each actually captures the other's point of view and frame of reference, sometimes in remarkable ways. For dharmic literary expression at certain points does indeed sound the depth of internal conflict, difference, and ultimate submission to divine sovereignty, while the Abrahamic traditions can and sometimes do attain great heights in the expression of natural flow, unity, and participation in divine creativity. The Bhagavad Gita is one such text; the Song of Songs perhaps another. These moments are, however, all the more striking for sounding a note not often heard in their respective contexts. Short of those moments, we can continue to look to their differences as ways to expand our response to literature and to the theologies and worldviews it displays and mediates.

Notes

1 The terms *religion* and *theology* used here in their adjectival forms are somewhat misleading applied outside their original context in Western thought. They are used here as indicators and not in a rigorous sense. Still, they have value in establishing the kind of coordinates that have been out of fashion for a time but that have enduring value at least in first approaches to other traditions.

2 As most readers will be aware, the Mahayana and Ramayana, the epic poems of India, are a seedbed of narrative for the vernaculars, and for novels, film, and television on the subcontinent, throughout Asia, and in the Hindu diaspora. Broadcast serially on Indian television in the 1990s and now available as a set of podcasts, one dramatization became one of the most widely viewed productions of a single work in all of South Asia. See inter alia Paula Richmond, ed., *Questioning Ramayanas: A South Asian Tradition* (Berkeley: University of California Press, 2001), 1–2.

3 The best exposition of this view is probably Richard King, *Orientalism and Religion: Post-Colonial Theory, India and "The Mystic East"* (London: Routledge, 1999).

4 Andrew Nicholson, *Unifying Hinduism: Philosophy and Identity in Indian Intellectual History* (New York: Columbia University Press, 2013).

5 Sanskriti has recently been redubbed the Sanskrit cosmopolis in the work of Sheldon Pollock, perhaps the most influential scholar of Sanskrit today. Pollock's magnum opus is *The Language of the Gods in the World of Men: Sanskrit, Culture and Power in Pre-Modern India* (Oakland: University of California Press, 2009).

6 Laurie L. Patton, personal communication.

7 "Gerontion," *The Complete Poems of T.S. Eliot 1909–1959* (New York: Harcourt Brace, 1971), 124.

8 Francis X. Clooney, "Why the Veda Has No Author: Language as Ritual in Early Mīmāṃsā and Post-Modern Theology," *Journal of the American Academy of Religion* 55.4 (Winter, 1987): 659–684.

9 Pollock's work has not gone uncontested on this count by defenders of Sanskrit tradition, most notably by Rajiv Malhotra, a fierce advocate for Hinduism, though not himself a scholar or Sanskritist by training. Malhotra points out that Pollock's central methodological move, which is to hive off the secular dimension of the Sanskrit corpus from its religious dimension, prevents him from seeing important aspects of the role of literature in Hindu culture, in part because Pollock's approach is governed by a relentless dismissal of spirituality and religion as inherently precritical, irrational, and mystifying. See Malhotra's *The Battle for Sanskrit: Is Sanskrit Dead or Alive, Oppressive or Liberating, Political or Sacred?* (San Francisco, CA: HarperCollins, 2015).

10 Daniel Ingalls, "Sanskrit Poetry and Sanskrit Poetics," introduction to *An Anthology of Sanskrit Court Poetry: Vidyākara's Subhāṣitaratnakoṣa* (Cambridge, MA: Harvard University Press, 1945), 33–35.

11 Ibid., 34.

12 For a fuller discussion of rasa, see Susan L. Schwartz, *Rasa: Performing the Divine in India* (New York: Columbia University Press, 2005).

13 Proverbs 9:10.

14 Exodus 20:4.

15 Charles Malamoud, *Cooking the World* (Oxford: Oxford University Press, 1996).

16 See Cleo Kearns, *T.S. Eliot and Indic Traditions: A Study in Poetry and Belief* (Cambridge: Cambridge University Press, 1987).

17 Dante Alighieri, *Paradiso*, trans. Robert Hollander and Jean Hollander (New York: Doubleday, 2007), 3.85, p. 63.

18 A.W. Ryder, *Shakuntala and Other Writings* (London: J.M. Dent & Sons, 1912), xx–xxi; cited in K. Krishamoortthy, *Kalidasa* (New York: Twayne Publishers, 1972), 108.

10

RICHARD K. PAYNE

Buddhism

The modern study of Buddhism reflects the values of Western and Western-ized scholars, values that determine why certain texts are selected to represent the tradition and what it means to read religiously. Many people in the West naïvely presume that religious texts can be understood just by reading them. The plausibility of this presumption is supported by cultural familiarity with the biblical narratives. Someone raised in a Euro-American religious culture can pick up the Bible or other Christian religious literature and read it without scholarly paraphernalia. This presumption, however, is not valid when approaching the majority of non-Western religious texts, even in translation.[1] Buddhist texts, and indeed the majority of non-Western religious literatures, require readers to become familiar with cultural traditions and reading practices markedly divergent from their own. When Buddhist texts are read on the basis of their congeniality with core Western values such as individualism, egalitarianism, and simplicity, they are, quite simply, misused.[2] A similar problem occurs with selection: the familiarity of texts such as Dhammapada, the Diamond Sutra, and the Tibetan Book of the Dead means that they have already been interpreted into a religious discourse about texts, textuality, and reading that is informed by Christian preconceptions. As such, they do little to challenge the presumptions that privilege a certain set of ideas about faith, practice, identity, time, and so on, themes constitutive of one kind of religious existence, but themes neither universal nor universalizable.

I.

To understand a text in its Buddhist context, it is important to recognize the systems according to which Buddhist thinkers have themselves organized their textual heritage. The large mass of Buddhist literature has led both traditional and modern scholars to create multiple canons, systems of organization, and bibliographic categories.[3] One basic categorization of Buddhist literature is that of the "three baskets" (*tripiṭaka*): discourses or teaching stories (*sūtra*s), rules of the order (*vinaya*), and the higher teachings (*abhidharma*). Gregory Schopen has noted that the metaphor of basket was in use prior to the creation of written texts, so the image, delightful as it otherwise is, of the three collections being transported in three baskets cannot be historically accurate. Schopen suggests instead that the image is one of an excavation at which baskets filled with dirt or rocks are passed from hand to hand, and thus the teachings are passed from teacher to pupil.[4]

Both the teaching stories and the rules of the order are presented in narrative form. Generally in Buddhism, authority has been based on the "speech of the Buddha" (*buddhavacana*). The narrative framework indicates the authenticity of the teachings given or the rule established, not just by presenting it as spoken by the Buddha, but also by giving the kind of convincing detail that leads one to accept that there was a specific event when the Buddha answered questions or resolved problems. One criterion for including texts in a canon such as the "three baskets" is authenticity: is a text the words of the Buddha or is its origin questionable?[5]

As widespread as the tripiṭaka categorization is, it is hardly adequate to the complexities of Buddhist literature.[6] A more encompassing system of twelve parts includes teaching stories, aphorisms in prose and verse, prophetics, verses, utterances, fables, stories of previous lives, stories of marvels, extended teachings, framing stories, heroic tales, and instructions.[7] Despite these and other systems of categorization, there is no consensus as to what might constitute a Buddhist canon. Buddhism has never had a bounded scripture such as the Bible or the Qur'an.[8]

2.

The particular texts considered here, the tantras, have not already been domesticated by comparative religious readings. Indeed, Loriliai Biernacki has described the tantras as "a mishmash of complex ritual prescriptions in a literary form quite alien to twenty-first-century Western literary expectations."[9] Even in translation, these texts require readers to see their own culture as just one among many, down to and including the most fundamental presumptions regarding what religion is; the nature of the self, of others, of the world; and the goal of human existence.

The tantras also fail expectations regarding "spiritual literature." In the modern West, "spiritual" now refers to individualized transformative experience, and spiritual practice is done privately in expectation of experiencing personal transformation. While there are many practices in the Buddhist tradition that may be interpreted this way,[10] much in the tantras is explicitly ritual in nature and does not conform to expectations that religious literature promotes personal spiritual transformation.

Perhaps a personal anecdote will help the reader to see this difference. When my grandmother passed away, I had already read the Tibetan Book of the Dead a couple of times. It was, after all, trumpeted by counterculture figures such as Timothy Leary as a key to expanding consciousness and was a popular part of hip culture.[11] In response to my grandmother's death, I decided to read the text aloud, which I'd heard was how it was used. It was only in doing so that what now seems obvious became apparent to me. "Invisible" to me in silent reading was the liturgical structure of the text, with directions to the ritual officiant on the one hand, and parts the officiant is to read aloud into the deceased's ear on the other. My own naïveté regarding what reading meant in a ritual context was suddenly confronted by the reality of the text as liturgical – but only when I was actually reading it aloud, rather than silently. The text is a ritual manual intended to assist the deceased to either awakening or a better rebirth and is not a privatized spiritual practice with the goal of personal transformation. Thus, key to understanding a religious text from a foreign culture is attending to the textual practices of that culture, including ritual and cultic uses, and to reading practices per se.[12] Catherine Bell argues that in Taoist practices the ritualization of texts and the textualization of rituals are "more than passive representations or formulations of their milieu, they are also the strategic means by which persons or groups act upon their environment."[13] Thus, also central to understanding religious texts from unfamiliar cultures, including Buddhist religious literature, is attending to differing conceptions of agency.

3.

I take here an expansive view of the idea of "Buddhist literature." The tantras are not instances of "religious literature" in the sense of fiction with religious significance. Rather than looking at works of fiction, we will consider one of the early sacred texts of the Esoteric strain of Buddhist praxis, the Vairocanābhisaṃbodhi-tantra. But in what sense then is this text an instance of literature?

Several works already address "Buddhist literature" in the narrow sense of fiction.[14] But outside the familiar conventions of contemporary categorizations, the distinctions between fiction and nonfiction tend to become much less clear. If we think of literature as originating in an act of the imagination, one creating an imaginal world made public, then many works usually considered "nonfiction" are works of literature. In addition, the tantras and other Buddhist works are narratives in the same way that historiography is narrative, as demonstrated by Hayden White.[15] As with the term "literature," "narrative" also does not mean fictional.

Even from the earliest strata of Buddhist literature, authors present the teachings in narratives.[16] The teaching stories largely share a narrative frame that initiates the story by identifying the location, participants, and events leading to Śākyamuni Buddha giving a particular teaching. These stories are not only narratives, but also derive from an earlier oral culture, having attributes consistent with being recited from memory over the several centuries between the time of the Buddha and the composition of the written record.[17] Rather than a horizon crossed once, this interface between oral and literate cultures recurs at many points in the history of Buddhist literature.[18] In addition to narrative texts as such, there are also many important systematic reflections on the teachings, including scholastic organization and summarization of them.[19] Many of these reflections, however, also evidence a narrative structure, that of ground, path, and goal.

The tantras give little consideration to the "big questions" of religion or philosophy, as these are commonly understood in Western culture. From outside that cultural context, it is evident that the central and defining concerns of religion and philosophy are grounded in preconceptions determined by Christian thought. Taking an example from the Vedas, Frits Staal rejects the primacy usually given the Ṛg veda's putative "Hymn of Creation" (RV 10.129). The privilege given this hymn in Western language literature "is a cultural construct due to religious prejudice in that it starts with *creation*. It is a concept that pops up automatically in the mind of a Euro-American, religiously minded or not, as well as many other speakers of English, because it is well known that the sacred books of Judaism and Christianity start with the creation myth of *Genesis*."[20] Thus, in selections of world religious literature, the hymn has been decontextualized and then recontextualized into a religious worldview in which the Creation is key. In this new context, the hymn acquires a specific meaning and importance at variance with its significance in Vedic religious culture.

Similarly, because the Enlightenment reinterpreted religion as primarily about morality,[21] popular culture in the West assumes a moralistic reading of religious texts in which they are expected to be moralistic allegories – perhaps more obscure, but basically the same as Aesop's Fables.

Paul Griffiths has described Christian practice as the "reordering of will and appetite away from self and toward God (first) and other humans (second)."[22] Inculcating the skills required for this reordering involves three kinds of practice: worship, prayer, and "reading or hearing the Bible for nourishment." Thus, Christians view the Bible as "a peculiarly authoritative witness to God's actions and intentions." The Bible provides the norm against which everything else can and is to be judged: "the Bible is a *norma normans non normata*, a norm that norms but is itself not normed."[23] Reading the Bible, or hearing it read, is how a Christian can understand God's intentions, hear God's voice speaking across the distance between human and divine.

The Buddhist tradition, however, does not promote that same relationship between a text and the individual practitioner. Texts are considered important as guides to practice, as records of teachings, or as compendia of aphorisms drawn from the Buddha's teachings, but not for understanding the intentions of a divine being. While some of the tantras are presented as being taught by buddhas embodying or identical with the totality of existence (*dharmadhātu*), they are not viewed as revelations of divine intent.

In addition to the Christian understanding described by Griffiths, religious texts have a variety of functions, including cultic functions.[24] One cultic instance is the treatment of texts as relics of the Buddha, in which case possession is itself the point of having a text, not reading it for didactic or doctrinal content. Physical relics were understood to include first the body relics remaining following the Buddha's cremation and also objects with which the Buddha had been in direct physical contact (robe, bowl, etc.). The category then expanded to include "relics of commemoration," that is, objects which bring the Buddha to the practitioner's mind.[25]

From commemoration relics, the category was further extended to include "dharma relics," that is, oral practices (such as chanting mantra and *dhāraṇī* or reciting sutras) and textual records that provide access to the teachings of the Buddha, the Dharma.[26] As one form of the "dharma body" in which buddhas exist (*dharmakāya*), textual records could be used in the same fashion as relics, in commemorative worship that "keeps the Buddha in mind" or by vivifying a memorial monument (*stupa*) by being buried in its base. Indeed, some of the historically most significant texts have been excavated from the bases of stupas.[27] As dharma relics, these texts served a cultic function.[28] Similarly cultic is the practice of copying texts, an act considered to generate merit.[29] For example, referring to itself, the Aparimitāyuḥ sutra indicates that "the copier or sponsor ... keeps it in his home as the focus of ritual action and as a powerful apotropaic presence."[30]

In the sixteenth century, translations of the Bible into vernacular languages revolutionized religious reading first in Europe and later in America.[31] The eventual result, focusing attention on the individual believer reading a sacred text for spiritual formation, does not automatically apply outside that world. Possession, veneration, copying, recitation of a text, and even the dramatic performance of a text were important in the practices of Buddhist textuality.[32]

Reading in this ritual context, however, whether out loud or silently, differs from reading as a spiritual exercise revealing God's intent, or in order to extract doctrinal content. This differs even more markedly from reading with the goal of extracting philosophical or therapeutic content, as is often the case in academic and popular apprehensions of Buddhist texts in the present. Such reading practices – spiritual, doctrinal, philosophical, or therapeutic – differ markedly from the complex intersections of ritual, narration, instruction, evocation, argumentation, and so on of traditional Buddhist practice. So, how then should we read the tantras?

4.

The term "tantra" is a bibliographic category, appearing in the titles of a large number of works. The complementary bibliographic term is "sūtra." The separation between sūtra and tantra is fuzzy, so much so that some texts, such as the Vairocābhisaṃbodhi-tantra, are called both tantras and sūtras. "Sūtra" literally means "sewing together" and is employed metaphorically for collecting the aphorisms or sayings of a teacher. Similarly, the warp threads on a loom are called tantra, and the metaphor of "weaving together" also becomes a bibliographic category. The term is further extended to identify the kinds of teachings found in texts called tantras, though this is not a perfect match.[33]

Given the obsession of popular culture with sex, a common association to tantra is something like the "yoga of ecstasy." Control and power are important themes for the tantras, and sex is a frequently recurring expression of those concerns. There is a difference, however, between its treatment in the tantras and its appropriation as the "yoga of ecstasy." Rather than maximizing pleasure or enjoyment, the tantric thematics of sex focus on controlling its power. In other words, the tantras embody neither the prudery nor the libertinism that polarize Western cultural responses to sex. Additionally, despite the common associations, some tantric texts, such as the Vairocanābhisaṃbodhi-tantra, do not include any of the explicitly sexual content found in many others.

In Indian literature generally, the term "tantra" encompasses a wide range of disparate forms of writing.[34] For the most part, the tantras were created without any organizing principle, other than the ritual and yogic practices they prescribe and the deities to which those practices are devoted.[35] Historically, there was no singular tantric movement, but rather a variety of differing groups of practitioners which come to be identified retrospectively as constituting some more general collective phenomenon. The literary consequence is that the tantras are created without any overarching organizing principle. Different scholars then attempted to organize these texts into some sort of overall coherence,[36] with perhaps as much as a century or more between the appearance of the first tantras and the first doxographic systematization in the middle of the eighth century.[37]

The categories used to systematize the tantras reflect scholastic and polemic concerns, not any "objective" organizational structure. The categories are scholastic, as they attempt to impose order on the original diversity. The categories are also polemic, as they promote certain ways of valuing the different tantras, placing the ones promoted by a particular school at the peak of the system. The most familiar four-part system has in part become familiar because it is employed by the Gelug sect, that of the Dalai Lama who has been so influential in bringing awareness of Tibetan Buddhist traditions to the West. These four are action, performance, yoga, and highest yoga. This fourfold system is in fact one of the later systems to be developed, entering Tibet only in the tenth century.[38]

Buddhist praxis, that is the tight dialectic between doctrine and practices, has a narrative structure of ground, path, and goal. Ground identifies the condition of "ordinary, foolish people" who, lacking awareness of impermanence, have not established themselves on the path leading to the goal of awakening. This contrasts with the threefold biblical narrative of paradise, fall, and atonement, which is pervasive throughout Western culture and is so deeply imbedded that, seeming natural, it blends invisibly into the structuring of narratives as understood by Western readers.

While the biblical narrative begins in paradise, the Buddhist version begins with a condition of ignorance (*avidyā*). Such ignorance leads repeatedly to frustration, dissatisfaction, and suffering (*duḥkha*). This is an epistemic situation, rather than the moral one leading to the fall from paradise, sinful disobedience to God's will. Once one realizes the unsatisfactory nature of ordinary existence, one seeks to become free from the unceasing round and makes the first steps on the path to awakening. In contrast, return from the fallen state requires an atonement for sin, rather than an increasing comprehension of the conditioned nature of existence. Thus, the Christian narrative structure is essentially moral in nature, while the Buddhist one is epistemic. Of course, given their long histories and extensive traditions of systematic thought, both traditions include a great deal of commentary on what each element of the narratives mean and how they are best put into action. The purpose here is to establish that the narrative structure fundamental to Buddhist praxis differs from the Christian narrative structure.

Thus, key to reading the tantras is attention to how the elements being discussed fit into the narrative of ground, path, and goal. As mentioned earlier, much of the tantric material is concerned with ritual performance. Like meditation, ritual is one form of practice on the path from ignorance to awakening.

5.

There are both a Chinese translation and a Tibetan translation of the Vairocanābhisaṃbodhi-tantra, the text to which we now turn. Although Sanskrit citations are extant, there is no Sanskrit version of the work. References here are to the English translation of the Chinese.[39] Structural differences between the Chinese and Tibetan translations are detailed by Alex Wayman.[40]

Although some believe the Vairocanābhisaṃbodhi-tantra was composed by a single author,[41] the idea of singular authorship as universal to all literatures is itself a cultural artifact. If we no longer assume unitary authorship as universal, it seems much more plausible that the work is a compilation of a variety of ritual practices by several different agents, probably over a long period. The text as we have it today does not vary between, for example, the Tibetan and Chinese translations because the urtext was mishandled by later copyists or poorly understood by later editors, but rather because each represents a textual event.[42] Or to use a chemical metaphor, each version marks one moment when the text "crystallized" and fell out of the saturated solution of Indic religious culture.

As with the teaching stories, the Vairocanābhisambodhi-tantra is written as a dialogue between the Buddha and an interlocutor. In this case the Buddha is Vairocana, the "Illuminator," the cosmic Buddha identical with all being (dharmadhātu). The interlocutor usually initiates the dialogue by asking questions. Here it is "Vajrapāṇi," whose name means "he who holds the vajra." The vajra represents a thunderbolt and is a central symbol for tantric Buddhism. Its origins are thought to be in the Indo-European cult of a sky god whose weapon is the thunderbolt. Figures such as Zeus/Jupiter in Greco-Roman mythology, as well as other sky gods closer to the Indic streams of symbolism leading to Buddhist tantra, are all portrayed wielding the thunderbolt. More proximately, "vajra" also identifies an implement used in tantric ritual that is symbolically linked to the thunderbolt as a handheld weapon, a mace or cudgel, similar to Thor's hammer. The vajra is conceptualized as stronger than anything else and is therefore sometimes described as adamantine or "diamond-like." This iconography links Vajrapāṇi with the Greek Herakles, but serving in the role of the Buddha's protector.[43] Vajrapāṇi also bears the epithet "Lord of Mysteries" (Guhya-kādhipati), by which he is addressed in this text.

The first chapter gives teachings on the absence (emptiness) from any actually existing entity of a permanent, unchanging essence, and the arising of awakening in the mind of the practitioner. A longstanding representation of Buddhism is that it has three separate "vehicles" (yānas): Hīnayāna or Theravāda, Mahāyāna, and Vajrayāna or tantra. Under this overly neat representation, these are sequential stages of either decay or progress, depending on an author's values.[44] Emptiness and the arising of the thought or mind of awakening (*bodhicitta*, sometimes rendered as "bodhi-mind") are familiar Mahāyāna doctrines and demonstrate the difficulty of treating tantric Buddhism and Mahāyāna as distinctly separate. The concepts of emptiness and its analog impermanence are central to understanding the process by which inherent awakening is realized through tantric practice.

The "equality of body, speech, and mind" is the identity of the body, speech, and mind of the tantric practitioner and those of the Buddha and is fundamental to the way that tantric practice is conceived to be effective. This identity is an expression of the teachings of emptiness and impermanence found in the Perfection of Wisdom literature, originating in the first centuries of the Common Era,[45] considered to be one of the earliest strains of Mahā-yāna Buddhist thought, and carried forward into this tantric text of the mid-seventh century. Not only are the ideas of emptiness and impermanence consistent, but the style in which they are presented is also. For example, Vajrapāṇi initiates the dialogue with a long series of questions regarding the source of the Buddha's wisdom and miraculous abilities to teach sentient beings in any form appropriate to their needs. The Buddha replies that

> The *bodhi*-mind is its cause, compassion is its root, and expedient means is its culmination. Lord of Mysteries, what is *bodhi*? It means to know one's mind as it really is. Lord of Mysteries, this is *anuttarā samyaksaṃbodhi* (unsurpassed, perfect, and full awakening), and there is not the slightest part of it that can be apprehended. Why? [Because] *bodhi* has the characteristic of empty space, and there is no one to comprehend it, nor is there any understanding of it. Why? Because *bodhi* has no [differentiating] characteristics. Lord of Mysteries, all *dharmas* are without characteristics. That is to say, they have the characteristic of empty space.[46]

Frequently, Western interpreters have described this kind of response as paradoxical and, generalizing on the model of religious neo-Platonism, as having the intent to cause the mind to suddenly leap to a new level of understanding. It is problematic, however, whether such a neo-Platonic dialectic can be universalized as these interpretations presume.

Rather than a paradox, if approached from the perspective of Madhyamaka, one of the most important schools of Mahāyāna thought, the expression is a fairly straightforward and didactic assertion concerning emptiness. Dharmas, the smallest constituents of the cognitively inflected ontology of Buddhist thought, were considered by early thinkers to be metaphysically ultimate, that is, the substance grounding lived experience. Analyzed to the level of dharmas, all existing entities, including persons, are impermanent, subject to change. The significant development of the Perfection of Wisdom and Madhyamaka is to assert that even dharmas are impermanent, that is, "empty" of any permanent, eternal, absolute, or unchanging status. When the Buddha here speaks of the characteristic of the empty sky, this is simply a way of saying dharmas are also impermanent.

The first chapter introduces another theme found in Mahāyāna, but which is central for much of tantric Buddhism. This is the reinterpretation of the narrative structure of ground, path, and goal such that ground and goal are identical with one another and the path leads the practitioner from not apprehending the inherently awakened nature of ordinary mind to initially comprehending the idea and then living in and through that awareness. The impermanence of all things applies to both the sentience of a buddha and that of the ignorant foolish person. This establishes their fundamental equality, their fundamental identity, and since all existing entities are empty of any unchanging essence, there is nothing that inherently hinders movement from the sentience of an ignorant foolish person to that of a buddha. The relation between impermanence and the identity of practitioner and deity is found elsewhere in the text as well. For example,

> Just as the eyes, ears, nose, tongue, body, mind, and so on are an assemblage and agglomeration of the four elements, so too is it thus empty of own-nature, and there is only that which is grasped by name; it is just like empty space, and there is nothing to be attached to, like a reflection. The Tathāgata accomplishes perfect awakening in uninterrupted mutual dependent arising. If something arises from conditions, then it arises like a reflection. Therefore, the deity is oneself and oneself is the deity, and they generate each other.[47]

Having established the identity of ground and goal in the first chapter, the balance of the text introduces the practitioner to the means by which the path may be followed to its end. The analysis of human existence into body, speech, and mind provides the organizing structure for specific ritual technologies that enable practitioners to realize their own body, speech, and mind as identical with the body, speech, and mind of a buddha. In ritual practice, the body identity is established by forming hand gestures (mudrā), the symbolism of which is a complex system ascribing significance to each hand, each finger, and indeed to each finger bone. The gesture, involving the positioning of hands and fingers, is then related to different actions and to different deities. The symbolism is found in Buddhist iconography[48] and is also related to the gestures of Indian dance. Identity of mind is established in meditative visualizations, most importantly the practitioner visualizing him- or herself as identical with the main deity evoked in the ritual. In understanding the centrality of body, speech, and mind for tantric ritual the power attributed to speech is particularly important.

While the goal of tantric practice is to realize what is already true – that one is already awakened – the efficacy of the ritual technologies is based in conceptions of the power of speech deeply rooted in Indic religious culture. From the earliest record of religious thought in India that we possess, the Vedas, speech (*vac*) has a special status.[49] Just as texts that embody speech have cultic efficacy beyond the information they contain,[50] the power of speech in religious ritual is not limited to its ability to communicate information. Speech is often conceived in primarily semantic terms, that is, as having the communication of information as its primary function. Attempting to fit – or force – ritual uses of language into this or other categories deriving from Western linguistics, however, creates problems of classification.[51] Rather than primarily conveying information, speech in the Indic religious context is a primary cosmogenic force.[52]

Two practices from the Vairocanābhisaṃbodhi-tantra based on this conception of the power of speech involve the syllable A and the visualized placement of mantric syllables on the body. The Sanskrit syllabery (the sequence of syllables functionally corresponding to the English alphabet) begins with the syllable A, for which reason it is understood as that primal source from which all existing entities emanate. The second significance ascribed to the syllable A results from it being the foundational vowel sound of all syllables. To simplify, the syllables KI, KU, KE, KO are all considered to be variants of KA in which the vowel has been modified. Therefore, in addition to being the source of all existence, the syllable A is omnipresent. The third dimension of significance follows from the syllable A serving as a negative prefix, just as in Latin-based English usage. For example, one who knows, a "gnostic," becomes one who doesn't know by adding the prefix a-, creating an "agnostic." The usage in Sanskrit is exactly parallel and provides the third meaning of the syllable A, that it represents the end of all existence. Thus the syllable A is the source of being, present in all being, and the end of being.[53] This is the significance behind Vairocana Buddha saying:

Good sirs, this letter *A* has been empowered by all Tathāgatas. [With it] bodhisattvas cultivating bodhisattva practices via the gateway of mantras are able to perform Buddha deeds and manifest physical bodies everywhere, and all Dharma revolves on the letter-gateway *A*. Therefore, Lord of Mysteries, if bodhisattvas cultivating bodhisattva practices via the gateway of mantras wish to see the Buddha, wish to make offerings [to the Buddha], wish to realize the generation of the *bodhi*-mind, wish to associate with [other] bodhisattvas, wish to benefit beings, wish to seek *siddhi*, and wish to seek the knowledge of an omniscient one, they should diligently practice in this essence of all Buddhas.[54]

In addition to highlighting the importance of the syllable A, this brief section includes several additional elements important to understanding this text, the tantric tradition, and Buddhism more generally. The term *tathāgata* (thus gone one) is an epithet ascribed to buddhas who have attained release from karmic bondage and who therefore can move freely through the cycles of existence (*samsara*). Bodhisattvas are those who have a commitment to attain awakening (*bodhicitta*) and are the companions of buddhas and support one another in their practice. The "gateway of mantras" refers to tantric practice and highlights the centrality of speech in the tradition.[55] The ability to manifest bodies everywhere is one of the powers enjoyed by advanced bodhisattvas, who, motivated by compassion, manifest these bodies in order to provide guidance to sentient beings, leading them to awakening. Although by capitalizing the term "Dharma" in the statement that "all Dharma revolves on the letter-gateway A," the translator seems to have interpreted it to refer here to the teachings of a buddha, it can also be understood to mean all existing entities – dharmas. In this interpretation, rather than being a sectarian claim, it is an assertion regarding the cosmic centrality of the syllable A. *Siddhi* are the extraordinary powers that tantric practitioners are said to attain, and thus those who have attained such powers are called *siddhas*. These powers are of two kinds. Mundane magical powers include such useful abilities as flying, finding treasure, attracting a lover, and overcoming enemies. Much more highly valued, however, is the supreme attainment – awakening.

The practice of visualizing syllables emplaced on the practitioner's own body demonstrates that tantric practice is not "spiritual," if we take by that the transcendence of embodied existence for a "higher" or "more refined" spiritual state. Instead tantra is fully embodied – it is in and by means of the body that awakening is attained. The intersection of the potency of speech and the centrality of the body is evidenced in chapter XVII, "The Allocation of Letters." Here we find instructions for the practitioner to visualize syllables from the sequence in various specific bodily locations. The sequence begins, for example,

The letter *Ka* is below the larynx; the letter *Kha* is on the palate;
The letter *Ga* is identified with the neck; the letter *Gha* is inside the throat;
The letter *Ca* is identified with the tongue; the letter *Cha* is in the middle of the
tongue.

This proceeds through a variety of parts of the body, and ends with

The letter *Aṃ* is the locus of *bodhi*; and the letter *Aḥ* is *parinirvāṇa*.
Knowing this entire method, the practitioner will accomplish perfect awakening;
The assets of an omniscient one will always be in his heart,
And the world will call him "omniscient."[56]

The Chinese commentary explains that *bodhi* (awakening) is the crown of
the head and *parinirvāṇa* (complete cessation) the entire body (258, nn. 113,
114). This seems an overinterpretation, however, especially as there are
other places in the text in which concrete and abstract are mixed together
in a similar fashion.

6.

The Vairocanābhisaṃbodhi-tantra is one of the early tantric Buddhist texts
and provides an example of how central Mahāyāna Buddhist teachings, such
as emptiness and impermanence, inform tantric praxis. The identity of the
ground and goal is evident in the assertion that the practitioner is already –
and always has been – awakened. Realization of this, the path, is accomplished through practice, particularly practice that involves ritual identification of the practitioner's own body, speech, and mind with the body, speech,
and mind of the Buddha.

In sum, religious literature does not comprise a single, coherent body of
works that can be understood by readers without adapting to very diverse
religious cultures. Religious cultures have employed a variety of textual and
reading practices that differ from those of contemporary Western or Westernized society. The latter commonly presumes a privatized goal of individual spiritual transformation attained through disciplinary practices that are
fundamentally psychological in nature. This is conceived as forming a spiritual trajectory from primal bliss, through a fall by moral failing, to reconciliation and atonement.

Buddhist literature employs a different trajectory, an epistemological
rather than moral one. The course of that trajectory moves from ignorance
through training to realization, that is, ground, path, and goal. Individual
works may discuss the entirety or instead focus on one or another element.
In the case of the tantras, much of the practice is ritual in character. Practice
is framed as making real for the practitioner the fact of already being

awakened – that the ground and the goal are identical. This identity is the positive expression of the absence of any permanent, eternal, absolute, or unchanging essence from anything that actually exists.

For the reader of religious literature, this is not the only alternative conception to that of individual spiritual transformation now dominant in the Western and Westernized world. A critical sensibility, one that doesn't simply presume that all religious literature can be understood in the same way because all religions are ultimately the same, is a more truly appreciative sensibility.

Notes

1 This presumption is also not true of the Bible itself. As Paul Griffiths asserts, "we Christians need to learn the skill of reading the Bible in a particular way, as well as a good deal of information about the Bible and about reading" (*Religious Reading: The Place of Reading in the Practice of Religion* [New York and Oxford: Oxford University Press, 1999], 19). This does not, however, preclude many people from accepting an expansive form of textual fundamentalism, i.e., expecting that the ready accessibility of the Bible extends to all religious texts.

2 Jan Nattier, *A Few Good Men: The Bodhisattva Path according to* The Inquiry of Ugra (Ugraparipṛcchā) (Honolulu: University of Hawai'i Press, 2003), 6–7.

3 Daniel M. Veidlinger, *Spreading the Dhamma: Writing, Orality, and Textual Transmission in Buddhist Northern Thailand* (Honolulu: University of Hawai'i Press, 2006), 20; citing François Bizot, *Le figuier a cinq branches* (Paris: L'École Française d'Extrême Orient, 1976), 21.

4 Gregory Schopen, "On the Absence of Urtexts and Otiose Ācaryas: Buildings, Books, and Lay Buddhist Ritual at Gilgit," in *Écrire et transmettre en Inde classique*, Études thématiques, no. 23, ed. Gérard Colas and Gerdi Gerschheimer (Paris: École Française d'Extrême-Orient, 2009), 189–219.

5 Ronald M. Davidson, "An Introduction to the Standards of Scriptural Authenticity in Indian Buddhism," in *Chinese Buddhist Apocrypha*, ed. Robert Buswell (Honolulu: University of Hawai'i Press, 1990).

6 Richard Salomon, "An Unwieldy Canon: Observations on Some Distinctive Features of Canon Formation in Buddhism," in *Kanonisierung und Kanonbildung in der asiatische Religionsgeschicht*, ed. Max Deeg, Oliver Freiburger, and Christoph Kleine (Vienna: Österreichischen Akademie der Wissenschaft, 2011).

7 Robert E. Buswell, Jr. and Donald S. Lopez, Jr., *The Princeton Dictionary of Buddhism* (Princeton, NJ: Princeton University Press, 2014), 276.

8 Donald S. Lopez, Jr., *Buddhist Scriptures* (London: Penguin Books, 2004), xii.

9 Loriliai Biernacki, *Renowned Goddess of Desire: Women, Sex, and Speech in Tantra* (Oxford and New York: Oxford University Press, 2007), 9.

10 Christopher Hatchell, *Naked Seeing: The Great Perfection, the Wheel of Time, and Visionary Buddhism in Renaissance Tibet* (Oxford and New York: Oxford University Press, 2014).

11 Donald S. Lopez, Jr., *The Tibetan Book of the Dead: A Biography* (Princeton, NJ, and Oxford: Princeton University Press, 2011), 8–10.

12 Gil Fronsdal, *Dawn of the Bodhisattva Path: The Early Perfection of Wisdom* (Berkeley, CA: Institute of Buddhist Studies and BDK America, 2014), 122. Robert F. Campany, "Notes on the Devotional Uses and Symbolic Functions of Sūtra Texts as Depicted in Early Chinese Buddhist Miracle Tales and Hagiographies," *Journal of the International Association of Buddhist Studies* 14.1 (1991): 28–72.

13 Catherine Bell, "Ritualization of Texts and Textualization of Ritual in the Codification of Taoist Liturgy," *History of Religions* 27.4 (1988): 366–392; see 390.

14 See, for example, Mark Knight, *An Introduction to Religion and Literature* (London and New York: Continuum, 2009); Mark Knight and Louise Lee, eds., *Religion, Literature and the Imagination: Sacred Worlds* (London and New York: Continuum, 2009); Kimberly Beek, "Telling Tales Out of School: The Fiction of Buddhism," in *Buddhism beyond Borders: New Perspectives on Buddhism in the United States*, ed. Scott A. Mitchell and Natalie E.F. Quli (Albany: State University of New York Press, 2015); David R. Loy and Linda Goodhew, *The Dharma of Dragons and Daemons: Buddhist Themes in Modern Fantasy* (Boston: Wisdom Publications, 2000); Lawrence Normand and Alison Winch, eds., *Encountering Buddhism in Twentieth-Century British and American Literature* (London and New York: Bloomsbury, 2013); and Gary Storhoff and John Whalen-Bridge, eds., *The Emergence of Buddhist American Literature* (Albany: State University of New York Press, 2009), and *Writing as Enlightenment: Buddhist American Literature into the Twenty-first Century* (Albany: State University of New York Press, 2011).

15 Hayden White, *Metahistory: The Historical Imagination in Nineteenth-Century Europe* (Baltimore, MD: Johns Hopkins University Press, 1973).

16 Steven Collins, *Nirvana and Other Buddhist Felicities: Utopias of the Pali Imaginaire* (Cambridge: Cambridge University Press, 1998), 126.

17 Veidlinger, *Spreading the Dhamma*.

18 In addition to the legacy of oral culture evident in the early literature as having been recorded as entire texts, there is also evidence in later literatures, both sutra and tantra, of having been compiled from earlier texts, including some that are themselves evidently oral in nature. Thus, some texts are examined in terms of stratigraphy, that is, the different historical "layers" of the text as known today.

19 Collins, *Nirvana and Other Buddhist Felicities*, 121–124.

20 Frits Staal, *Discovering the Vedas: Origins, Mantras, Rituals, Insights* (London: Penguin Books, 2008), 90–91.

21 Jan-Olav Henriksen, *The Reconstruction of Religion: Lessing, Kierkegaard, and Nietzsche* (Grand Rapids, MI, and Cambridge, UK: Eerdmans, 2001).

22 Griffiths, *Religious Reading*, 18.

23 Ibid., 19.

24 Veidlinger, *Spreading the Dhamma*, 5.

25 Jason Neelis, *Early Buddhist Transmission and Trade Networks: Mobility and Exchange within and beyond the Northwestern Borderlands of South Asia* (Leiden and Boston: Brill, 2011), 57.

26 Cf. Daniel Boucher, "The Pratītyasamutpādagāthā and Its Role in the Medieval Cult of Relics," *Journal of the International Association of Buddhist Studies* 14.1 (1991): 1–27.

27 Lewis Lancaster, "The Editing of Buddhist Texts," in *Buddhist Thought and Asian Civilization: Essays in Honor of Herbert V. Guenther on His Sixtieth Birthday*, ed. Leslie S. Kawamura and Keith Scott (Emeryville, CA: Dharma Publishing, 1977).

28 James Apple, "The Phrase dharmaparyāyo hastagato in Mahāyāna Buddhist Literature: Rethinking the Cult of the Book in Middle Period Indian Mahāyāna Buddhism," *Journal of the American Oriental Society* 134.1 (2014): 25–50.

29 Fronsdal, *Dawn of the Bodhisattva Path*, 122.

30 Schopen, "On the Absence of Urtexts and Otiose Ācaryas," 197.

31 See Diarmaid MacCulloch, *The Reformation: A History* (New York: Penguin Books, 2003).

32 Collins, *Nirvana and Other Buddhist Felicities*, 541.

33 Stephen Hodge, trans., *The Mahā-Vairocana-Abhisaṃbodhi Tantra, with Buddhaguhya's Commentary* (London and New York: RoutledgeCurzon, 2003); Gerald James Larson, "The Terms 'Tantra' and 'Yoga' as Portmanteau or Homographic Expressions," paper presented for the Tantric Studies Group at the Annual Meeting of the American Academy of Religion, Chicago, IL, November 2, 2008.

34 See Larson, "The Terms 'Tantra' and 'Yoga'"; Ronald M. Davidson, "The Problem of Secrecy in Indian Tantric Buddhism," in *The Culture of Secrecy in Japanese Religion*, ed. Bernhard Scheid and Mark Teeuwen (London and New York: Routledge, 2006) 74, n. 1.

35 Tadeusz Skorupski, "The Canonical Tantras of the New Schools," in *Tibetan Literature: Studies in Genre*, ed. José Ignacio Cabezón and Roger R. Jackson (Ithaca, NY: Snow Lion, 1996), 99.

36 Jacob Dalton, "A Crisis of Doxography: How Tibetans Organized Tantra during the 8th–12th Centuries," *Journal of the International Association of Buddhist Studies* 28.1 (2005): 115–181.

37 Steven Weinberger, "The Yoga Tantras and the Social Context of Their Transmission to Tibet," *Chung-Hwa Buddhist Journal* 23 (2010): 131–166; see 138.

38 Ibid., 138–139.

39 Rolf W. Giebel, trans., *The Vairocanābhisaṃbodhi Sutra* (Berkeley, CA: Numata Center for Buddhist Translation and Research, 2009 [2005]). Available at www.bdk.or.jp/bdk/digitaldl.html. Note: The pagination of the print version and electronic version differ; here I am using the pagination of the electronic version, as the publisher now considers that version the standard for this publication.

40 Alex Wayman and R. Tajima, *The Enlightenment of Vairocana* (Delhi: Motilal Banarsidass, 1992), 20–27.

41 Ibid., 8–9.

42 Lewis Lancaster, "Critical Editing of Buddhist Texts." Available at academia.edu, accessed January 31, 2015. www.academia.edu/7284930/Critical_Editing_of_Buddhist_Texts

43 Ronald M. Davidson, *Indian Esoteric Buddhism: A Social History of the Tantric Movement* (New York: Columbia University Press, 2002).

44 Christian K. Wedemeyer, *Making Sense of Tantric Buddhism: History, Semiology, and Transgression in the Indian Traditions* (New York: Columbia University Press, 2013), 50.

45 Fronsdal, *Dawn of the Bodhisattva Path*, 18.

46 Giebel, *The Vairocanābhisaṃbodhi Sutra*, 5.

47 Ibid., 176.
48 Cynthea J. Bogel, *With a Single Glance: Buddhist Icon and Early Mikkyō Vision* (Seattle and London: University of Washington Press, 2009).
49 Bruce Lincoln, "How to Read a Religious Text: Reflections on Some Passages of the Chāndogya Upaniṣad," *History of Religions* 46.2 (2006): 127–139.
50 Paul Copp, "Manuscript Culture as Ritual Culture in Late Medieval Dunhuang: Buddhist Talisman-Seals and Their Manuals," *Cahiers d'Extrême-Asie* 20 (2011): 193–226.
51 Laurie Patton, "Speech Acts and Kings' Edicts: Vedic Words and Rulership in Taxonomical Perspective," *History of Religions* 34.4 (1995): 332.
52 Yitzhak Freedman, "Altar of Words: Text and Ritual in Taittirīya Upaniṣad 2," *Numen* 59 (2012): 322–343.
53 Richard K. Payne, "*Ajikan*: Ritual and Meditation in the Shingon Tradition," in *Re-Visioning "Kamakura" Buddhism*, ed. Richard K. Payne (Honolulu: University of Hawai'i Press 1998); "The Shingon *Ajikan*: Diagrammatic Analysis of Ritual Syntax," *Religion* 29.3 (1999): 215–229.
54 Giebel, *The Vairocanābhisaṃbodhi Sutra*, 94.
55 Cf. David Seyfort Ruegg, "Aspects of the Investigation of the (Earlier) Indian Mahāyāna," *Journal of the International Association of Buddhist Studies* 27.1 (2004): 3–62.
56 Giebel, *The Vairocanābhisaṃbodhi Sutra*, 163–164.

11

SUSAN HANDELMAN

Judaism

Writing this chapter as the representative of "Judaism" makes me feel something like the reluctant Moses at the beginning of the biblical book of Exodus. In chapter 3, God calls to him from a burning bush as Moses, an Egyptian-Jewish fugitive, herds his sheep in the desert. Announces God: I have come to deliver the suffering Jewish people in Egypt from slavery, and you, Moses, will be my agent and messenger to Pharaoh. But Moses declines. A long argument ensues: God keeps urging and assuring; Moses keeps objecting. According to Jewish tradition, this goes on for seven days. Finally, God's patience wears thin, and Moses, reluctantly, agrees.

Each of the biblical prophets, of whom Moses is the foremost, was reluctant. In the end, they managed to carry out their mission by speaking out of their own particular historical situation to their generation, although their words carry meaning beyond their own times. I too am hesitant; I can speak only from my position as a Jewish woman and English professor in the twenty-first century. At the same time, I'm aware of standing in a chain linking me to all the previous and forthcoming generations of Jews.

I.

I preface my discussion of "Judaism" with this remark about generations and generativity because I want to reorient our discussion of literature and religion here away from a discourse about "texts." A rabbinical student in a *yeshiva* (religious Jewish academy) in Israel once offered his rabbi an "interpretation of the text." The teacher responded, "It's not a 'text.' It's your mother!" In other words, a Jew's relation to the sacred writings and traditions she or he lives and interprets is as intimate, personal, reciprocal, and complex as the deepest family relation – in fact, it *is* a family relation. Regardless of personal belief or practice, each Jew is part of the collective Jewish people, each Jew is inextricably tied up with all the Jews who came before and who will come after. And as in a family, you are always a "daughter" or "son" despite any disputes or attempts at disavowal.

To write about "Judaism," "religion," and "literature," then, I need to start by reconstructing those terms from a Jewish perspective. Terminology is important, because each English or Hebrew word carries along with it a whole train of meaning, culture, and conceptuality. Even when a certain translation might seem approximate, there can be worlds of theological, philosophical, and cultural difference. So Judaism, first of all, is not a "religion." Indeed, the common Hebrew word used to signify "religion," *dat* (דת), is Persian in origin and does not even appear in the Bible until the late Book of Esther where it signifies "law, judgment." It's worthwhile noting that in this satirical biblical book, *dat* refers to the laws of an especially incompetent and ridiculous king.

"Torah" is the Hebrew word used in ancient and modern Jewish sources to refer to Judaism's holy oral and written teachings, stories, laws, practices, beliefs, and traditions. It comes from the Hebrew root *y-r-y* (י- ר -י), meaning "to cast" or "to shoot," as in "to shoot an arrow." The Hebrew alphabet has no vowels. Hebrew builds words and verb forms out of consonantal roots vocalized differently to generate meaning and vocabulary. To make a rough analogy in English, think of the two consonants *c-t* . If you had to guess what word it meant, and added vowels, it could be "cat," "cot," "cut," "coat" – as noun or as verb – "acute," "act," and so forth. In Hebrew, one form of the root *y-r-y* means "to aim, direct toward"; in another it becomes "to proclaim, to teach" (*herah, hora'ah*). A teacher (*moreh*) both aims "at us" and "with us" – to direct us. The Hebrew word for "parent" (*horeh*) comes from a close root, *h-r-y,* meaning to conceive, generate.[1] This little etymological exercise emphasizes the deep Jewish connection between parenting, generativity, teaching, learning, writing, interpreting, aiming, believing – and living within time and history. "Torah" is not reducible to "religion," "literature," "text," or "law." It is generative learning and living in relation to God, the word, the world, and one another, encompassing the most seemingly banal details of life, from how to tie a shoelace or behave in a privy to the most far-flung cosmic speculations. On another level, for the rabbis, Torah preexisted the world, "written" in "black fire on white," and was the "blueprint of creation" (*Tanhuma* Gen. 1).

In sum, "Torah" is not a "book" and Jews are not, as commonly thought, the "People of the Book," a moniker given by Muslims but never used in rabbinic sources. Nor does rabbinic tradition use the word "scripture" ("writings") to designate the text of the "Bible" (also a non-Jewish word), but rather *Mikra* (מקרא) from the root *k-r-a* (ק-ר-א), meaning "reading." *Mikra* signifies retaining in the act of reading the sense of an immediate *oral,* personal communication between God and the human. To make a simple analogy, you are experiencing me right now through my "written self," but if I were to talk with you face to face and discuss the same ideas, it would be an entirely different experience, with different meaning. How could I unite the two?

Simply to "read" Hebrew writing already requires deciphering, sounding, and vocalizing the words. In Hebrew, the root *k-r-a* also means "calling," calling by name or calling out (*keri'ah*). Reading is a form of calling out and being called, called to account and summoned to be transformed. For the rabbis, Hebrew is also the language of holiness and revelation, mediating the experience of God. So Hebrew words – even the physical shapes and numerical values of the letters – are living forms of creative power, like God's creative "callings/namings" in the first chapter of Genesis.

I prefer to name Jews the "People of the Mouth" rather than the "People of the Book." *Mikra* is also just one part of Torah, which in Jewish tradition encompasses both what's called "oral Torah" (*Torah she be'al peh*) and "written Torah" (*Torah she b'ktav*). In a general sense, *written* Torah refers to the biblical corpus; *oral* Torah refers to the ongoing rabbinic interpretations, debates, commentaries, laws, stories, and speculations – up to the freshest insight a Torah teacher or student might create at this very moment. Collections and codifications of oral Torah eventually had to be written down, lest these teachings be lost. But as we'll see, their rhetorical forms intentionally conserve and reenact the primary orality, a sense of immediate face-to-face personal speech and dialogue, open to change and renewal at every moment, a "living Torah," a form of "continuing revelation."[2]

2.

If we return to the story of Moses in Exodus 3, we notice that it, too, is a "face-to-face" dialogue between God and Moses, a series of questions, retorts, further questions, and challenges in an intense, intimate, emotional encounter charged with ethical urgency; lives are at stake. That, too, is the kernel of how the oral Torah works. At bottom, it is about not "text" and "interpretation" but urgent personal encounter, reciprocity, argument, questioning, and continuing search.

1. And Moses kept the flock of Jethro his father-in-law, the priest of Midian; and he led the flock far away into the desert, and came to the mountain of God, to Horev.[3]

2. And the angel of the Lord appeared to him in a flame of fire out of the midst of a bush; and he looked, and, behold, the bush burned with fire, and the bush was not consumed.

3. And Moses said, "I will turn aside, and see this sight, why the bush is not burnt."

4. And when the Lord saw that he turned aside to see, God called to him out of the midst of the bush, and said, "Moses, Moses." And he said, "Here am I."

5. And he said, "Do not come any closer; take off your shoes from your feet, for the place on which you stand is holy ground."

6. And he said, "I am the God of your father, the God of Abraham, the God of Isaac, and the God of Jacob." *And Moses hid his face; for he was afraid to look upon God.* [emphasis added]

7. And the Lord said, "I have surely seen the affliction of my people who are in Egypt, and have heard their cry because of their taskmasters; for I know their sorrows. ..."

10. Come now therefore, and I will send you to Pharaoh, that you may bring forth my people the children of Israel out of Egypt."

11. And Moses said to God, "Who am I, that I should go to Pharaoh, and that I should bring forth the people of Israel. ... "

Rabbinic commentary on this episode – its gaps, ambiguities, images, words, meanings – is vast. To get some sense of it, we'll sample a form of oral Torah called *midrash*, coming from the root *d-r-sh*, meaning to "search out," "inquire," "demand." *Midrash* is an intense searching of the biblical text for meaning beyond the plain surface sense, indeed, a "demand."[4] Let's look with rabbinic eyes at a phrase in this story that is *not* obviously "literary" but more a descriptive afterthought, Exodus 3:6: "Moses hid his face and was afraid to look upon God." At first glance, the verse seems to describe Moses' emotional reaction, his sense of religious awe – a pious and praiseworthy action. What could be more obvious? But to put ourselves in a rabbinic frame of mind means to become somewhat like Sherlock Holmes, who tells Watson, "There is nothing more deceptive than an obvious fact."[5] The rabbis, like Sherlock, teach us to ask questions, look for clues, anomalies, deeper patterns, hidden connections underneath the surface story. For as God is one, so too there is a larger hidden unity beneath the prolific plurality of the world. In midrashic inquiry, at bottom, we're looking for meaning amid the fractures of the words, the world, our lives, and history. Or, to pick up the images of our biblical episode, we're striving to "hear God's voice and see God's face" in the thicket, in the brambles – despite, through, and with the fire.

So what ripples of discomfort do we feel in reading verse 6 even in an English translation? The previous verses clearly state that Moses doesn't have any inhibitions about turning aside to stare at the burning bush; the story even tells us in verse 4 that God approved. So it's Moses' own idea to hide his face, not God's command. You might retort, "What is the problem? Isn't he being just naturally pious?" But if so, wouldn't it make more narrative and logical sense for Moses to hide his face out of religious awe *immediately* upon hearing the voice of God? That is, shouldn't it have been written: "And God called to him out of the midst of the bush and said 'Moses, Moses.' And Moses hid his face; for he was afraid to look upon God." So we have to ask: Why does Moses hide his face, *only later*? Are we missing something in the dialogue or in the relationship between God and Moses?

These are some questions underlying the sample rabbinic midrash below on verse 6. For readers unfamiliar with midrashic style, the questions, debates, and answers may be confusing, like suddenly falling down a rabbit hole and into Wonderland. The rabbis assume that the reader knows the entire Bible backward and forward. They do not summarize the events or footnote their references, but abbreviate in terse code. I have filled in the sources below in brackets and highlighted key words/verses/parts of verses the rabbis cite as clues to generate meaning. The rabbis here compare Moses' behavior at the burning bush with a later narrative – the story of the people's worshipping the Golden Calf (Exodus 32–34). Above all, this midrash from the collection called *Exodus Rabbah* poses a demanding and radical question: Did Moses act rightly in hiding his face?[6]

"**And Moses hid his face**": R. Yehoshua ben Korha and R. Hoshaya [discussed this]. One said, Moses did not do right [*lo yafeh asah*] when he hid his face [*panav*]. For if he had he not done so, God would have revealed to him what is above and what is below, what has been, and what will be in the future. So when Moses later asked to behold [God], as it is said, "**Show me, I beg You, Your glory**" [Ex. 33:18],[7] God replied to Moses, "I came to show you, but you hid your face. Now I say to you that '**man shall not see Me and live**' [Ex. 33:20]. For when I wanted, you did not want."

R. Yehoshua of Sikhnin in the name of R. Levi said: Even so, God did show him: as a reward for "**and Moses hid** [*va-yaster panav*] **his face**" [Ex. 3:6] we read [later], "**the Lord spoke unto Moses face to face** [*panim el panim*]" [Ex. 33:11]. And as a reward for "**he was afraid** [*va-yarei* – Ex. 3:6] we read, [later] "**and they were afraid** [*va-yir'u*] **to come close him**" [Ex. 34:30]. And as reward for "**he was afraid to look**" [*me-habeet* – Ex. 3:6] we read, "**and he looks** [*habeet*] **upon the likeness of God**" [Num. 12:8].

> R. Hoshaya the Elder said: Moses did right [*yafeh asah*] when he hid his face. For God said to him: "I came to show myself to you [*leharot lekha panim*], and you honored me and hid your face. I assure you that in the future, you will be close to Me on the mountain for forty days and forty nights, without eating or drinking. And in the future you will have pleasure from the radiance of the *Shechinah* [the indwelling Divine presence], as it is said, **"and Moses did not know that his face [*panav*] was radiant"** [Ex. 34:29]. (*Exodus Rabbah* 3:1)

In the debate about the propriety of Moses' hiding his face, these rabbinic sages living in the Land of Israel from the late second and third centuries CE are using scriptural proof-texts from the same narratives to bolster their conflicting claims. They find subtle verbal and thematic links between the seemingly unconnected stories of the burning bush and the worshipping of the Golden Calf (Ex. 32–34). In the later story:

> Ex. 32:1 And when the people saw that Moses delayed to come down from the mount, the people gathered themselves together to Aaron, and said to him, "Arise, make us gods, which shall go before us; and as for this Moses, the man who brought us out of the land of Egypt, we do not know what became of him."

The Golden Calf is made; God informs Moses what has happened, says to leave him alone and descend, for he will now destroy this people in his anger, and make another nation out of better stuff – out of Moses himself.

Moses refuses the offer to become the progenitor of a new people – nor does he leave God alone. This is a reversal of the burning bush episode where it was Moses who had wanted to be left alone. Moses argues, pleads strenuously with God to forgive the people. God finally relents. Sensing an opportune time of special intimacy and grace, he seizes the moment: "Now therefore, if I have truly gained Your favour, *show me now, I beg, Your ways*, that I may know You, and continue in Your favor" (Ex. 33:13, emphasis added). "Your ways" here mean the secrets that guide God's dealings with humanity, how the universe is governed, the workings of good and evil and forgiveness. As he senses a further opening, Moses presses on: "*Show me, I beg You, Your glory [kevodekha]*" (Ex. 33:18, emphasis added). He asks for even more: an immediate, intimate, exclusive experience of God's essence. God's response: Yes – up to a point, but then *no further*!

19. And he answered, "I will make all my goodness pass before you, and I will proclaim before you the name Lord [YKVK], and I shall be gracious to whomever I am gracious [although they may not deserve it], and I shall show mercy to whomever I will show mercy."
20. But he said, "You cannot see my face [*panai*]; for man shall not see me and live."

21. And the Lord said, "See, there is a place near me. Station yourself upon the rock;

22. And as my Glory [*kavod*] passes by, I will put you in a cleft of the rock, and shield you with my hand until I have passed by.

23. Then I will take away my hand, and you shall see my back; but man shall not see me and live."

In the aftermath, Moses ascends for another period of forty days on Mount Sinai, hews the second set of tablets, and then returns to the people. But something has happened to Moses' face: "Moses was not aware that the skin of his face was radiant since he had spoken with Him."[8] This new awesome radiance of Moses' face frightens the people, and Moses then "puts a veil on his face" (34:30; 34). He now will take the veil off only when going to the Tent of Meeting to speak with God or upon coming out to teach the people.[9]

3.

Needless to say, this is another very rich and complex narrative and helps illustrate why and how the rabbis in our midrash create meaning. Characteristic of oral Torah, the midrash interweaves two seemingly disparate stories to engage us in a "face-to-face" debate. One story is used to interpret the other through subtly finding linked literary themes and motifs, such as "face," "seeing/showing," "revelation," "glory," "fear." Reading the account of the rabbis' midrashic debate is like opening up a Russian *matryoshka,* a wooden nesting doll: you start with the large one, open it in the middle and inside is another one; you open that up and find another, and so on and so on . . . like Moses trying to penetrate further and further into the mysteries of God.

My ultimate aim, as we work through this material, is to consider how this classical rabbinic form of interpretation – exotic as it may first seem – may connect to the study of literature and especially to the goals of that study. Annie Dillard, in her memoir *The Writing Life* asks:

> Why are we reading, if not in hope of beauty laid bare, life heightened and its deepest mystery probed? . . . Why are we reading if not in hope that the writer will magnify and dramatize our days, will illuminate and inspire us with wisdom, courage, and the possibility of meaningfulness, and will press upon our minds the deepest mysteries, so that we may feel again their majesty and power? What do we ever know that is higher than that power which, from time to time, seizes our lives, and reveals us startlingly to ourselves as creatures set down here bewildered? Why does death so catch us by surprise, and why love? We still and always want waking.[10]

I am enamored of this particular midrash, for I read it as a kind of Jewish counterpart to Dillard's words. R. Yehoshua ben Korha is arguing that Moses' hiding his face at the burning bush was his response to God's offer to explain to him these "deepest mysteries." If so, now the stakes are suddenly even greater than whether or not Moses will accept the urgent mission to save the Jews from slavery. That's why R. Yehoshua ben Korha criticizes Moses' behavior: if Moses had *not* hidden his face, he says, God would have revealed to Moses "what is above" – the deepest theological and cosmological secrets – and "what is below" – the secrets of how the world works, God's conduct of the world. He would have revealed "what has been and what will be in the future" – the meaning of history, the secrets of redemption.

The questions underlying this midrash are those I ask myself continually about the relations among "Judaism," "literature," and "religion": what and how can literature tell us about the great mysteries of life? How much can it know and reveal, and where are its limits? Do literature and criticism also have a mission in the world to redeem and save? What are the ethics of reading and writing, of knowing and not knowing, of teaching and learning? The midrash invites us to study these questions, to read between the lines, look carefully at the language of this passage and become participants in the back and forth of the debate. The rhetorical construction of the text forces us to do so; this is "oral Torah" as it searches and amplifies meaning in the gaps of the written Torah.

How does R. Yehoshua support his radical interpretation that Moses did not act rightly in hiding his face? He changes the linear narrative sequence and jumps *ahead in time* to the story of the Golden Calf. Why choose that particular story for proof? And why make such an abrupt juxtaposition between the two stories? Employing a formalistic literary approach, we see that the stories of Moses at the bush and the Golden Calf have strong thematic parallels and linguistic links. In the aftermath of the Golden Calf, there is another intense, intimate, emotional argument and dialogue between Moses and God: once again the Jewish people's fate is at stake; their lives are in danger; Moses is tested in his leadership. This time, though, God is the reluctant one, not Moses. Moses pleads aggressively with God to save and forgive the people. After God finally accedes, Moses daringly presses on and asks God to reveal his "glory" and his "ways"; Moses asks for another awesome personal revelation of God, but this is a reverse mirror image of the burning bush story. At the end of the Golden Calf story, both Moses and God hide their faces. The people now relate to Moses after the calf as Moses related to God at the burning bush – fearful to look at his great radiance.

There is another reason why R. Yehoshua has juxtaposed the two stories. A main principle of rabbinic interpretation states, "There is no before or after in Scripture" (*Sifri BaMidbar* 9; *Pesakhim 6b*). In other words, the biblical narrative is not written in a linear, chronological way. So deciphering the meaning of biblical episodes requires the interpreter to search in many simultaneous dimensions, including different ways of juxtaposing them "anachronistically." The eminent Jewish historian Yosef Hayim Yerushalmi puts it this way: the rabbis played with time "as with an accordion, expanding and collapsing it at will."[11] This is not arbitrary play; there are close literary parallels and links between the two stories. On a deeper philosophical, existential, and theological level, time itself is a flexible category. As Einstein helped us understand, "Time and space are modes by which we think and not conditions in which we live."[12]

The rabbis are probing the deeper *meaning of* history in a world that God set in motion. They are straining to catch glimpses of the face of God in history and the meaning of human suffering. The biblical word for "history" is *toladot*, literally meaning "generations," from the root *y-l-d*, "to give birth." What is history bringing forth? To what is it giving birth? How is it moving along the trajectory of a divine plan from creation to redemption? History is not only the record of the generations of Jewish people through their long journey in time, their dispersions, and travails; it is part of a meta-history, a universal human and cosmic drama with its terrors and catastrophes but to which there is a promised redemptive end – and for which God assigned the Jewish people a special task. Even Sherlock Holmes asks: "What object is served by this circle of misery and violence and fear? It must tend to some end, or else our universe is ruled by chance, which is unthinkable."[13] So R. Yehoshua ben Korha rebukes Moses for hiding his face when God was willing to reveal those secrets of history, to tell him "what is above and what is below, what has been and what will be in the future." He reads the biblical dialogue of God and Moses after the Golden Calf as a *direct continuation and response to* their earlier dialogue at the burning bush:

> So when Moses later asked to behold [God], as it is said, **"Show me, I beg you, Your glory"** [Ex. 33:18], God replied to Moses, "I came to show you, but you hid your face. Now I tell you that '**man shall not see Me and live**' [Ex. 33:20]. For when I wanted, you did not want."

Moses did not do well, should *not* have hid his face at the burning bush – because *later on*, when Moses *did* want to see and know the deepest mysteries of God and the universe, God was then unwilling. Case proved? Elementary, my dear Watson?

Not quite. R. Yehoshua of Sikhnin, in the name of his teacher, R. Levi, and R. Hoshaya have a comeback. In a characteristic move of oral Torah, they argue the opposite, using the same scriptural parallels. Moses' behavior was *indeed right*; God *did* reward him for it, and *did* reveal Himself more deeply.

> Even so, God did show him: as a reward for **"and Moses hid [*va-yaster*] his face"** [Ex. 3:6] we read, **"the Lord spoke unto Moses face to face"** [Ex. 33:11]. And as a reward for **"he was afraid"** [*ve-yarei* – Ex. 3:6] we read, **"and they were afraid [*ve-yeru*] to come close him"** [Ex. 34:30]. And as reward for **"he was afraid to look"** [*me-habeet* – Ex. 3:6] we read, **"and he looks [*mehabeet*] upon the likeness of the Lord."**

To sum up this counterargument: our original verse from Exodus 3:6, "And Moses hid his face; for he was afraid to look upon God," has been parsed here as *three* separate actions: (1) "hid his face," (2) "for he was afraid," (3) "to look upon God." These three acts of Moses, this opposing argument goes, were actually meritorious. They are what led later to his three rewards: (1) for "And Moses hid his face" (Ex. 3:6), he was rewarded with the radiant illumination of his face (Ex. 34:29–30); (2) for "he was afraid" (Ex. 3:6), he merited the Israelites' awe of coming too near him (Ex. 34:30); (3) for "to look upon God" (Ex. 3:6), he was given a vision of God's glory, "The likeness of the Lord he beholds" (Num. 12:8). Here – in a reversal of the previous critical reading – Moses' hiding his face at the burning bush was the very act that led to his being given the greatest prophetic powers and the special illumination of his own face.

What do we do with these two opposite interpretations which the midrash, in another characteristic of oral Torah, leaves perplexingly unresolved? I would suggest that each allows a glimpse of a "different face of God," as it were, a God who indeed reveals and conceals himself in so many different ways and times in our lives, in the world, in the Bible, in history, and in "literature," a God who is always larger than our grasp. Moreover, the effect is seductive; the play of revelation and concealment in the midrash, as in the biblical narrative, draws us in, whets our desire to probe further. Like Moses who presses more and more for God to reveal himself in the aftermath of the Golden Calf, we seek more and more to know, to penetrate the mystery. We return and reread, circle in again, look between the lines, over and over. We, too, get a tantalizing glimpse from the cleft of the rock, and then it goes dark; we search again. In this desire to know and see more, there is also an energy of "eros," and in the process we become more and more part of, "united with," what we read; it becomes ours. This is "knowledge" in the sense of the Hebrew word *da'at*, as in the famous verse from Genesis, "And Adam knew (*yada*) Eve" (Gen. 4:1). As Elyakim Simsovic puts it, "You know something, *da'at*, when it is no longer a knowledge you possess, but has become an integral part of your very self, your identity."[14]

4.

Here we have moved beyond the analogy of Torah to a detective story. The fascination is not just that of Holmesian intellectual play in solving a mystery. It becomes a relation of love. We sense a depth of meaning glimmering between the gaps, a hidden face . . . like the concealed face of a beloved. "Knowledge" is the ostensible goal of the Academy. But what relation is there between knowing, interpreting, living, loving? Can we ever really know without eros, the energy of wanting and drive for connection? Can we ever deeply understand a work of literature without somehow loving it, let alone another human being, or God, or Torah?

There is a famous parable about this eros of learning and interpretation in the *Zohar*, one of the classic texts of the Jewish mystical tradition (*Kabbalah*). The speaker of the story is a hidden holy sage, disguised as a donkey driver:

> [Torah] may be compared to a beloved maiden, beautiful in form and appearance, concealed secretly in her palace. She has a single lover unknown to anyone – except to her, surreptitiously. Out of the love that he feels for her, this lover passes by her gate constantly, lifting his eyes to every side. Knowing that her lover is constantly circling her gate, what does she do? She opens a little window in that secret place where she is, reveals her face to her lover, and quickly withdraws, concealing herself. None of those near the lover even sees or notices, only the lover, and his inner being and heart and soul go out to her. He knows that out of love for him she revealed herself for a moment to arouse him.
>
> So it is with words of Torah: she only reveals herself to her lover. Torah knows that one who is wise of heart circles her gate every day. What does she do? She reveals her face to him from the palace and beckons to him with a hint, then swiftly withdraws to her place, hiding away. None of those there knows or notices – he alone does, and his inner being and heart and soul follow her. Thus Torah reveals and conceals herself, approaching her lover lovingly to arouse love with him. (*Zohar* II:99a "*Saba d' Mishpatim*")

Only the lover earns the right to see more and more of the beautiful maiden, who in turn reciprocally arouses him in increasing intimacy.

At the same time, this intimate relation to the Torah grows through struggle, as we see in the conflicting interpretations over Moses hiding his face. In a famous talmudic passage, "R. Hiyya bar Abba said: 'Even the parent and child, the teacher and disciple who study Torah at the same gate become enemies of each other. And they do not move from there until they come to love each other'" (*Kiddushin* 30a–b). In rabbinic language this conflict and struggle to understand the Torah is known as the "war of Torah." But how can war lead to love?

A contemporary talmudist and Jewish thinker, R. Yitzhak Hutner (1906–1980), explains this "war of Torah" not just as another method of study but as the essential foundation of generative, creative Torah. The "love at the end" comes, he writes, not *despite* the conflict but *because of* and *through* it. That love flourishes on the very soil of the conflict (*makhloket*), for "all love reaches its apex at the time the two sides are partners in creating." This type of love is a non-Freudian and nonromantic eros; it is not about dissolution into the other, possessive conflict, or an act of theological "grace" but about partnership in generative creation. It moves even beyond notions of "reciprocity" or "dialogue" and puts "love," "generativity," and "fecundity" at the center of the reading, interpreting, learning, and teaching relation. It may also be a model, I would suggest, for the ways we might read and teach literature.

But we are not quite finished with our midrash. Yet another understanding of Exodus 3:6 comes from R. Joseph B. Soloveitchik (1903–1993), who bases his reading on an expanded version in the Talmud *Berakhot* 7a, which fills out God's response as: "When I wanted, you did not want; now you want and I do not want." When God first calls out to Moses at the burning bush, he is ready, says R. Soloveitchik, to reveal himself in the fullness of absolute truth. This was Moses' chance to penetrate the depths, to comprehend clearly the ways of God, of good and evil, and to find the answers to all the great questions of life. But instead, Moses hid his face. R. Soloveitchik suggests the reason why: he did not want all the answers to be known, all the secrets to be revealed. He chose to remain in the darkness of human finite understanding; he feared to become an "all-knower." But why make such a choice? Answers R. Soloveitchik, Moses understood that if he were to "know" everything in the absolute sense, he would lose his ability to feel compassion and love for his fellow creatures, those still bound by the limits of human understanding, those who still suffered. Had Moses understood everything, he would have seen that from the ultimate, divine, "nonhuman" perspective everything that appeared as negative in the end was ultimately patterned for good, including death, poverty, suffering, loneliness. And then he could not have performed kindness, felt compassion, or protested against God. R. Soloveitchik poignantly writes, "Loving-kindness comes to humanity at a heavy price: lack of knowing." Moses gave up the most precious and elevated human desire: to know the all and to know God ultimately; he sacrificed this for the sake of love for his fellows, to be able to suffer with and do good for them.

This, R. Soloveitchik continues, is the deeper meaning of God's telling Moses *after* the Golden Calf, "you cannot see my face and live," but see only a glimpse of "God's back" from a fissure in the rock where God places him: "When I wanted, you did not want; now that you want, I do not want." That is not a petulant rejoinder. Rather, God is reminding Moses of his earlier choice: he cannot have both absolute knowledge and human kindness at the same time. Nevertheless, continues R. Soloveitchik, Moses' choice to sacrifice absolute knowledge for the sake of his relation to his people coincides with the refinement of Moses' own character and desires; it transforms Moses' own person into something purified and illuminating. That also explains the other seemingly opposite rabbinic opinion – the one praising Moses' decision to "hide his face" and affirming that God indeed rewarded him for that action. For due to this action, Moses received the highest prophetic powers and shining illumination of his own face. In sum, like any good talmudic commentator (and detective) R. Soloveitchik here also reconciles the contradiction between the two opinions and finds the deeper unity underlying them. Both positions are true: (1) Moses hid his face and that pious act granted him prophetic powers and the shining illumination later on, and (2) he hid his face and missed an opportunity that God offered to explain to him the deepest mysteries of the world, and so was refused later, when he asked again. R. Soloveitchik understands the midrash to mean that the ultimate compassion and love for one's fellows comes not from knowledge but from a certain kind "not-knowing."[15] I'd like to suggest that an essential issue for the study of literature and religion, indeed for all academic study, is how to make that "not knowing" more than a series of negative critical gestures or an empty shell, how to make the "critical" searching light of intellect also a "shining illumination of the face" and not a place where the dizziness of the mind spins on itself. How might the university become a place where we search for knowledge and yet also nurture respect for concealment and mystery?

These are all very serious issues, but there is yet one more way to read our midrash and think about the relation of Judaism, literature, and religion: humor. When God retorts, "When I wanted you didn't want; now you want and I don't want!" it may be that the rabbis are also winking at us. Humor is a constitutive element in Judaism, found throughout the biblical and rabbinic corpus. It's helped Jews to endure through history. On a deeper level, if indeed we saw from the ultimate distance, were given absolute knowledge, we would have no more questions about good and evil, life and death, the meaning of suffering or history. If all the mysteries were finally revealed, our mouths would "then be filled with laughter," as the Psalmist puts it (Ps. 126:2) in describing the messianic redemption. This humor is not derisive or cynical. It can be the smile that comes from amazement, wonder, surprise at things unusually juxtaposed or out of natural proportion. Such humor is also an antidote for arrogance; it offers a welcome distance from one's own narrow life and ego.

So there is much in the subtle wink of God's answer to Moses in our midrash. When we wink, we hint to the other person to "read between the lines"; we might be signaling the opposite of the surface meaning ("Don't take what I am saying *too* seriously"), indicating there's a secret meaning here only for you and me, or emphasizing our intimate relation. It's a way of expressing certain things that can't be said directly or literally. And here I want to locate another kind of nexus of literature, religion, and Judaism. All involve the struggle to put into language so many things that are "beyond" expression and require indirection. That's one of the secrets of stories, and why the deepest teachings are usually indirect, revealing and concealing at once.

Midrash plays with language in a quite "literary" way, but in the end one can't equate midrash or any form of literature with summaries or interpretation of the "ideas" found "in" them. All good literary writing, reading, and criticism, as well as good pedagogy, uses language not to "arrive at conclusions" but to create experiences in reading that are inseparable from the ideas being presented or played with.[16] But for the rabbis, all this is in service of something more than aesthetic or creative pleasure, intellectual challenge, or psychological self-understanding. I am tempted to call rabbinic forms of interpretation "messianic" modes of reading. They create/enact an experience that moves us beyond the linear tunnels of history and our limited selves; they are "performative" in both *style* and *content*. In our sample midrash, the *content* is about the opportunity to know the all and understand the secrets of history; in *style*, its nonchronological readings, abrupt juxtapositions, and plays with multiple dimensions of words and phrases all open up depths and reveal other narratives and other "faces" of the human and the divine. This activity has an inextricably ethical dimension in helping us, too, "illumine our faces" and sanctify the ways we treat others.

5.

To return to our opening illustration, "It's not a text; it's your mother!" Like your mother, it doesn't leave you alone; it calls you back again and again. You catch a glimmer of light, fall back into confusion, put it together another way, see more deeply, return yet again. "Torah" is not a book, not any defined essence, not a "text," and not "religion." But it encompasses all those, because it is *shared space between you and God.*

There are complex, ancient Jewish laws still in effect about how the religious scribe (*sofer*) painstakingly hand writes a Torah scroll and its 304,504 black letters: there is special ink, quill, and parchment; there are laws about how to form the letters; and there are laws about the blank spaces. The letters must not be allowed to touch each other; all must be surrounded by white space (*Menakhot* 29b–30a). If one letter of the 304,504 touches the next at any point, the entire scroll is invalidated. R. Soloveitchik understands this law on a deeper level: the white space is all the unwritten and continuing oral Torah.[17]

Blank space. Here, too, is where the reader and the writer become partners in literature and also in Torah. Here, too, is another way "Judaism," "literature," and "religion" themselves intersect; there is an "empty space" between them. The connections I have made in this chapter are only spaces "in between." You, my reader, will read "between the lines" and create your own connections.

Notes

1 The vowels are heard when the Hebrew words are pronounced in oral speech. But when a reader looks at the vowel-less written version, she or he already has to interpret the letters, decipher possible meanings. A given set of letters can be vocalized in different ways, as in our above example of *c-t*. This characteristic of Hebrew makes for a richness, for tonalities, harmonic resonances, leitmotifs, and plays with meaning that can't be captured in translation. You have to "hear" to read, as it were, and sense the "perpetual murmur from the waves beyond the shore" (Abraham Joshua Heschel, *Man Is Not Alone: A Philosophy of Religion* [New York: Farrar, Straus and Giroux, 1976], 8).

2 The *Talmud*, redacted in the fifth century CE, is the great repository of oral Torah with 63 tractates and more than 6,000 printed pages. The word "Talmud" comes from the root *l-m-d*, meaning "learning." Learning, commenting on, debating, and analyzing Talmud is at the heart of Jewish life and identity.

3 The original Hebrew version of the Torah scroll has no numbered chapters and verses. That format of editing the Bible was originated later by Christian theologians. In rabbinic reading, this lack of chapter, verse, and conventional punctuation opens the biblical text to further interpretive possibilities.

4 There is a traditional rabbinic division of the different dimensions of Torah into four levels: *peshat, remez, drash, sod* – also referred to by the acronym *PaRDeS*: "garden," i.e., the "fertile garden of meaning." These four Hebrew words roughly translate as: (1) surface or plain, literal meaning; (2) hinted, allegorical meaning; (3) homiletic meaning; and (4) secret, mystical meaning – though the levels overlap, like skins of an onion.

5 Sir Arthur Conan Doyle, "The Boscombe Valley Mystery," in *The Adventures of Sherlock Holmes* (New York: Heritage Press, 1950), 310.

6 The most accessible English *Midrash Rabbah* is edited by H. Freedman and M. Simon, 10 vols. (New York: Soncino Press, 1983); translations from Exodus by the author following those of S.M. Lehrman in vol. 3.

7 English translations by the author, following *The Jerusalem Bible/Tanakh*, revised and edited by Harold Fisch (Jerusalem: Koren Publishers, 1992).

8 I have capitalized "Him," but since Hebrew letters have no capitalization, there are interesting grammatical ambiguities here about who is speaking to whom and when and about the dynamics of interaction between the speakers.

9 We don't usually visualize Moses with a veil or think of his face as hidden. The Hebrew verbal root for "shining" or "radiating" is *k-r-n* (*karan*). In the noun form, vocalized as *keren*, it can mean both "ray" and the word "horn." A misreading of this word gave us Michelangelo's famous sculpture of Moses with horns on his head.

10 Annie Dillard, *The Writing Life* (New York: Harper Perennial, 1990), 72–73.

11 Yosef Hayim Yerushalmi, *Zakhor: Jewish History and Jewish Memory* (Seattle: University of Washington Press, 1982), 17.

12 Dimitri Marianoff and Palma Wayne, *Einstein: An Intimate Study of a Great Man* (New York: Doubleday, Doran, 1944), 62.

13 Sir Arthur Conan Doyle, "The Cardboard Box," in *The Adventures of Sherlock Holmes*, 561.

14 Elyakim Simsovic, personal communication (February 19, 2015).

15 Rabbi Joseph B. Soloveitchik, "Ha-Yehudi Mashul L'Sefer Torah" [Hebrew], in *Beit Yosef Shaul: Kovetz Hiddushei Torah*, ed. Elchanan Asher Adler (New York: Gruss Kollel, R. Yitzhak Elchanan Seminary, Yeshiva University, 1993), 68–100. R. Soloveitchik himself wrote his dissertation on nineteenth-century German philosophy when he was a university student in Berlin in the 1920s. The philosophical quest to "know the All" was central in the German academy of his time.

16 My close paraphrase of Thomas Ogden describing the writing style of British psychoanalytic theorist, D.W. Winnicott. Thomas H. Ogden, "Reading Winnicott," *The Psychoanalytic Quarterly* 70 (2001): 299.

17 Rabbi Joseph B. Soloveitchik, *Nefesh Ha-Rav: Likkutei Ma'amarim* [in Hebrew], ed. Hershel Shachter (Jerusalem: Reshit Yeruyshalyim, 1994), 290–291.

12

LORI BRANCH AND IOANA PATULEANU

Eastern Orthodoxy

For many Eastern Orthodox Christians, the Romanian priest Father Roman Braga has been a living Father Zossima, a radiant man cut from the cloth Dostoevsky tailored into Alyosha's spiritual guide in *The Brothers Karamazov*. Born in 1922 to free peasants in Moldavia, his life followed the upheavals of his country, from the "Burning Bush" spiritual revival of 1945–1948 and the Communist Revolution of 1947 to the horrors of Pitești Prison, the Communist reeducation experiment that Aleksandr Solzhenitzn called "the most terrible act of barbarism in the contemporary world."[1] After he was exiled by Ceaușescu in 1968, he eventually became spiritual father to a Romanian women's monastery in Michigan, where a steady stream of pilgrims flowed to make their confessions and receive his counsel until his death in 2015.

Before the Revolution, Father Roman was certified to teach Romanian language and literature, and he often emphasized the importance of literature for transmitting what is good, true, and beautiful in any culture, a conviction that predated his academic training. Recalling a life-changing encounter with Father Nicodemus Sachelarie, his confessor at the Condrița monastery and now a saint in the Romanian church, Father Roman recounted:

> Once I had committed a great sin, and I went to him very ashamed. He knew me; he read my heart, and he said, "I understand. You are very young and not very mature. I do not want to give you any penance, but please read *The Brothers Karamazov*. And I give you the homework of analyzing the character of Alyosha; after two weeks come to talk with me." I can say that this was a turning point in my life.[2]

That a monk in rural Romania recommends Dostoevsky in confession, and that this literary encounter is a life-changing event for one who will suffer for the faith and teach thousands, bespeaks the connectedness of literature to life in Orthodoxy, and what we might call the living literariness of Orthodox spirituality.

I.

Eastern Orthodoxy comprises the second largest Christian group worldwide and is one of the fastest growing religious groups in North America[3] but remains largely *terra incognita* for Western people, a third term outside the Catholic-Protestant binaries that shape Western religion. The division between Western (Roman) and Eastern (Orthodox) Christianity in the Great Schism of 1054 was the result of a gradual drifting apart exacerbated by claims of papal supremacy and the Roman insertion of the *Filioque* into the Nicene Creed.[4] The Eastern Church thus maintains a rich, living connection to the ancient Christianity that the New Testament calls "the Way," "the traditions (*paradosis*) that you have been taught, whether by word or epistle," and "the faith once and for all delivered to the saints."[5] But the Church's inflections and experience of that mere Christianity are distinctive from that of its Western sisters: without Scholasticism, the Reformation, Counter-Reformation, or Vatican II; having suffered Muslim conquests, the Ottoman Empire, and seventy years of Soviet atheism; and developing along its own organic lines for 2,000 years, Eastern Orthodoxy is a treasure-house for all, a Christianity robustly experiential and rooted in what Vladimir Lossky calls the "mystical theology" of union with the Triune God in Christ.[6]

The great theme of Orthodox spirituality is the return to Paradise, its great goal and longing, salvation, understood as the mystery of the communion of free beings, divine and human. From ancient times, this journey has been described as a three-fold path of purification, illumination, and *theosis* – transfiguration and deification through communion with the living God. Eastern Christian art, liturgy, and architecture is above all joyfully Eucharistic and fleshes out the all-encompassing drama of this quest, the living experience that "God is our king from before the ages, working salvation in the midst of the earth," a salvation which humans desperately need.[7]

In the Orthodox understanding of the fall, Adam and Eve turn away from direct, life-giving communion with God to distrusting God. They believe the lie of the serpent, the *diabolos* or divider, who suggests that God is keeping something from them, that there is a higher knowledge than knowledge of God – the knowledge of both good and evil – and that when they have that knowledge, they will be like God, apart from God.[8] What comes through the fall is thus the deathly rending of relationship between rational beings and their Creator, which affects the entire cosmos. In pulling away from the Giver of Life, human beings deform their God-given freedom and become beset by need and egocentric passions.[9] The healing of this division begins with the long-prophesied incarnation of Christ: the Son of God's voluntarily entering into that rent world and assuming all its suffering and death, triumphing over them by his humble self-sacrifice and resurrection. In his one person and two natures, human and divine, Christ renews disintegrated human nature and literally reunites that which was made for communion – the human person – with God. Thus baptism is a "new birth," in which believers are united to Christ, the "new Adam"; they die to their egocentric self and "put on Christ," the healed humanity once again capable of knowing God experientially.[10]

In uniting human beings to Christ, baptism purifies and regenerates their being, including the freedom without which they would not be in God's image. To heal and exercise that freedom, God works with believers in *synergia*, giving them the ongoing remedy (*pharmakon*) of *repentance*: in Greek, *metanoia*, literally "change of mind and heart."[11] As patristic scholar Jean-Claude Larchet puts it, "everyone is always in need of repentance," and the preaching of the gospel both by St. John the Baptist and by Jesus therefore began with the preaching of repentance. "The Fathers see in repentance a *process of conversion*," Larchet writes, "whose aim is less sin itself than the return to God."[12] As St. Symeon the New Theologian wrote in the eleventh century, "Through repentance, man acquires anew the splendor proper to him."[13] Instead of viewing the world as Adam and Eve did – the place where God keeps good things from them – human beings can now come to approach the world as the place where God reveals himself to them, where God is "working salvation in the midst of the earth." Through *metanoia*, believers exercise their gradually restored freedom to ask to be further illumined and to regain their likeness to God: to become ever more free and integrated beings, whose very nature is love. "Thus repentance is the road to love," writes the great twentieth-century confessor and theologian Dumitru Staniloae; "it serves love [and] leads from an insufficient love to more love."[14]

The contemporary Athonite monk and Cypriot bishop Athanasios of Limmasol puts it this way:

> The experience of the love of Christ is the greatest experience that a human being can have. It is infinite, and it has no boundaries or limits ... because God has no boundaries. We may be tired of the things of this world, but we can never tire of the experience of God. The love of God is a state of perpetual enthusiasm. It is a state of continued enchantment and doxology in the infinite and absolute taste of God's eternal love.[15]

Salvation then is God's work, "by grace, through faith," in which human beings are called to cooperate freely through repentance;[16] it is one way they participate in the divine nature, working with God to reshape their being.[17]

This participation is creative and eloquently expressed in the roughly twenty volumes of poetry and song that comprise the texts of the Orthodox liturgical year. At the beginning of Lent, setting sail on the "great sea of the fast," much-loved Matins hymns ask, "Open to me the doors of repentance ... for I have profaned myself with coarse sins, and consumed my entire life with procrastination"[18] – tarrying with desires that do not satisfy, with ways of viewing the world that do not give life. One of the Vespers hymns even supplicates Paradise itself:

> O most honoured Paradise,
> comeliness transcendent in splendor,
> the dwelling-place perfected by God,
> unending joy and enjoyment,
> the glory of the righteous,
> the joy of the prophets,
> and the dwelling-place of the saints,
> beseech the Creator of all,
> by the tune of the rustling of thy leaves,
> to open for me the gates which I closed by sin,
> and that I be worthy to partake of the tree of life and joy,
> which I enjoyed in thee of old.[19]

By its splendor, the place where believers can dwell with God calls forth their prayers and longing, and that beautiful, wordless rustling of its leaves is itself a prayer. Literature – hymnody, poetry, language in its fullness – may evoke and be this kind of prayer, by the Creator's grace it bears, drawing listeners and readers toward the beyond to which it points. It is both doxological and noetic, challenging human beings to repentance by gentle beauty: both to tarry in stillness with the longing for the eternal and to set out for it by ongoing change of mind and heart toward God and the world, by acts that engage their psychosomatic unity. As Father Roman put it,

> The Holy Fathers did not theorize; they were practical men: fasting, metania [prostrations], confession and communion were not simply words for them. ... God is not an acquisition of our intellect, nor is Christianity a manual of rules and ethical principles; on the contrary, *God is our life* and our actions are authentic when we are able to say together with St. Paul, "I live, but not I; Christ lives in me" (Gal. 2:20).[20]

Orthodox Lent is thus full of metanoia and metania, repentance and prostrations. Reciting a fourth-century prayer of St. Ephrem the Syrian several times a day, believers prostrate themselves, asking God for "purity, humility, patience, and love" and "to see my own sins, and not to judge my brother." Such athletic prayer is perhaps not as attractive as the poetry of

Paradise. But at the heart of Orthodox spirituality is the recognition that they are inseparable: that the humus of the earth of which I am made, to which (etymologically and literally) in humility I bow down in repentance before God and my neighbor, this temporal materiality is the very path that mediates my ongoing conversation with my Creator – my repentance, my freedom, my return to Paradise "in the midst of the earth."

It is in this context of ongoing conversion that Father Nicodemus' recommendation to the young Roman to read *The Brothers Karamazov* and ponder Alyosha's character makes sense – and that two millennia of Orthodox literature makes sense. Augustine fretted about the corrupting allure of the *Aeneid*, but for the Eastern Church, St. Basil the Great's "Address to Young Men on the Right Use of Greek Literature" has been more influential.[21] For St. Basil, not only are poetry and fiction potential bearers of truth, goodness, and beauty, but even pagan literature may be so. Christians have the freedom and even responsibility to read widely, "altogether after the manner of bees" in search of nectar, taking away "whatever benefits our souls and is allied to the truth."[22] Thus, drawing on their rich Byzantine educations, St. Basil's friend St. Gregory Nazianzus produced a vibrant Christian literature under Julian the Apostate, and in *The Life of Moses* St. Gregory of Nyssa crafted a lovely emblem of the joy of eternal progress in relationship with God. Likewise St. Ephrem the Syrian, St. Romanos the Melodist, St. Symeon the New Theologian, and acclaimed Orthodox writers of the last two centuries – Nikolai Gogol, Fyodor Dostoevsky, Alexandros Papadiamandis, Eugene Ionesco, Mircea Eliade – have produced literature that explores creation and the human-divine relationship, along with some whose relationship with Orthodoxy was more complex, including Leo Tolstoy, Anton Chekov, Nikos Kazantzakis, and many lesser known in the West. The Orthodox believer and literary theorist Mikhail Bakhtin saw liturgy and literature as embodying a profound dialogism and *heteroglossia*, engaged in the search for and the making of meaning. From an Orthodox mindset, literature may thus become a place of revelation and repentance – as it was for Father Nicodemus and the young Father Roman – inasmuch as through reading and writing it we come to hope that we may be changed and glimpse how that might be done. This is a personal way of reading that is not limited to sacred texts, nor can it be reduced to what Michael Warner has called a secular, distanciated mode of "critical reading."[23] If we interpret the world in light of the hope for salvation – for the communion of free beings with God and each other – then what Papadiamandis calls "the prose of everyday reality" may mediate to us a vision of beauty and the possibility of living toward that beauty. Literature itself cannot mechanically transmit to us God or *theosis*. But just as icons in the Orthodox tradition are called "windows to heaven," literature may glimmer with hints of the God who wishes to reveal himself to us personally and with the vision of a humble, extraordinary humanity that sometimes turns, and then runs, walks, and tarries in that light.[24] By calling to readers through beauty, hope, and even images of deathliness they may recoil from, literature can be a real part of their repentance and journey to Paradise.

In the rest of this chapter, we examine works by two Orthodox authors, the Greek short story writer Alexandros Papadiamandis (1851–1911) and the Romanian priest and memoirist Nicolae Steinhardt (1912–1989). Exemplarily Orthodox in their literary spirituality and spiritual literariness, these writers span the twentieth century and explore themes germane to religious life today, especially the relation of faith to secular custom and the response of faith in the face of suffering. As different as their lives and writings are, in them we see writers undeceived about human fallenness yet in love with the human ability, even amid vicious weakness and suffering, to reorient one's heart and mind – to set out toward Paradise and to tarry with the transcendent divine, immanent in the created world.

2.

Alexandros Papadiamandis was an Orthodox priest's son and a *psaltis*, or cantor, on intimate terms with those twenty volumes of Orthodox liturgical poetry by virtue of chanting them each year in the church. The fourth of nine children, he was born on the small island of Skiathos in 1851, where he died in 1911 after a career as a journalist, fiction writer, and literary translator. Popularly called "the Greek Dostoevsky," Papadiamandis is loved by many Greeks in the same intense way many believing Russians love Dostoevsky, as capturing the collective experience of Eastern Christianity. Beyond the anatomy of human egotism and fallenness so vivid in their fiction, what interests Papadiamandis, not unlike Dostoevsky, is the ability of the conscience to waken and the heart to turn – or not to turn.

The novella *The Murderess* (1902–1904) dramatizes the chilling potential of freedom in Hadoula, a sixty-year-old herbalist who decides after years of treating the poor that it is better to kill infant girls than to allow them and their families to endure the hardships that attend being female – the greatest being the necessity for a dowry which, amid such poverty, makes each girl into a dire burden. Escalating into a spiral of crimes, Hadoula finally flees into the mountains of Skiathos, pursued by policemen. Stranded in a rocky hideout, low on food, desperate for deliverance, piling lie upon lie in a situation that looks more hopeless than the lives she has ended, Hadoula nonetheless feels "a hope leap up in her."[25] She decides to flee to a nearby monastery via a treacherous tidal path: "there she would confess all her troubles. It was time to repent" (123). When she finally reaches the neck of sand linking the monastery to the island, it is nearly high tide and the path stands just an inch above sea level. Literally fleeing for her life, Hadoula nonetheless "stood and hesitated. 'Won't it be low tide again in a little while?' she said. 'Why should I hurry now and get all wet?'" (125).

The remarkable thing about *The Murderess* is not simply the way Papadiamandis maintains the plot breathlessly unresolved until the final paragraph, but the way that the masterful ending draws us back to this moment three pages before, when Hadoula procrastinates on her path to repentance. As horrifying as Hadoula's actions are, as startling as it is to hear the Jesus Prayer in her mouth or her resolution to repent, we have been *hoping* she would do so, holding out hope for her as for ourselves. And the novella's starting place is not Hadoula's wrongdoings but Papadiamandis' hometown and the greater societal evil of the dowry system, which makes human beings into financial burdens (or opportunities for gain). From a Christian perspective in which all are made in the image of God, *The Murderess* calls for cultural repentance about the dehumanizing effects of the dowry custom, at the same time that it calls our attention to the risk to which the recognition of such systematic ills makes one prey. For the great danger for Hadoula is not simply that she dawdles on the path to repentance while the tide rises, but that earlier, in tarrying too long with the grim view of the world around her, she becomes more deathly than the system she rightly laments. It is the hopelessness of that system that speaks in Hadoula when she asks, in spite of her hope, "Why hurry and why get wet?" – the briny waters a perfect emblem of the baptism, suffering, and mediation she recoils from all along.

But in other stories by Papadiamandis, we see dawdling and even dowries transfigured by repentance. This is the beautiful heart of "Fey Folk," which uses the word "dawdle" repeatedly to describe Agallos, a middle-aged husband who drags his feet each day on his way home from errands.[26] His family lives far from the village because, as part of her dowry, his wife Afendra brought the remote mountain-stream mill that now provides their living. Agallos is in no spiritual hurry, either; he goes to church once a year when church comes to him, as it were, on the village feast day. The family is regarded by their neighbors as "fey folk," not "afraid of spirits" and "on good terms with them." When Agallos dawdles, it's not because he's talking with fairies but rather because he's daydreaming about his glory days, when he was a handsome catch sought after by village girls. On the Christmas Eve in which "Fey Folk" takes place, Agallos fails to come home; Afendra, like her husband often lost to reality in daydreams of her beauty as a bride, frets and cries, and her aged mother Synodia at last decides to brave the snowy dark to search for her son-in-law. Much of the story recounts the main characters' lonely thoughts during the search for the missing husband – their worries, grudges, fantasies of themselves. When we finally catch up with Agallos, we discover that he was indeed "dawdling like a bride" on his way home when he stopped by an abandoned church and saw a light inside. Investigating, he finds the lamps all lit and half a dozen monks chanting Christmas vespers. "Convinced that he'd gone, while still alive, to Paradise," Agallos inquires who the monks are, and

> ... [w]hen [he] had satisfied his curiosity, he made up his mind to leave and go down to the mill and bring his wife and children all together up to the church of the Holy Virgin, because the strange monks were going to keep an all-night vigil and celebrate the liturgy towards daybreak. But as he was about to leave, he thought again to himself: "I'll stay a bit longer" and then "a bit longer" and it was already approaching midnight without him having felt at all tired. For he found the sweetness and decorum of the chanting most pleasing. (245, 246)

In a humorous turn, Agallos' habitual dawdling is transfigured as his ability to tarry, not in solipsistic daydreams but in the liturgy. But he does at last go home, help wash the children, and lead them back to the church for confession and communion, returning home together as the sun rises.

By the end of "Fey Folk," the principal characters have all been reoriented toward themselves and others. Instead of dawdling alone, Agallos brings his family to tarry together in the church; instead of focusing on themselves, Synodia and Afendra confess their sins against Afendra's rival and for penance do what they can to help her get married. Earlier in the story, Afendra thinks to herself,

> It's no small matter, stealing away the orphan girl's good fortune to get married yourself. But then again what are you to do? How else can you live? Life's like that; it's war. To attain perfection, to put the other before yourself ... it's like deciding not to live in this world. It's like going and drowning yourself. Just thinking about it clouds your wits. It's enough to send you out into the wilderness. (240–241)

However unlikely, it's this sort of dying to self and living toward others that Afendra and Agallos undergo. At one point the wind blows snow from the trees into the faces of Synodia and her friend as they search for Agallos, and as if reflecting on both snowflakes and faces, the narrator recalls Homer's account of Proteus, in which Homer "wished to show that one primary seed, embedded in the world by the Creator and procreating in infinite combinations, would produce such an infinite variety of individual types and forms that no two leaves are alike, as that truest of sayings goes" (238). For Papadiamandis, we are all uniquely protean, all fey folk, people fated to die and "tetched," fairy people who may transform in a twinkling of an eye from lonely dawdlers avoiding each other to families walking home together in the morning light. Crucial to Papadiamandis' sensibility is the way this fairy magic is mediated through the material, quotidian world of hearing chant and bathing children. In the related story "At St. Anastasa's," we witness villagers' petty rivalries and eventual reconciliations alongside their painstaking hike through the mountains to celebrate Pascha (Easter) in an abandoned church. The signature of Papadiamandis' Orthodox realism is always this oscillation: from singing "Christ is risen" to hollering to every-one to mount the donkeys and clamber up the hill; from standing in a heavenly church in prayer to suddenly being distracted by a rival; from receiving Holy Communion to passing the flask in a gesture of forgiveness at the meal afterward. It is the attempted return to Paradise, precisely in its material, everyday labor, in its prosaic reality, that is the appeal of the story and that reveals how repentance turns us, toward love and our neighbor.

In a rare metafictional prologue to the story "Easter Chanter," Papadia-mandis addressed highbrow critics' complaints against his writing:

> What talent, pray, or power or originality can there be in someone's taking the trouble to describe in detail how a village priest went to celebrate the liturgy in a country chapel for a little community of peasants or shepherds, who and how many took part in the festival, and what their customs were like? ... We want a story which is all poetry, not the prose of everyday reality. (265–266)

This "prose of everyday reality" Papadiamandis sees as the heart of their complaint and the grit of good writing, and it is not so much a function of Papadiamandis' much-remarked aesthetic realism as it is of what we may call his incarnational realism, the living literariness of his Orthodox spiritu-ality, a sense of writing one's story and life synergistically with God, in the daily details of living and turning one's heart and mind toward God and others. Even in responding to his critics, Papadiamandis leaves them their freedom, merely staking out his own. Eschewing both displays of "original-ity" that critics would praise and moralizing fiction's treading upon readers' freedom, he says simply, "For my part, as long as I live and breathe and am of sound mind, I will never cease, especially during these resplendent [pas-chal] days, to praise and adore Christ, to depict nature lovingly, and to represent with affection those customs which are authentically Greek" (267): a manifesto, of sorts, for an Orthodox literature – doxological, lovingly mimetic, and repentant, sorting through personal habit and cultural custom in search of what is authentic and true. The modesty of the short story form seems fitting for Papadiamandis' interest in *metanoia*: it exposes illness and can't help but hope and pray for a cure (for both Hadoula and the dowry system), but in Papadiamandis' gentle hands, it doesn't approach the scope of a grand theory or novel. It seems a form appropriate for whispering: *the divine, the most lofty, is always humble, humus, of the earth and relation.* Where Papadiamandis fleshes out that faith in the impoverished rural context of postindependence Greece, Steinhardt's memoir provides a gripping account of what it meant for a Jewish-Romanian intellectual to find and live out the same faith in the horrors of a Communist prison camp.

3.

Modernity often associates the experience of suffering with an inevitable loss of faith. Starting with Voltaire's reaction to the 1755 earthquake in Lisbon, most writers questioned the goodness and competence of a God who allowed suffering to exist when he could easily have created a perfect world. In our times, many individuals do not hesitate to confess a loss of faith when suffering affects them personally and argue that they can only wave goodbye to a God who has betrayed them and dashed their expectations of happiness.

The experience of suffering in twentieth-century Eastern European communist prisons, gulags, and extermination camps, however, produced paradoxical results. Public intellectuals who were labeled traitors to the new regimes and thrown into communist prisons and extermination camps walked out of institutions designed to crush religious belief either more ardent in their faith or having discovered a faith at which they had previously scoffed. Professed atheists (such as the Romanian philosopher Petre Țuțea, who jokingly asked friends and family to sacrifice a rooster to Aesculapius for him) were released from prison joyful and humble Orthodox Christian believers. Procrastinating intellectuals converted in prison, as was the case of the Jewish Romanian novelist, literary critic, and doctor in constitutional law Nicolae Steinhardt (1912–1989).[27]

Steinhardt was imprisoned between 1960 and 1964 for refusing to testify against his friend, the philosopher Constantin Noica – whose literary and philosophical gatherings he had frequented – and lived through the horrors of the worst prisons in communist Romania.[28] Interrogations were followed by beatings. Prison life was rife with more sophisticated forms of torture, which went beyond beating and starvation to sleep deprivation and solitary confinement, and being forced to eat excrement, climb up walls using one's finger nails, and stand for hours without support. Steinhardt converted immediately after his incarceration; upon his release from jail, he became a charismatic monk and priest and continued his literary career with a renewed and profoundly Orthodox Christian understanding of literature. "You don't need to have spent too much time in prison," Steinhardt argues in his groundbreaking memoir pointedly entitled *The Journal of Happiness*, published after his death, in 1991, "to begin to grasp deeper realities":

> What a human being is, what the human condition truly is, the way things are with us – and that Christ is there, two steps away from you, that He sees you, that He saw you, that He has always seen you – is something that one understands in a matter of minutes. (72)[29]

The experience of communist prisons produced a series of well-known literary works, the most famous of which is the Russian author Aleksandr Solzhenitsyn's novel *One Day in the Life of Ivan Denisovich* (1962) and his three-volume collected testimonies of survivors of Soviet prisons, *The Gulag Archipelago* (published in the West in 1973). Solzhenitsyn's work, which denounces the failures of the Communist system, its abuses and crimes, shows, as Daniel Mahoney puts it, the power of "literature as a humanizing vehicle of truth."[30] While Steinhardt's memoir undoubtedly reveals the powerful role of literature as a "vehicle of truth" to expose injustice and political corruption, its erudite and loving rereading of twentieth-century literature, life, and politics aims to unveil the truth of human nature in its unlimited potential for transformation and transfiguration in the likeness of God. Steinhardt, one can say, goes where Solzhenitsyn fears to tread. His touching sketches of life, which depict people in their ordinary moments of grace-filled peacefulness as well as moments of severe crisis, articulate the human condition as an eminently theological one, of a being who was created free to choose, to love, to create, to suffer, and yet to be happy. Through baptism, the human being becomes a child of God, called to do the impossible and be deified: "The Impossible. That is what is demanded of us. Otherwise there is no escape, no exit, no beatitude" (36).

The memoir begins with Steinhardt's deep anguish in the face of impending suffering: a journey from interrogation to sentencing in which, Christ-like, the author goes through fear of pain to trial, torture, and disappearance into the tomb of the prison. His falling into the depths of a Communist Hades, however, leads to repentance for his own sins and the sins of mankind and to baptism. In spite of his disbelief that such an absurd experience could happen to him, Steinhardt refuses to be lured by his interrogators' promises of release and instead embraces the casual courage of his Jewish father and the cultural roots of the Orthodox Romanian society in which he grew up. The morning of his final interrogation, his father gives him a brilliant final piece of advice while still "in his pajamas, small, fat, and joyful": "Make sure that you don't put me to shame. Don't be a scared Jew and don't shit your pants" (25). Throughout the interrogation, he resists the temptation to interpret his situation through the abstract lens of a surrealist painting, or a linguistic game pertaining to the *Nouveau Roman,* which could lead him to believe that his actions had no real consequences. Rather, he appeals to the common sense, pluck, and colorful language of the lower classes from the neighborhood in which he grew up. This common sense, he argues, was informed by a profoundly Christian understanding of morality and loyalty: "Whatever Judas might say, no matter how refined, impersonal, disinterested, and grandiloquent his motives may have been, the common sense of the people will always be able to translate his beautiful reflections into the hideous and mud-bearing word *traitor*" (312). Contrary to the tenets of psychoanalysis, Steinhardt argues, after hundreds of years of living a humble liturgical life in search of communion with God, the subconscious of a people can become clean "like the depths of a clear lake" (rather than ugly and murky) and peaceful, "the most important inheritance that the Savior bestowed on humankind" (163). For the rest of his life, Steinhardt will commend instances of the courage to face and uphold the truth in both historical figures and literary characters.

The experience of suffering leads Steinhardt to a quick awareness that Christ had died on the cross for him as well, and that he had fully experienced and redeemed its absurdity: "If He had maintained – in part at least – his impassibility on the cross, if He had not fully tasted of human despair, the event that took place on Golgotha would not have been – for philosophers, for priests, and for the masses – an opportunity to stumble and fall, but a 'scenario' or ritual, hence acceptable, palatable" (55). It is precisely from this marginalized, despicable, and grotesque position of suffering that Steinhardt understands the ability of the cross to recenter and transfigure the human heart, awaken its potential for love and kindness, and reveal the true walls that imprison it: "... if we understand just a little bit all the misery of envy and anger, the shameful, devastatingly shameful and pathetic ridiculousness of jealousy, envy and meanness, as they must appear to the one on the cross and as they certainly appear to the one in prison or on his or her deathbed" (376), he exclaims, our understanding of reality will be transformed. The figure of Don Quixote, with his ability to reveal a true, transfigured reality for his readers, through faith and language, frequently visits the pages of the *Journal.*

In a brief preface entitled "political testament" Steinhardt offers secular and humanly achievable solutions to the problem of suffering, which here he associates with any form of totalitarianism: the courage advocated in the works or words of Solzhenitsyn, Alexander Zinoviev, Matei Calinescu, Winston Churchill. The emphasis of the *Journal,* however, is on the mystical solution of faith as an "exit" from "any form of incarceration." Faith, however, can only be testified to, not offered as a political solution, "because it is the consequence of grace" (6). The memoir thus offers the reader a testimony not only of the beauty and dignity of human courage, but also of the profound theological implications of courage: the acknowledgment of human freedom. "We are asked to believe in complete freedom" (63), Steinhardt explains, accounting for the fact that he fell in love with Christ while behind bars, precisely at a time when he experienced no comfortable material props to sustain his faith, no promises of worldly happiness, and no physical freedom. Steinhardt's conversion happens after he had been beaten and tortured, had undergone a hunger strike, and suddenly found himself in a room that defied definition: "it is a cave, a canal, a subterranean gut, cold, and profoundly hostile, it is a sterile mine, the crater of a dead volcano, and a rather accomplished depiction of a discoloured Hell" (30). In this room, Steinhardt's understanding of faith and subsequent experience of grace is preceded and informed by examples of human generosity and dignity that overwhelm him. In the overcrowded "cell no. 34," he discovers intellectuals, aristocrats, and priests who spend their days offering courses in their own fields, teaching each other all the poems and psalms they knew, narrating all the books they had ever read. (Steinhardt himself will narrate Eugene Ionesco's plays to a highly engaged and fervent audience.) He meets young people who tend to the sick and dying at the expense of their own health and lives.

The generosity and self-sacrificial love he witnesses become for him a definition of true nobility and the core of Christian experience. Revisiting his existentialist readings, especially Jean-Paul Sartre's depiction of the nauseous and tainted world in which we live, Steinhardt draws the conclusion that "the existentialists' description is not an exaggeration; it's only the solution that is wrong. Or rather they don't know the solution: the piercing of the wall to Christ the comforter.... And it is a wonder: some of the existentialists were in prison: how come they did not find the way to go through walls?" (145–146).

The human spirit can go through walls precisely because Christ is present everywhere. It is in this horror-filled environment that Steinhardt has an experience of grace, which occurred in the ghastly environment of the infamous prison Gherla:

> The next night I fall asleep exhausted. And then, that very night, I am given a miraculous dream, a vision. I don't see the embodied Christ, but an immense light – white and bright – and I feel extremely happy. The light surrounds me from all sides, it is total happiness, and it sets aside anything else; I am bathed in the blinding light, I float in light, I *am* light and I exult. I know that it will last forever, it is a *perpetuum immobile*. *It is I*, says the light not through words, but through the senses – I understand that it is the Lord and that I am inside the

Taboric light, that I don't just see it, but that I live in it. And above anything else, I am happy, happy, happy. (94–95)

The experience of both suffering and joy leads Steinhardt to a renewed appreciation of literature and art. Literature, he points out, is the expression of human creativity in which authors imitate God: "Truly great writers build a world and creatures, just like God does" (60). The *Journal* asks a question that is still alive in the minds of students of literature and religion: "Many prison inmates as well as literary critics wonder: where is God in the work of Proust? Or in the novels of Mauriac? Where is He? Let me tell you where He is. He is not on such and such page, because the authors are not theologians. He is nowhere. He is everywhere, the same way as He is in the world" (59). Just as the walls of a prison cannot prevent man's communion with God, art, too, Steinhardt believed, is permeated by God's presence. Literary texts, one can say, are capable of bearing witness to what Steinhardt calls "THE GREATEST MIRACLE of Christ God ... the transformation of the creature" (45).

4.

Literary criticism today is grasping for language to speak about connections of literature to life that go beyond ideology replication and critical distance. Secular accounts including Rita Felski's *Uses of Literature* and Deidre Lynch's *Loving Literature* wade along the shores of religious discourse in recovering a language of literary "enchantment," while Alan Jacobs' *A Theology of Reading* dives deep into those waters to speak of loving texts and writers.[31] Eastern Orthodoxy is rich in its vibrant, living relation to literature, providing language to speak about its spiritual and communal dimensions. It models reading and writing that respect human freedom and eschew moralizing. Growing from a theology of divine-human communion and a spirituality of love and repentance, many Orthodox literary texts, like icons, call to readers with subtle, gentle pictures of beauty and repentance; in Steinhardt's words, in freedom they create worlds and characters, also free, in the midst of suffering and love, which mirror and call upon readers' interpretive freedom. This literature and the sort of reading it encourages cannot be cashed out as an academic methodology, but it may supplement the shortcomings of criticism that limit reading to critical analysis and speak to the readerly sensibilities that surpass them.

Notes

1 For scholarship and testimony about Pitești Prison, see www.thegenocideofthe souls.org/public/english/the-pitesti-experiment/.

2 Father Roman Braga, *Exploring the Inner Universe: Joy, the Mystery of Life* (Rives Junction, MI: Holy Dormition Monastery Press, 1996), 26.

3 See, for instance, the National Council of Churches statistics for 2006: www.ncccusa.org/news/060330yearbook1.html. A recent study of Orthodox demographics in the United States is Alexey D. Krindatch, *The Orthodox Church Today* (Berkeley, CA: Patriarch Athenagoras Orthodox Institute, 2008): www.orthodoxinstitute.org/files/OrthChurchFullReport.pdf.

4 The *Filioque* is a dogmatic claim about the Trinity, namely, that the Holy Spirit proceeds from both the Father "and the Son." This addition to the Creed was accepted by the Pope of Rome in 1014 and is rejected by the Orthodox and Oriental churches in favor of the original formulation.

5 Acts 9:2 and passim; 2 Thessalonians 2:15; Jude 1:3.

6 Vladimir Lossky, *The Mystical Theology of the Eastern Church* (Crestwood, NJ: St. Vladimir's Seminary Press, 1997).

7 Psalm 74:12.

8 Gen. 3:4–5.

9 Jean-Claude Larchet, *Therapy of Spiritual Illnesses: An Introduction to the Ascetic Tradition of the Orthodox Church* (Montreal: Alexander Press, 2012), 1.92–93.

10 Romans 5:14, 6:3; 1 Corinthians 15:45–49.

11 Larchet, *Therapy of Spiritual Illnesses*, 2.69–70, 2.72.

12 Ibid., 2.73, 74, emphasis added.

13 St. Symeon the New Theologian, *Catecheses*, quoted in Larchet, *Therapy of Spiritual Illnesses*, 2.83.

14 Dumitru Staniloae, *Orthodox Spirituality: A Practical Guide for the Faithful and a Definitive Manual for the Scholar*, trans. Jerome Newville (South Canaan, PA: St. Tikhon's Seminary Press, 2002), 137.

15 Kyriacos Markides, *Inner River: A Pilgrimage to the Heart of Christian Spirituality* (New York: Random House, 2012), 276–277.

16 Ephesians 2:8.

17 2 Peter 1:4.

18 *Divine Prayers and Services of the Catholic Orthodox Church of Christ*, compiled and translated by Seraphim Nassar (Englewood, NJ: Antiochian Orthodox Christian Archdiocese, 1979), 606.

19 Ibid., 638.

20 Braga, *Exploring the Inner Universe*, pp. 116–117, emphasis added.

21 Though, regrettably, not influential enough to have prevented Justinian I from closing the philosophical Academy of Athens in 529.

22 St. Basil the Great, "Address to Young Men on the Right Use of Greek Literature," translated in Frederick Morgan Padelford, "Essays on the Study and Use of Poetry by Plutarch and Basil the Great," *Yale Studies in English* 15 (1902): 99–120 (105).

23 Michael Warner, "Uncritical Reading," in *Polemic: Critical or Uncritical?*, ed. Jane Gallop (New York: Routledge, 2004), 13–38.

24 On the Orthodox theology of icons, see Michel Quenot, *The Icon: Window on the Kingdom*, trans. a Carthusian monk (Crestwood, NJ: St. Vladimir's Seminary Press, 1996).

25 Alexandros Papadiamandis, *The Murderess*, trans. Peter Levi (London and New York: Writers and Readers, 1983), 119. Subsequent references are to this edition.

26 Alexandros Papadiamandis, *The Boundless Garden: Selected Short Stories*, vol. 1, ed. Denise Harvey and Lambros Kamperidis (Evia, Greece: Denise Harvey Publishers, 2007). Subsequent references to his stories are to this edition.

27 In the anti-Semitic atmosphere that characterized Europe in the first half of the twentieth century, Steinhardt grew up with a keen sense of being neither Romanian nor Christian. Even if he was drawn to Christ, the *Journal* records his skeptical musings from the 1930s: "yes, but why would He want me?"

28 Steinhardt was condemned to thirteen years of hard labor and was released early when a presidential decree granted amnesty to all political prisoners in 1964.

29 Nicolae Steinhardt, *Jurnalul Fericirii* (Cluj Napoca: Dacia, 1992), Translation by Ioana Patuleanu; subsequent references to this edition and translation.

30 Daniel J. Mahoney, *The Other Solzhenitsyn: Telling the Truth about a Misunderstood Writer and Thinker* (South Bend, IN: St. Augustine Press, 2014), 80.

31 Rita Felski, *Uses of Literature* (Hoboken, NJ: Wiley-Blackwell, 2008); Deidre Shauna Lynch, *Loving Literature: A Cultural History* (Chicago, IL: University of Chicago Press, 2015); Alan Jacobs, *A Theology of Reading: The Hermeneutics of Love* (Boulder, CO: Westview Press, 2001).

13

PAUL J. CONTINO

Roman Catholicism

Pope Francis dislikes "theist gnosticism." His biographer notes that, as Archbishop of Buenos Aires, he rejected any "disembodied thinking that in Church terms could be expressed as 'God without Church, a Church without Christ, Christ without a people.' Against this elite, 'airspray theism' Bergoglio set what he called *lo concreto catolico*, the 'concrete Catholic thing,' which [he insisted] was at the heart of the history and culture of the Latin American people."[1] Indeed, "the concrete Catholic thing" can be discerned through the whole of Catholic culture. In its varied embodiments over space and time, the Catholic literary imagination remains rooted in the story of the Incarnation, of the God who "became flesh and dwelt among us,"[2] who redeemed humanity within the contours of a particular time and place, who ascended into heaven and remains in relationship through the Church – its sacraments and the mediation of its "great cloud of witnesses," the saints, both "the living and the dead."[3] Persistently, Catholic fiction images persons oriented toward sanctity, the universal call to holiness made possible by the Incarnation.

Like all Christians, Catholics affirm the reality of the Triune God who, in an outpouring of interpersonal love, created, redeemed, and sustains all humankind through the event of the Incarnation. However, Catholics understand redemption not solely in the light of Christ's atoning act on the cross but also through the prism of his entire life, as related in the Gospels and discerned in the present. In a first-century epistle, St. John testifies to what the apostles "have heard, what we have seen with our eyes, what we have looked at and touched with our hands, concerning the word of life."[4] "The world is charged with the glory of God," writes the Jesuit poet Gerard Manley Hopkins, and this is so not only because God made the world, but because he entered it – born from the body of his mother Mary, raised in a town called Nazareth, and befriended by disciples with whom he spoke, healed, ate, grieved, and rejoiced. The Catholic imagination posits "the priority of Christ" and invites the members of Christ's body, the Church, to "rekindle the Christic imagination" by remembering that God has visited God's people in the most surprising way, "infinity dwindled to infancy."[5] In this chapter, I will discuss the ways in which the Incarnation infuses the Catholic literary imagination in Dante's *Commedia*, Dostoevsky's *The Brothers Karamazov*, and an array of more recent narrative works and will suggest ways in which the works themselves operate sacramentally, moving their attentive readers toward the receptivity of grace.

I.

In his *Confessions*, St. Augustine exhorts his fellow pilgrims to "come down that you can ascend, and make your ascent to God."[6] The older Augustine describes his younger self Platonically striving in solitude to scale the heights of divine knowledge. And failing: "My weakness reasserted itself, and I returned to my customary condition" (7.17.23). For all his admiration of – even gratitude to – the Platonic writers, he cannot find anything in them like the Word made flesh dwelling among us. Later, when Augustine humbly falls beneath a tree in a Milan garden, he relies upon the guidance of a child, and he picks up and reads St. Paul's Letter to the Romans. In so doing, he experiences his dependence on God's grace and so finds the strength to turn to God fully. His own story of conversion thus follows the descent/ascent pattern of the Incarnation.

Similarly, Dante tries to climb up and out of a dark wood but is stopped in his tracks by the successive appearance of three beasts. Like Augustine, he needs the help of others, and the Christian community of heavenly saints responds to his plight. Divine love moves the Virgin Mary to help him. Mary asks Lucia, who petitions Beatrice, who commissions Virgil, and it is he who points Dante in the right direction. Dante must first descend into the infernal realm of damnation before he can ascend Mount Purgatory and rise to Paradise.

Why so? In Canto 1 of the *Purgatorio*, Virgil explains that Dante seeks his "liberty" (71) and that there was "no other way" (62) to liberate him but first to travel through hell.[7] The pattern is incarnational. As William Lynch writes in *Christ and Apollo*, a classic guide to the Catholic literary imagination, "the great fact of Christology [is] that Christ moved down into all the realities of man to get to His Father."[8] Augustine exhorted his readers to take Christ's descent and ascent as their own model. Like the young Augustine, Dante the pilgrim does not fully understand sin for what it is and requires this knowledge if he is to grow receptive to God's ever-available grace.

In the *Inferno*, Dante the pilgrim sees sin in all its solipsism and rejection of community. As he ascends Mt. Purgatory, however, he is greeted by souls who exude courtesy and hospitality. Every creature in Purgatory awaits a nuptial union with the loving Creator in Heaven. Each ascends three steps, an emblem for the sacrament of reconciliation. The first white step symbolizes penitence: all souls in Purgatory are sorry for the sins they've committed, for the good they've left undone. The second step, rugged, purple-black, symbolizes confession: all souls in Purgatory have confessed and publicly acknowledged their sins. The third step is blood-red and represents satisfaction or penance: each soul in Purgatory sets out to accomplish a purifying work. The human capacity to freely *cooperate* with grace is a recurring theme in the Catholic imagination. Dante depicts these souls as uniting with each other in their desire to respond to and cooperate with Christ's redemption through their efforts. In turn, God respects and fulfills the desire of his creatures. Thus these souls freely unite their sufferings with the salvific suffering of Christ. In *Purgatorio* we encounter a hope-filled, therapeutic suffering whereby, through grace, souls complete the human task of conformity to Christ through their final expiatory efforts. Forese Donati, one of the gluttonous who fasts while beholding a fruitful tree, explains this to Dante:

> "The fragrance coming from the fruit
> and from the water sprinkled on green boughs
> kindles our craving to eat and drink,
>
> and not once only, circling in this space,
> is our pain renewed.
> I speak of pain but should say solace,
>
> for the same desire that leads us to the trees
> led Christ to utter *Eli* with such bliss
> when with the blood from His own veins He made us free." (23.67–75)

The crucified Christ can utter *Eli* –"*Eli, Eli, lamma sabachtani?*," "My God, my God, why have you forsaken me?"[9] – with joy as the cross fulfills his vocation to restore the freedom of human beings. He restores their divine image, and so the souls in Purgatory begin to shine in the image of God.

In *Paradiso*, Dante evokes a fully purified community, grounded in the reality of a God who not only created us, but became one of us in the Incarnation. Throughout his ascent, Dante meets persons who conform to the model of Christ. Dante writes in terza rima but refuses to rhyme any word with "*Cristo*," thus revealing his reverence for the divine name.[10] But he is doing more, argues John Freccero: he is making a point about the way in which the Incarnation of Christ transforms time and changes history forever.[11] In the light of the Incarnation, we can discern Christ's presence recapitulated in those lives that conform most fully to his: in the past *prefigurings* of Christ – Abraham's willingness to sacrifice Isaac or Moses leading Israel from Egypt[12] – but also in the *postfigurings*. So, for example, Dante hears the Dominican St. Thomas Aquinas tell the story of St. Francis of Assisi, who weds Lady Poverty, founds an order, and bears Christ's wounds (Canto 11). Beatrice herself is analogous to Christ, and St. Bernard tells the pilgrim that Mary's face is that which "most resembles" the face of her Son (32.85). It is crucial, however, to remember that any human analogy of the divine indicates similarity but an even greater dissimilarity to the divine. For Dante, Beatrice, and all the saints are not idols but icons, pointing the pilgrim *to* God, the source of grace. Thus Beatrice's smile is radiant when Dante's "love was so set on Him / that it eclipsed Beatrice in forgetfulness" (10.59–60).

Near the conclusion of the *Paradiso*, Dante discerns an astonishing image, a fiery point of light, from which "depend the heavens and all nature" (28.42). Dante's understanding of the cosmos is now radically inverted. For this *"punto"* – the luminous, loving mind of God – and not our "little patch of earth" (22.151), is the true center of the universe, the "hidden ground of love"[13] in whom "we live and move and have our being."[14] Dante's attention is increasingly drawn into that central point until, through the loving mediation of the saints, the point reveals its trinitarian and incarnate form: three circles, each "reflected by the other / as rainbow is by rainbow, while the third seemed fire, / equally breathed forth by one and by the other" (33.118–20). Dante discerns the human image to be incarnately inscribed within the Trinity, tries to understand how this might be, and, in his insufficiency, finds himself transformed, the pilgrim become poet, ready to write his *Commedia*:

> Here my exalted vision lost its power.
> But now my will and my desire, like wheels revolving
> With an even motion, were turning with
> The Love that moves the sun and all the other stars. (33.142–145)

Sustained by divine love, wielding words with all their limitations, Dante the poet offers the *Commedia*, an invitation to his fellow pilgrims to follow his path to God.

2.

If Dante sought readerly conversion, so too did Dostoevsky, especially in his final novel. When readers surrounded him and testified to the transformative power of *The Brothers Karamazov*, he wrote joyfully to his wife Anna:

"A host of people, youths and greybeards and ladies, rushed toward me exclaiming, 'You're our prophet. We've become better people since we read *The Karamazovs.*'"[15] In the chapter "Cana of Galilee," Alyosha Fyodorovich Karamazov – the novel's "hero" – receives a vision akin to that of Dante's.[16] Alyosha's spiritual elder, Father Zosima, has commissioned him to "sojourn in the world like a monk" (285), but his first days are blackened by failures, and by the third day, he rebels against what he perceives to be God's injustice. Zosima has died, and his reputation is shamed when his body decays prematurely, "by three o'clock in the afternoon" (330). Alyosha goes to Grushenka, a woman with whom both his father and his brother fancy themselves in love, with the aim of ruining himself. But to his surprise the two exchange small acts of loving attention that prove restorative. As did Dante with Beatrice, Alyosha finds grace in the face of a beloved woman, Grushenka, who "raise[s] his soul from the depths."[17] Back in the monastery, beside the elder's coffin, he encounters the risen Zosima, who joyfully directs Alyosha's attention to the transfigured, risen Christ. Alyosha awakens after a vision of paradise, a Cana of communal beatitude. Like Dante, he is now ready to embrace his vocation – not as a poet but as "a monk in the world" (Norton, 247).

Brief, poetic "Cana of Galilee" invites a close reading and suggests that this avowedly anti-Catholic author nevertheless reveals a deeply Catholic vision, certainly consonant with his own Orthodox tradition but also full of Dantean resonances,[18] revealing its "interior affinity" to Catholicism.[19] Moreover, it displays what I have called Dostoevsky's incarnational realism, grounded as his faith is in Christ the Word made flesh.[20] In "Cana" he perceives the wedding of the finite and eternal, and the reverberations remain with him "for the rest of his life."

Alyosha arrives back in the monastery a little after 9 p.m. In a novel in which "triads dominate" and one can discern a "Trinitarian theology,"[21] the number nine (which Dante links with Beatrice in his earlier *Vita Nuova*) squares, and thus accentuates, the number three. Zosima's shaming culminates around 3 p.m., the hour of Christ's death; near 9 p.m. Alyosha will witness Christ's resurrected life.[22] Despite his late arrival, "the gatekeeper let him in by a special entrance"– one among many casuistic loopholes in a novel shot through with scenes of surprising grace. Like the disciples in the upper room after Christ's crucifixion, Alyosha is "timid" when he opens the door to the room where Zosima's body lies in the coffin. Father Paissy reads from the Gospel of John, and Alyosha kneels and prays. Read in the light of *Paradiso*'s final canto, the "slow and calm rotation" of impressions within Alyosha's soul, the "sweetness in his heart," the "joy singing in his mind," recalls Dante's soul as it rotates "like wheels revolving / with an even motion," "by the Sun and the other stars." Alyosha falls before the coffin "as if it were a holy thing," made sacramental by virtue of the holy man who lies within. Alyosha loves the story of the wedding of Cana, the miracle that Jesus never expected to perform, just as Alyosha never expected to experience a miracle with Grushenka (358); these miracles are both gratuitous and purposeful. In what might be called an Ignatian composition of place, a Catholic spiritual exercise that invites the imagining a specific scriptural place,[23] Alyosha employs his senses to imagine the scene at Cana: he hears Mary noting the lack of wine and sees Jesus' quiet, meek smile when he responds by saying, "Mine hour is not yet come." But his mother knows that Jesus descended into our human condition, that he "came down ... not just for his great and awful deed" but for just such prosaic events as this one, "the simple, artless merrymaking of some uncouth, uncouth but guileless beings who lovingly invited him to their poor marriage feast."[24] Mary's mediatory, motherly presence is prominent in Alyosha's comforting, "assuaging" vision, just as it is at the beginning of *Paradiso* 33, and is notable in a novel of brothers bereft of mothers.

Throughout the chapter, readers can discern a "both/and" perspective running through Alyosha's experience of "the wholeness of things" (Norton, 309), rooted in the Incarnation and deeply characteristic of the Catholic imagination.[25] Once the water is made wine, Alyosha feels "the walls of the room opening out." To his surprise, Alyosha sees Zosima at the wedding feast, which is now turned heavenly banquet and over which the transfigured, risen Christ presides. Here Dostoevsky's "both/and" imagination can discerned in three ways. First, Christ is presented as both immanent and transcendent. Zosima exhorts Alyosha to be not afraid and to begin his work by looking at the image of the risen Christ: "our Sun, do you see him?" Earlier, Zosima had insisted that if "we ... did not have the precious image of Christ before us, we would perish and be altogether lost" (320); now he affirms the paradoxical power of that image: "Awful is his greatness before us, he became like us out of love, and he is rejoicing with us, transforming water into wine, that the joy of his guests may not end." Second, Alyosha's emotional state is marked by both joy and pain, wholeness and self-emptying: "Something burned in Alyosha's heart, something suddenly filled him almost painfully, tears of rapture nearly burst from his soul." Third, as he awakens and gazes for thirty seconds upon the body of Zosima, he recognizes his friend as both dead, "stretched out with an icon on his chest," and risen, as Zosima's "voice was still sounding in his ears."

Here this symphonic chapter reaches its final movement. "Yearning for freedom, space, vastness," Alyosha hurries outside, and in the starlit August night we discern three more "both/and" moments. First, Alyosha perceives the nuptial union of infinite and finite, the way "seeds from other worlds" sprout on earth, and how all thus "lives and grows only through its sense of being in touch with other mysterious worlds" (320). Seeing "shining stars," "golden domes," sleeping flowers, he hears the way "the silence of the earth seemed to merge with the silence of the heavens, the mystery of the earth touched the mystery of the stars." Second, Alyosha – like Zosima in his dying moment – both descends and ascends: a profound impulse of love and memory propels him to fall upon the feminine earth in an open-armed gesture that suggests both *eros* ("he long[s] to kiss it, to kiss all of it") and *agape* ("He wanted to forgive everyone"), the synthesis of which is *caritas*.[26]

Third, and finally, Alyosha's experience is both solitary and communal. No one sees his ecstasy; another priest Father Paissy, notices him leaving the elder's room but tactfully "look[s] away again at once, realizing that something strange was happening with the boy." Alone upon the earth Alyosha weeps for his fellow creatures, for "the stars that shone on him from the abyss," and for his fellow human persons: "He wanted to forgive everyone and for everything, and to ask forgiveness, oh, not for himself! But *for all* and for everything, 'as others are asking for me'...." I see the phrase "for all" as providing the linguistic key to the novel, and its continued repetitions forges a "both/and" unity that suggests both that divine grace is freely given for all and that we each are responsible for all. Later in the novel, Alyosha responds to his brother Ivan's searing cry for justice by pointing to the Christ who comes as "ransom for many," the "Being [who] can forgive everything, forgive all *and for all*," "because he himself gave his innocent blood for all and for everything" (246, emphasis in original). The phrase "for all" is also repeated by Zosima, but in a context that suggests the necessary human cooperative, synergistic response to the Incarnation: "There is only one salvation for you: take yourself up and make yourself responsible *for all* the sins of men" (320, emphasis added). "For all" is the phrase that links the dual claims of the Christian life, the gift received as task: Christ's work redeems all and we must work responsibly for all. "For all" is also drawn from the Eucharistic prayer in the Orthodox liturgy – "In behalf of all and for all"[27] – as is the phrase "unto ages of ages," repeated three times in this chapter and again on the final page of the novel. Alyosha's mystical moment in solitude is situated in the communal context of the liturgy of the Church.[28]

In "Cana of Galilee" Alyosha has grown fully capable to apprehend and respond to the real. Like Dante, who in his final canto sees that God's light "contain[s], / by love into a single volume bound, / the pages scattered through the universe" (33.85–87), Alyosha senses the integral wholeness of reality, as "those innumerable worlds of God all came together in his soul."

Discerning that "grace is everywhere,"[29] he rises up "a fighter, steadfast for the rest of his life," remembering always that "someone visited my soul at that hour." Three days later, he departs the monastery to begin his work.

In this chapter, Dostoevsky invites the reader to perceive the reality of things, the way the Incarnation has linked the earthly with the infinite. The novel's "prosaics of conversion" present the sublime, humble image of Christ, in whom Dostoevsky saw "nothing more beautiful."[30] Christ descends into the limited and particular contours of human life and – in the words of Hopkins – "plays in ten thousand places," including the "limbs," "eyes," and "face" of Grushenka, Zosima, and Alyosha. In the incarnational realism of *The Brothers Karamazov* – accentuated here through a Catholic critical lens – the salvific image of Christ calls the reader to contemplate this presence and, possibly, be reformed in the process.

3.

The portrayal of characters oriented toward sanctity continues to inform Catholic fiction in both classic and contemporary novels. These characters reflect the variety of possible forms that "the good life" of holiness can take, for in each work the path to sanctity is particular to that character. A number of "Catholic works" focus upon characters committed to the vocation of priest or nun. In the great but underread Italian novel *The Betrothed* (1827), Alessandro Manzoni portrays the historical Cardinal Federigo Borromeo of Milan, who extends radical kindness to the villainous "Unnamed," and – like Father Zosima – mediates a gracious transformation: the Unnamed "raised his eyes to that man's face, he felt himself more and more penetrated by powerful yet gentle feelings of veneration" (414). In the twentieth century, we find images of priests who believe they are falling short of their vocation. In Graham Greene's *The Power and the Glory* (1940), the unnamed "whisky priest" considers himself an utter failure but remains committed to the beleaguered poor of Mexico. Ultimately, he gives up his life to provide the sacraments and sacramental presence that the oppressive government has forbidden them. He is moved to do so because he sees the image of God in each person he serves. Imprisoned, he reflects: "When you visualized a man or a woman carefully, you could always begin to feel pity – that was the quality God's image carried with it. When you saw the lines at the corners of the eyes, the shape of the mouth, how the hair grew, it was impossible to hate. Hate was just a failure of the imagination."[31] Similar is Father Jerome Strozzi, the hero of Jean Sulivan's *Eternity, My Beloved* (1966). For Father Jerome, the divine image is present everywhere, as he explains to the narrator toward the end of the novel,

"As I've often told you, I instinctively see Jesus, Son of God, in every human being. God has no other image except the face of a person, every person."[32]

By his acceptance of martyrdom for his faith, Greene's whisky priest stands in contrast to Father Rodrigues, the Jesuit missionary to Japan in Shusaku Endo's *Silence* (1966).[33] Rodrigues symbolically renounces his faith by stamping upon an image of Christ. Paradoxically, he feels closer to Christ in the aftermath of his apostasy because he joins Christ in his humiliation for the sake of others. Perhaps the most memorable example of a priest who feels failed yet remains attentive to others is the nameless hero of Georges Bernanos' *Diary of a Country Priest* (1936). Yet the final words of his diary suggest a movement toward graced self-acceptance: "I am reconciled to myself, to the poor, poor shell of me. How easy it is to hate oneself! True grace is to forget. Yet if pride could die in us, the supreme grace would be to love oneself in all simplicity – as one would love any one of those who themselves have suffered and loved in Christ."[34] His final words echo St. Therese of Lisieux: "All is grace."

The tone of graced self-acceptance pervades the concluding scenes in stories of others who take on the religious life. In J.F. Powers' "Lions, Harts, and Leaping Does" (1963) the dying Father Didymus finally discerns the saintliness of his simple caretaker, Brother Titus;[35] in Edwin O'Connor's *Edge of Sadness* (1961), the recovering alcoholic priest Father Hugh Kennedy embraces his position at poor, declining Old St. Paul's parish and reflects: "I might, through the parish and its people, find my way not again to the simple engagement of the heart and affections [which he had found at previous parishes], but to the Richness, the Mercy, the immeasurable Love of God. . . ."[36] In Ron Hansen's *Mariette in Ecstasy* (1991), the heroine speaks in similarly graced, accepting tones as she writes to one of the sisters she had known in the convent where, thirty years earlier, she had been sent away because her mystical visions were judged fraudulent and disruptive to the community:

> . . . Christ reminds me, as he did in my greatest distress, that he loves me more, now that I am despised, than when I was so richly admired in the past.

> And Christ still sends me roses. We try to be formed and held and kept by him, but instead he offers us freedom. And now when I try to know his will, his kindness floods me, his great love overwhelms me, and I hear him whisper, Surprise me.[37]

Persistently, the Catholic narrative imagination suggests the presence of grace as characters pass through limitation, including the limits of human sinfulness. Sigrid Undset's epic trilogy, *Kristin Lavransdatter* (1922), tells the story of a fourteenth-century Norwegian woman who, against her father's wishes, enters a troubled yet passionate marriage with the excommunicated Erland, bears him eight sons, and lives through her husband's death and some of her children's before she herself dies during the Black Plague of 1349. Near death, just before receiving her final communion, Kristin gives away her wedding ring so that Masses might be said for a poor woman whom she had courageously defended from a violent mob. She perceives the imprint of the letter "M," the symbol of the Virgin, on her finger, and reflects:

> She had been a servant of God – a stubborn, defiant maid, most often an eye-servant in her prayers and unfaithful in her heart, indolent and neglectful, impatient toward admonishments, inconstant in her deeds. And yet He had held her firmly in His service, and under the glittering gold ring a mark had been secretly impressed upon her, showing that she was His servant, owned by the Lord and King who would now come, borne on the consecrated hands of the priest, to give her release and salvation.[38]

Similarly, Charles Ryder, the narrator of *Brideshead Revisited* (1945) and eventual convert to Catholicism, finally accepts the fact that "the worse I am, the more I need God."[39]

Narrative images of saints often suggest the saint's participation in the suffering of Christ. In "Parker's Back" (1965), the story she wrote upon her deathbed, Flannery O'Connor tells the story of O.E. Parker, who, to please his sternly religious wife, has an icon of a Byzantine Christ tattooed upon his back, the only spot on his body bereft of a tattoo. For his trouble, he is soundly beaten by Sarah Ruth, who turns out to be vehemently iconoclastic and condemns any imaging of the divine as idolatrous. Unexpectedly, Parker emerges as an image of Christ. When he submits to his wife's beating, he embodies the descent of Christ in the Incarnation, a movement known as *kenosis*: he empties himself of the will to resist and defend himself. The "large welts that form on the face of the tattooed Christ" form, of course, on his own flesh, and thus suggest his participation in the sacrifice of Christ, as does his later leaning and weeping against the "single tall pecan tree on a high embankment," itself an image of the cross.[40] In Oscar Hijuelos' *Mr. Ives' Christmas* (1995), the title character receives the grace that enables him to forgive his son's murderer and, in the novel's final scene, to discern the figure of the risen Christ, "placing his wounded hands upon Ives' brow."[41] In David Adams Richards' *Friends of Meager Fortune* (2006), the title character bears a beating for the cowardice of a fellow logger on Good Friday Mountain; broken, he "wink[s]" up at the man for whom he has suffered.[42] In "My Parents' Bedroom," the final story in Uwem Akpan's searing collection, *Say You're One of Them* (2008), a Rwandan girl witnesses the horrific murder of her mother by her own father. She sees, in the end, her little brother "playing with the glow of the crucifix, babbling Maman's name."[43]

Catholic fiction sometimes represents the power of the sacraments themselves, especially the Eucharist. In Larry Woiwode's *Beyond the Bedroom Wall* (1975), Alpha Neumiller recalls her conversion to Catholicism and her First Communion: "She'd converted because of the feeling of light, a light she'd sensed but couldn't quite see. The more she studied the Bible and the catechism, the stronger the light became. ... Since her First Communion, the light had stayed."[44] In Andre Dubus' novella *Voices from the Moon* (1984), twelve-year-old Richie Stowe has a similar reverence for the Eucharist and a strong calling toward the priesthood.[45] He begins a difficult day at Mass and concludes it lying in a baseball field, gazing at the night sky while holding the hand of the girl he loves. In the close of the novella, Richie learns that the *caritas* to which the Eucharist calls him includes both an acceptance of the cross – the renunciation that active love entails – and a grateful openness to the grace mediated by his girlfriend, Melissa. In a star-filled scene that recalls both Dante's final vision and Alyosha's descent to and embrace of the earth, Richie gratefully recognizes that he can love both Christ and Melissa.

4.

As Thomas Rausch notes, "Catholicism traditionally says 'both/and.' Not scripture alone but scripture and tradition, not grace alone but grace and nature, not faith alone but faith and works as well as faith and reason."[46] Allow me to add another pairing: Christians pray in gratitude for God's kingdom that is both present and yet still to come. In this life, limited as humans are within the constricted contours of time, place, and commitment, they nonetheless receive glimpses of eternal life, union with God and each other, the *telos* to which all people are called. At the end of his *Commedia*, Dante glimpses the communion of saints surrounding the Triune God of Love, but he must then return to his temporal exile in Italy and fulfill his authorial vocation. At the end of *The Brothers Karamazov*, just after they have celebrated the funeral service for a nine-year-old boy, Alyosha speaks to a group of twelve boys and exhorts them to remember their friend and the goodness and kindness that each one of them in their grief reveals to each other at that moment. The eldest and most precocious of the boys, deeply moved by Alyosha's words, asks Alyosha if it's really true that they will rise again after death. Alyosha, fulfilling his vocation as a monk in the world, promises them the joy of the resurrection: "Certainly we shall rise, certainly we shall see and gladly, joyfully tell one another all that has been." And then he walks with them, "hand in hand" to a traditional funeral dinner of pancakes (776). A contemporary image of communal pilgrim hope also occurs near the end of Alice McDermott's *Someone* (2013). Marie has a terrible, terribly real dream: that her son, Tom has been killed – by drowning or drunk driving. Weeping, keening, she pleads with her brother Gabe – who has left the priesthood – to "Ask": to "make it not real" (228), to intercede for her that Tom might be saved. She awakens. Tom is alive. It feels like a miracle: "I had asked and it had been given. His life restored" (229). She is "foolishly certain that it had not been a dream at all" (230), and in her experience – as in Dante's final vision and Alyosha's dream of Cana – the reader discerns subtle gleams of life everlasting.

In literary works born of a Catholic imagination, characters recurrently glimpse the promise of eternity within the impinging contours of their limited lives. But such a vision is ultimately "catholic" in the root sense of that word in that it runs "through the whole" of the Christian imagination – be it Catholic, Orthodox, or Protestant.[47] Witness the luminous work of Marilynne Robinson. Her saintly character John Ames – an elderly, small-town Iowa pastor who reads both Bernanos and Calvin – loves life and longs to "talk about the gift of physical particularity and how blessing and sacrament are mediated through it" (69). He reflects, Hopkins-like, on the sheer shining beneficence of reality and challenges his reader to summon the grit to accept the graced gift of the real: "It has seemed to me sometimes as though the Lord breathes on this poor gray ember of Creation and it turns to radiance – for a moment or a year or the span of a life. . . . Wherever you turn your eyes the world can shine like transfiguration. You don't have to bring a thing to it except a little willingness to see. Only who could have the courage to see it?"[48]

Here too we find this chapter's emphases: the realistic acceptance of limits, the proper place of suffering, the fallen yet sacramental beauty of creation, the inspiration of the saints, and the gift of grace.

Notes

1 Austen Ivereigh, *The Great Reformer* (New York: Henry Holt, 2014), 310.
2 John 1:14.
3 A phrase from the fourth-century Nicene Creed.
4 1 John 1:1.
5 Here I draw on the titles of three recent works of Catholic theology: Robert Barron, *The Priority of Christ: Toward a Postliberal Catholicism* (Grand Rapids, MI: Brazos, 2007); Edward T. Oakes, S.J., *Infinity Dwindled to Infinity: A Catholic and Evangelical Christology* (Grand Rapids, MI: Eerdmans, 2011); and Robert P. Imbelli, *Rekindling the Christic Imagination: Theological Meditations for the New Evangelization* (Collegeville, MN: Liturgical Press, 2014).

6 Saint Augustine, *Confessions*, trans. Henry Chadwick (New York: Oxford University Press, 1991), 4.12.19. All references to this edition.

7 Throughout, I cite the verse translation of the *Commedia* by Jean and Robert Hollander (New York: Anchor, 2000–2007).

8 William Lynch, S.J., *Christ and Apollo: The Dimensions of the Literary Imagination* (Wilmington, DE: ISI Books, 2004; 1960), 23.

9 Mark 15:34.

10 See Cantos 12.71–75; 14.104–108; 19:104–108; 32:83–87.

11 See John Freccero, *Dante: The Poetics of Conversion* (Cambridge, MA: Harvard University Press, 1986), 258–271.

12 Genesis 22 and Psalms 114–115.

13 The phrase is Thomas Merton's, the title of a collection of his letters: *The Hidden Ground of Love: The Letters of Thomas Merton on Religious Experience and Social Concern*, ed. William H. Shannon (New York: Farrar, Straus and Giroux, 1985).

14 Acts 17:28.

15 *Selected Letters of Fyodor Dostoevsky*, ed. Joseph Frank and David I. Goldstein and trans. Andrew R. MacAndrew (New Brunswick, NJ: Rutgers University Press), 504.

16 Except where noted, I cite the translation of *The Brothers Karamazov* by Richard Pevear and Larissa Volokhonsky (New York: Vintage, 1991).

17 For this phrase, I cite the Garnett/Matlaw translation, revised by Susan McReynolds Oddo, *The Brothers Karamazov*, Norton Critical Editions (New York: W.W. Norton, 2011), 302. Further citations from this edition will be noted "Norton" and cited within the text.

18 Ivan compares Orthodox depictions of hell with those of Dante at the start of his "Grand Inquisitor" (247). For the sake of coherence, I'll dispense with page references to this brief chapter. All quotations are taken from pp. 359–363 of the Pevear/Volokhonsky translation.

19 I draw the phrase "interior affinity" from Pope Benedict XVI, who cites Dostoevsky in his 2007 encyclical *Spe salvi* and who comments on the recent progress in ecumenical relations between the Western and Eastern Churches in *The Light of the World: The Pope, the Church, and the Signs of the Times: A Conversation with Peter Seewald*, trans. Michael J. Miller and Adrian J. Walker (San Francisco, CA: Ignatius Press, 2010), 87. Dostoevsky has proven influential to numerous Catholic writers, from theologians Hans Urs von Balthasar, Henri DeLubac, and Romano Guradini to novelists Georges Bernanos and Walker Percy to social justice advocates Dorothy Day and Martin Sheen. Both John Paul II and Benedict XVI cite Dostoevsky in encyclicals. For details, see "Dostoevsky," in *The New Catholic Encyclopedia: Supplement 2011* (Farmington Hills, MI: Gale Cengage). Recently Pope Francis has urged people to "read and reread Dostoevsky" "because he has a [great] wisdom." See: www.catholicnewsagency.com/news/full-transcript-of-popes-inflight-press-remarks-released/.

20 I analyze incarnational realism more fully in "The Prudential Alyosha Karamazov: The Russian Realist from a Catholic Perspective," in *Dostoevsky Monographs*, ed. Jordi Morillas (St. Petersburg, Russia: Dmitry Bulanin, 2015), 49–78.

21 David S. Cunningham, "*The Brothers Karamazov* as Trinitarian Theology," in *Dostoevsky and the Christian Tradition*, ed. George Pattison and Diane Oenning Thompson (Cambridge: Cambridge University Press, 2001), 141.

22 Another Dantean numerological link: If one includes the novel's prologue, "From the Author," *The Brothers Karamazov* is comprised of 97 chapters. Not the perfect 100 that comprise the *Commedia*, but just right for the open-ended *Brothers Karamazov*: the "missing" three chapters may be seen as gesturing toward the continuing, unfinalizable work of the Trinity.

23 For an analysis that suggests that Dostoevsky's attitude toward the Jesuits is more complex than usually acknowledged, see Paul J. Contino, "Incarnational Realism and the Case for Casuistry: Dmitri Karamazov's Escape," in *Dostoevsky's* Brothers Karamazov: *Art, Creativity, and Spirituality*, ed. Pedrag Cicovacki and Maria Granik (Heidelberg: Universitätsverlag Winter, 2010), 131–158.

24 The repetitions here – "uncouth, uncouth" – and elsewhere recall Book 6, the life of Zosima written by Alyosha in the form of a *zhitie*, or saint's life, the style of which is "rhythmic, sounds and words are repeated, especially *umilenie* (tender emotion) as noun, verb, adjective, and adverb." See Nathan Rosen, "Style and Structure in *The Brothers Karamazov*," in the Norton Critical Edition, 729.

25 See von Balthasar on Irenaeus: "[T]he reconciliation of the world and God, of nature and grace ... has its foundation in the one Incarnation. This indestructible interweaving of things is the true touchstone of what is Catholic" (*Scandal of the Incarnation: Irenaeus against the Heresies* [San Francisco, CA: Ignatius Press, 1990], 3). See Chapter 2 in this volume, especially Wilson's final observation of a Catholic aesthetics "that concerns itself ... with form as a whole and, finally, the whole of reality, created and uncreated."

26 See Pope Benedict, *Deus caritas est*: "Yet *eros* and *agape* – ascending love and descending love – can never be completely separated. The more the two, in their different aspects, find a proper unity in the one reality of love, the more the true nature of love in general is realized" (section 7). I develop my discussion of *caritas* (as the synthesis of *agape* and *eros*) in the second part of "Dostoevsky: *The Brothers Karamazov*," in *Finding a Common Thread*, ed. Robert C. Roberts and Scott Moore (South Bend, IN: St. Augustine Press, 2011), 254–271.

27 See Alexander Schmemann, *For the Life of the World* (Crestwood, NY: St. Vladimir's Press, 1997), 41. In *Dostoevsky: Language, Faith, and Fiction* (Waco, TX: Baylor University Press), 35–37, Rowan Williams discerns other Orthodox echoes in the "Cana" chapter.

28 Henri de Lubac writes: "Catholic spirituality has not to choose ... between an 'interior' and a 'social' tendency, but all their extended forms, in their extensive variety, will share in both." See *Catholicism: Christ and the Common Destiny of Man*, trans. Lancelot Shepherd and Sister Elizabeth Englund, OCD (San Francisco, CA: Ignatius Press, 1988), 343.

29 "*Tout est grace*," words attributed to St. Therese of Lisieux.

30 *Selected Letters of Fyodor Dostoevsky*, ed. Joseph Frank and David I. Goldstein and trans. Andrew R. MacAndrew (New Brunswick, NJ: Rutgers University Press), 68.

31 Graham Greene, *The Power and the Glory* (New York: Penguin, 1991), 131. My discussion of this array of more recent fiction, and some earlier parts of this chapter, are presented in different form in "Fiction and Catholic Themes,"

in *Teaching the Tradition: A Disciplinary Approach to the Catholic Intellectual Tradition*, ed. John Piderit, S.J., and Melanie Morey (Oxford: Oxford University Press, 2012), 151–169.

32 Jean Sulivan, *Eternity, My Beloved*, trans. Sr.Francis Ellen Riordan (St. Paul, MN: River Boat Books, 1999), 125.

33 Shusaku Endo, *Silence*, trans. William Johnston (New York: Taplinger, 1980).

34 George Bernanos, *The Diary of a Country Priest*, trans. Pamela Morris (New York: Carroll and Graff, 2002), 296.

35 J.F. Powers, *The Stories of J.F. Powers* (New York: New York Review of Books Classics, 2000).

36 Edwin O'Connor, *The Edge of Sadness* (Chicago, IL: Loyola Press, 2005), 637.

37 Ron Hansen, *Mariette in Ecstasy* (New York: HarperCollins, 1991), 179.

38 Sigrid Undset, *Kristin Lavransdatter III: The Cross*, trans. Tiina Nunnally (New York: Penguin, 2000), 422.

39 Cited by Paul M. Puccio, "Brideshead Revisited," in *Encyclopedia of Catholic Literature*, ed. Mary R. Reichardt (Westport, CT: Greenwood Press, 2004), 742. The two volumes of this *Encyclopedia* offer numerous discussions of Catholic fiction and offer a very good resource for anyone planning a course in Catholic fiction.

40 Flannery O'Connor, *The Complete Stories* (New York: Farrar, Straus and Giroux, 1971), 510. My reading comports with Michon Matthiesen's insights into the relationship between sacrifice and joy in her reading of O'Connor in Chapter 7 in this volume.

41 Oscar Hijuelos, *Mr. Ives' Christmas* (New York: HarperCollins, 1995), 248.

42 See Susan Handelman's discussion of "the subtle wink of God's answer to Moses" in Chapter 11 in this volume. And another alluring wink: in *Paradiso*, Dante asks if non-Christians can be saved and is soon answered by the appearance of pagans Trajan and Ripheus, "blessed lights" forming the brow of the Eagle, who "wink in concord" with the Eagle's words on the mystery of God's salvific grace. (Here I use Allen Mandelbaum's translation [New York: Everyman's Library], 20.146–147.)

43 Uwem Akpan, *Say You're One of Them* (New York: Little, Brown, 2008), 354.

44 Larry Woiwode, *Beyond the Bedroom Wall* (New York: Farrar, Straus, Giroux, 1975), 256.

45 Andre Dubus, *Selected Stories* (New York: Vintage, 1995).

46 Thomas Rausch, "Catholic Anthropology," in *Teaching the Tradition*, 36–37.

47 See Walter Ong, S.J.'s remarks upon being awarded the Conference on Christianity and Literature Lifetime Achievement Award in 1996: "The term 'Catholic,' already featured in the very early Church's creeds, today can refer more to present actuality and less to a promising future than it used to. Today Christianity is discernibly 'through-the-whole' – a better definition of 'Catholic' than 'universal' is." Available at www.christianityandliterature.com/Walter_Ong.

48 Marilynne Robison, *Gilead* (New York: Farrar, Straus and Giroux, 2004), 245.

14

MUSTANSIR MIR

Islam

To the Islamic scripture, the Qur'an, language is of central importance. The Qur'an relates how earlier prophets performed miracles to validate their claims to prophecy. Curiously though, Muhammad, the bearer of the Qur'an, never showed any such miracles, even when challenged by his opponents to do so. The only miracle he did present was the Qur'an itself. This fact assumes significance when we remember that the first addressees of the Qur'an were, unlike the believing Israelites addressed by the Torah, unbelieving Arabs. These Arabs were fiercely proud of their linguistic prowess – the word *'Arab* literally means "the articulate," the non-Arabs being called *'Ajam*, literally, "the dumb" – and their first encounter with the Qur'an was at the level of language or form rather than at that of content or message. What initially impressed the Arabs was the Qur'an's literary beauty, which eventually led them to accept the Qur'an as divine revelation. From the very outset, then, the literary aspect of the Qur'an has been inextricably bound up with the thought of the Qur'an – as borne out by the well-known theological-literary doctrine of the matchlessness of the Qur'an. Understandably, the Qur'an has served, not only for Arabic literature but, derivatively, for Persian, Turkish, Urdu, and other Islamic literatures as well, as a model of literary excellence and has influenced, at several levels, the vast and variegated literature produced in the many Islamic languages over centuries.

A short chapter cannot capture the variety and breadth of Islamic literature. I will, therefore, select two poems, one medieval Arabic and the other modern Urdu, to illustrate aspects of the intricate relationship that exists between language, religion, and culture in that literature. *The Wine Ode (al-Khamriyya)* by the Egyptian Sufi 'Umar ibn 'Ali ibn al-Farid (1181–1235) and *Satan's Advisory Council (Iblis ki Majlis-i Shura)* by the South Asian poet-thinker Muhammad Iqbal (1877–1938) might appear to belong in different worlds, but they are connected, across time and space, by their preoccupation with a set of themes central to the Islamic religious and literary heritage, with the Qur'an standing at the center of that heritage.

Ibn al-Farid's *The Wine Ode* deals with spiritual enlightenment, or love of God, whereas Iqbal's *Satan's Advisory Council* deals with the subject of creating a body politic on the basis of Islamic ethical and egalitarian principles, these principles ultimately deriving from the Islamic religious vision. *The Wine Ode* is addressed to the individual, or an individual who is a member of a select group – that of Sufi adepts – practically in isolation from the wider society, whereas *Satan's Advisory Council* is addressed to individual Muslims whose identity is defined and shaped through a close engagement with the social and political forces and challenges that make up the fabric of their environment. *The Wine Ode* speaks of an enduring state of human-divine intimacy achieved through drinking the wine of divine love; consequently, the poem's mood is uniformly serene, and may even be said to be marked by quiet jubilation. *Satan's Advisory Council* talks of a conflict-ridden world whose vicissitudes will eventually pave the way for an ethically fair and socially equitable system – that of Islam; the poem's mood, after fluctuating between self-assurance and anxiety, eventually becomes one of expectancy and hope. Philosophically, then, *The Wine Ode* may be said to belong in the realm of being and *Satan's Advisory Council* in the realm of becoming. *The Wine Ode* envisions the spiritual relationship of love between God and man in a state of perfection that suffers little essential change since the perfection is conceived in a metahistorical framework. *Satan's Advisory Council*, on the other hand, projects the emergence – or, rather, reemergence – of Islam as a just and compassionate system of life for humanity against the historical backdrop of conflict between rival systems of thought and practice. As such, *Satan's Advisory Council* possesses a dynamic quality or developmental dimension that *The Wine Ode* lacks. In spite of these differences, the two poems represent, in an elemental sense, motifs that run deep and long in Islamic intellectual and spiritual history. Stripped down to the bare bones, Ibn al-Farid's *The Wine Ode* celebrates individual enlightenment and Iqbal's *Satan's Advisory Council* underscores the importance of social salvation. Both these motifs are, each in its own way, authentically Islamic: they represent two major trends in the larger body of Islamic literature, and reading the two poems together furnishes a more rounded view of the nature of that literature.

I.

To see how these motifs are worked out in the poems, we turn first to Ibn al-Farid and *The Wine Ode,* a paraphrase of which may be found in

Section 4. Ibn al-Farid was born in Cairo, where he was educated and to which he returned after spending many years in Mecca. He lived a simple, solitary life, experienced trance-like states, and danced in ecstasy in public. Like several other well-known figures in Islamic history, Ibn al-Farid, a scholar of the law, is said to have "converted" to Sufism, such conversion stories meant to illustrate mysticism's superiority to law, while at the same time dispelling the notion that law and spirituality are necessarily in conflict. It will be instructive to look at the opening verse of *The Wine Ode* in some detail:

> *Sharibna 'ala dhikri l-habibi mudamatan*
> *Sakirna biha min qabli an yukhlaqa l-karmu*

> We drank, as we remembered the Beloved, a wine,
> Which intoxicated us even before the vine had been created.

Three words in the first hemistich are notable, the verbal noun *dhikr* (remembrance), the preposition *'ala* (upon), and the noun *mudama* (wine). *Dhikr* may mean both "remembrance" and "mention," that is, either "We drank wine when *we* remembered the Beloved" or "We drank wine at the mention of the Beloved." *'Ala* denotes "upon," meaning that we drank wine upon remembering the Beloved, but may also connote that the drinkers drank the wine in celebration of their relationship with the Beloved (toasting the name of the Beloved, to use modern terminology). As for *mudama* (wine), it is grammatically indefinite and can be interpreted as a noun qualified by the entire second hemistich: we drank a wine that had us intoxicated even before the creation of the vine. But the indefinite noun can also be seen as standing alone, concluding the sentence beginning with "We drank." The second hemistich then begins a new sentence, in which case the indefiniteness of *mudama* provides a kind of emphasis called *tafkhim* (magnification). In this case, the first hemistich would mean: We drank *a* wine, that is, a certain special wine – the indefiniteness of the word suggesting that the supremely exquisite wine was beyond compare and, therefore, beyond definition, indefiniteness of expression being the only recourse left for referring to it.

Furthermore, although *mudama* means "wine," the root of the word, *d-w-m*, has the essential meaning of "continuity," "perpetuity," "eternity," and, according to the lexicographers, one reason why wine is called *mudama* is that, of all the beverages, it is the one that can be, and is worthy of being, imbibed continually, regularly, or permanently. That the wine existed before the existence of the vine means that it is a spiritual wine drunk by spirits and not a material wine to be consumed by bodies. This wine, then, stands for the intuitive love of God embedded in human nature from preeternity. According to Qur'an 7:172, a favorite verse of the Sufis, in preeternity, God took out from the loins of Adam's children all human beings ever to be born and asked them if they acknowledged him as their Lord, and all responded in the affirmative: *a-lastu bi-Rabbikum qalu bala shahidna*, "Am I not Your Lord?" They said, "But yes, we bear witness." The words *a-lastu*, "Am I not?," have generated the Persian expression *sharab-i alast*, "The wine of *a-last*." In light of this Qur'anic verse, the wine in Ibn al-Farid's poem becomes the wine of a covenant between God and humanity, and intoxication by this wine means that human beings have willingly, and out of love of God, accepted the terms of that covenant.

Finally, the phrase *dhikr al-habib* (remembrance or mention of the Beloved) makes a clear reference to the phrase *dhikra habib* (remembrance of a beloved) in the famous opening line of the ode of Imru' al-Qays, often called the greatest of the pre-Islamic poets. The poet, accompanied by his friends, happens to revisit the dwellings, now in ruins, of his tribe and his beloved's tribe, and tears well up in his eyes as he reminisces: *qifa nabki min dhikra habibin wa-manzili*, "Halt, my friends, that we may weep over a beloved and a dwelling!"[1] But while Ibn al-Farid's *dhikr al-habib* makes an unmistakable allusion to Imru' al-Qays' *dhikra habib*, the referents in the two verses are different – a female beloved in Imru' al-Qays and God in Ibn al-Farid.

The most notable thing about Ibn al-Farid's *The Wine Ode* is its inversion of the Islamic legal prescription concerning wine. Wine-drinking is prohibited in Islam (Qur'an 5:91), which calls it a sin (Qur'an 2:219). Ibn al-Farid maintains, to the contrary, that not to drink the wine spoken of in the poem would be a sin (v. 25). His bold assertion is predicated on the Sufi view that the wine in question is that of divine love and is not material in any sense: it is limpid like water but is not liquid; it is subtle like the air but is not air; it gives off light but not as would a flame; and it is spirit but does not inhabit a body (v. 22). Intoxication with this wine drives sorrow away, making one lord of the world (v. 31; see also v. 7). Intoxication, rather than sobriety achieved through abstinence, is the valid norm, and those whom this wine intoxicates need not feel ashamed that they have committed a forbidden act by drinking it (v. 5). Those who live their lives in a state of sobriety and fail to become intoxicated with the wine are unfortunate and have wasted their lives (vv. 32–33). The poem turns the conventional Islamic legal vocabulary concerning wine on its head. But it does much more than legitimize the drinking of the wine in question; it gives that wine center stage in the Islamic framework of thought by appropriating for it several Islamic motifs.

Numerous verses in the Qur'an call this world a repository of signs (*ayat*) pointing to the ultimate reality, namely, God. This relationship between the signifier and the referent is reinterpreted by Ibn al-Farid in the poem, the wine's bouquet and resplendence now serving as the signs that lead one to the ultimate reality (v. 3).

Verses 7–20 of the poem are a sustained disquisition on the extraordinary, wonder-working qualities of the wine, and several verses in the passage explicitly or implicitly borrow from the Qur'anic discourse about miracles and may, in one or two verses, be alluding to the Bible as well. The wine has the power of reviving the dead (v.9), a miracle that the Qur'an attributes to Jesus (3:49), and, like Jesus (Qur'an 3:49), the wine cures even one born blind, endowing him with sight (v. 14); the Arabic word used in the Qur'an for "one born blind" is *akmah*, and this is the word used in Ibn al-Farid's verse. In verse 16, the word used for the act of healing performed by the caster of spells is *abra'a*, the word used by the Qur'an when it speaks of Jesus' healing of the born blind and lepers (3:49). The poem says that the wine makes the mute talk (v. 11) and makes the deaf hear (v. 14), miracles attributed to Jesus in Mark 7:32–37. These biblical miracles are not mentioned in the Qur'an, but they are not in conflict with the Qur'anic account of the miracles of Jesus – they, in fact, have an affinity with the Jesus miracles related in the Qur'an, most obviously with the miracle involving the born blind, and so may be called virtual Qur'anic miracles. While it is difficult to say whether Ibn al-Farid had direct knowledge of the Bible or part of it, some of the biblical stories of Jesus, as part of the popular religious culture, may have reached educated Muslims in his day. At any rate, it would be a natural extension of thought on the part of Ibn al-Farid to mention Jesus' healing of the deaf and the mute in conjunction with his healing of the born blind.

Verse 19 speaks of two qualities produced by the wine – *jud* (generosity) in a miser and *hilm* (patience, forbearance – or patient forbearance) in one full of anger – both qualities considered praiseworthy in Islam as in pre-Islamic Arabian culture. The word *jud* does not occur in the Qur'an, though the concept of generosity as such is very much part of the conduct prescribed in the Qur'an, which praises those who spend their wealth at all times, at night and during day, both secretly and openly (2:274). As for *hilm*, it is mentioned in the Qur'an as one of the attributes of God: he is *halim*, one who possesses *hilm* (2:225, 235, 263, and several other verses), and Abraham and Ishmael are each called *halim* (Abraham: 9:114; 11:75; Ishmael: 37:101). Qur'an 3:134 combines the virtues of generosity and patient forbearance, praising "those who spend of their wealth in ease and hardship and choke down their anger"), and one wonders whether, in combining the two virtues in verse 19, Ibn al-Farid was consciously following the Qur'anic verse. There is one other point to consider. The Arabs in pre-Islamic times saw wine and generosity as closely related: to get drunk and then give away one's wealth in a state of drunkenness – that is, in a state of disinhibition, when one does not fully realize what one is doing – was considered a laudable act. In combining wine and generosity, then, verse 19 of the poem evokes the motif of wine-drinking leading one to perform generous acts.

There is possibly deliberate ambiguity in verse 26. References to Christian monks are found in pre-Islamic Arabic poetry. In early Islamic poetry, those references came to include mention of wine-drinking, which, of course, could not be associated with Islam. The verse seems to have two almost equally valid trajectories of meaning, which, depending on one's perspective, may or may not be in conflict with each other. First, since, as several verses in the poem have already indicated, one does not actually have to drink the wine in order to become intoxicated with it, Christian monks, though they have not drunk the wine, have nevertheless become intoxicated with it and, as such, are the equals of Muslim mystics. On this interpretation, Ibn al-Farid would be including, under the broad rubric of the Sufi doctrine of divine love, members of an otherwise non-Muslim religion among the people of faith. Second, Christian monks, though they have tried to drink of the wine of divine love, and deserve credit for their attempt to do, have fallen short of their goal, whereas Muslim mystics – the verse implies – have both attempted to drink and succeeded in drinking the wine, Muslims thus being superior in rank to Christians. It seems that, in Ibn al-Farid's view, the first, mystically inclusivist interpretation would have an edge over the second, legally and theologically exclusivist interpretation, if on no other grounds than those of the verse's opening phrase, which wishes the Christian monks well, *hani'an li-ahli d-dayr*, "Good drinking to the people of the monastery," and concluding words, which commend the monks for at least making the attempt to drink the wine, *wa-lakinnahum hammu*, "but they did try."

2.

In contrast with the inclusive Sufi mysticism of *The Wine Ode*, Muhammad Iqbal's *Satan's Advisory Council* sounds a more overtly political note (a paraphrase of the poem can be found in Section 5). Muhammad Iqbal (1877–1938) was born in Sialkot (in present-day Pakistan) and educated in that city and in Lahore. He went to Europe for higher studies and, during his three-year stay there (1905–1908), graduated from Cambridge University, qualified at the bar from London's Lincoln's Inn, and earned a PhD in philosophy from the University of Munich. He wrote poetry in Persian and Urdu and prose in Urdu and English. He was active on the country's political scene as well: he wrote on political issues, served as an elected member of a provincial assembly, and, most important, proposed the creation of a separate homeland for India's Muslims – hence his reputation as the spiritual father of Pakistan.

The titles of Iqbal's poetic volumes – such as *The Sound of the Caravan Bell*, *Gabriel's Wing*, *The Secrets of Selflessness*, *Persian Psalms*, and *The Stroke of Moses* – indicate that he had taken it upon himself to perform a prophetic role for the worldwide Muslim community. It was Iqbal's wish to rouse Muslims from their long slumber and impress upon them the need to become, once again, active and productive members of the world polity. To this end, he urged Muslims to develop their potential both as individuals and as a collectivity, outlining in detail what has come to be known as his philosophy of selfhood (*khudi*). He urged Muslims, on the one hand, to reevaluate their civilizational heritage and, on the other, to learn from the experiences of other nations, with a view to charting their own destiny in the world.

Of the many novel themes in Iqbal's poetry, one pertains to Satan. Satan is an important figure in the Qur'an, where his personal name is Iblis (cf. Greek *diabolos*). Here, following, is the opening verse of *Satan's Advisory Council*:

> *Yih 'anasir ka purana khel yih dunya'-i dun*
> *Sakinan-i 'arsh-i a'zam ki tamanna'on ka khun*

> This ancient play of the elements, this vile world –
> A shattering of the fond hopes of the highest heaven's dwellers!

Iblis' words "This ancient play of the elements" (*yih 'anasir ka purana khel*) allude to a classic issue in medieval Muslim philosophy, namely, that of whether the world has existed since eternity, as the Greeks thought, or whether it was brought into existence at a certain time in the past by the conscious will of a mighty God, as Islam teaches. (The Arabic counterpart of the Urdu word *purana*, ancient, is *qadim*, which is typically used in Muslim philosophy in the sense of "eternal.") Iblis, as is indicated in several places in the poem, would not deny that God created the world, but, by uttering these opening words, he tries to diminish God's role as the world's creator, supporting, out of defiance rather than conviction, the view that the four elements – earth, water, air, and fire – have always existed and that their impersonal interplay constitutes a sufficient explanation of the workings of the world.

The Urdu word *khel* carries the twin meanings of interplay and drama: it is implied, first, that the world can be explained with reference to its constituent elements, there being no need to invoke an outside agency such as God to account for the world's existence, composition, and workings; and, second, that, since the world is like a stage on which a drama is being enacted, no serious or deeper purpose underlies the creation of the world, a view that contravenes the Qur'anic statement that God did not create the world playfully (21:16, 55; 44:38). The words "this vile world" (*dunya'-i dun*) reflect Iblis' contempt for the world, and this is ironic because his contempt for it does not lead Iblis to ignore or neglect the world; on the contrary, he is deeply interested in controlling it. Incidentally, the two words making up the Urdu phrase contain a wordplay. Both words are originally Arabic: *dunya* literally means "that which is closer *or* lower in physical terms" (hence the technical meaning of the earthly world), and from this meaning comes the transferred meaning of "that which is lower in value." The word *dun*, which qualifies *dunya*, means "low," the alliterative qualifier intensifying the meaning of lowness denoted by *dunya*. This base world, says Satan, represents a total frustration of the hopes and wishes of the angels, the inhabitants of the highest heaven, where God, too, dwells – the implication being that the angelic frustration is accompanied by divine frustration. The frustration consists in the fact that the great hopes that the heavenly host had attached to the human beings' creation and to their performance during their tenure on earth have come to naught – and they have come to naught, Iblis is gloatingly insinuating, because of his successful strategy to thwart the human project on earth. This is an allusion to Qur'an 2:30–39, in which, at God's behest, the angels prostrate themselves before Adam, God's caliph on earth, whereas Iblis refuses to do so, God subsequently sending all to earth, with enmity sown between Adam and Eve on the one hand and Iblis on the other. But in calling the human project a failure, Iblis is trying to preempt God, for the final verdict on that project is supposed to be announced on the Last Day and Iblis is already declaring victory in his conflict with humanity.

In his works, Iqbal seeks to present Islam as a religion with a dynamic and progressive spirit and a humane and egalitarian system of life. *Satan's Advisory Council* is part of that overall Iqbalian project, verses 46–53 recounting some of the principal features of that project as enunciated by the unlikeliest of speakers – Iblis himself. But Iqbal bemoans that the Muslims have forgotten the true nature of their own religion, that the religion that once made them a dominant power in the world has now been reduced to a set of mechanically performed rituals, and that especially their leaders, including both legal scholars and spiritual guides, have become tools in the hands of oppressive, autocratic rulers (vv. 7–13). Iqbal is unhappy that Muslims have for long viewed capitalism as sanctioned by their religion, even though capitalism flies in the face of the Qur'an (v. 46). In the poem, Iblis notes with satisfaction the decadence and abject state of the Muslims, but he is still apprehensive that the Muslims will rise again, challenging his dominion and implementing Islam in its true spirit (vv. 43, 48). Needless to say, Iblis' apprehension is Iqbal's hope.

There is no doubt that the Muslim world today is witnessing an internal struggle for the soul of Islam. In several of his works, both prose and poetical, Iqbal identifies various dimensions of that struggle – political, economic, legal, theological, and spiritual. Several verses in *Satan's Advisory Council* refer to the complex nature of the malaise from which the Muslim body politic is suffering: both the Sufi and the doctor of the law have become obedient servants of autocratic rulers (v. 10); Muslim theologians continue to discuss pointless issues (vv. 56–59); and the Islamic egalitarian outlook, meant to unify society, has been compromised by a divisive capitalistic outlook (v. 46). The grand result of all this has been devastating for the Muslims as a whole: their creativity has been sapped, their vision has become blinkered, and their ability to grasp, deal with, and adjust to the ever-changing circumstances of practical life at various levels has been severely impaired (vv. 60–62).

Iqbal's critique of Muslims and Muslim societies occurs within a concrete context – that of the West-dominated modern world. During his stay in Europe in the early years of the twentieth century, Iqbal keenly observed European life, culture, and politics, and throughout the rest of his life he remained interested in developments taking place in European societies. *Satan's Advisory Council* reflects Iqbal's view of the relationship between several competing philosophies in the Europe of his day. Democracy, originally introduced as an antidote to kingship, has become subject to manipulation by the powerful, with the result that kingship, with all the evils attending on it, has come in again stealthily through the back door (vv. 15–19). Capitalism, which divides the members of a society into haves and have-nots, has the blessings of Iblis, who, on the one hand, creates in the rich an insane love of wealth and, on the other, teaches the poor to accept their fate with resignation (v. 4). Communism teaches the have-nots to rebel against their rich overlords, thus threatening the capitalist system, which has Iblis' approval. Fascism, the Fourth Advisor on Satan's Council suggests, could be used to counter communism (vv. 24–25), but, as the Fifth Advisor points out, communism is going to prove a tough nut to crack, requiring Iblis' urgent attention (vv. 32–36). At this point, Iblis declares that Islam, not communism, is the real danger and that his and his followers' best efforts must focus on undercutting Islam's egalitarian vision for humanity. Briefly but trenchantly, Iqbal distinguishes between the communist and Islamic doctrines of the equality of human beings: communism, with its narrow economic outlook, uses conflict between the proletariat and the bourgeoisie to put its agenda into effect – the slaves uprooting the tents of their masters (v. 23) – but Islam, by declaring that a rich man's wealth is polluted unless he shares it with the poor, presents an ethical program for societal change in which the rich themselves become responsible custodians of wealth; the program, thus, ushers in a wholesale revolution of thought and conduct (vv. 51–52). *Satan's Advisory Council*, then, can be read as Iqbal's forecast of Islam's eventual triumph over the powerful philosophies of capitalism, communism, and fascism.

Iqbal's characterization of Iblis in the poem can be taken as a poetic *midrash* on the Qur'anic account of Iblis. According to Qur'an 15:39; 38:82, when God banished him from his presence, a vengeful Iblis vowed to mislead all of humanity but was told by God that he would have no sway over God's chosen people. Iqbal's interpretation of the Qur'anic portrait of Iblis adds a few dimensions to that portrait, but these are not incompatible with the Qur'an. Thus, Iqbal's Iblis, situated within the framework of modernity, carries out his promise of misleading humanity by creating and blessing political and economic systems such as imperialism, capitalism, and even democracy, which sow dissension and corruption and disrupt peace and harmony in human societies.

Arabic dictionaries explain the name Iblis as "one who has despaired," that is, one who has forever despaired of receiving God's forgiveness for his defiance of God's command to bow down before Adam. Seen in this light, Iqbal's Iblis, though outwardly confident and assertive, is not without his insecurities. In his opening speech, he claims to be master of the world: all events occur in accordance with his plans and wishes. Yet in that speech he makes an incidental remark – namely, that God, the artificer of the world, has decided to destroy the world (v. 2) – whose ironic potential is brought out only later, in his concluding speech. For the destruction in question is destruction from Iblis' standpoint: Iblis is afraid that Islam, a religion that declares all human beings to be equal under God, putting an end to man's enslavement of man, will once again rise and pose a threat to his sovereign control of the world; God, by allowing Islam to emerge victorious over rival philosophies and systems, is, Iblis says ominously, going to put a spanner in Iblis' works. Iblis' several advisors, while they each have distinctive personalities and their disagreement with one another makes for brief but high drama in the poem, are, in a sense, an objectification of Iblis' own conflicted state of mind. It is as if Iblis were holding a conversation with himself, the conversation culminating in a reassertion of Iblisic pride, the reassertion, in turn, accompanied by an urgently felt need to plan to control and direct the future course of events in the world. As such, the concluding part of *Satan's Advisory Council* constitutes an ironic comment on the poem's beginning: Satan inaugurates the proceedings of the council by claiming that his dominion over the world is unchallenged. By the end, however, his proud claim has been deconstructed, his initial show of confidence replaced by a deep and barely hidden anxiety. It is God, not Iblis, who remains sovereign.

3.

Taken together, the two poems studied in this chapter – one celebrating the covenantal relationship of love between humans and God and the other calling Muslims back to a just society in which all human beings are equal under God – revolve around the twin poles of personal enlightenment (*The Wine Ode*) and social redemption (*Satan's Advisory Council*), which are fundamental to Islamic culture. The poems draw their power, both of thought and of language, from the Qur'an, in which they are so deeply embedded.

4.

Paraphrase of The Wine Ode

[1]Upon remembering the Beloved we drank a wine, which intoxicated us even before the vine had been created. [2]Itself a sun, the wine has the full moon for its cup, which is being passed around by a crescent moon – many a star appearing when the wine is mixed with water. [3]Absent its bouquet, I would not have been guided to its tavern; and absent its brilliance, one would not be able to imagine it. [4]Time, however, has reduced it to a shadow of its self, its hiddenness comparable to concealment of secrets in the chests of the wise.

[5]The mere mention of this wine would intoxicate the people of a tribe – no sin or disgrace attaching to them. [6]It rose up from amidst the jars, disappearing, its name alone surviving in actuality. [7]If, some day, the thought of it crosses a man's heart, it would fill him with great joy, his sorrow gone. [8]If the drinkers were to look at the seal of its container, the seal itself, aside from the wine, would intoxicate them. [9]If it were sprinkled on a dead man's grave, the man's soul would return to him, his body reanimated. [10]Illness would depart from a hopelessly sick person placed in the shadow of the wall covered by its vine. [11]Brought near its tavern, an invalid would begin to walk, and, at the mere mention of its taste, the dumb would begin to speak. [12]Its fragrance exhaled in the East, one with a cold in the West would regain his sense of smell. [13]A man whose palm were tinged upon his touching of its cup would not stray in the night, his hand now holding stars. [14]One born blind would become sighted if it were secretly unveiled before him, and, hearing it poured would make the deaf hear. [15]If a group of horsemen were

to aim for its land and the group included one snake-bitten, poison would not harm the latter. [16]If the caster of spells were to inscribe the letters of its name on the forehead of one possessed, the man would become well. [17]If its name were written on top of an army's banner, the writing would intoxicate those under the banner. [18]It refines the character-traits of the drinkers, and so one lacking resolution is guided by it to the path of resolution. [19]It makes generous one whose hand has known no liberality, and it makes forbearing one who lacks forbearance in anger. [20]If the fool among a people were to kiss its strainer-cover, the kiss would make him privy to the meaning of its noble qualities. [21]They say to me, "Describe it, for you know well how to describe it." Yes, I do have knowledge of its attributes: [22]purity, but no water; subtlety, but no air; light, but no fire; spirit, but no body.

[23]These are the wine's good qualities, which lead its extollers to describe it, everything they say of it, whether in prose or in poetry, becoming beautiful. [24]Upon hearing it mentioned, one who did not know it is enraptured, as one longing for the woman called Nu'm is whenever Nu'm is mentioned. [25]They said, "You have imbibed a sin!" Not at all! I have only drunk what, to me, it would have been a sin to abstain from. [26]Good cheer to the people of the monastery! How often they have become intoxicated by it, without having drunk it, though they had intended to! [27]I had been intoxicated with it even before I came into being, and the intoxication will remain with me forever, even if my bones should rot. [28]You must drink it pure; but if you wish to mix it with water, then your turning away from the moisture of the Beloved's mouth would be an act of iniquity. [29]So get hold of it at the tavern, and have it displayed before you to the accompaniment of songs, for, served together with songs, it is a great treat. [30]This wine and worry never dwelt together in the same place for a day; likewise, grief never dwelt together with songs. [31]Even if you are under its intoxication for just one hour, you will see time turn into your obedient slave, all authority belonging to you. [32]One who lives sober has no life in the world; and one who does not die intoxicated with it lacks prudence. [33]So let him cry over himself, the one whose life is wasted and who has had no share or part of it.

5.

Paraphrase of Satan's Advisory Council

Iblis[3]

[1]This ancient play of the elements, this wretched world – it represents a shattering of the hopes and wishes of the angels residing in the highest heaven! [2]That craftsman, who called it the world of "Be!," is today bent

upon destroying it. [3]I made the Europeans dream of imperialism; I broke the spell of mosque, temple, and church. [4]I taught the destitute the lesson of resigning to fate; I instilled in the rich the craze of capitalism. [5]Who can put out the scorching fire of one whose commotions are fueled by the inner passion of Iblis? [6]Who can bring low the ancient date-palm, whose branches, watered by us, have risen high?

First Advisor

[7]This Iblisic system is, no doubt, firmly established. Because of it, the masses have become more deeply inured in their servile attitude. [8]Falling prostrate has been their lot from time immemorial; to offer the prayer without standing upright – that is what they are constrained to do by nature. [9]Ambition has no chance of being born, to begin with; and if it is born, it either dies or never matures. [10]Our relentless effort has borne this fruit, that the Mulla and the Sufi have become slaves to kings. [11]This was just the kind of opium suitable for the Eastern temperament, for, otherwise, theology is in no way inferior to the tediously repetitive chorus, *qawwali*. [12]What if the hustle and bustle of pilgrimage and circumambulation still exists – the sheathless sword of the believer is blunted! [13]Of whose despair does this new edict furnish conclusive evidence – "Jihad is forbidden to Muslims in this age!"?

Second Advisor

[14]Is the clamor about the rule of the people something good or bad? You are not well informed about the fresh troubles brewing in the world!

First Advisor

[15]I am, but my insight into the world tells me that no danger is posed by what is only a guise for kingship. [16]We ourselves dressed kingship up as democracy when Adam became self-aware and self-observant. [17]The reality of kingship is quite different; it is not dependent upon the existence of the so-called ruler or sultan. [18]Be it the parliament of a nation or the court of King Parwez – the sultan is one who eyes the field of others. [19]Have you not seen the democratic system of the West? It has a bright face, but its inward is darker than Genghiz's!

Third Advisor

[20]There would be no cause for worry if sultanship remained alive in spirit. [21]But how does one counter the mischief of that Jew – that Moses without an epiphany, that Christ without a cross, the one who is no prophet, and yet carries a scripture under his arm? [22]How can I describe that infidel's veil-rending looks, which would usher in a day of reckoning for the nations of

East and West! ²³How much further could human nature degenerate, for the slaves have cut the ropes of their masters' tents?

Fourth Advisor

²⁴For its antidote, look to the halls of the Great Rome: We have again shown Caesar's dream to Caesar's progeny. ²⁵Who is clinging to the waves of the Mediterranean Sea – rising like a pine at times, lamenting like a rebeck at others?

Third Advisor

²⁶I am not quite convinced of his prudence, considering how he has exposed European politics!

Fifth Advisor

(addressing Iblis)

²⁷You, whose ardent breath sets the world's affairs in order – you have, whenever you wished, disclosed all hidden things. ²⁸Your fiery warmth has turned clay and water into a vibrant, passion-filled world, and your instruction has turned the simpleton of paradise into an astute being.²⁹ He, who is known to simple-minded people as Providence, does not know human nature more intimately. ³⁰Those whose only vocation was to declare God holy, glorify Him, and circumambulate His throne – your fierce sense of honor has made them hang their heads in everlasting shame. ³¹Although the sorcerers of Europe are all your acolytes, I no longer trust their sagacity. ³²That mischief-making Jews, that incarnation of Mazdak's spirit – his craze is about to leave every mantle in tatters. ³³The wild raven is becoming the peer of eagle and hawk – how fast does the mood of the times change! ³⁴What, in our ignorance, we had taken to be a handful of dust has spread all over, covering the vast heavens. ³⁵The impending ordeal has caused such dread that mountains, gardens, and streams are all ashiver. ³⁶My Lord, the world that is solely dependent on your leadership is about to be turned upside down.

Iblis

(to his advisors)

(1)

³⁷This world of scent and color is under my complete control – the earth, the sun and the moon, and the layered skies. ³⁸East and West will watch the show with their own eyes when I warm up the blood of the European nations. ³⁹By heaving a single shout of *hu*, I could fill with craze all – the

elders of the church and the leaders in politics both. ⁴⁰Let the fool who takes it to be a glass workshop try to break the cups and pitchers of this culture. ⁴¹The needle of Mazdakean logic will not darn the necklines ripped by nature's hand. ⁴²How can the communist street-loafers frighten me – their lives in disarray, their heads muddled, their *hu* out of tune? ⁴³If I sense any danger, it is from this Community, in whose ashes there still exists a spark of ambition. ⁴⁴Here and there in this nation one can still see those who make their ablutions with tears shed at dawn. ⁴⁵One privy to events in the womb of time knows that the impending ordeal is not Mazdakism but Islam.

(2)

⁴⁶I know that this Community is not a bearer of the Qur'an: the same old capitalism makes up the faith of the believing Muslim. ⁴⁷I know that, in the dark night of the East, the sleeve of the elders of the Sanctuary is missing the white hand of Moses. ⁴⁸But I am afraid that the exigencies of modern times will disclose the Prophetic Conduct. ⁴⁹Beware, a hundred times beware of the Prophetic Code of Law: it protects women's honor, challenges men, and breeds men. ⁵⁰It spells death to slavery in every form – leaving neither emperors with the titles of Faghfur and Khaqan nor any beggars sitting by the wayside. ⁵¹It cleanses wealth of every pollution, and makes the rich trustworthy custodians of wealth. ⁵²The earth belongs to God, not to kings! – what could be a greater revolution of thought and conduct? ⁵³It would be best if this Code remained hidden from the world's eyes. We are lucky enough that the believer himself lacks conviction. ⁵⁴It is better for him to continue to be embroiled in theological issues and in far-fetched interpretations of the Book of God.

(3)

⁵⁵The man whose declaration of "God is Most Great!" breaks the spell of this six-sided magical realm – may his dark night never brighten up. ⁵⁶Is the Son of Mary dead or does he have eternal life? Are God's attributes distinct from His Being or His very Being? ⁵⁷Is the one to come the Christ of Nazareth or a Reviver with the qualities of the Son of Mary? ⁵⁸Are the words of the Book of God created or eternal? In what doctrine lies the blessed Community's salvation? ⁵⁹Do these Lat and Manat, deities sculpted by theology, not suffice for the Muslim in this age? ⁶⁰Keep him alienated from the world of action, so that all his chessmen on the board of life are routed. ⁶¹Our safety consists in this, that the believer should remain a slave until the Last Day, having renounced this inconstant world in favor of others. ⁶²Only that poetry and that Sufism will serve him well which hide from his view the spectacle of life. ⁶³My fear, every moment, is that this Community will wake

up – a community the true essence of whose religion consists in holding the universe accountable. [64]Keep him stupefied with meditation and reflection at dawn; confirm him further in the monastic temperament.

Notes

1 *Diwan Imri' al-Qays*, ed. Muhammad Abu l-Fadl Ibrahim. Dhakha'ir al-'Arab series 24, 4th printing. (Cairo: Dar al-Ma'arif, 1984). Incidentally, the indefiniteness of "a beloved" (*habib*) and "a dwelling" (*manzil*) in Imru' al-Qays' line is of the same type as that of *mudama* in the opening verse of Ibn al-Farid's poem.

2 The paraphrase is made from Giuseppe Scattolin's critical edition of Ibn al-Farid's complete poetical works, *The Diwan of Ibn al-Farid: Readings of Its Text Throughout History* (Cairo: Institut Français d'Archéologie Orientale, 2004; Textes Arabes et Études Islamique 41), 158–161 (Arabic section). Verses 23–30, probably an interpolation, have been left out, following the practice of some commentators (this means that the verses following v. 30 in the Scattolin edition have been renumbered in this paper, v. 31 in Scattolin now becoming v. 23, and so on). A short bibliography on *The Wine Ode* is as follows: Rushayyid b. Ghalib, ed., *Diwan [of Ibn al-Farid]*, 2 vols. in 1 (Cairo: al-Matba'a al-Khayriyya, n.d.), which contains the commentaries of Hasan al-Burini and 'Abd al-Ghani al-Nabulusi; Ibn Kamal Basha al-Hanafi, *Sharh Khamriyyat Ibn al-Farid li-Ibn Kamal Basha Hanafi*, ed. Idris Maqbul (Irbid, Jordan: 'Alam al-Kutub al-Hadith, 2011); Amir Sayyid 'Ali Hamadani, *Masharib al-Adhwaq* [Persian], ed. Muhammad Khwajavi (Tehran: Mawla, 1983); Reynold A. Nicholson, *Studies in Islamic Mysticism* (London: Curzon Press, 1994; first published by Cambridge University Press, 1921). Th. Emil Homerin, an Ibn al-Farid specialist, has written extensively on the poet and his work. See his *From Arab Poet to Muslim Saint* (Columbia: University of South Carolina Press, 1994); *Passion Before Me, My Fate Behind* (Albany: State University of New York Press, 2011); and *'Umar Ibn al-Farid: Sufi Verse, Saintly Life*, Classics of Western Spirituality Series (New York: Paulist Press, 2001).

3 The paraphrase is made from Iqbal's complete poetical works, *Kulliyyat-i Iqbal – Urdu* (Lahore: Sheikh Ghulam Ali & Sons, 1973), 647–657; the particular volume in the *Kulliyyat* in which the poem occurs is *Armaghan-i Hijaz* [*Gift of the Hijaz*]. While an extensive literature dealing with the major themes of Iqbal's poetry exists, there is a surprising dearth of detailed discussion or systematic treatment of Iqbal's individual poems. I am aware of three studies of *Satan's Advisory Council*, but none of them makes a close study of the poem's text *qua* text. The studies are as follows: A. Bausani, "Satan in Iqbal's Philosophical and Poetical Works," translated from the Italian by R.A. Butler, in *Selections from the Iqbal Review*, ed. Waheed Qureshi (Lahore: Iqbal Academy Pakistan, 1983), 286–336 (*Satan's Advisory Council* is one of the poems studied in this essay); Asloob Ahmad Ansari, *Iqbal ki Terah Nazmen* ["Thirteen Poems by Iqbal"] (New Delhi: Ghalib Academy, 1977), 182–203; and Rafi-ud-din Hashmi, *Iqbal ki Tawil Nazmen* [*Iqbal's Long Poems*] (Lahore: Globe Publishers, 1970), 148–173.

15

WILLIE JAMES JENNINGS

Protestantism

The word of God is in my hands and everything has changed. In many ways this idea is at the heart of the Protestant literary imagination. While Protestants may imagine their origins from Luther and his forerunners, the origins of their literary sensibilities lay closer in spirit to William Tyndale with both his vernacular translations and his theological vision expressed in works such as *The Obedience of a Christian Man*. Tyndale articulated two abiding sensibilities: first, that the word of God may be placed in the everyday language of the people and, second, that all our words and thoughts may be soaked in a scriptural imagination such that we need no ecclesiastical or political ruler to hear God's voice and know the divine dictums. Such sensibilities grew like a swelling tide that covered over countless women and men, drenching them in a biblical world the contours and extent of which many were never able to escape, even if they wanted to, even if they disavowed all claims to any real connection between human words and God's voice. The drenching was complete.

The Protestant literary imagination is a storied imagination, imbued with the compelling narratives of the Bible and a compellingly biblical way of narrating life. The Bible came to life – living, breathing, and moving – and this is what constituted the Protestant. Of course, there is a central element of theological protest against a lax Catholicism in the origination of Protestantism, but biblical literacy is the birth parent who taught Protestants the stories of their lives and which became the story of their life. Like so many others, the Bible was the book that introduced me to the book. It was the pedagogue that guided me in the joy of reading, writing, and discovery. Biblical literacy gave birth to literacy for me, but not only for me but also for much of the Protestant world. The Protestant story is the story of literacy in unanticipated hands, but with mixed consequences and mangled results. This chapter considers those mixed consequences and mangled results and their legacy in the literary vision of those who carry the imprint of its effects.

My goal is not to rehearse the influence of the Protestant Bible on Western writers or Western literature. Nor am I aiming at an argument for the continuing value of the Bible for understanding various literary traditions. That rehearsal and those arguments have been made elsewhere. I am concerned here with the social and political effects of the Protestant Bible and specifically the vernacular Bible for the emergence of world literature. It is that emergence that illumines the complications and possibilities of a Protestant literary imagination.

I.

Christianity is a translating religion. It does not exist apart from translation. Indeed the Christian faith's originating impulse beats with the heart of a God who became flesh in the specific history of a people called Israel. Jesus of Nazareth is the translating God, a God known in and through life in the womb of Jewish people. As historians Lamin Sanneh and Andrew Walls have so eloquently noted, Christian faith exists in the mode of translation as a Jewish faith traveled between languages, finding home in the semiotic systems of many.[1] A faith so characterized carries with it capacities for flexibility, malleability, and adaptability. These capacities, Christians believe, flow out of God's willingness to speak within the messiness of creaturely life and the instabilities of human communication. God's words are also inexplicably human words. The Protestant literary imagination circles around this conundrum and has always gloried in the journey of the translator. The translator is indeed a crucial but shadowy figure in Christianity, not due to nefarious activity but because she or he has been the necessary but unacknowledged background to making the faith come to life for so many people.

The translator working in places near and far gave birth to the vernacular Bible, and the vernacular Bible is at the heart of the blessing and the curse of a Western literary vision that builds and destroys at the same time. My goal here is not to rehearse the history of Protestant translations of the Bible but to register the longitudinal effects of that history on the literatures of many peoples, many of whom were to become Protestant Christians. The peoples I have in mind are all those affected by the long reach of colonial history. The emergence of the Protestant vernacular Bible (and with it what I call the vernacular habit of mind) coincides with the emergence of colonialist nationalism and the formation of racial consciousness.

The Bible translated peoples into a new world, and the effect of translating the Bible into the languages of indigenous peoples translated them into new configurations of their worlds.[2] Those new configurations centered on possession and ownership. European colonial settlers who came to the new worlds of Africa, the Americas, and other colonial sites came imagining themselves as the new Israel and predestined by God to take possession of the new worlds and its peoples for the sake of the gospel. Theological visions of providence and stewardship set the stage for a form of Christian witness and formation that encircled land, animal, and people inside domains of property and encased people in racial description and vision. The Bible in the modern world and the work of its translation grew on this diseased soil.

Encircled land, animal, and people and racially encased bodies was the volatile mixture that helped fuel the engine of nationalism. Nationalism is fundamentally about possession, and its logic infected the work of translators from the colonial moment forward. As the humanist Antonio de Nebrija wrote in the preface to his book on the grammar of the Castilian language, a book created by the use of the printing press and presented to Queen Isabella of Castile in 1492, "I have found one conclusion to be very true, that language always accompanies empire, both have always commenced, grown and flourished together."[3] Nebrija's insight (if we want to call it that) grew out of the counsel he heard given to the queen by her confessor, Fray Hernando de Talvera, bishop of Avila, who explained to her the value of Nebrija's innovative text. Rather than a Latin grammar, he had produced a grammar in the everyday language of the people. Bishop Talvera's explanatory logic was clear. He stated, "After Your Highness has subjected barbarous peoples and nations of varied tongues, with conquest will come the need for them to accept the laws that conqueror imposes on the conquered, and among them will be our language."[4]

If nationalism is fundamentally about possession, then the act of inscribing and codifying the language of a people is about self-possession and more. The lexicon from Portuguese and Spanish colonial expansion forward was aspirational. It was about raising the sightline of a people toward a wider horizon of significance. For Spain and the other colonialist empires, their language would expand to cover their new possessions, new lands, and new peoples. In such a vision, the Bible, which is the word of God for the people of God, became the Bible of the people, owned by a people. The renowned English pastor, poet, and hymn writer Isaac Watts (1674–1748) is a small example of this vision at work. In his translation of the Psalms he imagined this great treasure in the hands of British people for the deepening of their devotion to God and their country. He offered a vernacular Psalms that cultivated a sense of ownership. Take, for example, a few excerpts from his version of Psalm 147, Part 2.

O Britain, praise thy mighty God,
And make his honor known abroad,
He bid the ocean round thee flow;
Not bars of brass could guard thee so.

The children are secure and blest;
Thy shores have peace, thy cities rest;
He feeds thy sons with finest wheat,
And adds his blessing to their meat.

He bids the southern breezes blow;
The ice dissolves, the waters flow;
But he hath nobler works and ways
To call the Britons to his praise.

To all the isle his laws are shown,
His gospel through the nation known;
He hath not thus revealed his word
To every land: Praise ye the Lord.[5]

Gone from the Psalm is the addressee Israel. "Praise the LORD, O Jerusalem; praise thy God, O Zion" (Psalm 147:12 KJV) has been replaced with an admonition to the British people. This change of address reflects the replacement of Israel by the Christian church as the chosen people of God, which theologians term "supersessionism," which embedded itself inside the work of translation and grew with the vernacular habit of mind. Israel is replaced with another people, not only equally people of God but preferred people of God given their commitment to the gospel. Watts performs a sensibility that grew with Protestantism and its literary imagination – that the vernacular Bible is the word of God for every people, resting in their language and exalting their own voice as incarnate site of the divine voice. This is not a bad thing, but coupled with its colonial contexts it became a mangled and diseased thing.

The Bible became an agent and engine of cultural nationalism. The Bible from the modern colonial enterprise forward would be caught up within the struggle between colonial nations for geographic and literary supremacy. As Pascale Casanova suggested in her groundbreaking work, *The World Republic of Letters*, once Latin was pushed from its imperial position as the lingua franca of learned reflection and communication, new languages tussled for its exalted position.[6] The French, English, Spanish, and Dutch, along with other lesser colonial powers, pressed the importance of their language. They did this less concerned with their language's preeminence and more with its global significance as a linguistic and semiotic site for world instruction, that is, the instruction of colonial subjects. Their languages and from it their literatures were imagined as the vehicles to bring the undeveloped peoples of the world into civilization and their full human-ity. Literature and learning took national form, and nationalist desire guided learning and literature.[7] The Bible did not simply stumble into this mix. It helped solidify it, tying together devotional strings from love of God to love of my people's language to love of our land to love for the expansion of our land into new spaces. A vernacular Bible joined with vernacular space as two sides of a colonizing operation.

The story, however, is more complicated than simply colonial takeover. A gospel work was yet being carried out under these sick conditions and that work was to give to peoples the Bible in their mother tongue. Translation can be a holy act, echoing the actions of a God revealed in its vulnerability and marking Christian identity with its most powerful sign. This holy action, however, was caught up inside an unholy act. The translation of the Bible occured inside the translation of native space into occupied, colonized space. So the literacy offered up was inside a strange intimacy constituted by whiteness. Words paint pictures, yet the irony of the vernacular Bible is that it often painted a picture of a white male God. The words of a people were forced to journey inside the literary imagination of whiteness and move toward an aesthetic that would press indigenes to imagine the true, the good, and the beautiful always in and through the bodies, language, and literature of Europeans.

The Bible opened up a Christian world to native peoples as also their world. Unfortunately, that Christian world in both its Roman Catholic and Protestant forms was also a racial world in which their languages were arrayed as so much backdrop to the centrality of the words of white colonial settlers who relentlessly turned indigenous eyes to the old world as the true origin of language that signifies truth. So even with Bible in hand, indigenous peoples experienced a sleight of hand through which their words were asked to mimic the languages of Europeans and their semiotic systems. What does all this have to do with literature and the Protestant literary imagination? Everything. The Bible in these new native hands opened up possibilities of literary existence through the codifying of indigenous voice in lexicon and grammar. The Bible helped many peoples imagine their voice in print. But they imagined along constrained lines and contested angles of thought.

Those constraints pivoted on possession. Who owned the language? Was it owned by the white colonial settlers as the ones who imagined themselves parents of a literate native population ready now to enter the world republic of letters? These eternal teachers were ready to guide the indigenous voice into proper literary expression. Or was it owned by the indigenes, who saw this literary configuration of power in all its colonialist trappings and sought to seize its control and announce a break with its imperialist designs? I am not proposing a narrative of development from indigenous orality to literacy, from silence to voice. Nor am I suggesting an absence of literacy and literary traditions in places that enjoyed centuries of writing. Christian intellectuals who have defended the good work of missionary translators have been much too quick to tease out a good from colonial occupation in narratives that claim they brought literacy to "remote parts" of the world. The point here is that even when literacy and the vernacular Bible offered genuine goods, the enterprise as a whole emerged under constraints that burdened Protestant Christianity and mangled the literary imaginations of so many people of color and others. I have in mind three complications created by the Protestant literary enterprise, enfolded as it was in the colonial enterprise.

2.

The first complication is that the options presented by the colonial enterprise drew native peoples toward two equally bad choices: assimilation or cultural nationalism. Both choices were within the trajectory established by the struggle of colonial nations for literary significance. As Casanova suggested, the idea inspired by Johann Gottfried Herder (1744–1803) that every people should through its literature express its own cultural genius made sense to colonial powers as well as to their formerly colonized subjects.[8] But who are my people, literarily speaking? Such a circle of belonging has always been difficult to trace not because it is difficult to identify but because it is constituted by racial reasoning and colonial Eurocentric logics. Visions of peoplehood were being pressed toward nationalism throughout the colonial theater, and such a vision of peoplehood hinged on ideas of ownership.

To be a people is to own something. What do we (indigenous peoples) own in relation to the colonial powers? This kind of question exposed a comparative logic that was already bondage, repeating the imperial relations that were at work reconfiguring land, animals, and habitation into private property. Language too, and the texts produced using one's own language, became a question of ownership. This meant that peoples the world over were bequeathed a struggle against a derogatory view of their own words in print as secondary or even tertiary in significance to the literature of the old (European) world. Their worlds were at stake with their words. They entered a battle against a false universal created in the literary imagination of whiteness that repeatedly provincialized indigenous texts and refused their alternative epistemologies, ontologies, and ways of articulating truth as compelling invitations to see the world in greater fullness.

There have been and continue to be impressive efforts at reconciling the good of old world literature with the good of literature by those who self-identify as subaltern or third world or who come from former colonial sites. The efforts at reconciliation are complicated because they often reflect the evaluative turmoil both internally and externally of those shaped within the pedagogical regimes of the West.[9] That turmoil could aptly be characterized as trying to create art, artistic possibilities, or fresh vision while inhabiting the evaluative schemas born of Western education, which reach far beyond matters of technique and form and into ways of life, faith, and love. Speaking and writing in multiple voices is not the source of turmoil, as Henry Louis Gates, Jr., so powerfully argued; rather, it is the words that torment the word, that is, the forms of evaluation that walk alongside and sometimes within the literary imaginations of so many.[10]

This state of affairs grew out of the strange mixture of creating a vernacular Bible within colonialism so that the very action that should have helped constitute a new sense of belonging across boundaries through scripture worked to deepen such boundaries, and in many cases racialized them. The Bible emerged as a book for each people rather than a book that created a new people in a material sense. The act of translation was denied its perfect work of constituting learners of language as a way of life. Just as the translator who in learning a people's language enters into their world, possibly being transformed by life with them, so too the Christian enters a zone of translation in which she lives learning the language of another people, Israel, and of a God who joins them together in order to learn each other's languages in life together. To translate the Bible was to be wonderfully caught between multiple worlds and bound to the twofold task of giving witness to a people called Israel in another language and giving witness to another people through their own words. The Protestant impulse to place the Bible in every hand was close to the original impulse of the gospel in effect, that is, a profound joining of hands and lives. That impulse, however, could not overcome the mangled literary space into which it was formed.

That mangled literary space produced a possessive vision of the Bible that helped to cultivate nationalist desire and form in literature. It also cultivated segregationist mentalities right at the site of devotional reading practices, forming orbits of affection first around whiteness and then suborbits around various formerly colonized peoples' own literature. Here was a vision of literacy and the literary that drew lines of difference – racial, cultural, and nationalistic – that became grotesque demarcations. It fostered strange hierarchies of literary value and drew pained and sometimes forced distinctions among the literary works of formerly colonized peoples as well as from peoples of European descent. A problem with textuality formed right at the site of this possessive and segregated vision of the Bible, an undisciplined use of the idea of scripture. If the first work of creating literary space is to draw out the importance of each people's literary voice, then what happens when that voice takes on biblical proportions?

3.

Colonial literary relations were not simply or even primarily the result of Protestant Christianity. Roman Catholicism was at the founding moment of the enterprise. So it would not be accurate to see the possessive and segregationist frame as a Protestant invention. But the second complication Protestantism brought to this venture was a vernacular operation that helped foster a biblical-like devotion to the literature of a people. Reading the vernacular Bible as scripture taught many to read other texts like scripture, not only with a seriousness and careful attention to detail, but also with a sense of majesty that borrows a bit of the holy gleam from the word of God, as well as with a sense of finality that became the soil for legal and juridical writings. Reading texts with reverence is not a new thing, nor is it the problem; it is the work reverence is put toward, that is, the ways in which reverence moves from respect to veneration and thereby becomes worship, becomes idolatry. Such ways of reading and writing were permeated with nationalist longings for significance. Colonial nations wanted their texts to be read like scripture, especially by their colonial subjects.

They also wanted their texts to be taught like scripture. There was and is an intense pedagogical desire embedded in the work of translation. The desire of the translator to learn the language of a people was bound to the desire to teach them the Bible. That desire to teach found in colonial settlers was Christian in character but colonialist in form, constituting what I have called a pedagogical imperialism by which the world outside Europe was (and in some Western contexts still is) imagined as in need of instruction, with Euro-Christians and their progeny being eternal teachers and the rest of the world being eternal students. So the good desire to teach the Bible grew cancerous inside the desire to educate colonial subjects in the literatures of their colonial master, infecting such ideas as growth, maturity, and enlightenment with a racist valence. This sick pedagogical trajectory created a scripture-like vision of canon formation that imagined and continues to imagine in many national contexts the impossibility of authentic education without deep familiarity with and instruction in various classic European and North American texts.

My point here is not to rehearse the arguments about the value or demerit of canon formation for teaching. Nor am I pressing against or toward a more inclusive vision of canon, though I am certainly in favor of more inclusion.

I am drawing attention to the scriptural imagination that fuels the racist hierarchy that still attends canonical thinking in literature, education, and intellectual life in the Western world. That scriptural imagination borrows from a theological vision of tradition through which creeds, confessions, and councils (the written results of deliberations of Christian intellectuals) form the guiding texts that must be read and understood in order to write theology well. This is the logic of orthodoxy applied to textual production, and this sensibility traveled into colonial literary relations and found virulent manifestation in the ways indigenes were taught to revere old world European texts and severely critique any native writing that failed to meet this standard.

This borrowed logic of orthodoxy has yielded far more than ethnic and racial chauvinism performed in the evaluation and appreciation of literary works. It has unleashed a scriptural imagination that is applied to law and public policy. The U.S. Constitution is a powerful example of a text that continues to be read like scripture. It and other founding documents of the Republic are texts framed to gesture toward an eternality that wishes to mirror the word of God. Indeed a whole host of documents that govern everything from financial markets, public policies, and corporations are treated like scripture, especially by those Christians who have very weak firewalls between how they read scripture and how they read other documents around which flow enormous political, social, and economic power. These texts can exist for many people in the realm of immutability, and it requires enormous energy and effort to alter the social trajectories they helped to create and sustain. This literary sensibility is more than contractual. It is fundamentally theological, inspired by a Protestant imaginary – by scripture alone. By scripture alone in this regard is not scripture isolated from all else, but scripture as the central facilitating reality of social life, life together, and life with God. There has been, however, a third problem with imagining that central facilitating reality after colonialism and the emergence of the vernacular Bible, and that is that such imagining performs most often a solitary confinement.

4.

Protestantism glories in the joy of reading. It bears the imprint of a Jewish religious aesthetic that binds ecstasy to texts in hands and near real bodies. Protestants read and find life and pleasure in the act. They also read as a constituting act of obedience to God. They read and remember. This is the demand placed by Adonai on Israel, and Protestant Christians continue that long obedience. The word of God is for the whole community and indeed the whole world, but it must be eaten (taken in) by each woman, man, and child in the community. This is a sensibility that framed the reading habits of many a descendant of Protestantism, and it illumines the energy that remains strong within Protestant Christianity and the literary imagination of other Christian communities as well. This love of reading bound to an abiding piety only strengthened with the advent of the vernacular Bible and the printing press. Together they formed the material conditions inside colonial literary relations that gave life to a relentless individualism.

I am not suggesting that Protestant Christianity or the Protestant literary imagination is the progenitor of modern individualism, which has a much more complicated genealogy. Protestantism did and does, however, promote a form of individualism that generates an image of the reader in solitude, and with the advent of colonialism that solitude mutated into a solitary confinement. The reading practices of Protestant Christianity have been troubled since colonialism and slavery. The prohibition against teaching slaves to read and write in the United States was an indelible example of the deep contradictions that framed Western Christianity. The place of reading as vital to Christian life and obedience was denied Christian slaves because they were commodities, although they were in fact Christians. Slaves who learned to read and write were a danger to the economic life of the Republic because they could with such abilities argue for their humanity and their rights to exist in freedom. This contradiction flowed into another contradiction: that is, if slaves wanted to learn to read and write, especially read the Bible, they risked life and health to do so. In fact, many slaves did take on such risk and learned to read and write, but they did so in secret.

Reading (and writing) in secret in slaveholding society existed at the nexus between racial segregation, oppression, and a possessive vision of the scriptures. From this nexus, a readership emerged separated, segregated, and atomized in the very practice of reading texts. That atomization grew out of the nationalist vision that was woven inside the vernacular operation. A possessive vision of the scriptures worked itself down into individual bodies. That atomization also drew life from the existence of the Bible in commodity form, a thing to be bought and sold, reachable to every interested pair of hands. In this regard, the slave and the Bible shared a similar existence as commodities and bound toward individual uses.

I own what I read and I read what I own. That joined commodity existence of slave and Bible illumined the segregationist mentality that grew inside Christian practice. Here the commodification of the slave and the atomization of scriptural reading practice worked seamlessly. More is at play in this history than the use of the Bible as sourcebook for racial and gender oppression. This is a practice of reading that could be conservative but also oppositional, especially when slaves read the Bible. It could both adhere to the status quo and overturn it, but in almost all instances the reading would be solitary.[11]

Protestantism engendered an image of parallel readers, each searching the scriptures for themselves, moving along their own journey in the exploration of texts, and seeking their way toward a democratic vision of interpretation where unity was imagined in shared agreement of the meaning of passages of scripture. Such an image covered over a more compelling possibility of seeing themselves as *readers together*, readers who in the very act of reading constituted an invitation to a shared life. This reading together would have turned attention less to texts and more toward readers, less to textures of syntax and semiotics and more toward the textures of multiple lives seeking to hear and discern, read and understand their own existence and the life of God together. There would still have been interpretation, but it would have been enfolded in the wider reality of readers together, rather than solitary readers enfolded in the technologies of interpretation bound to the commodification of texts, which remains the current state of affairs in many Protestant reading habits of scripture.

The wider implication of this legacy for the Protestant literary imagination points to its tragedies but also its accomplishments and possibilities. As I noted at the beginning of this chapter, the number of authors who drew and still draw on a Protestant scriptural imagination for their work is too numerous to outline and superfluous to examine at this point.[12] But we could ask, What are some of the abiding characteristics of this scriptural imagination that are worth continued reflection?

5.

First, that imagination glories in translation. The biblical world repeatedly gets translated into this world, and indeed this world is rendered always as the biblical world in vernaculars that conceal that translation. To the discerning eye, the biblical world can be spied out in the narratives as well as the events both mundane and spectacular of many a literary work, and the Protestant rhythm can be heard even in authors who have imagined they have moved away from a Christian formation or a Christian influence directly or indirectly.[13] Translation, of course, is not the sole domain of the Protestant, but its contribution to the work of Christian translation witnesses a unique intensity. The practice of translation spilled over from the Bible into the basic structures of literacy and from there into the everyday speech of many people(s), exposing a vernacular flexibility that never ceases to yield literary surprises.

Second, the Protestant literary imagination played a crucial role in the formation of colonial literary relations and the continuing pedagogical struggle over how literature helps to educate people. We still live with what Pascale Casanova calls the Greenwich meridian of literature, and I would add the meridian of theological writing as well, both of which imagine the center in Europe and America, and the rest of the world organized from this space of global facilitation.[14] The love of the word and the desire for the book are hallmarks of the Protestant aesthetic, and they should be appreciated. Social worlds have been revolutionized and created afresh through this aesthetic, and boundaries once thought impassible have been crossed through the simple act of reading and understanding. Yet boundaries have also been created and peoples' worlds turned deficient and inferior through this same aesthetic infected with a racial semiotic. Indeed white supremacy has embedded itself in our commitment to the book and the exaltation of the word in the Western world. We have not sufficiently analyzed this enmeshment nor found a way to imagine canon formation of texts for learning that break open and break apart this demonic connection.

Third, this imagination inspired the idea of literature owned by a people. As I noted earlier, Protestants were not the only translators who formed Bibles in the vernaculars of peoples. Protestants did however perform the ideas of ownership and possession in ways that shaped how many imagined peoplehood as witnessed in and through texts. More significantly, Protestants resourced a desire for national form in literature that would help a people announce its significance on the global stage. Of course, literature that glories in national form does not negate the power of texts, translated and otherwise, to speak powerfully to a multitude of different peoples and overcome death-dealing hostility and boundaries between groups. In fact, for a literary work to be named for and by a people can and often has been a powerful invitation to deepening appreciation and respect of that people. But a nationalist vision of literature that imagines difference struggles with thwarting the long reach of white imperialism's evaluative regime, which constantly presses our visions of the true, the good, and the beautiful to circulate around white bodies. Not enough writers and artists have been able to escape the derogatory gaze that often accompanies that circulation, unleashing an evaluative turmoil that yet judges the maturity, growth, and enlightenment of their own peoples in ways that reflect the pedagogical imperialism of former colonial powers.

The legacy of the Protestant literary imagination is mixed. Translation, pedagogy, and nationalist visions can prove both liberating and, when infected with the racial semiotic, enslaving. The question remains a compelling one for us today: Can a world formed by the word also be reformed through that word?

Notes

1 Lamin Sanneh, *Translating the Message: The Missionary Impact on Culture* (Maryknoll, NY: Orbis Books, 1990); Andrew F. Walls, *The Cross-Cultural Process in Christian History: Studies in the Transmission and Appropriation of Faith* (Maryknoll, NY: Orbis Books, 2002).

2 An expanded version of this argument is found in Willie James Jenning, *The Christian Imagination: Theology and the Origins of Race* (New Haven, CT: Yale University Press, 2010).

3 Cited in Henry Kamen, *Empire: How Spain Became a World Power, 1492–1763* (New York: HarperCollins, 2003), 3.

4 Ibid., 3.

5 Cited in Jennings, *The Christian Imagination*, 219.

6 Pascale Casanova, *The World Republic of Letters*, trans. M.B. DeBevoise (Cambridge, MA: Harvard University Press, 2004), 45ff.

7 Timothy Brennan, "The National Longing for Form," in *Nation and Narration*, ed. Homi K. Bhabha (London: Routledge, 1990), 44–70. See also John Willinsky, "The Educational Mission," in *Learning to Divide the World: Education at Empire's End* (Minneapolis: University of Minnesota Press, 1998), 89–112.

8 Casanova, *The World Republic of Letters*, 75ff.

9 A good example of this can be seen in Edward W. Said's essay, "Among the Believers: On V.S. Naipaul," in *Reflections on Exile and Other Essays* (Cambridge, MA: Harvard University Press, 2003), 113–117. See also Timothy Brennan, "The Critic and the Public: Edward Said and World Literature," in *Edward Said: A Legacy of Emancipation and Representation* (Berkeley: University of California Press, 2010), 102–120.

10 Henry Louis Gates, Jr., *The Signifying Monkey: A Theory of African American Literary Criticism* (New York: Oxford University Press, 1988); *Loose Canons: Notes on the Culture Wars* (New York: Oxford University Press, 1992)

11 Allen Dwight Callahan, *The Talking Book: African Americans and the Bible* (New Haven, CT: Yale University Press, 2006)

12 See, for instance, Valentine Cunningham, "The Novel and the Protestant Fix: Between Melancholy and Ecstasy," in *Biblical Religion and the Novel, 1700–2000*, ed. Mark Knight and Thomas Woodman (Burlington, VT: Ashgate, 2006), 39–57.

13 Nelson Burr, "New Eden and New Babylon: Religious Thoughts of American Authors: A Bibliography," *Historical Magazine of the Protestant Episcopal Church* 55:1 (1986): 57–77.

14 Casanova, *The World Republic of Letters*, 83ff.

16

SUSAN VANZANTEN

World Christianity

Despite the historical myopia that associates Christianity solely with European Christendom, Christianity was a world religion from its very founding. Originating with a small group of Jewish men and women living in radically new egalitarian ways under Roman rule, Christianity rapidly spread in the first-century world, as St. Paul and others founded Christian communities throughout the Mediterranean Roman Empire. By the third century Christianity had made its way to Armenia, a distant Roman province in Western Asia, where, for the first time in history, it was named an official state religion. Constantine's Edict of Milan (A.D. 313) assuring religious freedom for Christians prompted more conversions in Spain, Italy, the Balkans, and North Africa. Traders and missionaries brought Christianity to areas as distant as the British Isles, Persia, China, and Ethiopia, where Christianity was made a state religion in A.D. 330. But northern Germany, central Europe, and Scandinavia did not embrace Christianity until between the fifth and tenth centuries.[1] Subsequent eras of exploration and colonialism from the seventeenth to the nineteenth century eventually brought Christianity to North America, Central and South America, and the rest of Africa and Asia.

Yet demographers and religious historians today speak of "World" or "Global" Christianity in terms of the explosive twentieth-century growth of Christianity in the "Global South" of Africa, Asia, and Latin America concomitant with its waning presence in North America and Europe. In 2010, according to the Pew Forum on Religion and Public Life, 61 percent of Christians lived in the Global South, compared with about 39 percent in the Global North. This represented a sweeping change: in 1910, about two-thirds of the world's Christians lived in Europe, but by 2010, only about 26 percent of all Christians lived in Europe, the former center of Christianity for over one thousand years.[2] World Christianity today spans multiple continents, theological traditions, nationalities, ethnicities, and cultures.

World Christianity, in both its historical and current manifestations, begins with the premise that Christianity is not exclusively a Western religion. As African religious historian Lamin Sanneh explains, World Christianity denotes indigenous peoples' discovery of Christianity rather than their capitulation to European Christianity.[3] World Christianity assumes that because humans are linguistic, cultural, and social entities, they can apprehend and articulate Christian faith only within a particular historical context. Oxymoronically, World Christianity is vigorously local: it embodies and enacts the universal Christian identity through the cultures, customs, and traditions of particular people. Locally inflected modes of worship, thought, action, and art emerge as African, Asian, and Latin American Christians read the scriptures, celebrate the sacraments, and form religious communities. Indigenous languages, narratives, images, and metaphors articulate new understandings of Christianity in theological prose but also in stories, poems, legends, songs, and tales, both oral and written, as authors interact with the primary text of scripture, received church practices, and indigenous religious traditions. Just as the early church's embodiment within Roman culture resulted in new texts such as St. Augustine's *Confessions*, and as the medieval church's entrance into Anglo-Saxon life resulted in *Beowulf* and *Caedmon's Hymn*, the contemporary relocations of World Christianity produce new kinds of literature. This chapter will consider two African exemplars of this phenomenon: a poem that originates within a Protestant Pentecostal tradition and a novel inflected by Roman Catholic practices and beliefs. Both texts are enriched by readings that take World Christianity into account.

I.

In postcolonial theory, the weaving together of local materials, biblical elements, religious traditions, and literary modes is often described as hybridity. As formulated by Homi Bhabha, hybridity refers to new transcultural identities that emerge in colonial and postcolonial situations. Hybridity begins when a colonial authority attempts to translate the identity of the colonized into a universal framework but fails, producing instead a hybrid mutation. This peculiar replication of colonial identity evokes anxiety in the colonial power. Hybridity's liminality is threatening because it breaks down the clear duality of self/other, colonial power/colonized subject, but it also can offer the colonized a kind of destabilizing power. Bhabha claims that hybridity strategically reverses the process of domination and, through mimicry, questions and exposes the artificiality of colonial power, becoming a subversive tool through which colonized people might challenge oppression. Mimicry is a form of camouflage, distinct from "turning white" or sinking into the swamp of acculturation. One of Bhabha's most important contributions to cultural studies is his recognition that cultures do not have fixed boundaries that either are preserved within a multicultural quilt or are repressed in an encounter with power. Instead, cultures constantly gravitate toward new mixtures – of identities, literary forms, and even religions. In a famous example, Bhabha discusses the hybrid response of rural nineteenth-century Indians to a Hindi translation of the Bible, a response that entailed both acceptance and challenge.[4]

While Bhabha's work on hybridity provides useful elements of analysis, the work of Andrew Walls, one of the foremost scholars of World Christianity, offers a more nuanced way to approach the literature of World Christianity. Walls defines a key difference between proselyte and convert. Proselytes substitute something new for something old, jettisoning old beliefs and practices to adopt new ones; they, in effect, assume cultures have fixed boundaries. Converts, on the other hand, redirect the truths of their current beliefs and practices, turning them in the direction of Christ.[5] Religious synchronism merely adds the new to the old and stirs, in a supplemental process that might produce a subversive hybridity, but Christian conversion transforms or redirects rather than eliminating the old or mimicking the new. In postcolonial theory, hybridity begins with the imposition of a colonial identity (or literary form), but in World Christianity, the material, literary, and social practices of a local culture are pointed in a new direction as the old is transfigured into something new. To the extent that an emergent local Christianity produces new spiritual and theological insights, it may well provoke Western anxiety, but rather than a subversive imitation or mimicry, postcolonial conversion creates and celebrates a new reality.

Sub-Saharan Africa has experienced phenomenal church growth over the past century, making it one of the more influential centers of World Christianity today. As colonial powers withdrew, independence was achieved, and modernization occurred; religion in Africa did not disappear. Few African countries have ever become truly secular, either politically or culturally, and most Africans remain thoroughly religious. In fact, more Africans have converted to Christianity since the end of colonial rule than in the entire colonial period, and similar sustained growth has occurred in the Muslim population. In African culture, neither art nor religion is regarded as a distinct sphere; such objects and practices as ceremonial masks, dances, drumming, singing, praise proclamation, and tale-telling involve both the aesthetic and the religious, the material and the transcendent. For African literature, then, the very categories of "religion" and "literature" create a false dichotomy. Working simultaneously with the lens of African World

Christianity – its texts, religious communities, beliefs, worship practices, and ethical systems – and with the tools of literary analysis, we can fruitfully explore African texts. Although I am not an African Christian, I have worshipped in Africa, and I am a part of World Christianity in that as I affirm the Nicene Creed, say the Lord's Prayer, and partake of the Eucharist each Sunday, I participate with millions of Christian sisters and brothers across the globe. As a North American Episcopalian with Reformed roots, I write as an African literary scholar who welcomes expressions of World Christianity and what I might learn from them.

While Western literature no longer has many instances of oral literature beyond rap and poetry slams, in Africa, oral literature remains a highly respected art form. Oral poets such as the *imbongi* of South Africa and the *griots* of West Africa are central figures at public ceremonies, as was seen in praise singer Zolani Mkiva's performance at Nelson Mandela's funeral in 2013. Far from becoming anachronistic, oral literature (more accurately termed *orature*) has thrived in the modern era, playing a central role in political, medical, cultural, theatrical, and religious practices; permeating contemporary popular culture; and being widely distributed through YouTube videos and websites.[6] Ruth Finnegan, one of the first modern scholars of African oral literature, points out that scholars incorrectly assumed that the importance of religious orature would diminish with the spread of Christianity, but instead African religious oral art forms continued to flourish and evolve.[7]

2.

One remarkable African work of orature is *Jesus of the Deep Forest*, a long poem by Afua Kuma (1900–1987), a non-literate woman from a small town in eastern Ghana. *Jesus of the Deep Forest* was first recorded and transcribed in the Akan (Twi) language, in which it was performed during the late 1970s, and was later published in both Twi and English by Asempa Publishers in 1981.[8] Since this publication, the Akan version, *Kwaebirentuw ase Iesu*, has regularly sold out; the English translation has been less popular. Madam Kuma, as she was politely termed, belonged to the Church of Pentecost, an African Independent church that remains the single largest Protestant denomination in Ghana. In *Jesus of the Deep Forest*, the demands and capacities of a complex indigenous literary form produce new theological insights, generating what Ghanaian theologian Kwame Bediako calls "grassroots theology."[9] Concurrently, the creative modifications of this ancient literary form to address fresh contemporary realities demonstrate religion's generative artistic power. As Christianity is articulated through a traditional genre, with local referents, and in an indigenous language, the poem redirects its originating culture in a new direction rather than manifesting a subversive hybridity. In *Jesus of the Deep Forest*, the Christian gospel is expressed from within an African consciousness and is shaped by African experience. The poem's deft weaving of local and biblical elements generates a reciprocal expansion.

Jesus of the Deep Forest celebrates the attributes of Jesus in the conventions of the Akan *apae*, a type of orature esteemed as one of the highest forms of Ghanaian literary expression. *Apae* means *prayer* or *praise*, and the title page of the English translation includes the subtitle: *Prayers and Praises of Afua Kuma*. While praises are also chanted in informal settings, as when a mother celebrates her child, most African cultures contain a formal genre of praise poetry recited by an official member of the entourage of a king or chief. In Ghana, the praise poet is called an *Okyeame*, which means "the royal spokesman."[10] Madam Kuma thus presents herself as a member of the official entourage of Jesus, and she frequently performed her praise-poetry prayer at Church of Pentecost evangelistic crusades. Traditionally a male art form, *apae* has been resistant to change,[11] making the innovations of Madam Kuma even more remarkable. A genre formerly performed by a male *Okyeame* to praise a chief's political and spiritual leadership has been redirected by a female poet to celebrate Jesus as the ultimate political and spiritual ruler. The *apae* has been transfigured into a hymn, speaking for a gathering of worshippers in the voice of the communal "we," summarizing the mighty deeds of God, exhorting faithfulness, and proclaiming praise.

In discussing *Jesus of the Deep Forest*, we must acknowledge the limits of literary analysis of orature. When an oral performance is transcribed and translated, we miss "the full actualization of the poem as an aesthetic experience."[12] We cannot take into account multiple elements of the performance – gestures, facial expressions, voices, tones (especially significant in African languages), rhythms, and musical accompaniment. Furthermore, we miss the social context and interactions with a particular audience. Oral poems have standard themes, motifs, and events; they follow accepted literary conventions of style, structure, and genre. But in a performance, the poet might suddenly employ a new image, insert a creative aside, order events differently, or add new twists to well-known actions. Oral poets are highly skilled performers; they excel in playing arresting new changes on familiar themes, and their audiences delight in and respond to such abilities. Nonetheless, the literary critic can analyze a specific version of a poem: the work as delivered and recorded on one occasion. The recording, transcription, translation, and publication of *Jesus of the Deep Forest* have produced a stable literary text.

Like most praise poems, *Jesus of the Deep Forest* does not have an overall narrative structure, although it contains several embedded narratives. *Apae*s are typically based on particular historical events, which are alluded to but not recounted during the performance. Performers rely on their audience's knowledge of the underlying narrative to locate the praise historically.[13] The original narrative shimmers behind the performance. The hidden narrative of *Jesus of the Deep Forest* is clearly the biblical story, and attentive and knowledgeable audiences will recognize allusions to the Pharaoh's defeat by Moses, the provision of manna for the Jews in the wilderness, Jesus' triumphal entry, his feeding of the five thousand, the parable of the Prodigal Son, and Jesus' resurrection. But the poem's central element is the praise name, a laudatory title most often given to people but sometimes used to describe clans, animals, or objects. Praise names highlight the striking qualities and notable deeds of the celebrant and include personal names (*mmrane*) and strong appellations (*abodin*) – epithets or nominals of complex compound constructions, such as *Akyerɛkyerɛkwan* (O You-who-show-the-way). Praise poems consist of a series of praise names, praise lines, and praise verses that are loosely linked together into stanzas. The line divisions in print are probably governed by the original oral delivery, in which a group of words would be pronounced in one breath, followed by a pause. In different performances, the stanzas might be ordered differently because their purpose is not narrative but rather descriptive, conveying a broad picture of the actions and character of the hero rather than a chronological account of his life. Each praise name, verse, and stanza extends previous articulations without employing causal links. Praise poetry relies on a cumulative effect, building emotional momentum through repetition, amplification, and accumulation.

Jesus of the Deep Forest opens with a strong declaration of purpose:

> WE are going to praise the name of Jesus Christ.
> We shall announce his many titles:
> they are true and they suit him well,
> so it is fitting that we do this. (5)

The river of names that inundates the poem includes both the personal name *Jesus*, which appears more than one hundred times, and about fifty Akan appellations. The poem's naming redirects the conventions of traditional orature toward a Christian reality. The personal name *Jesus* often appears as an apostrophe or interjection: "Jesus! You are the one / who has gone out to save the nations" (6), "Jesus: you are solid as a rock!" (7), "O Jesus!" (10). Many of the Akan praise names employ complex noun formations:

Source-of-great-strength: **Okuruakwaban** (7)
Owesekramo: the untiring Porter (9)
Okokurokohene: powerful Chief! (11)
Ankankyerε-Damfo-Adu, the friend of all (39)
Okwatayi-mu-agyabenaa [one who is not limited to a single place] (39)

The sheer number and variety of Akan praise names indicate Jesus' power, ubiquity, and majesty, as well as establish Madam Kuma's verbal adroitness. The fact that the English poem retains the Akan names is significant, indicating concepts that cannot be adequately translated, titles that move beyond English denotation, elements of Jesus' essence that can be expressed only in Akan. When Jesus is named in a new language, his identity is explored within a new thought system. The limited human comprehension of a limitless Lord enlarges as Jesus is named, imagined, and celebrated in the Akan world and language. Bediako points out that all the Akan honorifics in *Jesus of the Deep Forest* were traditionally used for royal human rulers, both ancestral and present day, so Madam Kuma proclaims Jesus' rule over both the spirit realm and the political realm.[14] The Akan praise names reflect a central concept in World Christianity: God is present in indigenous languages and cultures. Jesus is "the Word" in every language.

The *apae* is also a highly metaphorical genre, and the poem's abundant animal metaphors frequently have local origins: Jesus is a python, mamba eggs, crab, lamb, whale, ram, "great Lion of the grasslands," leopard, and elephant. Non-animal metaphors occur even more frequently:

> The great Rock we hide behind:
> the great forest canopy that gives cool shade:
> the Big Tree which lifts its vines
> to peep at the heavens,
> the magnificent Tree whose dripping leaves
> encourage the luxuriant growth below. (5)

This stanza demonstrates Madam Kuma's skillful use of parallelism and repetition, two central techniques of orature. The "great forest canopy" is metonymized into the parallel "Big Tree" and "magnificent Tree," which form an incarnational link between heaven and earth, lifting upward to the heavens in the third and fourth lines and bestowing blessings on the earth below in the fifth and sixth lines. Jesus is of the deep forest because he *is* the forest: "You are the deep forest which gives us tasty foods" (37). He is also frequently depicted with metaphors of water, light, wind, and the moon, for the spiritual and natural world interpenetrate in Akan culture. Madam Kuma also uses metaphors based on human-made objects, and she draws from both traditional and modern, male and female, Akan life to construct them: Jesus is an iron rod, elephant gun, loom, pestle, hoe handle, string of beads, grass hut, grinding stone, sword, house, farm, lantern, city, Caterpillar (construction equipment), and the great cross-beam of a traditionally constructed hut. Most of these metaphors are local, not alluding to biblical metaphors (sword and lantern may be exceptions). The interpenetration of local metaphors with the insistent refrain "Jesus" and the occasional metaphor with both local and biblical resonances (lion, rock, sword) embody the redirection of local and traditional elements to a new end. The stream of metaphors demonstrates the abundant ways in which Jesus provides food, shelter, and protection. Names alone cannot capture his manifold nature.

The primary topic of traditional praise poetry is the military exploits of the king or chief, along with his generosity and hunting skills. While all three themes appear in *Jesus of the Deep Forest*, the poem most frequently depicts Jesus as a "wonderworker," one who performs miracles, especially miracles that provide for his people:

> Wonderworker, you are the one
> who has carried water in a basket
> and put it by the roadside
> for the travelers to drink for three days.
> You use the *kono* basket to carry water to the desert,
> then you throw in your net and bring forth fish!
> You use the net to fetch water and put it into a basket. (5)

The miracles appear in the daily and ordinary, with repeated narratives of miraculous feeding. The marvelous deeds of Jesus, the "signs and wonders" that he performs, also include his power to heal. One of the most arresting images of healing draws on Madam Kuma's experiences as a midwife:

> A woman is struggling with a difficult labour,
> and suddenly all is well.
> The child, placenta and all, comes forth
> without an operation. He is the Great Doctor! (14)

Jesus is a "Guide for the blind" (10), has "medicine for hunger" (27), and "fills his basket with sickness, / and dumps it into the depths of the sea" (32). The theological emphasis on Jesus as healer turns the traditional African belief that healing always has a spiritual dimension into an expression of charismatic Pentecostalism.

As Madam Kuma participates in the living tradition of the *apae*, she both redirects and recreates. Her reference to the crucifixion transposes that event into the present day in order to explore the mysterious movements of sin and salvation:

> Jesus! We have taken you out
> and nailed you to a cross.
> On a cross we have nailed you.
> The cross is your fishing net;
> you cast it in the stream, and catch men.
>
> The cross is the bridge we cross over
> to search for the well of his blood.
> The blood-pool is there.
> If it were not for the cross
> we would never have the chance to wash in that blood. (35, 37)

The semantic repetition, linear parallelism, and shifting metaphors capture the richness and mystery of Christ's sacrificial act, as the cross represents a tortured death, an evangelistic call, and a route to new life. The fishing net, bridge, and well are familiar African realities, but also evoke fishing for men (Mark 1:17) and washing in the blood of the lamb (Rev. 7:14).

The Christological emphasis of the poem is striking, given the Church of Pentecost's emphasis on the experience and gifts of the Holy Spirit. Nonetheless, its theology clearly is Trinitarian; it refers both to "**Onyankopɔn**: the great God," who is named *Jehovah* (30) as well as to the third person of the Trinity: "Jesus! / Let your Holy Spirit come and help us, / to lead us to victory" (39). But in its concentration on the identity and work of Jesus, the poem's grass-roots theology parallels a similar emphasis in academic African theology.[15] The Jesus repeatedly identified in this poem with Akan appellations feeds the hungry, heals the sick, protects against dangers and threats (human, natural, and supernatural), defends the poor, forgives sins, arbitrates among the nations, and rules with justice. His attributes are celebrated in African settings, with African flora and fauna, in English and Akan, with biblical stories and Akan folklore.

3.

While Madam Kuma redirects a traditional genre to express theological concepts in newly embodied ways, thus participating in the formation of World Christianity, Chimamanda Ngozi Adichie employs the classic genre of the Western bildungsroman (novel of growth) in *Purple Hibiscus* (2003) to interrogate different expressions of Christianity and to affirm a vigorously local African Christianity. *Purple Hibiscus* tells the story of Kambili, a timid fifteen-year-old Nigerian girl who lives in a luxurious modern family compound with her domineering father, frightened mother, and beloved brother Jaja. Kambili's father, Eugene, has emerged from poverty with the help of a mission-school education, becoming a wealthy and powerful "Big Man" both in the city and in his rural village. He owns several factories, publishes a liberal newspaper, and serves as the spiritual exemplar and financial patron of St. Agnes Catholic Church. Eugene is a hefty, inflexible man who physically punishes his children when they are not first in their class and strikes his wife when he feels threatened or disrespected. When Kambili and Jaja visit their widowed Aunty Ifeoma and her children in Nsukka, brother and sister discover a fundamentally different way of life: full of laughter, music, debates, and freedom. They begin to question their father's repressive ways, particularly his attitude toward his own father, their grandfather Papa-Nnukwu, whom Eugene rejects as a pagan. Over the course of the novel Kambili survives a vicious beating by her father that hospitalizes her, and she eventually becomes the head of the family after her father dies, poisoned by her mother who can no longer bear his abuse. Jaja claims responsibility for the murder and is imprisoned. In the tradition of the bildungsroman, Kambili discovers her voice and identity, and her maturation includes spiritual and religious elements.

Contemporary Nigeria constitutes the heart of African World Christianity, and the novel reflects that vitality and diversity, from the "Pentecostal churches that spring up everywhere like mushrooms"[16] to the simple structure of St. Peter's Catholic Chaplaincy, with its plain wooden crucifix, to the stained-glass windows and ornate marble altar of St. Agnes. While some readers see *Purple Hibiscus* as an exposure of the sadistic, oppressive, and coercive nature of Christianity,[17] the text is actually more multivalent. Papa Eugene and Aunty Ifeoma are both devout Catholics but differ substantially in their religious practices and attitudes. Eugene attempts to reject his Igbo aesthetic and religious heritage and to become a Western believer, ferociously enacting every religious practice to the minutest detail: abjectly kneeling to take communion, reciting twenty-minute blessings before meals, and insisting that the entire family say novenas during long car rides. He is a pillar of the St. Agnes community, where speaking Igbo is not acceptable and hand clapping is kept to a minimum. At Nsukka, however, Kambili finds new ways of practicing Catholicism; morning and evening rosaries are said, but they are "peppered with songs, Igbo praise songs that usually called for hand clapping" (140), songs like Madam Kuma's *apae*. Kambili's cousin Amaka paints a Virgin and Child with dark skin; in contrast, an oil painting in Eugene's room features a white Madonna with her child, and a blond, life-size Virgin Mary presides over St. Agnes. Eugene's prayers condemn "ungodly people and forces" and describe the eternally raging fierce fires of hell; Aunty Ifeoma prays for the university at which she works, for Nigeria's future, and for "peace and laughter today" (61, 127). The biggest contrast between Eugene and Ifeoma, however, lies in their attitude toward and treatment of their father. Eugene will not allow Papa-Nnukwu in his house, refuses to allow his children to have a relationship with him, and repeatedly denounces him as a hell-bound pagan. Ifeoma accepts and respects her father's traditional ways, obtains and pays for his medical care, and even takes him into her overcrowded home when he is dying. She prays to Mary for his healing, prompting Kambili to wonder how Our Lady could intercede on behalf of a heathen. Ifeoma replies that "Papa-Nnukwu was not a heathen but a traditionalist, that sometimes what was different was just as good as what was familiar, that when Papa-Nnukwu did his itu-nzu, his declaration of innocence, in the morning, it was the same as our saying the rosary" (166). Ifeoma transforms and redirects her father's traditional practices toward a different end.

Eugene is a proselyte, in Walls' terms, not a convert. He has rejected most aspects of his Igbo heritage – from speaking the language to decorating his house to praying to his ancestors to respecting and honoring his father. In his overly zealous adherence to Western ways, Eugene attempts to construct forcibly the cultural boundaries that postcolonial theory insists are permeable, thus producing violence and abuse. His mimicry of English Catholicism undeniably reveals its oppressive elements. Yet Eugene's Western ways also include a commitment to liberal democratic society and opposition to corrupt, brutal military rule. Eugene is an internationally recognized human rights leader, advocate for the freedom of the press, and anonymous benefactor to children and the disabled. Bhabha views mimicry as exposing the artificiality of symbolic expressions of power, but what should we call acts of emulation that embrace concern for others and respect for human life? Might such values – found in both Western political theory and traditional Igbo mores – rather manifest two historical embodiments of Christian ethics? Nonetheless, Eugene, as so many colonial powers before him, recognizes the life-enhancing aspects of cultural exchange as going in only one direction. Ifeoma, on the other hand, is a convert who has embraced and redirected central elements of Igbo life and practices in the direction of Christianity, with Igbo praise songs, exuberant dancing, and enthusiastic clapping, as well as in her loving respect for and care of her father.

While Madam Kuma's poem subtly relies on the shadow narrative of the Bible, Adichie's narrative is explicitly constructed around the Christian liturgical year. Section titles place events on, before, or after Palm Sunday. Kambili's maturation occurs as she follows the traditional Christian journey through the Christian year: Christmas, Epiphany, Palm Sunday, Good Friday, and Easter. Her spiritual journey begins at Epiphany, the season associated with the sudden manifestation of the light of Christ, when the events of that day prompt the first visit to Nsukka and a later pilgrimage to Aokpe (106–107). Initially, Kambili's relationship with God is prompted more by her worship of her father than genuine spiritual experience, and she repeatedly associates God with European culture. Father Benedict, the sickly-looking white priest at St. Agnes, cannot pronounce Kambili's name properly, and she imagines that God also has a British accent and is unable to say her name. Given the significance of naming in African culture, this is telling. Later, when Aunty Ifeoma describes a view as revealing "how God laid out the hills and valleys," Kambili envisions "God laying out the hills of Nsukka with his wide white hands, crescent-moon shadows underneath his nails just like Father Benedict's" (131). God, for Kambili as for her father, is white, British, and distant. When Father Amadi, the handsome African priest at St. Peter's, tells her that he sees Christ in the faces of the scruffy teenagers he coaches in football, Kambili is astonished: "I could not reconcile the blond Christ hanging on the burnished cross in St. Agnes and the sting-scarred legs of those boys" (178). Constrained by aesthetic, linguistic, and cultural blinders, she is unable to see the image of God in Africans.

The novel's liturgical structure cumulates in an apparition of the Virgin Mary on the day after Easter. Ifeoma and her children, along with Kambili, Jaja, and Father Amadi, have traveled to Aokpe, a rural village that became a popular Nigerian pilgrimage destination between 1994 and 1995 after a local girl witnessed an apparition of the Virgin Mary. Amid hundreds of pilgrims, the young girl, clad in white, is led out, and Kambili describes the windless rustling of a huge flame-of-the-forest tree, a mysterious shower of fire-colored leaves, and the sun turning white, assuming the color and shape of the host: "And then I saw her, the Blessed Virgin: an image in the pale sun, a red glow on the back of my hand, a smile on the face of the rosary-bedecked man whose arm rubbed against mine. She was everywhere" (274–275). Employing both Pentecostal and sacramental imagery, the liturgical colors of red and white, this scene places the Virgin Mary as decisively in the African world as in the European world of Lourdes or Fátima. This Mary is not the blue-eyed blond of St. Agnes but instead is associated with the African landscape and people.

Kambili's final role as the resilient, responsible, and loving figure that holds her family together is accompanied by a new affirmation of her Catholic identity. She leaves St. Agnes where she had been martyred like the parish's namesake, to become a member of St. Andrews, named after the brother of Peter associated with strength and valor. While some readers may find Kambili's religious affirmations too closely associated with her adolescent crush on Father Amadi, Kambili denies that any "lovey-dovey" emotions lie behind the fact that they correspond and that she carries his letters around. She affirms that she loves Father Amadi but not as a rival with God. Amadi's letters remind her "of my worthiness" and "give me grace" (303), she attests.

4.

Despite the substantial growth that occurs in Kambili and the African Christianity of Ifeoma, Father Amadi, and Aokpe, the novel does not overly simplify the complexities and challenges of World Christianity. Kambili's cousin Obiora offers a more cynical view of the possibility of a genuine African Christianity, when he likens the inseparability of religion and oppression to the process of making *okpa*, a mixture of cowpea flour and palm oil that is steam-cooked for hours until the individual elements are inextricably fused together. Even Father Amadi's vigorous African Christianity has its blinders. He wants Amaka to choose an English confirmation name, but she refuses, pointing out that when the missionaries first came, they didn't think Igbo names were suitable for a religious identity: "What the church is saying is that only an English name will make your confirmation valid. 'Chiamaka' says God is beautiful. 'Chima' says God knows best, 'Chiebuka' says God is the greatest. Don't they all glorify God as much as 'Paul' and 'Peter' and 'Simon'?" (272). On Easter Sunday, Amaka is not confirmed, despite insisting that God can recognize her name in Igbo. At the conclusion of the novel, Father Amadi leaves Nigeria to become a missionary in Germany, where an old woman will refuse to shake his hand because she does not think a black man should be her priest. Despite such resistance, Christianity is no longer the proprietary possession of white Europeans, reflecting another reality of contemporary World Christianity. Obiora highlights the ironic reversal with a mock proclamation: "From darkest Africa now come missionaries who will reconvert the West" (279). Amaka, however, notes that "The white missionaries brought us their god . . . [w]hich was the same color as them, worshiped in their language and packaged in the boxes they made. Now that we take their god back to them, shouldn't we at least repackage it?" (267). The grassroots theology and complex literary texts that emerge from the context of African World Christianity, including Madam Kuma's *apae* and Adichie's novel, are such a repackaging.

Contemporary global Christianity as articulated and represented in literary texts thus affirms what Christianity has always been: a universal reality revealed only in the embodied particulars of human life and culture. Post-colonial hybridity, while a sometimes useful category of analysis, when taken alone fails to identify and apprehend the nuances of conversion and transformation that are World Christianity at its best.

Notes

1 Peter N. Stearns, *Cultures in Motion: Mapping Key Contacts and Their Imprints in World History* (New Haven, CT: Yale University Press, 2001), 38–39.
2 Based on levels of economic development, the Global North is typically defined as North America, Europe, Australia, Japan, and New Zealand; the Global South is the rest of the world. *The Pew Forum on Religion and Public Life, Global Christianity: A Report on the Size and Distribution of the World's Christian Population*, 19 December 2011. Web.
3 Lamin Sanneh, *Whose Religion Is Christianity?: The Gospel beyond the West* (Grand Rapids, MI: Eerdmans, 2003).
4 Homi K. Bhabha, "Signs Taken for Wonders: Questions of Ambivalence and Authority under a Tree outside Delhi, May 1817," *Critical Inquiry* 12 (1985): 144–165.
5 Andrew F. Walls, "Old Athens and New Jerusalem: Some Signposts for Christian Scholarship in the Early History of Mission Studies," *International Bulletin of Missionary Research* (October 1997): 148.
6 Russell H. Kaschula, ed., *African Oral Literature: Functions in Contemporary Contexts* (Cape Town: New Africa Books, 2001).
7 Ruth Finnegan, *Oral Literature in Africa*, World Oral Literature Series (Cambridge: Open Book Publishers, 2012), ebook, chapter 7.
8 Afua Kuma, *Jesus of the Deep Forest: Prayers and Praises of Afua Kuma*, trans. Jon Kirby (Accra: Asempa Publishers, 1981). The English version does not include line numbers, so subsequent in-text references will be to page numbers. While several scholars have discussed the poem's theology, few literary studies exist beyond Akosua Anyidoho, "Techniques of Akan Praise Poetry in Christian Worship: Madam Afua Kuma," in *Multiculturalism and Hybridity in African Literature*, ed. Hal Wylie and Bernth Lindfors (Trenton, NJ: African World Press, 2000), 71–86.
9 Kwame Bediako, *Jesus and the Gospel in Africa: History and Experience* (New York: Orbis, 2004), 17.
10 Akosua Anyidoho, "Linguistic Parallels in Traditional Akan Appellation Poetry," *Research in African Literatures* 22.1 (1991): 67.
11 Akosua Anyidoho, "Tradition and Innovation in 'Nnwonkoro,' an Akan Female Verbal Genre," *Research in African Literatures* 25.3 (1994): 156.
12 Finnegan, *Oral Literature in Africa*, chapter 1.
13 Karin Barber, "Text and Performance in Africa," *Bulletin of the School of Oriental and African Studies* 66.3 (2003): 329–330.
14 Bediako, *Jesus*, 14.
15 John Baur, *2000 Years of Christianity in Africa: An African History 62–1992* (Nairobi: Paulines, 1994), 304.

16 Chimamanda Ngozi Adichie, *Purple Hibiscus* (New York: Anchor, 2003), 29. Subsequent page references are to this edition.
17 See, for example, Lily Mabura, "Breaking Gods: An African Postcolonial Gothic Reading of Chimamanda Ngozi Adichie's *Purple Hibiscus* and *Half of a Yellow Sun*," *Research in African Literatures* 39.1 (2008): 203–222. More nuanced readings include Cheryl Stobie, "Dethroning the Infallible Father: Religion, Patriarchy and Politics in Chimamanda Ngozi Adichie's *Purple Hibiscus*," *Literature & Theology: An International Journal of Religion, Theory, and Culture* 24.4 (2010): 421–435; and Cynthia R. Wallace, "Chimamanda Ngozi Adichie's *Purple Hibiscus* and the Paradoxes of Postcolonial Redemption," *Christianity and Literature* 61.3 (2012): 465–483.

SELECT BIBLIOGRAPHY

The archive on religion and literature is vast. This bibliography represents a selection of books that have informed the chapters in this volume and that offer an introduction to literature and religious traditions. For additional sources, see the endnotes for each chapter.

Religion and Literature

Asad, Talal. *Genealogies of Religion: Discipline and Reasons of Power in Christianity and Islam*. Baltimore, MD: Johns Hopkins University Press, 1993.

Detweiler, Robert, and David Jasper, eds. *Religion and Literature: A Reader*. Louisville, KY: John Knox Press, 2000.

Griffiths, Paul. *Religious Reading: The Place of Reading in the Practice of Religion*. Oxford: Oxford University Press, 1999.

Jones, Lindsay, ed. *Encyclopedia of Religion*, 2nd ed. New York: Macmillan, 2005.

Knight Mark. *An Introduction to Religion and Literature*. London and New York: Continuum, 2009.

Masuzawa, Tomoko. *The Invention of World Religions, or, How European Universalism Was Preserved in the Language of Pluralism*. Chicago, IL: University of Chicago Press, 2005.

Miles, Jack, et al., eds. *The Norton Anthology of World Religions*. 2 vols. New York: W.W. Norton, 2014.

Smith, Wilfred Cantwell. *The Meaning and End of Religion*. San Francisco, CA: Harper San Francisco, 1978; 1962.

Secular and Postsecular

Asad, Talal. *Formations of the Secular: Christianity, Islam, Modernity*. Stanford, CA: Stanford University Press, 2003.

Carruthers, Jo, and Andrew Tate, eds. *Spiritual Identities: Literature and the Post-Secular Imagination*. Bern: Peter Lang, 2010.

de Vries, Hent, and Lawrence E. Sullivan, eds. *Political Theologies: Public Religions in a Post-secular World*. New York: Fordham University Press, 2006.

Dressler, Markus, and Arvind-Pal S. Mandair, eds. *Secularism and Religion-Making*. Oxford and New York: Oxford University Press, 2011.

Fessenden, Tracy. *Culture and Redemption: Religion, the Secular, and American Literature*. Princeton, NJ: Princeton University Press, 2007.

Gorski, Philip, et al., eds. *The Post-Secular in Question: Religion in Contemporary Society*. New York: New York University Press, 2012.

Hungerford, Amy. *Postmodern Belief: American Literature and Religion since 1960*. Princeton, NJ: Princeton University Press, 2010.

McClure, John. *Partial Faiths: Postsecular Fiction in the Age of Pynchon and Morrison*. Athens: University of Georgia Press, 2007.

Neuman, Justin. *Fiction beyond Secularism*. Evanston, IL: Northwestern University Press, 2014.

Ratti, Manav. *The Postsecular Imagination: Postcolonialism, Religion, and Literature*. London and New York: Routledge, 2013.

Taylor, Charles. *A Secular Age*. Cambridge, MA: Belknap Press, 2007.

Hinduism and Literature

Farquhar, J.N. *An Outline of the Religious Literature of India*. Oxford: Oxford University Press, 1920.

Flood, Gaven, ed. *The Blackwell Companion to Hinduism*. Hoboken, NJ: Wiley-Blackwell, 2003.

Gonda, Jan, ed. *A History of Indian Literature*. 10 vols. Wiesbaden: Otto Harrassowitz, 1973–1988.

Pollock, Sheldon. *The Language of the Gods in the World of Men: Sanskrit, Culture and Power in Pre-Modern India*. Oakland: University of California Press, 2006.

Schwartz, Susan L. *Rasa: Performing the Divine in India*. New York: Columbia University Press, 2005.

Buddhism and Literature

Buswell Robert E., Jr., and Donald S. Lopez, Jr. *The Princeton Dictionary of Buddhism*. Princeton, NJ: Princeton University Press, 2014.

Cabezón, José, and Roger Jackson. *Tibetan Literature: Studies in Genre*. Ithaca, NY: Snow Lion Publications, 1996.

de Bary, Theodore, ed. *The Buddhist Tradition in India, China, and Japan*. New York: Random House, 1969.

Lopez, Donald S., Jr. *Buddhist Scriptures*. London: Penguin Books. 2004.

Strong, John. *The Experience of Buddhism: Sources and Interpretations*, 3rd ed. Independence, KY: Wadsworth, 2007.

Veidlinger, Daniel M. *Spreading the Dhamma: Writing, Orality, and Textual Transmission in Buddhist Northern Thailand*. Honolulu: University of Hawai'i Press, 2006.

Judaism and Literature

Bialik, Hayyim Nahman, and Yehoshua Hana Ravnitzky, eds. *The Book of Legends/ Sefer Ha-Aggadah: Legends from the Talmud and Midrash*. Trans. William G. Braude. New York: Schocken Books, 1992.

Grossman, Maxine, and Adele Berlin, eds. *The Oxford Dictionary of the Jewish Religion*, 2nd ed. New York: Oxford University Press, 2011.

Holz, Barry W. ed. *Back to the Sources: Reading the Classic Jewish Texts*. New York: Summit, 1984.

Schwartz, Howard. *Tree of Souls: The Mythology of Judaism*. Oxford: Oxford University Press, 2004.

Skolnik, Fred, ed. *Encyclopaedia Judaica*, 2nd ed. 22 vols. Detroit, MI: Macmillan, 2007.

Stavans, Ilan, ed. *The Oxford Book of Jewish Stories*. Oxford: Oxford University Press, 1998.

Christianity and Literature

Balthasar, Hans Urs von. *The Glory of the Lord*. 7 vols. San Francisco, CA: Ignatius, 1983–1990.

Frye, Northrop. *The Great Code: The Bible and Literature*. New York: Harcourt Brave Jovanovich, 1982.

Gabel, John B., et al. *The Bible as Literature: An Introduction*. 5th ed. Oxford: Oxford University Press, 2005.

Haas, Andrew, David Jasper, and Elisabeth Jay, eds. *The Oxford Handbook of English Literature and Theology*. Oxford: Oxford University Press, 2007.

Jeffrey, David Lyle, ed. *A Dictionary of Biblical Tradition in English Literature*. Grand Rapids, MI: Wm. B. Eerdmans, 1992.

Kurian, George Thomas and James D. Smith, eds. *The Encyclopedia of Christian Literature*. 2 vols. Lanham, MD: Scarecrow Press, 2010.

Mitchell, Margaret, et al., eds. *The Cambridge History of Christianity*. 9 vols. Cambridge: Cambridge University Press, 2009.

Islam and Literature

Allen, Roger M. *An Introduction to Arabic Literature*. Cambridge: Cambridge University Press, 2000.

Beeston, A.F.L., et al., eds. *The Cambridge History of Arabic Literature*. 6 vols. Cambridge: Cambridge University Press, 1983–2006.

Bruijn, J.T.P., ed. *General Introduction to Persian Literature*. London: I.B. Tauris, 2009.

Calder, Norman, Jawid Mojaddedi, and Andrew Rippin, eds. *Classical Islam: A Sourcebook of Religious Literature*, 2nd ed. London: Routledge, 2012.

Cook, Michael, ed. *The New Cambridge History of Islam*. 6 vols. Cambridge: Cambridge University Press, 2010.

McAuliffe, Jane Dammen, ed. *The Encyclopedia of the Qur'an*. 5 vols. Leiden: E.J. Brill, 2002–2005.

Selected English Translations of Sacred Texts

Websites

www.accesstoinsight.org/: Buddhist texts from the Pali canon

www.bdk.or.jp/bdk/digitaldl.html: Buddhist texts from the BDK Tripitaka Translation Series

www.halakhah.com/ The English Babylonian Talmud
www.biblehub.com/: Biblical texts in Hebrew and Greek, many English translations, commentaries, concordances, and other interpretive aids
www.biblegateway.com: Biblical texts in many modern language translations

Print Sources

Ali, Abdullah Yusuf. *The Holy Qur'an: Text, Translation and Commentary*. Washington, DC: Amanah, 1989.

Ali, Maulavi Sher, and Malik Ghulam Farid, trans. and eds. *The Holy Qur'an: Arabic Text with English Translation and Short Commentary*. Tilford, Surrey, UK: Islam International Publications, 1994.

Bodhi, Bhikkhu. *In the Buddha's Words: An Anthology of Discourses from the Pali Canon*. New York: Wisdom Publications, 2005.

Conze, Edward, ed. *Buddhist Texts through the Ages*. New York: Harper Torchbooks, 1964.

Dawood, N. J., trans. *The Koran*, revised 5th ed. London: Penguin, 1990.

de Bary, William Theodore, et al. *Sources of Chinese Tradition*, 2nd. ed. 2 vols. New York: Columbia University Press, 1999.

Sources of Japanese Tradition, 2nd ed. 2 vols. New York: Columbia University Press, 2001–2005.

Dimmitt, Cornelia, and J.A.B. van Buitenen, eds. *Classical Hindu Mythology: A Reader in the Sanskrit Puranas*. Philadelphia: Temple University Press, 1978.

Embree, Ainslee T., and Stephen Hay. *Sources of Indian Tradition*, 2nd ed. 2 vols. New York: Columbia University Press, 1988.

Fox, Everett, trans. *The Early Prophets: Joshua Judges, Samuel, and Kings. The Schocken Bible*, vol. 2. New York: Schocken Books, 2014.

The Five Books of Moses: Genesis, Exodus, Leviticus, Numbers, Deuteronony. The Schocken Bible, vol. 1. New York: Schocken Books, 2000.

Fronsdal, Gil, trans. *The Dhammapada*. Boston and London: Shambhala, 2005.

Ganguli, Kisari Mohan, and Pratapachandra Raya. *The Mahabharata of Krishna-Dwaipayana Vyasa*. 18 vols. 1884–1896.

Giebel, Rolf W., trans. *The Vairocanābhisaṃbodhi Sutra*. Berkeley, CA: Numata Center for Buddhist Translation and Research, 2009.

Goldman, Robert P., and Sally J. Sutherland, trans. and eds. *The Rāmāyaṇa of Vālmīki: An Epic of Ancient India*. 6 vols. to date. Princeton, NJ: Princeton University Press, 1985– .

Haleem, M.A.S. Abdel, trans. *The Qur'an*. Oxford: Oxford University Press, 2008.

Hodge, Stephen, trans. *The Mahā-Vairocana-Abhisaṃbodhi Tantra, with Buddhaguhya's Commentary*. London and New York: Routledge Curzon, 2003.

Jamison, Stephanie W., and Joel P. Brereton, trans. *The Rigveda*. 3 vols. Oxford: Oxford University Press, 2014.

Keith, Arthur Berriedale, trans. *Rigveda Brahmanas: The Aitareya and Kausitaki Brahmanas of the Rigveda*. Cambridge, MA: Harvard University Press, 1920.

Lee, Peter, and William Theodore de Bary, eds. *Sources of Korean Tradition*. 2 vols. New York: Columbia University Press, 1997–2000.

Olivelle, Patrick, trans. *Early Upanishads: Annotated Text and Translation*. Oxford: Oxford University Press, 1998.

Patton, Laurie, trans. *The Bhagavad Gita*. London: Penguin, 2008.

Sarna, Nahum M. *The JPS Torah Commentary Series: The Traditional Hebrew Text with the New JPS Translation.* 5 vols. Philadelphia: Jewish Publication Society, 1996.

Schaeffer, Kurtis R., Matthew T. Kapstein, and Gray Tuttle, eds. *Sources of Tibetan Tradition.* New York: Columbia University Press, 2013.

Steinsaltz, Adin, and Tzvi Hersh Weinreb, eds. *Koren Talmud Bavli.* 19 vols. to date. Jerusalem: Koren Publishers, 2012– .

White, David Gordon, ed. *Tantra in Practice.* Princeton, NJ: Princeton University Press, 2000.

INDEX

Cambridge Companions to Literature

AUTHORS

TOPICS